Errata

pages IX + 112: **Instead of:** Allusions to Some Dialogues **read:** Allusions in Some Dialogues

pages XI + 199: **Instead of:** The References of the Platonic Writings to Selected Unwritten Doctrines **read:** Selected References of the Platonic Writings to the Unwritten Doctrines

page 4 line 13 **after the bracket read:** : The artistic form of the Platonic writings, in its unity, serves as a sensitizing . . .

page 9 line 12 from below: **Instead of:** Tennemann writes **read:** Schleiermacher writes

page 10 line 7 from below **read:** Actually, the first proposal, because of the chronological results of stylometric statistics obtained in the meantime, is not defensible. (Schleiermacher still understood the relation between the trilogy of the **Sophist, Statesman,** the **Philosopher** and the **Symposium** and the **Phaedo** in a sense opposed to what subsequently proved to be the case.)

page 41 line 5 from below **read:** the clarifying capacity of the reports

page 42 line 13 **read:** 340-45

page 50 line 11: **Instead of:** considerably increased **read:** considerably decreased

page 58 line 3 from below **read:** does not proceed not only . . .

page 61 line 17 **read:** it is evident, that these limits of the legitimacy . . . line 19 **read:** can be only a *subject*. . . .

page 90 lines 1 and 2: **to be crossed out**

page 97 line 7: **Instead of:** nothing **read:** anything

page 99 line 13 from below **read:** Considered more deeply, it is order, proportion, and symmetry . . .

page 101 line 26 **read:** in the simile of the cave 516A8, 532A4

page 103 line 17 **read:** at the present state of our knowledge, it depends on recognition . . .

page 105 line 17 **read:** the formulation of eight pathways by means of the combination of multiple perspectives

page 109 line 13 from below **read:** so unity itself in the role of the principle of being and in the role of the good itself . . .

page 110 line 9 from below **read:** are characterized . . .

page 113 line 14: **Instead of:** as is demonstrated **read:** is demonstrated

page 117 line 12: **Instead of:** whereas **read:** by

page 139 line 1: **to be crossed out**

page 139 line 11 **read:** according to which the set of all sets, which do not include themselves, does not include itself . . .

page 141 line 17: **Instead of:** for example with the theory of the proportions **read:** for example for the theory of the proportions

page 143 line 1 **read:** . . *verum convertuntur*), which, moreover . . .

pages 143/144: in the formulas (9.5a/b), (9.6), (9.7) the sign $\rightarrow$ is to be replaced by the sign for negation: $\neg$

page 144 line 10 **read:** "posterior", in conformity with proposition (9.4), is always . . .

page 144 line 20-22 **read:** For all both types of method – that of generalizing just as that of the reduction – is valid, then, the rule.

page 145 line 1: **to be crossed out**

page 147 line 2 from below **read:** . . relation between the Platonic and the transcendental ultimate foundations

page 153 line 5 **read:** . . the progressive-synthetic deduction of the principled follows beginning from the principles.

page 153 line 9/8 from below **read:** . . recovered, both in method as well as in the type of structures of the theories.

page 153 line 3 from below **read:** . . legitimately spoken about[50], even if . . .

page 161 line 2 from below **read:** are consistent: Plato . . .

page 177 line 5 from below **read:** . . in the dialogues always outlined only in a very concise way . . .

page 179 line 17 **read:** the theory of the principles which mediates historically, on the one hand, the philosophy of the Presocratics . . . line 19 **read:** . . with a greater degree of consistency . . .

page 180 line 9 from below **read:** with new rigor and consistency

page 181 line 16 **read:** creates better presuppositions with the respect to the past

page 182 line 11 from below **read:** if possible bygone form of philosophy, one ought instead . . .

page 232 note 20 line 1 **read:** in *Physics* IV 2 = Appendix 3.4

page 254 note 34 line 3 **read:** Ἀπόλλον (ἀ-πολλά: not-many . . . , line 5 **read:** ἀπόφασις τῶν πολλῶν

page 255 note 34 line 2 **read:** μέτρον, line 6 **read:** μέγιστον μάθημα!, αὐτὸ τὸ ἀληθές

page 264 note 5 line 4 **read:** . . a "stage" in a chronological succession), cannot certainly . . .

page 281 note 9 line 5 **read:** From what, in any case, Patzig is "very far" (loc.cit.), he shows in . . .

page 284 note 25 line 13 **read:** . . for the evolutionistic hypothesis than formerly were applied to Plato

page 284 note 25 line 27: **Instead of:** Eighth Letter **read:** Seventh Letter

page 299 line 8 from below **read:** in A. Graeser, ed.,

Plato and the Foundations of Metaphysics

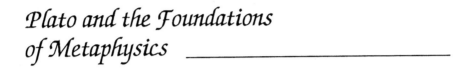

A Work on the Theory of the Principles and Unwritten Doctrines
of Plato with a Collection of the Fundamental Documents

Hans Joachim Krämer

Edited and Translated by

John R. Catan

STATE UNIVERSITY OF NEW YORK PRESS

Published by
State University of New York Press, Albany

For information, address State University of New York Press,
State University Plaza, Albany, N.Y. 12246

Library of Congress Cataloging-in-Publication Data

Krämer, Hans Joachim, 1929-
  [Platone e i fondamenti della metafisica. English]
  Plato and the foundations of metaphysics: a work on the theory of
  the principles and unwritten doctrines of Plato with a
  collection of the fundamental documents/Hans Joachim Krämer;
  edited and translated by John R. Catan
  p. cm.
  Translation of: Platone e i fondamenti della metafisica.
  Includes bibliographical references.
  ISBN 0-7914-0433-1 (alk. paper).—ISBN 0-7914-0434-X (pbk.:
  alk. paper)
  1. Plato. 2. Plato—Contributions in metaphysics.
  3. Schleiermacher, Friedrich, 1768-1834—Contribution in study of
  Plato's metaphysics. 4. Metaphysics. I. Catan, John R.
  II. Title.
  B395.K6713   1990
  184—dc20   89-77689
                                                        CIP

10 9 8 7 6 5 4 3 2 1

In Memoriam
Ann M. Catan (1904-1989)

Contents

Part One
The Loss and Recovery of the Indirect Platonic Tradition: The Position of Schleiermacher and Its Consequences

Part Three
The Philosophical Implications of the Platonic Theory of the Principles and Viewpoints for Its Interpretation

Preface to the American Edition _____

Hans J. Krämer

Thanks to the initiative of John R. Catan my chief work on Plato's philosophy (3rd Italian edition 1989) is presented now to the American — and English— speaking reader. With this, it can reach a worldwide scholarly and educated audience, which surely is to be considered in itself a success that could not have been anticipated by the author from the start. Especially, the ignorance of the languages in which the work has been published would not be a handicap to the scholars of Platonic philosophy anymore, as has been the case with regard to the Italian edition.

I am obliged to Professor Catan for personally having taken care of the translation of the book. His task was the more difficult because he translated primarily the Italian version, that is, he had to produce a translation of a translation. Later on, however, he made use of the German original, too, and by this achieved an optimum of adequacy and accuracy. I am fully satisfied with his translation and I hope that the reader will judge it in the same way.

Preface to the Italian Edition

Hans J. Krämer

I had willingly accepted the invitation of Giovanni Reale, one of the foremost international scholars of ancient philosophy, to present to Italian readers, in their language the results of my studies on Plato, conducted over many years. I wish to thank Professor Reale in a special way for taking charge of the translation and writing an introduction to the volume. The treatment that follows presupposes my preceding research on Plato and Platonism, but also contains many new perspectives and therefore must be considered as a self-sufficient and original contribution. On the other hand, I consider the book not a termination but a temporary resting place and interim balance. It will succeed quite well in its purpose if it moves the philosophical discussion about the significance of the Platonic theory of principles further along and if it were also to stimulate others to commence their research and inquiry into the subject.

Introduction:
The "Italian Plato" of Hans Krämer

Giovanni Reale

It has been some time now since I extended an invitation to Professor Krämer to prepare a synthesis of the interpretation of Plato according to the School of Tübingen (founded by him together with K. Gaiser and of which he is the philosophical leader) for the Italian reader. The invitation was immediately accepted, but because at the time Krämer was involved in reediting the section of Ueberweg's *History of Philosophy* concerned with the ancient Academy, he asked me to wait until he had finished this work. I thought, then, that he would produce a brief synthesis of a hundred pages or so, using the text of the lectures that he had given recently at the Catholic University of Milan. I thought, in sum, that it would be a companion to the small volume of Cherniss, *The Enigma of the Ancient Academy* published in an Italian translation in 1974. But Krämer's work turned out to be almost the historical and philosophical antithesis of Cherniss's, due to the conclusions which the School of Tübingen had reached, namely, an exact reversal of the conclusions at which Cherniss and his school had arrived. In the meantime, the Catholic University of Milan recently established a Center for Metaphysical Research just at the time Krämer had finished his reediting of Ueberweg.

Consequently, it seemed to be an opportune time again to ask Krämer, rather than to compose a short synthesis, to inaugurate the historical and philosophical section of the publications of the *center* by recasting the original project in a more unified manner, like the Platon-Bild of the School of Tübingen, which is undoubtedly the most metaphysical among those introduced in the modern epoch.

Krämer has generously accepted this new proposal, which is a more onerous although more compelling task than the preceding one. What resulted, as the reader can easily judge, is a work of the first magnitude in every sense of the word. It is certain to be numbered among the best works of the School of Tübingen, and it is probably a work that is richer and also formally more perfect than Krämer has written up to this time and certainly one that is philosophically more mature, insofar as it makes use of the results of his scholarship of almost thirty years of studying Plato, as well as his most recent reflections of a theoretical nature.

Who is Krämer? Since 1969 he has been a professor at the University of Tübingen, and no student of ancient philosophy and no reader of Plato is unaware of him. His first work *Arete bei Platon und Aristoteles* (1959), published at Heidelberg, immediately and forcefully brought him to the attention of the scholarly world, insofar as it contained remarkably mature theses to be treated in a first work. The two succeeding larger works, *Der Ursprung der Geistmetaphysik* (Amsterdam, 1964) and *Platonismus und hellenistische Philosophie* (Berlin-New York, 1971), have largely confirmed the expectations of scholars, while the reediting of the section of Ueberweg cannot avoid taking seriously the doxographical texts on Plato. If the doxography is rejected, then consistently one can no longer speak about thinkers like Socrates or Pyrrho, nor can one consistently speak about all those philosophers who have written nothing, and further, and more generally, one would have to renounce a great part of the reconstruction of the history of philosophy. In the second place, Aristotle, to whom the most significant doxographical reports concerning the unwritten doctrines of Plato go back would stand accused of not having understood Plato; but, contradictorily, they accept as solid all the reports of Aristotle on the followers of Plato. Finally, it is absurd to criticize the School of Tübingen by objecting that it claims to write about what Plato had stated ought not be written. In fact, it is possible to investigate scientifically the reasons by which Plato maintained that it was inopportune to write about certain arguments, and it is possible to comprehend them without transforming them into inhibiting bonds, since they are inserted in an archaic cultural context, without taking into account the fact that Plato himself, as we have previously said, never maintained that it was impossible to write about such arguments, but only maintained that it would be wholly ineffective (under the conditions of that period). This, and only this, is the meaning of the "esoterica" of Plato, although it is a term that Krämer consistently avoids because of its ambiguities, he instead uses the term *innerakademische*. What is the relationship of the two traditions according to Krämer? And what are the consequences that would follow for the reader of Plato? The gap between the written dialogues and the indirect tradition arising from the unwritten doctrines is that between "writing" and "orality," comprehensible only if the Socratic formation of Plato is kept in mind.

The dialogues are incomparably richer in their thematic content than the unwritten doctrines; but these and only these contain the crown of the system and, hence, the key that reveals it. This means that, notwithstanding their quantitative paucity, the indirect tradition contains some very important things from a qualitative viewpoint and even, in a certain sense, essential things, that is, the ultimate foundation, the subsequent fulfillment and completion of the ascending dialectic up to the final heights, about which there is silence in the dialogues.

Some have seen this position as dangerous, fearing that the dialogues would be diminished by it. Krämer maintains, on the contrary, that the dialogues become enriched. Plato loses nothing with respect to his artistry and gains as a philosopher. Only that halo of theoretical indetermination around the dialogues and certain apparently problematic traits are dissolved, wholly to the advantage of the concreteness and the specific determination of Platonic thought.

The question What is a dialogue?, which is itself an abbreviated way of expressing the whole "Platonic problem," acquires a new dimension; the problem at times debated about the unity or lack of it in the written works in the context of which every dialogue is seen and every problem is resolved now must be repositioned and resolved in function of the quite enormous and fruitful dialectical tension that involves the written dialogue and the "unwritten," writing and orality.

Part Two of the book is fundamental, in which Krämer condenses, like a true master, the results and the achievements of the Tübingen School and contains, consequently, pages of anthology. Important, especially, is the Chapter One entitled; "The Unified Structure of Platonic Philosophy," in which, with exemplary precision, he unveils the philosophical significance of the unwritten doctrines in their fullness.

Beyond the Ideas (which are a plurality and, hence, as such, in need themselves of something further), are principles or elements from which the Ideas themselves are derived. These are the One (which corresponds to that which in the Republic is called the Good) and the Dyad of the great-and-small, the principle and essence of multiplicity. The Platonic system culminates in a duality of ultimate irreducible correlative principles and, hence, in a species of original dualism. It is a dualism which is sui generis, that is, a proto-typical dualism (different from that which is "two," "duality" and "dualism" signified in the further scope of the things deduced from the principles). Thus all the subsequent categories, like similarity, difference, and others like them, are determinations that come after the principles, and, as such, cannot be applied to the principles. But Krämer again goes beyond this by affirming that the principle of contradiction itself and the excluded middle do not apply to the principles but only to those things derived from the principles, or they apply to the principles in a wholly special way, that is, once again, in a proto-typical manner.

So also it is for being. In fact, being arises from the cooperation of the two principles, and it is, therefore, a kind of mixture in which the one determines the multiple, by fixing indeterminate multiplicity and by equalizing the great-and-small. Being, hence, can be defined as unity in multiplicity. Now if that is so, the affirmation of the *Republic* according to which the Good is "beyond being" affirms what can seem to be said on a merely intuitive level, but it is actually confirmed by a well-defined doctrine that is in the background. In fact, the two supreme principles are beyond or above being, because being is what is generated precisely from the two principles, according to different levels of the mixture and, hence, according to a consequent hierarchical gradation, which proceeds from the supremely universal down to the sensible world.

The resulting hierarchical structure, according to Krämer, divides being into four levels: (1) that of the principles, (2) that of the Ideas, (3) that of the mathematical entities, (4) that of the sensibles. In their turn, these levels are distinguished into further grades of their own: (1) there are two principles and, among them, the One has absolute predominance; (2) among the Ideas are found the Ideal Numbers and the Meta-Ideas or most general Ideas; (3) the mathematical entities are divided into the objects that are within the scope of arithmetic, geometry, astronomy, and music (the soul seems to belong to this level as self-moving number); (4) the sensible world is distinguished into the sublunary world and the superlunary world.

The highest hierarchical grade is "prior," that is, endowed with an ontological priority with respect to the lower grades as they enjoy a necessary but not sufficient role for justifying the existence of the inferior grades.

In all the grades of being, as we have said, it is the "One" that is mixed at different levels with material duality by limiting it. The duality in the different levels enjoy a role of ever-renewable material in which the categorical novum that accompanies it is essential to the plan of the system, but which is not explained. In other words, how and why the duality differentiates the different levels is not explained by Plato.

But there is more. The doctrine of the principles implies a methodological pluralism and likewise one of polyvalent functions, both of which are very important.

The ultimate foundations are, at times, considered as the most simple "elements," and in this guise the process of reduction is connected to them (analyses that proceed to the individualization of the primary elements), a process applied chiefly to the analyses of dimensions and numbers, however applied by the Presocratics in their physical speculations. On the contrary, insofar as they are considered as the most universal and most general "genera," the primary principles imply the process that goes from the particular to again the most general and universal; this procedure proceeds especially to the Ideas and, in particular, to the supreme Ideas, and it is a Socratic matrix. These two methodological processes, for which the primary principles are both "first elements" and "supreme genera," are at times in competition, but for the most part, they are integrated into each other.

In addition to this plurality of methods, the plurality of argumentation procedures that do not coincide with them, but intersect with them, are likewise to be noted. On the one hand, Plato, at times, proceeds according to a reductive-regressive model, that is, from low to high; at times, instead, with a derivational-deductive model, that is, from high to low. The two procedures naturally can be applied both in an elementarizing way and a generalizing way.

The doctrine of the categories (which has as its highest correlatives "relational being" and "nonrelational being") is elaborated for the purpose of reducing the whole of reality in a methodical way to the highest principles.

In what concerns, on the contrary, the polyvalent functions of the principles, Krämer underscored in a faultless way that the One is, at the same time a cause of being, foundation of knowledge, and principle of value on condition that the nexus between ontology, epistemology, and axiology is fundamentally and structurally guaranteed precisely by the polyvalence of the principles. In particular, Krämer's making evident the role of the Good as a functional component of the One should be noted. Due to this, the limit which the One imposes on the unlimited (on the duality of the great-and-small) and its mediating function between the extremes makes it possible for the being that is derived from it to be structurally positive. Plato is, in this way, the true founder of the doctrine of the transcendentals (*ens, unum, verum, bonum convertuntur*).

The dominant concept which functions in a unifying way among the various aspects of the principles, Krämer explains, is limit that guarantees all the formal determinations of identity, existence, harmony, positivity, and similars. And the concept of measure is also structurally connected with the concept of limit. The One is the supremely perfect measure and on the lower levels it is also their measure. And likewise the following concept of norm is structurally connected with the concepts of limit and measure.

The concept of unity as measure, properly speaking, expresses the correlation between the first unconditioned principle and conditioned being and precisely insofar as it is such it functions as an intermediate between the one and the other by expressing the meaning of the ultimate foundation, and thus recapitulates in itself the basic ontological conception of Plato. Anyone who has found these theories abstract or even bizarre simply does not understand them, or they do not have a familiarity with the Greeks which is necessary in order to grasp how in these metaphysical propositions Plato expresses in a faultless way the key to life with sensibility, imagination, and thought that is precisely Greek and reveals its most profound depths.

In Chapter 7, Part Two of the book, Krämer shows in brief, the fruitfulness of his interpretation of the unwritten doctrines as the hermeneutic canon for the interpretation of some of the dialogues or of some of their central parts. Let us remember, in particular, that reread in the light that Krämer suggests, the central part of the *Republic* produces an extraordinary enrichment by revealing that hidden "capital" of which Socrates, in the dialogue, is limited to presenting only the "interest." The two-fold character of the principles is revealed as the key that deciphers the *Parmenides* , about which everything has been said and its contrary, as a result of beginning thus from presuppositions extraneous to the dialogue: here we have, instead, a precise position going back to that which has come from the very lips of Plato himself. The *Sophist* also appears in a wholly novel light: the famous five most general Ideas does not constitute the vertex of the Platonic system, as has been thought, but rather a choice among some of the Meta-Ideas made as illustrations and limited to the particular purposes that the dialogue proposed. But the other dialogues also, from the *Meno* to the *Philebus*, from the *Timaeus* to the *Laws* are illuminated by this new light.

In Chapter Eight, concerned with the historical position of the doctrine of the principles in the ambit of ancient philosophy, Krämer demonstrates that it is a revival of the theory of the Presocratics radically renovated and carried up to a new plane precisely through the passage toward Socrates. Plato emerges in this way as the creator of classical metaphysics which Aristotle historically reoriented, insofar as his doctrines depend, in the light of this new reading of Plato, on the Platonic-Academic doctrines in a structural manner. If the Hellenistic Age, then, had not benefitted from the unwritten doctrines concerning the principles, renovated Platonism had structurally taken them up (without counting, then, the Neo-Pythagoreans, who had appropriated them as well as attempting a modification of them in a monistic sense).

Part Three is of a an elegantly theoretical character. And here Krämer presents for the first time a whole series of perspectives in whole or in part unpublished. He proceeds to a comparison of the structure of the Platonism thus as he has constructed it, with the principal currents of thought which operative today, and specifically with analytic philosophy, with transcendental philosophy, with Hegelianism, with phenomenology and with Heidegger. What emerges from it is a further great surprise. In fact, reconstructed in this manner, Platonism lends itself to a very effective and fruitful comparison with the modern philosophical currents. Apart from the comparison with analytic philosophy which does not have precedents, and the novelty of which is hence clearly foreseeable, the conclusions to which Krämer came astonished not a few precisely through the comparison with transcendental philosophy and with Hegelian philosophy, however more times instituted, but which, in this new vision produced unforeseen results. Indeed, from the analysis of this part, modern philosophy is like a perennial commentary to Plato, made in a very different and very unexpected way.

The Appendices which complete the volume are all very important. In particular, they are to be considered an integral parts of the treatment in the first three parts, which both in their unity and in the way in which they are proposed (text and accompanying translation) are unique on the international level, and which hence cannot be omitted without rendering the theses of Krämer profoundly incomprehensible, while the remaining ones constitute a most useful complement, especially the fifth and the eighth.

But to return to the first three appendices, the reader must keep in mind what follows. Krämer, in the course of the volume, speaks throughout, (1) of the self-witness of Plato on the meaning of his writings and on the gap existing between the written word and spoken dialectic, (2) of the numerous passages of the dialogues in which Plato avoids speaking himself and by saying certain things touches on ultimate questions and thus points beyond the written word to a clearly existing "unwritten" word, (3) of the "relations" of the disciples to the unwritten *On the Good*. In the notes, in addition, there are continual references to these passages. To be able to read them together in a single appendix was therefore necessary, and furthermore in a bilingual edition [not included in the American version], in order to guarantee absolute objectivity. Moreover, the self-witnesses are presented *in toto* [completely], and their collection constitutes something new. The references in the dialogues to the unwritten doctrines are very clear and evident, and, hence, more evidential; also this collection constitutes a novelty, and is of great usefulness to the reader. The relations among the unwritten doctrines are all those essentially which are found in the collection of Gaiser; very few new ones are there in addition. Nevertheless, they are arranged differently in the Gaiser collection, according to a arrangement which better reflects the actual status of the research of the School of Tübingen; and also this constitutes a new thing, although partially so. The translation of the two long passages in the first appendix, the eleventh and the thirty first, were completed by me to assist in grasping the theses maintained by the School of Tübingen. Through some of these principal "reports," on the contrary, I have followed in the footsteps of Gaiser and Krämer. Keep in mind that some of the texts contained in the third appendix (and precisely some of the most important ones) are here translated for the first time into Italian.

The bibliography, selected by Krämer with great acumen, is presented in the fourth appendix in order to serve as an enrichment eventually for further research on the theme of the unwritten doctrines, while the select bibliography of all the scholarly works of Krämer has the purpose of presenting the most adequate possible image of the author [not included in this volume]. The indices of names and concepts permits the consultation of the work in an smooth manner [again not included in this volume].

Some friends, knowing of my invitation to Krämer and the effort expended on the translation of this work, asked me if I had by any chance been converted to the interpretation of Plato identified with the School of Tübingen, from which, on the contrary, I seemed in my *History of Ancient Philosophy* to be quite distant. As a matter of fact, I must say that in turning the work over in my mind that is presented here and rereading synoptically the documents to which the School of Tübingen appeals I have been convinced that they have substantially achieved their basic goal. When I asked Krämer to prepare a synthesis of his Platon-Bild, I thought that I could take a middle position between Cherniss and the School of Tübingen. But this book, chiefly with the novelty that it has achieved, and with the imposing synoptic balance which was accomplished, shows irrefutably that between the position of the followers of Cherniss and the interpreters of the School of Tübingen there lies a non-unifiable contradiction. He shows that Cherniss's position is a one which has now reached its Columns of Hercules, while the positions of the School of Tübingen offer more and further fruitful premises for research of various kinds and of various characters.

In particular, it seems to me that now it goes against the historical evidence to try to insist on the absolute autonomy of the Platonic dialogues with respect to the indirect tradition and to accept what follows. (1) There exists a precise indirect Platonic tradition, which goes back to the oral teaching presented to the whole Academy and which contains elements which go beyond the content of the dialogues but which in substance can be creditably maintained. (2) The "something more" which this tradition contains does not deny anything to the writer Plato and, in return, enriches Plato from the viewpoint of philosophical content by revealing the ultimate foundation of his system of thought and the related nexuses of an ontological, epistemological, and axiological character. (3) This "something more" not only is helpful in the comprehension of Plato in general, but it is also useful for the understanding of individual dialogues, sometimes precisely at critical junctures, or even in their basic intentions. (4) The unwritten doctrine of Plato discloses a system of reality conceived according to hierarchical levels derived from a supreme pair of principles (the unity and duality of the great-and-the-small), which influences every level, in which unity emerges in a marked manner, functioning as limit and, hence, as measure (with respect to that which is so conditioned) and, likewise, as norm. (5) The polyvalent structure of the system and of the connected methodology clarifies the polyformed content of the dialogues.

In my *History of Ancient Philosophy* I spoke of a Plato of three dimensions. But now I am convinced that the School of Tübingen has discovered a fourth, that, indeed which is concealed in the dimension of the "oral" and, which, as a matter of fact, provides the best support for the other three. Fortunately, I did have the time to add it to the fifth edition of the second volume of my *History*, which contains the treatment of Plato and which has just been published and I have demonstrated this thesis in detail.

The analytical investigation of the whole range of problems dealt with in this volume and their historical-philological foundations have led me to the conviction that the new interpretation suggested by the School of Tübingen is definitely a new hermeneutical paradigem which marks the beginning of a new epoch in Platonic studies. Obviously, this does not mean that I accept totally the theses of the School of Tübingen, no less their whole series of implications and corollaries. For example, it does not seem to me that there is sufficient room left for the soul. And analogously, the figure of the Demiurge seems restricted almost to the point of elimination. In addition, I do not see the religious-mystical dimension of Plato adequately supported, and I do not see the peculiar cognitive value of myth noted. Finally,–and especially–I do not see put in its necessary relief what Plato called his "second voyage," that is, the discovery of transcendence. Nevertheless, I see the possibility of integrating all of this with the discoveries of the School of Tübingen. I have carried out this plan in my monograph entitled *Per una nuova interpretazione di Platone. Rilettura della metafisica dei grandi dialoghi alla luce delle "Dottrine non scritte"* (Milan: Vita e Pensiero, 1989[6]).

But to be more precise, I should state that the School of Tübingen has now accepted my clarifications, and Krämer has clearly expressed his agreement with them in his review of my book (cf. *Rivista di filosofia neoscolastica*, 1980, pp. 341-53. now reproduced in the appendix of the last edition of my monograph, *Plato*, pp. 707-27).

In conclusion, Krämer, with his "Italian Plato," has gone well beyond the limits of a work of spreading the results of a school, in presenting a contribution which by taking up everything which has matured in the course of his preceding research he furnishes a series of valid indications and perspectives even for the future like an indispensable instrument of work and thus rather than a gift to the Italian friends of Plato, Krämer has made a gift to the friends of Plato of the whole world.

I want to warmly express my gratitude to Professor Krämer for the effective work of assistance given to me in the task of translator. He, in fact, knows the Italian language well, and came two times to Italy (at Luino) in order to discuss the translation and he modified a series of things in order to obtain a true and accurate Italian rendition. On a third occasion I journeyed to Germany for the final revision (the meeting between Krämer and me took place in Königsfeld/Schwarzwald). I wish to thank the administration of the Villa Fonteviva in Luino, who offered to Professor Krämer and me such elegant hospitality which made our work notably smoother.

One final remark is in order. This monograph (which summarizes the results of 30 years of work of the author) is not a book simply to be read, but it must be studied and even rather compellingly studied. Parts One and Two do not require the reader to have any specific prior knowledge, since the notes and the appendices furnish all the tools necessary for grasping the interpretation of Plato proposed by Krämer. On the contrary Part Three, given its strongly technical character and its robust theoretical concerns, require, in order to be adequately understood, a prior knowledge (and further a not superficial one) of analytic philosophy, of transcendental philosophy, of Hegelianism, of Husserlian phenomenology, and Heideggerian ontology besides the complete understanding and grasp of Parts One and Two.

Note by the Translator of the American Edition

I should like to thank Hans Krämer and Giovanni Reale for the opportunity to bring the views of the School of Tübingen to English and American scholars. I would also like to thank Mr. William Eastman of State University of New York Press and Ms. Ruth East, production-editor, and Gnomi S. Gouldin, copy-editor, for reading the manuscript and making stylistic and grammatical suggestions in the name of clarity. The faults of the translation are, of course, my own. My friend and colleague Dr. Joseph Gilbert read the manuscript in one of its versions and forced me to clarify some obscure syntax and I am grateful.

I am also in the debt of the publishers who allowed me to quote from their publications, especially Bollingen Series for the translations of Plato used in the Documents section, although where translations were not available in English I provided my own.

I did the compositing with the help of a Compaq Deskpro 386™ Computer, a Hewlett Packard Series IID LaserJet™ printer, and Font Effects™ from SoftCraft Inc.®

There may be some hesitation on the part of the reader to bother with an English translation of an Italian translation of unpublished German original. The German manuscript is still not published and the Italian version has been recognized by many as the best available presentation of the views of Krämer on the vexed issue of the "unwritten doctrines," so in that sense if the translation is a good one then it is loyal to the Italian version (which is the only printed version available at this date). But I felt compelled to check the German manuscript that Professor Krämer made available to me. There are some features missing that were included in the Italian text in the Appendices and Indices as a result of communications from Professor Krämer as well as some additions to the text of Professor Reale's "Preface to the Italian Plato" that he requested.

I dedicate this volume to the memory of my dearest mother I cannot imagine a loss greater than that of a mother, and although we had a stormy relationship over many years, we were able to reach a peace with and affection for one another, that will remain one of my fondest memories until we meet again.

Abbreviations

AAW = H. Krämer, "Review" of E. Dönt, *Platons Spätphilosophie und die Akademie* (1967), in: *Anzeiger für die Altertumswissenschaft* 4 (1968): 221-25.

AK = H. Krämer, "Die platonische Akademie und das Problem einer systematischen Interpretation der Philosophie Platons," *Kant-Studien*, 55 (1964): 69-101; reprinted in: K. Gaiser (ed.), *Das Platonbild zehn Beiträge zum Platonverständnis* (Hildesheim, 1969) 198-230.

APA = H. Krämer, *Arete bei Platon und Aristoteles. Zum Wesen und zur Geschichte der platonischen Ontologie*, [Abhandlungen d. Heidelberger Akademie der Wissenschaften, philosophisch-historisch Klasse, Jahrgang 1959, Nr. 6] (Heidelberg, 1959; Amsterdam, 1967²).

Appendix = Document section published in the present volume.

Denkbewegung = H. Krämer, "Die Denkbewegung der aristotelischen Ersten Philosophie und ihr geschichtlicher Hintergrund," in: *Akten des XIV. Internationalen Kongresses für Philosophie*, Wien 1968, vol. VI, (Wien, 1971) 355-60.

Eidos = H. Krämer, "Aristoteles und die akademische Eidoslehre. Zur Geschichte des Universalienproblems im Platonismus," *Archiv für Geschichte der Philosophie* 55 (1973): 119-90.

Epekeina = H. Krämer, "ΕΠΕΚΕΙΝΑ ΤΗΣ ΟΥΣΙΑΣ. Zu Platon, *Politeia* 509 B," *Archiv für Geschichte der Philosophie* 51 (1969): 1-30.

Gaiser followed by the number of a page = K. Gaiser (ed.) *Das Platonbild. Zehn Beiträge zum Platonverständnis* (Hildesheim, 1969).

Gaiser Menon = K. Gaiser, "Platon Menon und die Akademie," *Archiv für Geschichte der Philosophie* 46 (1964): 241-92; reprinted in: J. Wippern (ed.) *Das Problem der Ungeschriebenen Lehre Platons* (Darmstadt, 1972) 329-93.

Gaiser PUL = K. Gaiser, *Platons Ungeschriebene Lehre. Studien zur systematischen und geschichtlichen Begründung der Wissenschaften in der Platonischen Schule. Mit einem Anhang: Testimonia Platonica. Quellentexte zur Schule und mündlichen Lehre Platons* (Stuttgart, 1963; 1968²).

Gaiser Quellen = K. Gaiser, "Quellenkritische Probleme der indirekten Platonüberlieferung," in the volume miscellany: *Idee und Zahl*, Abhandlungen der Heidelberger Akademie des Wissenschaften, philosophisch-historische Klasse 1968/2 (Heidelberg 1968) 31-84.

GF = H. Krämer, "Die grundsätzlichen Fragen der indirekten Platonüberlieferung" in the volume of miscellany: *Idee und Zahl*. Studien für platonischen Philosophie von H. G. Gadamer, K. Gaiser, H. Gundert, H. J. Krämer, H. Kuhn [Abhandlungen der Heidelberger Akadamie der Wissenschaften, philososphisch-historische Klasse, Jahrgang 1968, 2. Abhandlung], Winter, (Heidelberg, 1968) 106-50.

GSAM = H. Krämer, "Zur geschichtlichen Stellung der aristotelischen Metaphysik," *Kant-Studien* 58 (1967): 313-54.

PD = H. Krämer, "Über den Zusammenhang von Prinzipienlehre und Dialektik bei Platon. zur Definition des Dialektikers *Politeia* 534 B/C," *Philologus* 110 (1966): 35-70; reprinted with a 'Nachtrag 1968' in the volume of miscellany: *Das Problem der Ungeschriebenen Lehre Platons* [Wege der Forschung, vol. CLXXXVI, herausgegeben von J. Wippern], (Darmstadt:Wissenschaftliche Buchgesellschaft, 1972) 394-448.

PHP = H. Krämer, *Platonismus und hellenistische Philosophie* (De Gruyter: Berlin-New York, 1971).

Ph.R. = H. Krämer, "Neues zum Streit um Platons Prinzipientheorie," *Philosophische Rundschau* 27 (1980): 1-38.

Retr. = H. Krämer, "Retraktationen zum Problem des esoterischen-Platon," *Museum Helveticum* 21 (1964): 137-67.

Test. Plat. = *Testimonia Platonica*, which is in Gaiser **PUL** (cf. above) 441-557.

UGM = H. Krämer, *Der Ursprung der Geistmetaphysik. Untersuchungen zur Geschichte des Platonismus zwischen Platon und Plotin*, (Schippers: Amsterdam, 1964, 1967^2).

VPA = H. Krämer, "Das Verhältnis von Platon und Aristoteles in neuer Sicht," *Zeitschrift für philosophische Forschung* 26 (1972): 329-53.

Part One

The Loss and Recovery of the Indirect Platonic Tradition:
The Position of Schleiermacher and Its Consequences

1 *The Arguments of Schleiermacher in the Introductions to the Translation of Plato*

The Essential Relations between the Artistic Form and the Philosophical Content in Plato According to Schleiermacher

F. E. D. Schleiermacher, the great liberal Protestant theologian and reformer of hermeneutics (1768–1834), in addition to the exegesis of the Old and New Testaments, has applied his hermeneutic method to the authors of classical antiquity. His works on Anaximander, Heraclitus, Diogenes of Apollonia, Hippo, Socrates, and Aristotle, however, are in the second rank, in terms of vigor and effectiveness, compared to the great translation of Plato, equipped with introductions and explanations (1804-1828[1]); (1817[2] ff.); (1855[3]).[1] This work has as its ideal a literary and documented translation.[2] But due especially to the interpretation of Plato contained in the general Introduction, if it has not wholly produced that image of Plato which belonged to the following epochs, it has at the very least bent it in a specific direction, even outside the area of those who speak and understand German.

The specific marks of the presence of Schleiermacherianism in the study and interpretation of Plato are the following.

1. The method of exposition in the dialogues of Plato's philosophy, insofar as it is an *artistic form*, is inseparable from the *content*; in fact, the dialogue is the uniquely appropriate form of *philosophical communication*. In particular, for modern man, the understanding of the *literary dialogue*, its method and content, goes hand in hand with understanding Platonic philosophy.

2. Within the confines of this conception, which reduces the philosophy of Plato to its literary aspect, there no longer remains any space for a complementary indirect tradition to arise due to the oral teaching of Plato. The indirect tradition is treated as or restricted to a negligible amount, or as happens in some followers of Schleiermacher, it is chronologically limited and neutralized by means of a late dating.

3. The system of Platonic philosophy is contained completely in the writings, but it unfolds in successive stages, according to a precise

didactic plan. In this regard, there are to be distinguished three principal groupings of writings (elementary writings, writings that indirectly express the system, writings that are presented in a constructive and objective manner), each of which is at times further divided into three classes: fundamental writings, complementary writings, and occasional writings. The unitary interpretation of Schleiermacher in principle, however, does not exclude the allowance of genetic modifications to the general plan.[3]

In particular, Schleiermacher, in his famous Introduction, claimed to "understand" for the first time the specific kind of *philosophical communication* in Plato (thus the central concept of the hermeneutic of Schleiermacher: the *subtilitas intelligendi* [the subtlety of the understanding] of the old hermeneutic tradition is applied), the artistic form of the Platonic writings, in its unity, and serves as a sensitizing and protreptic elevation of the reader. It has the task of stimulating him and bringing him to a spontaneous and active capacity for, and attention to, the understanding and assimilation of the teachings. The artistic form is revealed, above all, in the correct coordination of the parts with the whole, both within each individual work and in the relation between different works, and, finally, in the general plan itself considered, in all its ramifications. (In this regard, the connection between the part and the whole of the "hermeneutic circle" plays an essential role, which Schleiermacher, after Schlegel and Ast, in his hermeneutic has projected for the first time in a more incisive manner.) The artistic form is manifested, in the second place, in the dialogue form and, in general, in the conversational form that is proper to the Platonic writings, as well as in the inclusion of the mimetic aspects and the setting of the scene in this connection. A series of further techniques of speaking and presentation given in an implicit manner, veiled and elusive (apparent aporias, digressions, prior interruptions of the goal of the argument, and so on), is connected strictly with the artistic form.

This, according to Schleiermacher, has important consequences; not only for the philosophical content that remains in part unexpressed and is transposed into formal relations, but for the way in which it leads to the comprehension of the content grasped, in every instance, only through the consideration of the form. *All* content is mediated through the form and every philosophical affirmation is related, in the first place, to its dramatic place and setting in the sense of total dependence on it.[4] In this interpretation, there is an unending task that Schleiermacher himself never completed. He has clarified in a magisterial manner the structure of some dialogues, especially the *Parmenides,* the *Theaetetus,* and the *Sophist,* and he has shown, in general, some connections in the themes existing between dialogues, but, for the rest, he has left incomplete the program sketched out in the Introduction.[5] In the summary exposition of the philosophy of Plato, written in 1812, Schleiermacher proceeds, on the contrary, in a purely dogmatic manner, without further reflection on the form of the exposition proper to Plato.[6] Moreover, the discussion of the "Platonic question" about the unity of the literary work, in the meantime, has wandered far from the thesis of Schleiermacher's rigid general plan by going in different directions; and so involved both a more accentuated evolution (the writings were found, in fact, in the proposed interpretation of Schleiermacher, to have too much "purposiveness" and not enough "chance"), as well as an objective, less didactic, and more systematic order of the writings.[7]

The Interpretation of the *Phaedrus* Proposed by Schleiermacher and Its Inadequacy

Schleiermacher followed F. Schlegel in considering the Platonic *Phaedrus* as the methodological foundation of all the dialogues. So, he pressed hard to bring the reflections found at the end of the *Phaedrus* (274–78 = Appendix 1.1) about the relations between *written* and *oral discourse* into agreement with his hermeneutic hypothesis concerning the artistic form of Platonic philosophy and to submit them to it. Consequently, in the Introduction, beginning from the relation "model-to-image" existing between spoken discourse and written discourse of which the *Phaedrus* speaks (276A; cf. Appendix 1.1), Schleiermacher tried to extrapolate, as a postulate, a theory of the literary dialogue. He writes, in fact, expressly: "[Plato] must have endeavored to make even written instruction as close as possible to that better kind, and he must also have succeeded in that attempt."[8]

But K. F. Hermann had already correctly seen the fact that the term 'image' (*eidolon*) is used here in a purely pejorative sense (in the sense of something that is "merely a shadow"), and in this regard he has pointed out a series of obvious parallels that can be found, especially in *Republic* X.[9] We may add that this passage of the *Phaedrus* is concerned with the problem of discourse and writing still in a wholly general manner and only later passes on (276E; cf. Appendix 1.1) to the consideration of the method of dialectical discourse, understood as the only appropriate form of communication. The relation of "image-to-model" refers rather to the character of writing *as such* compared to discourse *as such*, without any further qualification of each. Hence a positive theory of the literary dialogue cannot be taken from this section of the *Phaedrus*, or from any subsequent one[10] (in fact, even "the best" among written discourses, of which 278A1 speaks [cf. Appendix 1.1], cannot refer exclusively to the written dialogue form). Schleiermacher did not understand essentially that the inequality of levels and the methodological hiatus existing between written and oral dialectical discourse (between "writing" and "speech") emerges in the concluding part of the *Phaedrus*. This means that a theory of dialogue based on the simple fact that the Platonic literary productions are in a dialogue form can be established or put forward only within an ambit already determined by the substantial and irrevocable pre-eminence of the dimension of oral dialectic. Therefore a theory of the literary dialogue, which in any case would be only implicit, cannot in any manner advance and overcome the explicit criticism in the *Phaedrus* or attempt to avoid its clearly stated strictures, and thus it cannot in any way compensate for them.

The literary dialogue is rather according to Plato's conception, primarily, something written and only secondarily (on a completely different and subordinated level, and generally *within* the sphere of the written) also a dialogue.[11] And this is so for many reasons.

1. It can give an answer only to a fraction of the possible difficulties that may arise in the reader, who is exclusively a witness and not an active participant in the fictitious dialogue.[12]
2. Also the idealized literary dialogue cannot substitute vicariously for the arduous and lengthy training, for the development and achievement of the processes of dialectical formation, but, at most, can be an introduction to them.[13]
3. The literary dialogue, as well as all written works, can involve results extraneous to the intentions of the author; it can be misunderstood, and consequently, have a "profaning" effect (*Phaedrus* 275E f.; cf. Appendix 1.1).

Plato, in this regard, can be pushed even up to the point of not giving to the written word (and even here, note, he refers only to the "best of writings" (278A1; cf. Appendix 1.1) the function of communication, for he gives it only the function of arousing the memory of things grasped in other ways (the mnemonic function of the written word). But Schleiermacher does not advert to this observation, which is fatal for his theory of the dialogue, just as he does not pay attention to the earlier mentioned objections.[14] The postulate developed by him, contrary to the explicit text of the *Phaedrus*, that Plato must necessarily have made his written teaching as similar "*as possible*" to that which is oral, skips over the decisive thesis of the *Phaedrus* itself, according to which this proximity is indeed *impossible* on the fundamental point, that is, on the issue of the *power of written communication*, and according to which every kind of written discourse, on this point, is essentially *unlike* the true dialogue. In the Introduction dedicated specifically to the *Phaedrus*, Schleiermacher himself allows us indirectly to understand that he did not find in the text of the *Phaedrus* any support in favor of his interpretation. In fact, he explicitly writes: "At that time Plato lost hope of ever being able in his written work to approximate" the type of oral teaching of Socrates, " but subsequently he learned to do it, and did not end thus with a belief in the complete incommunicability of philosophy."[15] And already in the dialogue immediately subsequent, namely the *Protagoras*, can be found "a perfect attempt to imitate even in writing the living and deeply felt discourse of the one who knows!"[16] This hypothesis, which simply in itself is not worthy of belief, lacks foundation in a definitive way through the verification of the late dating of the *Phaedrus*, obtained by the stylometric method. But this means that the critique of the *Phaedrus* directed against the written text takes into account all the works of Plato.[17]

In this way Schleiermacher, on the one hand, accentuating in a onesided manner the dialectical methodology of the second part of the *Phaedrus*, cannot take into account the organic unity of all the themes of this dialogue, since such a unity is found at a deeper level; on the other hand, he does not take into account the ultimate consequences that arise in the criticism of written works developed at the end of the dialogue (278B – E; cf. Appendix 1.1).[18] Plato in this passage defines the true philosopher as the one who has "something more valuable" (*timiotera*) than what has been written by him, and in consequence he thereby leaves the literary dialogue behind him even as regards content. The theory of Schleiermacher, according to which the literary and artistic dialogue of Plato is self-sufficient, is deeply shaken by these basic assertions.

The Meaning of the Criticism of Writing in the *Phaedrus* According to Modern Followers of Schleiermacher and the Interpretation of the School of Tübingen

The attempts of some modern followers of Schleiermacher to attenuate the importance of this part of the text of the *Phaedrus*, in the course of intensive discussions have been shown to be more and more unsupportable.

1. Plato, in the text of the *Phaedrus*, could not have alluded to simple explanations, clarifications, and defenses,[19] with which the philosopher different from the other authors of the writings mentioned there "comes to the aid" of his writings. In fact, this prevents the unequivocal differences of an hierarchical order between the things of "higher value" and the things of "low value" (τιμιώτερα-φαῦλα) of which the dialogue speaks.

2. Each written work, needs a special demonstration (ἀπόδειξις; cf. ἔλεγχος), to show that the written work itself is (relatively) "of minor value," precisely because there is something of "major value" that exists beyond the written work. In no way can this be thought to

be true because, in a purely general way, the character of the written work is considered in its difference with respect to oral teaching. The difference must be rather with regard to the philosopher, who with greater accuracy, is characterized by the superior wisdom that he possesses, which makes him capable of successful demonstration, and that therefore in its very nature is prior to oral discourse as well as to the written.[20]

3. A reason why the philosopher is held back from expressing himself wholly in his written work Plato has already mentioned in the preceding text (275E f.; cf. Appendix 1.1). The issue concerns the danger of being misunderstood by those who are incompetent and incapable of philosophy. Here, obviously, the responsibility of the philosopher in relation to his philosophy obliges him to react to a profanation of this kind.

4. T. A. Szlezák has recently verified, in numerous works, the meaning of the expression "come to the aid of his own discourse" (λόγῳ βοηθεῖν) using parallels from the *Republic* (362D, 368B f., 427E) and from the *Laws* (890D ff.).[21] The issue in all these cases is the fundamental connection that leads beyond the original theme, and goes back to the higher and more essential objects of philosophical reflection, in this way justifying the original ones. This semantic clarification of the *meaning* referring to the *content* of the Platonic *topos* entirely maintains its importance with respect to the *Phaedrus* 278 (cf. Appendix 1.1), independent of the fact that the parallel passages belong to a literary exposition.[22] Moreover, Aristotle offers a perfect parallel to *Phaedrus* 278, when, with respect to the followers of Plato, he writes that they "come to the assistance" of the cosmogony of the Platonic *Timaeus* by means of an atemporal interpretation, which moves from a chronological to a didactic level.[23] The *Phaedrus*, moreover, on this point, offers a series of parallels of a different kind, which, in their formulation, anticipate or repeat the assertions that can be read on page 278 (Stephanus edition), but that unequivocally regard an objective hierarchical relationship.[24]

5. The criticism of written discourse in the *Phaedrus* is linked by means of numerous topics to the ontological criticism of the poetic and figurative arts in *Republic* X,[25] thus as, also in the first part, the *Phaedrus* is tied again to the fundamental concepts of the *Republic*, and develops them. At the base of the distinction between dead written work and living dialectical discourse, between poetry, rhetoric, and philosophy is, hence, in the final analysis, a *hierarchy of the diverse levels of being*. And this hierarchy

of levels, since in the *Phaedrus* 276E (cf. Appendix 1.1) Plato includes the *Republic* itself in his criticism against the written word, carries even beyond to the theory of Ideas, which in this work is presented literarily, toward something charged with an even "greater value."[26]

6. The unwritten "thing of greater value" to which Plato alludes in the *Phaedrus* 278 (cf. Appendix 1.1) is linked by a series of topics with the central philosophical part of the *Seventh Letter* 340 – 345[27] ;(cf. later Appendix 1.2), which refers to the unwritten Platonic doctrine of the principles (τὰ περὶ φύσεως ἄκρα καὶ πρῶτα 344D). Because Plato, as can be proven, on the basis of the indications in the *Seventh Letter*, has professed the theory of the principles already in the year 366 (cf. see what is said in the passages 338C ff, 341A f., 345B; cf. these last two passages in the Appendix 1.2), it follows that the *Phaedrus*, by reason of its chronology, must already have taken into account such a theory. The parallel of the *Timaeus* 53D (cf. Appendix 2.10) connecting to this in another manner, which alludes to the analytical-dimensional regression (that is, to the procedure that rises by means of the analysis of the dimensions of bodies to their numerical constituents) of the unwritten doctrine, is a further confirmation.[28]

The Position of Schleiermacher in Relation to the *Seventh Letter* and the References in the Dialogues to the Unwritten Doctrines

Schleiermacher has not taken a position either in relation to *Phaedrus* 278 or to the *Seventh Letter*, even if a few years before W. G. Tennemann used the *Seventh Letter* as evidence to demonstrate the existence of a Platonic metaphysics standing behind the written works.[29] Schleiermacher, instead, left suspended (*in suspenso*) the authenticity of the *Seventh Letter* then contested by scholars such as Meiners ("let it be," Tennemann writes, "as it will with this letter")[30] even if leaving things in such an unclear state, the meaning of Schleiermacher's theory of the literary dialogue of Plato necessarily takes on an uncertain and provisional character. The same is to be noted about his treatment of the famous passages involving cessation of speech and the aspect of silence in which Plato refers to the unwritten doctrines standing beyond his literary work. Schleiermacher, with barely concealed resignation, is unable to integrate these assertions with his presentation of Plato. Thus, for example, he finds that "the reference to a discussion about ἀκριβές, or ἀκρίβεια here (*Statesman* 284D; cf. Appendix 2.8), stands rather lost,"[31] and he subsequently points out that in the introductory preamble, in which the simile of the sun in the *Republic* is demoted to the level of a second best way (506D f.; Appendix 2.4), "the satisfactory treatment of the latter [the Idea of the Good] is banished to I do not know what other place still far more beautiful, while here the Good is extolled only by means of images." [32] In the case of the *Republic*, this evasion on the part of Plato is all the more embarrassing for Schleiermacher, insofar as this work, together with the *Timaeus*, ought to represent the summarizing and constructive stage within his general outline. In the *Republic*, in fact, the system must reach its decisive heights, in which the increasing levels of rational explanation correspond to limitations, in a quite noticeable way, imposed on the mythic-poetic elements. It is evident, therefore, that the provisional character of the simile of the sun is opposed in a fatal way to the conception of Schleiermacher, which does not provide a "something more," which is to be found beyond the constructive works. Nevertheless, Schleiermacher ought to be given credit for being honest enough to recognize the incompleteness of the *Republic*, instead of seeking to neutralize this incompleteness by means of theories contrary to the text, the way his followers did by turning the assertions of the *Republic* 506D – E (cf. Appendix 2.4) into instances of "irony" presenting them as hints of "something which cannot be said."

The basic conception of Schleiermacher about the philosophy of Plato, namely, that it is to be found wholly in the literary works (the dialogues), also reveals a weakness on another point. The dialogue that was to have the title of the Philosopher and that is announced by Plato (*Sophist* 217A, 254B; *Statesman* 257A f.) was never written. As a consequence, Schleiermacher cannot reconcile himself to the existence of this omission in the general plan and necessarily felt impelled to give concrete form to the projected dialogue the *Philosopher*. He proposes, therefore, to see in the *Symposium* and in the *Phaedo* taken together the mimetic equivalent of the missing dialogue concerned with the definition of the philosopher, which must be, instead, of a systematic and definitional character. [33] Schleiermacher is well aware of the fact that, in this case, Plato had abandoned his original plan for a trilogy, or, at least, that he changed it in a significant way. He, therefore, subsequently in the Introduction to the *Phaedo* limited himself to proposing for consideration that Plato wanted to stimulate the reader to reconstruct for himself the figure of the philosopher, drawing from both prior and subsequent writings. Actually, the first proposal, that because of the chronological results of stylometric statistics obtained in the meantime Schleiermacher still understands the relation between the trilogy of the *Sophist, Statesman, Philosopher* and *Symposium* and *Phaedo* in a sense opposed to what subsequently proved to be the case, is not defensible. But the alternative consideration, which presupposes that the ideal figure of the philosopher is implicitly presented in the dialogues taken together, demands, as Schleiermacher himself appears to grant, a too excessive autonomy to the reader who must explicate it.

The Position of Schleiermacher in Relation to the Unwritten Doctrines and the Indirect Tradition

Schleiermacher has explicitly taken a position in relation to the question of an unwritten doctrine of Plato, in the Introduction, and, in discussion with Tennemann,[34] he tried to diminish and eliminate in whatever measure possible the indirect tradition, which contrasts with his general conception of Plato. The argument of Schleiermacher is substantially the following.[35] First he vigorously denied that "genuine historical traces which support the opinion about the existence of a difference between the esoteric and exoteric works of Plato [could be] found." He went back in this respect to Aristotle, who "never appeals to other sources but rather everywhere appeals, in a natural and straightforward way to the writings that have come down to us." Schleiermacher himself, nevertheless, retracts this clearly incorrect assertion and rectifies it within the same period, and admits what follows: "and even where, here and there, he cited other lost teachings or perhaps oral teachings, these citations do not contain anything which cannot be read in our writings or which departs entirely from them."[36] It is evident, then, that Schleiermacher is constrained to admit the existence of a "something more" that goes beyond the written works of Plato and that only the type of relation existing between the two traditions still remains a matter for discussion. Schleiermacher (in the passage cited) is correct in his assertion that the indirect tradition does not oppose the direct tradition, without having connections and relations with it, as though it were something radically different from it. But the bare assertion that there exists a substantial homogeneity does not resolve, without doubts, the problem that emerges concerning the relations of the two traditions, but, rather, obscures it. Schleiermacher seems to admit that, owing to the unifiability and affinity of the two traditions, the indirect tradition can be treated like a "negligible amount," while in reality, the real problem is hidden in the tension of its "divergence," which nevertheless, is "not a total divergence."[37] To which can be added that Schleiermacher tried to treat lightly, as exceptions, the reports of Aristotle on the unwritten doctrines of Plato (he did not name other informants), even though they are testimonies of significant weight like those from *Physics* A and *Metaphysics* A, M, and N. He, in addition, passed over in silence the fact that, in these reports, it is not a matter of any doctrine whatsoever, but of the fundamental one concerned with Plato's theory of the principles.

The inadequacy of the contradictory and obfuscating "explanation" of Schleiermacher did not escape his followers. They tried to free themselves from the indirect tradition in a way that was not so arbitrary, but by introducing further suppositions; either limiting the indirect tradition chronologically (that is, locating it at a late stage) or deriving it from the dialogues themselves on the basis of admitting that his circle of pupils misunderstood them. But in this strategy what Schleiermacher passed over in silence is in fact clear, that is, that there is simultaneously both agreement and disagreement between the two traditions.

Schleiermacher, however, has issued a challenge to the supporters of Platonic esotericism that their opinion must "be supported and developed in an orderly way by means of a coherent exposition of such a doctrine and all the allusions, even if very tenuous, which refer to it." The challenge was undoubtedly well motivated, since only in this way could the sphere of the esoterica be deprived of its indeterminacy and elevated to a concrete historical reality comparable to the writings, without being taken as a cover like a mere *asylum ignorantiae* (cover for ignorance), as some had done previously. We know not if Schleiermacher holds that such a systematic exposition and undertaking is possible, because he, as has been shown, did not pose the problem of the peculiar nature of the unwritten doctrines with the necessary accuracy. However, in the measure in which the indirect tradition is open to this possibility and Schleiermacher cannot deny this the monopolistic claim of the literary image of Plato proclaimed by Schleiermacher becomes problematic and is exposed to the possibility of a reorientation and revision. Schleiermacher could have undoubtedly maintained his discovery of the artistic form of the Platonic dialogue (which with its "holism" could in point of fact be supported by *Phaedrus* 264C, where it says that writing must be an ὅλον τι [*a whole*]), as consistent with the indirect tradition, if he had taken into account the hierarchical superiority of the self-testimonies and the references made by Plato himself in the dialogues (even in relation to some assertions in the *Phaedrus* 264, in fact the assertions of the *Phaedrus* 264C, are of relative and subordinate worth to that of Plato's self-testimonies). But, then, that discovery would have been limited in its nature and still remained subordinate to a fuller general position characterized by the philosophical primacy of the oral dimension, that is, of the living word. But also in this case it would have been taken as a trail breaking and permanent contribution to the understanding of the philosopher-writer Plato. Schleiermacher, instead, has overvalued the nature of his insights and has exaggerated his claims, creating the myth of a literary and artistic dialogue self-sufficient of itself, which is not supported historically. He himself in the Introduction established the relation of his thesis to the devaluation of the indirect tradition; like the incomprehension of the artistic form of the Platonic work led to the consequence that one had up to then to search for a loophole in the hypothesis of an esoteric doctrine, [38] thus, vice versa, the correct understanding of Plato the author renders superfluous every form of esotericism.[39] Here a claim of monopoly in favor of the literary dialogues is made to prevail that leads to the opposition and exclusion between the literary dialogue and the indirect tradition. The problem arises, then, whether in Schleiermacher what was purely hermeneutic went beyond the limits of the historian of philosophy, or if not, whether rather Schleiermacher the philosopher and metaphysician lost control and made history more dependent than is appropriate. Thus the next chapter is concerned with the clarification of this problem.

2 | Schleiermacher's Premises Inspired by the Idealistic Philosophy of Identity

"I always have a secret inclination to criticism; it is a very useful exercise to me personally, when conducted with discretion and I also believe, with this, to be able to accomplish some good, and here and there, to mediate between conflicting parts thus also many things in my Plato will be a mediation between the old and the new conceptions of philosophy."

Letter of Schleiermacher to Reimer,
September 1803

The Historical and Theoretical Conditions of the *Plato* of Schleiermacher

The translation of Plato by Schleiermacher should not be taken in an isolated manner, but it should be viewed in relation to all the works of Schleiermacher himself, as well as in relation to the spiritual milieu of the epoch around 1800s, especially in relation to the prior Romanticism and Idealistic philosophy. W. Dilthey has especially made a point of this in his great biography of Schleiermacher and in his treatment of the Berlin Academy of 1898, as has H. G. Gadamer more recently, in a supplementary way.[1] However, the presuppositions of the *Plato* of Schleiermacher, and especially the presuppositions of the formation of the categories and concepts that are at its base, have not been stated clearly and are not understood in all their connotations and implications. This depends above all on two main reasons; on the one hand, Schleiermacher, especially in the general Introduction, consciously remains within an historical scope, without further reflection on its basic conceptual apparatus; on the other hand, the theoretical and conceptual works of Schleiermacher especially *Ethics, Dialectic,* and *Aesthetic,* as well as *Hermeneutics, Psychology, Criticism of Moral Doctrine* of 1803, *Discourses on Religion,* and the *Doctrine of Faith,* and finally the *Reviews, Letters* and *Diaries* up to the present have not been taken into account in a systematic way in order to explain his *Plato.*

In the pages that follow there will be presented, for the first time, the results of this systematic comparison. On the basis of such a comparison we can to a large extent reconstruct the theoretical premises that Schleiermacher in his *Plato* was limited to apply without making them explicit, with the result, evidently, then, that the theory of the literary and artistic dialogue of Plato that belongs to Schleiermacher, contains the marks and signs of historical conditioning, which Platonic scholars have never become aware of in a worthwhile way.

The Genesis of the Hermeneutic Presupposition of the Autonomy of the Written Works in Schleiermacher

The principle of the autonomy of written works is among the indirect hermeneutic presuppositions. It was applied to the biblical corpus due to the reform of Protestantism. On the basis of this principle, the biblical text must be interpreted by beginning from the text itself (*sola scriptura*) and must be interpreted through itself (*sui ipsius interpres*), and all the various kinds of multiple senses of the written text (allegorical, anagogic, tropologic, etc.) must be rejected in favor of a purely literal interpretation. Beginning around the seventeenth century, this principle was also applied to the writings of Plato and it shattered the Neoplatonic interpretation of Plato.[2] Schleiermacher presupposed the evolution of this historical event as already concluded. In the capacity of a Protestant theologian fully familiar with the principle of this literal interpretation of written works, he has generalized it in his hermeneutics and made it a standard for every kind of interpretation.[3] The rejection of allegories, strictly connected with this principle, naturally was applied also to the writings of Plato. The methodological attitude of the Introduction to *Plato* of Schleiermacher, that is, that Plato must be correctly understood "only through an immediate and detailed knowledge of his works,"[4] applied in a traditional way the principle of the self-sufficiency of the written works also to the text of Plato.[5] But it was supported by the awareness that it was to be satisfied for the first time by means of a substantial interpretation.

The Romantic Conception of the Unity of Art and Philosophy as a Fundamental Presupposition of the Interpretation of Plato by Schleiermacher

The devaluation of the indirect tradition of Plato, however, in Schleiermacher himself was not based in a specific way on the principle of the literal interpretation of written works. This was to gain entrance only in the followers of Schleiermacher, who derived the indirect tradition from a "Neoplatonic" exegesis and from a distortion of the written works. Schleiermacher himself, as a theologian, was concerned with the *Sacred Scriptures* that were throughout of a doxographical and biographical nature and hence represented a secondary tradition, and that notwithstanding, must be taken into serious consideration. In addition, Schleiermacher even occasionally declared himself in favor of the primacy of the oral, that is, of the living word, with respect to written statements,[6] but, usually he ranked spoken and written discourse at least on the same level.[7]

The exceptional status given by Schleiermacher to the literary Plato is based rather on the exemplary artistic character of the written works of Plato and on his consequent idealized capacity for communication. The central conception of Schleiermacher, namely, to interpret "Plato also as philosophical artist," and "this same Plato, finally, as philosopher and artist,"[8] must be seen, therefore, in relation with the early Berlin Romanticism that flourished around Friedrich Schlegel, with whom Schleiermacher had strong ties of friendship and to whose suggestion the very translation of Plato is owed. The philosophy of life belonging to this circle—in opposition to the Enlightenment and to the intellectualized and specialized philosophy of the time—was determined by an option in favor of the super-rational character of religion, the arts and life, by the search for the infinite which is manifested also in the individuality of the finite, and by the aspiration to form a comprehensive synthesis, a universal mediation, for the unification and harmony of opposites. In particular, early Romanticism—F. Schlegel like Hardenberg (Novalis) who was highly esteemed[9] by Schleiermacher—proclaimed the unity of philosophy and art. This notion of art was chiefly applied to poetry, but F. Schlegel included in this concept of art, with Plato specifically in mind, even the art of philosophical discourse.[10] Now Schleiermacher, in the third of his *Discourses on Religion* (1799), places art, philosophy, and religion together and explains this association in the light of Plato.[11] On the other hand, his *Aesthetics* shows how one must understand more properly the literary works of Plato; as chiefly rhetorical works of art and in a more limited way as poetical.[12] This agrees with the judgment presented in the *Plato* and in the exposition of the *Platonic Philosophy* of 1812,[13] according to which, in the general plan of Plato, the poetic and mythic elements were made to recede gradually in favor of the rational *logos*, even if in a not wholly satisfactory manner. Therefore, in the conception of Plato presented by Schleiermacher, art and poetry were not in perfect harmony, but could diverge, even if the mimetic and dramatic characteristics[14] of the Platonic dialogue could lead also to poetic qualities. It is a matter of conviction, for Schleiermacher, that the work of Platonic art has an individualizing function;[15] but this means that it produces the infinite within the finite.[16] In addition, Dilthey[17] is correct when he admits that the notion of aesthetic production developed by Schleiermacher in the *Hermeneutics* and the *Aesthetics* was already operative in the Introduction to *Plato* with the distinction between *germinal decision* or mediation, original creation, embracing the basic decision concerning the content and the type of form and *composition*, that is, development, representation, and execution in particular. This means that the literary and artistic dialogue of Plato, according to Schleiermacher, already belongs to the stage in which the germinal decision (*Keimentschluss*)[18] is produced, with which once again the unity of content and form, philosophy and art is reinforced. Moreover, the *Aesthetics* confirms the impression of the Introduction that Schleiermacher conceived *art as techne* in the ancient sense, that is, as rational productive knowledge. Nevertheless, enthusiasm must precede *techne* and both must be involved in a harmonious relation in order that an authentic art can follow from it.[19] In addition, the *Aesthetics* conceives the writings of Plato as works of art with a scientific content, that is, they are art-works only accidentally;[20] they are, thus, works of art not insofar as they are presentations of science, but only of its procedure.[21]

The Role of F. Schlegel in the Formation of Schleiermacher's Interpretation of Plato

The part that F. Schlegel played in the formation of the conception of Plato by Schleiermacher was and still is controversial. The *Letters* show the philological inferiority of Schlegel, who as translator had not achieved the level necessary to realize the undertaking planned together with Schleiermacher, and therefore withdrew later on, but leave completely obscure the philosophical categories essential to the two authors. The degree of agreement, but also of differences, can be seen in the *Philosophical Lectures* of Schlegel between 1804 and 1806, which Windischmann had published posthumously for the first time.[22] According to Schlegel, the philosophy of Plato is a knowledge of the infinite, which can never be grasped in a definitive manner and which in its relation with the world allows itself to be represented only by means of images and allegories. To this end corresponds the dynamic artistic form of the Platonic writings, which in their interior structure and understood as a whole can point to the infinite, at least in an indeterminate manner. The protreptic character of Platonic philosophy excludes a rational system and therefore also a systematic esoteric teaching in the form of an unwritten doctrine of Plato. What the tradition seems to offer in this respect, Schlegel says, has come down to us through Plato's pupils, who "had little understanding" of their teacher, and therefore could not truly communicate his teaching. Schlegel hence agrees with the central tenet of Schleiermacher about the necessary connection of art and philosophy in Plato and about the rejection of the indirect tradition founded on it.

In several respects, however, he differs from him; in fact, while Schleiermacher looked for a basically didactic plan in the writings of Plato, and even for a system, Schlegel on the contrary, saw in Plato a thinker in continual development who was proceeding continually toward the infinite, without ever grasping it or fully achieving it.[23] In the second place, in Schlegel the artistic form is not a means or instrument of spiritual assimilation as it is in Schleiermacher, but it is a direct and necessary expression of the Absolute. Therefore, in Schlegel, the artistic form is immediately based on its metaphysical object, whereas in Schleiermacher, it seems to have only a didactic and hermeneutic function. The more radical and closed interpretation of Schlegel actually shows that he has largely adapted Plato to his own philosophical positions, although not in an acritical manner: the nostalgia for the infinite, the progress toward the infinite, the asystematic and essentially fragmentary character that Schlegel finds in many dialogues and finally, the connection of philosophy, art, and religion all this is motivated and conditioned by the personal position of Schlegel,[24] and therefore, we are under no obligation to regard it as history.

The idea of referring the Platonic corpus abruptly and thoroughly with the elimination of all the intermediate levels to the absolute infinite is an especially venturesome notion, and it goes beyond the self-testimonies of Plato in an unwarranted way, especially beyond the statements of the *Phaedrus*, which Schlegel placed at the commencement of the Platonic corpus, and beyond the declarations contained in it about the primacy of oral discourse. Nevertheless, the comparison of Schlegel with Schleiermacher again shows most clearly that the program of early Romanticism of the unification of philosophy and art has also been developed by other contemporaries taking Plato as a model, and the image of Plato shaped by Schleiermacher must be seen by taking into consideration this general background. Schlegel offers a very instructive parallel that gives evidence for the connection between an artificial reconstruction of the philosophy of Plato and the placement of the indirect Platonic tradition in the background.

The impression that the Introduction to the *Plato* of Schleiermacher, considered simply in itself, may produce, that is, that the Platonic artistic form for Schleiermacher, in contrast to Schlegel it is not metaphysically based, is erroneous. It is possible to demonstrate that behind the activity of Schleiermacher concerning the interpretation of Plato, just as in Schlegel, is a hidden theoretical attitude, which can be located within the context of the Idealistic philosophy contemporaneous with him, especially in the philosophy of identity expressed in its most perspicuous form by F. W. J. Schelling.

The Affinities and Convergences of the Theoretical Positions of Schleiermacher and Schelling

Dilthey, in his lectures held at the Academy of Berlin concerning the *Plato* of Schleiermacher, has already called attention to the historical and philosophical presuppositions at work in the actualization of Plato in the 1800s and likewise emphasized the role of the common element of *objective Idealism*. [25] The Announcement, made by Schlegel about the Plato translation he was going to do with Schleiermacher, published in the *Allgemeine Literaturzeitung* of 1800, supported as a matter of fact, "the necessity for disseminating the study of such a great author generally," "especially" in connection with the state of affairs created after the publication of the *Doctrine of Science* of Fichte[26]; and the *Communication* [Review] by Schleiermacher published in the same *Literaturzeitung* at the beginning of 1804, expresses the conviction that "right now a more accurate knowledge" of Plato "is the primary task."[27] In the letter addressed to the publisher Reimer, written a short time earlier, Schleiermacher announced that his Plato, indeed, was a "mediation between the old and the new conceptions of philosophy." [28] This explains the plan that Schleiermacher mentioned in the Communication, that is, a general, conclusive exposition and historical arrangement of Plato and his philosophy,[29] and as is documented in the long *Letter to Boeckh* regarding Plato written in 1808, in the second edition of the first volume of *Plato* published in 1817 and in the last volume published in 1828[30] he has maintained this plan to the end. The Introduction to the *Plato* of 1804, therefore, does not contain everything that Schleiermacher thought about Plato nor his final words on Plato, but is intentionally limited to the merely literary aspects, leaving aside the philosophical connections and specific references to the actual concerns he found in Plato.

But given a more attentive consideration, the perspective of the "new conception of philosophy" is at work even in the general Introduction, which is rigidly arranged according to a historical and literary viewpoint, whereas it emerges in an explicit manner in the *Introductions* to the individual dialogues and in the *Plato* of 1812. In the first place, it is immediately evident that the principles and the primary foundations that Schleiermacher ascribes to Plato in the basic early group of writings, are principles concerning method in the sense found in modern philosophy from Descartes to Kant and not principles concerning content in the sense of the old metaphysics of substance. But the schematic character of the supposed general plan of the writings, carried through three successive stages from the methodological foundation to its application to the "Sciences of Reality" (ethics and physics) up to the objective and constructive synthesis of the extensive works of the third group, also contains the attributes of the modern conception of *system,* so much so that Schleiermacher, in the *Lecture* of 1812, expressly presents Plato as the "first systematic philosopher."[31]

Consequently these two presuppositions concerning the concepts of method and of system, as can easily be grasped, are obstacles to the recognition of the existence of a Platonic theory of unwritten principles. In addition, the conception of the spontaneity and the "production of concepts"(!) on the part of the reader, which for Schleiermacher is decisive for the comprehension of the artistic form in Plato, in spite of all the historical justifications that it can have, cannot, in any case, deny its affinity to the Idealistic theory of the constitution of reality, and likewise to the modern principle *"verum et factum convertuntur"* ["truth and what is made are convertible"]. Finally, the category of *intention*, insofar as it already reflects the concept of "germinal decision" of the aesthetic of Schleiermacher, goes back to the practical philosophy of Kant and Fichte, since Schleiermacher constructed this concept on an analogy with the concepts of the "free act" and "self-determination."[32] Still more important, Schleiermacher wanted to recognize in the three stages of the overall plan three phases in the approach of the theoretical and the practical, which in the constructive period should be "thoroughly one."[33] Plato, therefore, leads the reader, through successive stages, to a conception that the contemporary philosophy of Fichte and Schelling made obligatory. More precisely, it is the unification of basic dialectical knowledge with the particular sciences of ethics and physics[34] that Plato, according to Schleiermacher, polarized into different pairs of dialogues, as Schleiermacher himself tried to show even in detail on the basis of the pairs of dialogues: *Protagoras* and *Parmenides*, *Gorgias* and *Theaetetus*, *Republic* and *Timaeus*. For the threefold partition of dialectic (logic), ethics, and physics Schleiermacher goes back to the Platonic Academy, but for the general concept of the "Sciences of reality" (*reale Wissenschaften*)[35] he appeals to contemporary philosophy. Schelling had coined this term in his *Lectures Concerning the Method of Academic Study* of 1803 and had used it often there.[36] Schleiermacher had accepted it in his extensive review of this work published in the *Jenaische Literaturzeitung* of 1804,[37] on which he was working at the same time he was completing the final redaction of his Introduction to Plato.

Further hints are found in the Introduction to the Parmenides published in 1805. Schleiermacher, in this dialogue, brought to light an actual message, namely "the highest task of philosophy," formulated as "the task of finding a unitary origin of thought and being" and of "deducing from it the immediate connection of man with the intelligible world."[38] The influence of Schelling emerges, also from the terminological viewpoint, in the admission of diverse "powers" of unity,[39] and finally, becomes explicit in the statement that the *Parmenides*, considered as the "most ancient attempt in philosophy to construct a knowledge mediating a connection of contraries," is "just like something which appeared in our own times."[40] A parallel is offered in the Introduction to the *Theaetetus*, published in 1805, where he remarks on the different attempts to define knowledge as the uninterrupted "gradual development of ordinary consciousness."[41]

The cultural ambiance surrounding the Introduction of 1804 as a result becomes clearly recognizable in its fundamental traits. Further features are offered by the exposition of Plato contained in the *Lectures on the History of Philosophy* of 1812 published by H. Ritter.[42] It is permissible to suppose that in them can be found the basis, or at least the equivalent of that which was to be the monograph on Plato, programmed right from the beginning, as the conclusion of the translation of Plato, but which Schleiermacher never published. Schleiermacher developed, in that place, a concise and systematic compendium of Platonic philosophy, divided, as in the Introduction, into dialectic, physics, and ethics. At the apex was the absolute unity of the opposites constituted by being and knowledge, represented by the Idea of the Good, which is identified with divinity.[43] To this absolute identity of subject and object were made to follow, in gradual succession, the ideal and real opposites. The formal (ideal) dialectic functions by mediating between absolute unity and the "Sciences of Reality," constituted by physics and ethics, which it reflects in a "speculative" manner. As in the ideal identity of being and knowledge, thus, analogically, there is existent also in the real a unity of spiritual and material in the form of life constituted by the soul and body. The issue is obviously the concern with different grades of the mixture and identity of the subjective and the objective; in fact, to Schleiermacher this especially implies that "there is nowhere in actual being a disjunction between the real and the ideal."[44] The fundamental general structure of all being that is deduced from an original unity, for Schleiermacher is more important than the differences conceived only gradually between the real and the ideal. The antidualistic tendency, in the ultimate analysis characterized by the philosophy of identity, that belongs to this interpretation of Plato, finds a corresponding place in the *Collected Fragments of Heraclitus* of 1808, in which the dominating theoretical interest seems to be concentrated on the deduction of the world from opposites and finally, from the original unity (also of thought and being).[45] Significantly enough, Schleiermacher examines the influence of Heraclitus on Plato at the end of this work.[46]

The exposition of the *Plato* of 1812 illustrates in a very precise manner the reduction to unity of the theoretical stage (dialectic) and the practical (physics and ethics as "Sciences of Reality"), which the Introduction of 1804 attributed to Plato; by this time it is manifestly assumed on the basis of the idea of a unity of the ideal and real, as Schelling had proclaimed it in his *System of Transcendental Idealism* of 1800 (ideal-realism, where ideal corresponds to theoretical and real corresponds to practical).[47] At the same time, the fact that the Platonism of Schleiermacher, interpreted in the sense of the philosophy of identity, must radically exclude the dualism of the principles of the indirect tradition of Plato, becomes comprehensible because of his theoretical commitments. Schleiermacher, actually, sees in Plato in a way different from Schlegel the undoubtedly systematic philosopher, but the dialogues seem to correspond to his requirements more than the metaphysics of the unwritten doctrine, which terminates in the ultimate opposition of the two principles.[48]

Wilhelm Dilthey, in his great biography of Schleiermacher, reconstructed the philosophical development above all of the early Schleiermacher, by using different approaches and different attempts.[49] This development, for a long time influenced by Kant (from about 1785 to 1793), went on to the acceptance of Fichte and in a complementary way Spinoza, and from him, to Schelling and to Plato. In the context of this development, the last two thinkers seem to outshine and overcome the influence of Spinoza, through their aesthetic-teleological aspects, and Schelling in his turn, will outshine and overcome the influence of Plato through the more rigorous conception of the Absolute and its systematic concretization in the constitution of the totality.[50]

In point of fact, a Spinozistic thinker, in the period of transcendental philosophy must inevitably come to the position of Schelling, and in the case of the acceptance of Plato the premises of the philosophy of identity must necessarily become dominant from the hermeneutic viewpoint. Schleiermacher, during his life, stayed closer to Schelling than to any other contemporary philosopher (with the exception of at most H. Steffens, a pupil of Schelling and his colleague at Halle). In the discussions concerning the positions of Schelling, Schleiermacher, beginning from a rather eclectic position, constructed his own system, as can be seen especially from the different editions of the *Ethics*, but likewise from the *Dialectic* of 1814. The *Letters* and the *Diaries* document the thorough study of the works of Schelling by Schleiermacher already in the first Berlin period.[51] Again the *Discourses on Religion* of 1799 show the influence of Schelling.[52] This was reinforced later on when Schelling beginning from about 1801 had become the predominant philosopher of the times, after the work of Hegel, *The Difference between the Philosophical Systems of Fichte and Schelling*. Schleiermacher and Schlegel saw in Schelling unlike Fichte who was considered "the onesided genius" of the *Doctrine of Science* [53] the philosopher of totality who had contrived to bring together into philosophy nature and history, art and poetry.[54] The point of conflict, for Schleiermacher, lay in the relation of the individual to the whole,[55] treated inadequately by Schelling, and which instead by the theologian, beginning from the *Discourses* up to the *Doctrine of the Faith* was insistently pressed.[56] In addition, besides Schelling's *Lectures concerning the Method of Academic Study* Schleiermacher had made a point of giving great importance to the Platonistically inspired Schellingian dialogue *Bruno or On the Divine and Natural Principle of Things* of 1802.[57] The hope of making Plato come alive, which Schleiermacher imposed on his translation of Plato that he was then completing, certainly received a new invigoration through this work. On the other side, it is well known that in the circle formed about Schelling the translation of Plato by Schleiermacher was looked upon with keen interest.[58]

In the context of these various convergences the fact is significant that Schelling, in the great works beginning from 1800, had described art as an "organon," a "mirror," and a "symbol" of philosophy, and had attributed a genuine philosophical function to it, more precisely the function of illustrating indirectly the fundamental identity of the ideal and the real, that is, the absence of the differentiation of thought and being in the Absolute. As Schelling explains in the fundamental and concluding part of the *System of Transcendental Idealism* of 1800, the work of art is the image of the Absolute, insofar as it, like an organism but in a much higher way, unites in itself the conscious and the unconscious, liberty and nature, the subjective and the objective. Schelling, therefore, defended, as did the first Romantics, the unity of philosophy and poetry, but for a more profound reason; namely, on the foundation of the philosophy of absolute identity. The *Bruno* carried forward these ideas, while the *Lectures Concerning the Method of Academic Study* analyzed them, assigning to philosophy in relation to art a small superiority in ideality (knowledge), but saw the symbolic relation of both as more strict than the more special one between theology and philosophy. Moreover, the Neoplatonism of Schelling attributes to mythology and art not only the function of symbolizing the Absolute but likewise of concretizing the ideal Absolute in the particular Ideas. Schelling shows further and this is the most important thing for the *Plato* of Schleiermacher that every science has its own artistic form, which is in turn "inseparable from its content," and with respect to philosophy he posits its proper form in dialectic.[59] The Introduction to the *Lectures* at Jena (1802 – 3) and at Würzburg (1804 – 5) of Schelling on the *Philosophy of Art*, finally develops in a summary way a complex philosophy from the viewpoint of art. It finds a difference between philosophy and art and, within art, between literary art (poetry) and figurative art, in the progressive triumph of the ideal or the real. Art takes the ideas of philosophy and puts them into an objective representation.

Now, a comparison with the theoretical writings of Schleiermacher shows that he has not only adapted the fundamental positions of the philosophy of identity of Schelling to his needs, but that he has also joined his aesthetic and hermeneutics to it and in this way preserved the central ideas of the metaphysics of the art of Schelling. This becomes clear at its best in different sketches of his *System of Moral Doctrine* that Schweizer, in 1835, tried to blend contaminating them within a whole inclusive unity and that O. Braun, in 1913, had published separately, making accessible for the first time the ample *Brouillon of Ethics* of 1805—06 and the *Doctrine of Virtue* of 1804—05.[60] The *Moral Doctrine* contained, still more than the *Dialectic*,[61] the ontology of Schleiermacher, in which the orientation modeled on the example of the *Ethics* of Spinoza is evident. Schleiermacher begins, as Schelling, from the identity of absolute knowledge and absolute being, which in the finite is separated into the opposition of the subjective and the objective, of the spiritual and the material, of the ideal and the real, of reason and nature; to these correspond the sciences of ethics and nature.[62] These oppositions interpenetrate one another according to different relations of the mixture ("relative oppositions") in which either the real or the ideal prevails Schleiermacher here follows Schelling's *Exposition of My System of Philosophy* of 1801 or the *Bruno* and therefore imitates, as "images," the original identity. These images or symbols of the Absolute are the organism (with the compenetration of soul and body), the universe, the natural form (as something that is teleologically organized), knowledge (as the relation between subject and object), the work of art, and, in general, every relation of expression, presentation, exposition, symbolization between what is interior and what is exterior. In this sense *art* is amply treated in the sketches of the *Moral Doctrine*,[63] and precisely, already in the *Brouillon* of 1805 and in the *Moral Doctrine* of 1804.[64] Art has a relation with the universe, and it is a symbol of the Absolute (of the unity of being, respectively of God)[65] in the particular, and therefore, as in Schelling, it reproduces the infinite in the finite.[66] Art is an objective individualization in this Schleiermacher is critically opposed to Schelling in the wake of Leibniz but, on the other hand, art depends "on the undivided act of the objective and subjective in intuition."[67] Art overcomes the opposition of being and knowledge, reality and ideality, and reconstitutes their identity; its productions are, in the highest degree, beyond all other productions.[68]

On the whole, the basic relation existing between the philosophy of identity and the concept of art of Schleiermacher is sufficiently clear, and, actually, already in the *Brouillon* of 1805 and *Moral Doctrine* of 1804, hence in the same year of the publication of the Introduction to *Plato*. These first drafts of the *Ethics* do not yet offer the systematic construction of the successive outlines from 1812 onwards, but they presuppose, partially and implicitly, what will become explicit at a later time, and in part continually allow us to glimpse fundamental ideas of the philosophy of identity.[69] The *Outline of a Critique of Previous Ethical Theory (Grundlinien einer Kritik der bisherigen Sittenlehre)* published in 1803 has an instructive reference to Plato. In this work Schleiermacher attributes to Plato the description of "the infinite being not only as being [!] [scil., as object] and as creator [scil., as subject], but also as poet, and the world as the handiwork of the divinity produced as work of art carried to an infinite degree," and Plato also looks for "a common principle and basis for nature and for ethics" [70] just like modern philosophers Spinoza and Fichte had done, although without the "conception of art and of a work of art."[71] Therefore, Schleiermacher attributes a universal concept of art to Plato, which he directly refers to infinite being and thought, on which both nature and morality is based. It is convenient here to add that the Introduction of 1804 conceived the work of Plato on the model of an organism,[72] which is in agreement with a similar function of the organism and the work of art in Schelling and Schleiermacher. In addition, the *Aesthetic* carried forward the analysis of the literary art of Plato, the preferred model, on this basis, as well as the arrangement in the typology of the symbolism of Schleiermacher. [73] Thus Plato likewise practiced, along with great symbolic art, a more modest one that was a burlesque and tied to the consideration of the particular.[74]

Concluding Summary

Let us summarize. Schleiermacher, on the basis of what we said earlier, not only brought Plato back to life in relation to the content of contemporary philosophy, but he likewise understood the artistic form of Plato's dialogues starting from his own premises of the philosophy of identity. And this result is totally independent of the question as to what measure the philosophy of identity and the philosophy of art of Schleiermacher has been influenced by the philosophy of Schelling or whether it was developed parallel to it.[75]

The artistic form of Plato, also in Schleiermacher, is not unmetaphysical and, as in Schlegel, has its own metaphysical and philosophical status. However in Schleiermacher, in the wake of Schelling, it is determined in a clearer manner and based on a more profound theory than that of Schlegel.

In Schleiermacher is an ontology of the artistic dialogue, which clothes the dialogue itself with a dignity that it could never have in the historical Plato. In fact, in the artistic dialogue, according to Schleiermacher, is symbolized "concretely" not only the infinite, but more especially, the absolute identity of subject and object. The dialogue hence corresponds to the structure of every finite being, which consists in being constituted by opposites, between which the dialogue in its own turn, mediates in the highest manner.

Just as the literary production of the author Plato, so also, reciprocally, does the hermeneutic reconstruction of his writings stand in the ontological relation of action and mediation, in which form and content, internal and external, subjective and objective intrinsically compenetrate and reproduce in an exemplary manner the absolute identity of the ideal and the real. The realization and the theoretical assimilation of the artistic form of Plato, taken in the strict sense, in Schleiermacher was somewhat beyond what is found in Schlegel, who critically distanced himself from Platonic dualism,[76] whereas in Schleiermacher it was changed in a monistic sense in an always increasing way, and for this reason Schleiermacher can fully identify himself with Platonism. For Schleiermacher there is a complete convergence of philosophy and art in Plato, insofar as art with its hermeneutic, throughout a philosophical anthropology, can be deduced from the fundamental axiom of Platonic doctrine understood on the basis of the philosophy of identity, and vice versa, consequently, it possesses an irreplaceable function for returning to the Absolute as identity.[77] *The fundamental reason for the excessive conclusions Schleiermacher has drawn from his theory of the literary and artistic dialogue of Plato consists indeed in these premises inspired by the philosophy of identity that are at the base of his interpretation of Plato.* The myth of the self-sufficient artistic dialogue, the comprehension of which is indispensable to the understanding of the philosophy of Plato, arose not only from the protoromantic program of the unity of philosophy and poetry, but is itself part of a metaphysics of art. The artistic dialogue, in Schleiermacher, must by its excessive evaluation and its exceptional dignity indeed bear the weight of this metaphysics, and thus it is far removed from the ontological criticism of art and writing that belonged to the historical Plato.[78] But the metaphysics of the philosophy of identity in the meantime has been overcome in various ways, on the one hand by Hegel, and on the other by Schelling himself in his last decades and again by the post-Hegelians. With the elimination of the metaphysical premises that marked it, the literary dialogue of Plato—some incontestable insights achieved by Schleiermacher being conserved—today must be considered as simpler and its relevance must be reduced.

After having examined and invalidated the historical presuppositions and conditions of Schleiermacher's theory of the dialogue, now is the opportune moment to offer a revision, which would appraise in a historically more adequate way the art of the dialogue of Plato, liberated from a metaphysics that was foreign to it. At the same time, the literary and philosophical function of the dialogue must be included within the comprehensive framework offered by the whole Platonic tradition and subordinated to it.

The First Dissenting Voices

The picture of Plato traced by Schleiermacher, in spite of its weaknesses, in the course of the nineteenth century, especially in midcentury began a progressive triumphal ascent. Ast (1816) and Socher (1820) oriented their works on Plato according to its perspective, Zeller with all his authority interceded in his *Greek Philosophy* right from the beginning (1846[1]) in favor of Schleiermacher, as well as Victor Cousin who in a French translation of Plato, took him, as his model. However, in the first half of the nineteenth century there was no lack of authoritative and penetrating critical voices who warned about the suppression of the indirect Platonic tradition and were concerned with incorporating the dialogues and the unwritten doctrines, the artistic form and the theory of principles in an adequate general schema.

A. Boeckh was such a voice. He was a follower of Schleiermacher at Halle, afterwards he became the major German philologist and methodologist of the nineteenth century in classical studies. In his review of the first volumes of the *Plato* issued in 1808 he approved, it is true, without any reservations the exceptional hermeneutic contribution produced by the discovery of the artistic form in Plato, and thus helped Schleiermacher to open the first breach. However, at the same time, Boeckh raised polite but accurate objections against the treatment given by Schleiermacher to the indirect tradition.[1] He pointed out, above all, certain points that alluded to a distinction between the *esoterica* and *exoterica* in the Pythagoreans and went back to the self-testimonies that Plato furnished in the *Seventh Letter* (341B ff.; cf. later Appendix 1.2) and in the simile of the sun in the *Republic* (506D; cf. later Appendix 2.4), where Plato expressly omits the definition of the essence of the Good. With this he put together the Aristotelian reports about the "unwritten doctrines" of Plato, of which he speaks in *Physics* (4.2; cf. later Appendix 3.4) and which were presented in lectures entitled—which coincided perfectly with the theme of the *Republic*—*On the Good* (περὶ τοῦ ἀγαθοῦ). From this Boeckh concluded that, in the oral lectures held in the Academy, Plato "presented in a clearer and explicit way what, on the contrary, he wrote in a way which was more difficult to understand," "and that in his oral teaching he placed the crown and key to what in his writings he did not bring to its highest point."[2] Boeckh, on the other hand, with good reason reproved Schleiermacher for having obscured the necessary differentiation between the writings and the unwritten doctrines and having expressed himself "as a Proteus," in a too indeterminate, obscure, and vacillating manner.

Boeckh, with this, left the impression that the problem of the indirect tradition could not be resolved by means of the discovery by Schleiermacher of the artistic form of the literary dialogue, but that, for the purposes of a methodologically adequate procedure, the indirect tradition and the direct must be joined together in an historically grounded manner. This direction indicated in the reflections of Boeckh was followed vigorously fifteen years later by C. A. Brandis in his work, *De perditis Aristotelis libris de ideis et de bono*.[3] Notwithstanding his bows in the direction of the interpretations of Schleiermacher on the Platonic writings,[4] Brandis presented an internal criticism of the reductive picture of Plato formed by Schleiermacher.[5] Brandis, for the first time, collected and commented on the testimonies referring to the unwritten doctrines (*On the Good*). He found in them the "fundamentals" of all the Platonic doctrines and projected a systematic comparison of the unwritten doctrines with the contents of the writings.[6]

The work of F. A. Trendelenburg, *Platonis de ideis et numeris doctrina ex Aristotele illustrata*,[7] stimulated by that of Brandis and published three years later was of no less importance. Trendelenburg conceded to Schleiermacher that he had put an end to the abusive use of the vague and obscure concept of esotericism in Plato and of having presented first of all the intrinsic connection of the writings. However he pointed out that this is not to fall into the opposite error which would be to absolutize the writings and to eliminate the indirect tradition as if it were an invention of the ancients.[8] Trendelenburg, in this respect, explains that the nucleus of the Aristotelian treatment of Plato could not be proved as a falsification, and that, consequently, it should be considered as authentic. In particular, he maintains that no contradiction exists between the Aristotelian treatment of Plato and the Platonic writings. Trendelenburg recognizes, moreover, like Brandis, that the unwritten doctrines involve a philosophical position more fundamental than the dialogues, which is clarified in an exemplary way by their comparison with the *Philebus*.[9] In this regard, Trendelenburg, like Boeckh, considers the relation between the written work and the oral doctrine as a relation of explication comparable to the relation existing between one group of writings and another group within the corpus.[10]

The problems that arise outside of the reductive picture of Plato, proper to Schleiermacher, and as such remain unresolved, found, in addition, eloquent expression in several works that the philosopher C. H. Weisse from Leipzig published during the period while Schleiermacher was still alive.[11] Weisse also tried to trace back the concept of the esoterica in Plato to its historically based kernel. He was interested chiefly in the Platonic notion of the material principle in comparison to that of Aristotle. Such a principle in its complete extension enters also into the constitution of the world of Ideas, Weisse, like previously Trendelenburg found, was a topic discussed only in the indirect tradition. Weisse proposed the cooperation of the formal and the material principle (unity and the great-and-small) on both levels of being—the ideal and the real—in such a way that in the ideal ambit the formal principle would prevail while, on the contrary, in that of the real the material principle would prevail (Weisse, in this respect, made use inappropriately, of the mythicizing expression *apostasy* [viz., falling away]).

A little different and more complicated position was taken up by K. F. Hermann in relation to the problem of the unwritten doctrine of the principles of Plato. In his work *Geschichte und System der platonischen Philosophie* I[12] which was destined to exercise a notable influence, he substituted for Schleiermacher's presupposition of a systematic plan of the Platonic writings the idea of the development of Platonic thought (agreeing in this respect with F. Schlegel). The tradition handed down by the pupils, in this way, is posited at the end, as the final stage of the evolutionary span of Platonic thought.[13] Consequently, in this way he limited the value of the oral doctrine in comparison to the written work, which could be done because the oral remained unwritten only temporarily, not enough to justify a differentiation between the *esoterica* and *exoterica* in Plato.[14] Hermann reserved the treatment of the unwritten tradition to the second volume of his work,[15] which, however, was never published. In a conference held in 1839 and published in 1849,[16] Hermann accepted, instead, as Boeckh and Hegel and against Schleiermacher, the thesis that between the oral activity and the written work there exists a relation of explanation (the oral lectures about the principles explain the written work) and, vice versa, between the former and the latter, a relation of application (the dialogues are the application of the principles). The unwritten doctrines treat of the highest principles, by which Hermann understood the complex of the Ideas together with the elements from which the Ideas themselves were derived, but without depriving, in this respect, the writings of the philosophical relevance due to them. Hermann, in this conference, assumed such distinctions as valid for the whole later period of Plato's life, which, however, means for the greater part of the writings of our philosopher. However, this concluding work of Hermann, which converges with the basic intentions of the other authors just mentioned, had hardly any consequences of note, quite different however than the work of 1839, which instead together with the *Greek Philosophy* of Zeller has determined the future of the indirect Platonic tradition for a long time.

E. Zeller

That all these starting points, in the succeeding researches, could not develop to the point of correcting and completing the picture of Plato shaped by Schleiermacher, depends principally on the work of E. Zeller. He had been influenced by Schleiermacher in a massive manner and had guaranteed the final victory to his interpretation in the whole world, apparently placing it in accord with the historical data. Zeller, as a theologian, through F. C. Baur and D. F. Strauss was a second generation follower of Schleiermacher, and also expressed several times his appreciation for him both from the historical and philosophical viewpoint as well as from the theological.[17] Already the *Platonic Studies* of 1839, which was the first work of Zeller, was dependent entirely on Schleiermacher, while from the philosophical point of view it moved along the path of Hegel. The third part, *The Exposition of Platonic Philosophy in Aristotle*, claimed to make a contribution to "frightening away the specter of an esoteric Platonism."[18] Based on parallel passages of the dialogues, that Aristotle, as can be documented, interpreted in an inadequate way, Zeller maintains the thesis that even the anomalies of the indirect tradition of Plato in their basic points (as, for example, the material principle of the great-and-small presented in the ambit of the Ideas according to the model of the Aristotelian concept of matter, the Good defined as the One instead of what is predicated as one, the intermediate position attributed to mathematical objects, the immanentism of the Ideas, the dogmatic interpretation of the "symbolization" of the Ideas by means of numbers) arise from a misunderstanding or adaptations of the dialogues, or of the oral teaching of Plato, on the part of Aristotle. Moreover, Zeller maintained that in the reports handed down there is no question of the original form of the Platonic doctrine, but, on the whole, of a late reelaboration of it. He, therefore, agreed with the genetic explanation of Hermann of 1839, but he went far beyond this, even contesting the authenticity of the indirect tradition on decisive points.

The attempt of Zeller of 1839, was destined to exercise a notable influence. It signaled in a double sense the inauguration of certain strategies of Schleiermacherianism, which tried to show that the picture of Plato traced by Schleiermacher was in accord with the factual data of the indirect tradition, and with this, to bring help to it.[19] The arguments of Zeller already show the characteristic analogical deduction *a minore ad maius* (from the lesser to the greater) that was fully developed by Cherniss, just as the attempt to eliminate the differences between literary and oral communication.[20] In Zeller, the Hegelian arguments are based on Idealistic premises (the postulate of the deduction of the levels of being, a symbolic relation existing between the Ideas and numbers as in the *Lectures on the History of Philosophy of Hegel*).[21] On the other hand, the dominant hermeneutic ideas of the genuine, original, and primal archetype in opposition to the succeeding degeneration and imitation, go back to a Romantic mind set. They find, once again, evident parallels in Schleiermacher; he, in fact, in his conference held in 1817 at the Academy of Berlin and published posthumously in 1835 under the title *On the Ethical Works of Aristotle*,[22] tried to demonstrate that the Aristotelian *Magna Moralia* was the authentic ethics for Aristotle, on which the *Nicomachean Ethics* and the *Eudemian Ethics* depended.

In the first edition of the *Greek Philosophy*, published seven years later, Zeller maintains unchanged in all essential points his thinking.[23] And this is also true except for some attenuations of some theses[24] of the subsequent editions.[25] The *Greek Philosophy*, moreover, gives details for the late dating of the indirect tradition, locating it in the period of the composition of the *Laws*, and tries to explain such a tradition like the *Laws* as pointing out the growing senility of Plato.[26] With this, the theory of principles remains, in any case, discredited and separated chronologically from the greater part of the written work, to the point that they cannot compete with them. The *Greek Philosophy* especially, in addition to the *Studies* of 1839, shows that Zeller has accepted in all its basic points the Platonic picture drawn by Schleiermacher: in the recognition of the artistic form[27] of the literary dialogue and its "psychagogic" [generative] action,[28] in the rejection of every esotericism connected to it and in the consequent treatment of the Platonic self-testimonies (the *Seventh Letter* is rejected as inauthentic, simply because it used a terminology connected to esotericism),[29] in the assumption of a distinct general plan on three levels,[30] in the articulation of the exposition in dialectic, physics, and ethics,[31] and finally, in the criticism mounted against the excess of myth and poetry in Plato.[32] Zeller, hence, proved himself to be a faithful follower of the tendencies proper to Schleiermacher. Zeller, in fact, knew that Schleiermacher followed the philosophy of identity,[33] to which he, as a Hegelian, was opposed; however the connection existing between this philosophy of identity and the *Plato* of Schleiermacher was not clear to him. The fundamental article of Hermann, published in 1849, maintained the last comprehensive antithetical position. It was rejected by Zeller in his *Greek Philosophy* on the basis of his Schleiermacherian position.[34] With his own solution, which reduced the range of the indirect tradition to an absolute minimum, Zeller dominated the studies on Plato well into the twentieth century. The reports of the unwritten doctrine were pushed to the periphery of the understanding of Plato, suspected of being inauthentic in important points, discredited philosophically as well by being joined to the aged Plato and to the circle of pupils inferior to him, and presented as having scarcely any intrinsic merit.

Also in the twentieth century the renovation of the interpretation and the reexamination of the indirect tradition of Plato, in the beginning, still remained wholly under the influence of the appraisal of Zeller, which in its previous suggestion, as we have seen, goes back to Schleiermacher and Schlegel. In fact, the interpretation of the reports of the unwritten doctrines given by Robin, Stenzel, Ross, and Wilpert included the oral teaching of Plato within the schema of the evolution of the dialogues. This doctrine diverges from the content of the published dialogues, in that interpretation is placed on the same level as that of the dialogues, but always forced to the end of the series of writings, as representative of the "final," "the last" stage of Platonic philosophy. Only the advanced age of Plato or his death—it is thus concluded—probably prevented the publication in written form of this final thought.

Only recently has this position been seen as illusory and as a construction of the philology of the nineteenth century, dominated by Schleiermacher and Schlegel, that is, as a solution that is irreconcilable with the reports just as they are with the self-testimonies of Plato and that arbitrarily keeps hidden the specific problems of the indirect tradition.

P. Shorey and H. Cherniss

The founder and the "creative genius" of American studies on Plato, P. Shorey (1857 – 1934) studied at Leipzig, Bonn, and Munich from 1881 to 1884, and at Munich, in 1884, with the dissertation "De Platonis idearum doctrina" achieved a doctorate, studying under the direction of W. Christ and K. v. Prantl. This work is an outline that reflects the German studies on Plato at that time and the dominant figure of Zeller, who is the author most frequently cited by Shorey.[35] The influence of Schleiermacher, who was well known to Shorey even as a theologian, as is proven from his most mature work,[36] acts indirectly, but in an undeniable manner in the dissertation. (Of the two scholars who guided Shorey, Prantl especially may be considered as a follower of Schleiermacher and after him also Christ).[37]

According to the interpretation of Shorey, the dialogues are fully sufficient for the purpose of a complete understanding of Plato's philosophy.[38] He concludes his dissertation with a characterization of the writings of Plato, which moves entirely along the tracks laid down by Schleiermacher and not by chance culminates in an interpretation of the end of the *Phaedrus*. According to this characterization, Plato can be advantageously distinguished from Aristotle by the fact that he, in many cases, presented his thought in myths, images, and playful forms to stimulate the reader to his own reflection, as in a real conversation. Indeed the greatness of Plato both as a dialectician and as a poet would consist in this.[39] Also in his major work composed twenty years later, *The Unity of Plato's Thought*,[40] Shorey characterizes Plato as an artist, in whom the sense of each passage emerges only from the whole dramatic context: a repetition of the hermeneutic principle of Schleiermacher, according to which every affirmation in Plato can be comprehended solely on the basis of the context in which it is located and its function as a part of the whole.[41]

Also, for Shorey, hence, the Platonic art of indirect communication cannot be separated from the philosophy of Plato; it even constitutes one of that philosophy's essential traits and merits. The other side of this position, however, even for Shorey, logically, is the categorical rejection of the indirect Platonic tradition and its reduction to some misunderstanding of some passages of the Platonic dialogues by Aristotle or by the distortion of some passages based on the criteria of Aristotelian philosophy and terminology.[42]

The decisive thrust that propelled Shorey to these conclusions came undoubtedly from Zeller's *Platonische Studien* of 1839, which he frequently cited in his dissertation.[43] Shorey accepted the methodological principle of the early Zeller in both its variants (misunderstandings-adaptations), but he was more radical and therefore tried to go beyond Zeller. (To the theses previously maintained by Zeller with regard to the material principle and the intermediate position of mathematical objects, Shorey added theses with respect to the One and to the Idea-Numbers, which were derived from the *Parmenides*, and later, even theses about the categories, which would have been derived from the *Theaetetus*).[44] Also the supposition of Zeller that the Aristotelian polemic was negatively influenced by Pythagorean tendencies of the ancient followers of Plato, Speusippus and Xenocrates, was taken into account by Shorey.[45] On the other hand, he not only interpreted the *Phaedrus* as Zeller (and Schleiermacher did), on the basis of a theory of the literary dialogue, but, as they did, he rejected as inauthentic the corpus of the *Letters*,[46] with the *Seventh Letter*—and this point Shorey maintained even afterwards—while not taking a position with respect to the references of some dialogues to the "unstated."[47] The difference between Zeller and Shorey consists chiefly in this: in Shorey the conceptual idealistic position has been substituted by criteria that are partly psychological and partly logical-ontological. A certain anti-metaphysical sensibility of Shorey falls with great violence especially upon the indirect tradition, and it is sometimes pushed with loaded language and biting irony.[48] The radicalization of the positions of Zeller must be motivated, among other reasons, by this basically antimetaphysical attitude.

Shorey, in the United States, exercised an enormous influence as a teacher and, especially, as an authority in the field of Platonic studies.[49] His critical destruction of the indirect tradition of Plato was carried on and developed chiefly by an indirect follower, H. Cherniss. Between Shorey and Cherniss exists, indeed, a precise connection with respect to his university. Among the teachers of Cherniss at Berkeley was R. M. Jones, who belonged to the limited circle of the followers of Shorey and under whose direction he obtained the doctorate, and G. M. Calhoun, who, in his dissertation, was also directed by Shorey.[50] The dissertation of Cherniss produced under the guidance of R. M. Jones, "The Platonism of Gregory of Nyssa," (1930) was a subject looked upon with great favor by Shorey himself.[51] The methodological principle of making the late traditions arise from the extant classical texts is also encountered in R. M. Jones, who, actually, in the history of the school, functions as a conduit between Shorey and Cherniss (and his students). Therefore, it is certainly not accidental that the Platonic picture of Cherniss coincides in all essential points with that of Shorey.

1. Both see the work of Plato in a unitary manner, that is, they begin from the presupposition of the essential unity of Platonic thought in all the periods of his life.
2. Both maintain that the *Letters*, even the *Seventh Letter*, are inauthentic.
3. Both explain the indirect tradition on the basis of the presupposition of misunderstandings or distortions introduced by the followers of Plato.
4. The historical position mediated by the ancient followers of Plato between the writings of Plato and the interpretation of these on the part of Aristotle either was taken into consideration (as Shorey has done following Zeller), or even carried to extreme consequences (as Cherniss has done following J. C. Wilson).
5. Both admit a threefold root for the Platonic theory of the Ideas: an ethical-definitional one, an epistemological one, and an ontological one.[52]
6. Both do not conceive the world of the Ideas in an hierarchical manner, but, taking as a base the *Sophist*, conceive them as a not rigid structure constituted by multiple coextensive supreme genera.[53]
7. Both overestimate the infallibility of the Plato of the dialogues and tend to underestimate Aristotle, often judging them on the basis of two different criteria.

The difference, in the first place, is that Cherniss brought together in a complete way and fully examined all the material regarding the question, and this undoubtedly is a significant advance. However, the origin of his formation as a researcher shows clearly that Cherniss is not very original in his basic categories. The basic position as well as the greater part of the special hypotheses[54] and even the specific arguments, are found in the tradition of Zeller and Shorey. The "aprioristic" supposition of the criticism of the indirect tradition by Cherniss, repeatedly denounced in the discussions of the last decades,[55] can be undoubtedly confirmed, verified, and explained by this historical and epistemological viewpoint. Actually, the critical attitude of Cherniss rests on an a priori supposition, concerning which he himself and his followers were hardly self-critical. P. Shorey was involved in this a priori supposition first of all, but before him F. E. D. Schleiermacher, together with a whole series of prejudices and choices of a basically intuitive character and even a metaphysics about which we spoke earlier, and that could not be entirely redeemed or critically overcome. The literary positivism of Cherniss, which admits as valid for Plato only the original literary texts, but not the doxographical reports, returned, in the final analysis, to the conception of the literary Platonic dialogue central to Schleiermacher's interpretation.[56] However, some presupposed and decisive reasons in Cherniss have been eclipsed and forgotten, resulting in Cherniss being seen as a kind of Schleiermacher *dimidiatus* [halved] and putting him in contradiction with his historical origins. The first paradox is in the fact that for Cherniss the artistic form of the Platonic dialogue no longer practically plays any role and that, in conformity with this, the principle of the dependency of the single affirmations on context is abandoned in favor of an arbitrary uncritical use of citations. A further paradox is derived from the fact that Cherniss tries to defend Plato against the criticism of Aristotle, but, in doing this, in every case he makes use of conceptual notions and criteria of formal logic derived from Aristotle, without regard to the specific dialectical methodology of Plato. The highest axiom of his predecessors, which is in Plato strictly uniting object and method, consequently is at least suspended, if not abandoned. In this, it is evident that a methodological modernism is at the fore, which contrasts sharply with the purposes of a Romantic and Idealistic origin that guide the direction of this research on the whole. If one looks at the whole course of the movement in its complexity, then one receives the clear impression that Cherniss argues, in part, against the wrong enemy. The purely intuitive postulate of F. Schlegel, according to which the followers would have "understood very little of Plato," was inspired, then, by the Romantic overestimation of the artistic form of the dialogue and the concept, likewise Romantic, of an infinite progress toward the absolute infinite. Cherniss has made the attempt to justify historically, in his own time, this Romantic postulate with an enormous argumentative display, but in doing this, he lost touch completely with the foundations of the postulate itself. We will clarify further the argument method of Cherniss, in a critical manner, in the next section.

The Reaction of the Twentieth Century (L. Robin, H. Gomperz, School of Tübingen, J. N. Findlay)

The Schleiermacherianism in the ambit of Platonic studies can be under-stood in both a wide sense and in a narrow sense. In the narrow sense, all the attempts to clarify the artistic form of the Platonic writings and to interpret and summarize the mutual connection of the means of literary communication and of the philosophical content in Plato can be brought together in it. This type of consideration has given signs of fecundity just in the past decades in a series of monographs written in German (Friedländer, Stenzel, Gundert, Schmalzriedt), in French (Schaerer, Goldschmidt), and recently, also in English (Sinaiko, Rosen, Burger). It belongs to the permanent acquisitions of Platonic studies. The possibility of cooperation between this current of research and that which points to the renewal of the indirect tradition of Plato and on the mutual integration of the two traditions to obtain a total perspective of the philosophy of Plato will be considered further in the Chapter 5.

On the contrary, Schleiermacherianism, as it is fundamentally con-sidered in this study, is taken in its wider meaning. It is characterized, as has been clarified in the preceding,[57] by the identification of the literary dialogue with Platonic philosophy itself and by the consequent elimination of the non-literary and originally oral Platonic tradition, which indeed was produced by means of such an identification. This Schleiermacherianism understood in the wider sense, after its almost unlimited triumph in the second half of the nineteenth century, has been seriously challenged, in a way that is always more marked, in the course of the twentieth century and recently it has begun to reveal serious deficiencies.

This developing crisis has been started by a renewed interest in the philosophical content of the indirect tradition, which is manifested first in French Platonic studies by V. Brochard, O. Hamelin, G. Milhaud, and G. Rodier. It is reflected and taken up in the monumental work of L. Robin, a follower of Brochard and Hamelin, *La théorie platonicienne des Idées et des Nombres d'après Aristote* (1908), which gave a systematic commentary to the Aristotelian reports about the theory of principles and numbers of Plato and the Academy. The purpose announced by Robin was to compare the Platonic writings with the picture of Plato given by his disciples, just as it emerged from the reports about the unwritten doctrine, and through this comparison to achieve historically objective criteria for the exegesis of the written work that by itself is ambiguous and, hence, open to different interpretations.[58] The 1908 book was meant only for preparing the ground for this task. Therefore it, consciously, contains neither the comparison with the dialogues nor any reference to them. Also in his succeeding books about Plato, Robin did not develop this comparison; however, he did this in a significant article limited to the consideration of the *Timaeus*, "Études sur la signification et la place de la physique dans la philosophie de Platon."[59] Robin had uncovered from the Aristotelian reports on the unwritten doctrines of Plato the systematic construction of Platonic metaphysics, structured according to the gradation of hierarchical levels; however, he could not liberate himself entirely from the genetic-evolutionary interpretation that was predominant chiefly within the confines of German Platonic studies. He, therefore, was inclined to join together the theory of principles and the construction of the system contained in the reports in its essential points with the late dialogues, beginning with the *Parmenides*, but not also with the dialogues prior to them.[60]

The contribution made by Robin to historiographic research on Plato is threefold. (1) He has newly recalled attention to the indirect tradition in an energetic manner, after an absence of almost a century and has commented on the material in a more accurate manner than his German predecessors of the nineteenth century. (2) In addition—unlike the estimation given by Zeller and his followers—he has taken into consideration seriously, without reservations, the philosophical content and hence has vigorously taken up the twofold source of the Platonic tradition, also from the viewpoint of its philosophical content. (3) Finally, he has traced the program of bringing together both of the traditions for the purpose of coming to a more profound hermeneutical explanation of the writings.

The influence of Robin on succeeding generations of French scholars of Plato is quite easily perceptible (as, for example, M. Guéroult, A. J. Festugière, R. Schaerer, P. M. Schuhl, P. Kucharski). On the contrary, his attempt in Germany was without any perceivable followers.

But, independent of this, in the cultural area influenced by the German language, in the period succeeding the First World War, a specific philosophical interest in the indirect tradition of Plato arose for many reasons.

1. J. Stenzel, in discussion with the neo-Kantian interpretation of Plato had given a picture of the development of Plato, which led from "arete" to "diaeresis," and finally, to the *atomon-eidos* in Aristotle.[61] To interpret the passage from Plato to Aristotle in a more specific way, Stenzel, in his second book on Plato, *Zahl und Gestalt bei Platon und Aristoteles* (1924, 1959³), made ample room for the indirect tradition and sketched a general outline of the late philosophy of Plato characterized by the diaeretic method, but, he

characterized its content by the doctrine of numbers and the principles.

2. The revolutionary genetic interpretation of Aristotelian philosophy in the book by W. Jaeger in 1923 opened various possibilities to reduce the philosophy of the Stagirite himself to its Platonic-Academic origins. Thanks to this, naturally, the interest in a presumed "late philosophy" of Plato and the Academic circle of his followers also became fashionable.

3. Wilamowitz, in his book on Plato in 1919, recognized the authenticity of the *Seventh Letter*, and with that, not only smoothened the way for a political interpretation of Plato, but also for the first time introduced in its entirety into the scholarly discussion the most important of the self-testimonies of Plato about the unwritten doctrine, in addition to that of the *Phaedrus*. But it is clear, from the indications of the *Seventh Letter*, that Plato has professed the theory of principles to which he here makes allusion, without changes, at least fifteen years before the redaction of this *Letter*, that is, for at least the course of the last two decades of his life.

The chronological conclusions in favor of an earlier dating of the unwritten doctrine, and beyond that, in favor of a systematic unity of Platonic philosophy were drawn in outline by the Austrian philosopher H. Gomperz, in 1928.[62] Two years later Gomperz presented at the *International Philosophical Congress* at Oxford a short paper, in which he made the One-Good of the unwritten doctrine coincide with the Idea of the Good of the *Republic* and also advanced suppositions in favor of a dating of the theory of the principles still prior to it. The philosophy of Plato, in the light of the unwritten doctrine, is presented in its overall lines as a "deductive system."

The thesis of Gomperz, evidently because of its lack of elaboration, did not have any adherents, and it remained almost unacknowledged for a long time.[63] Vice versa, the current started by Stenzel continued on its path in various ways, first, with the monograph of M. Gentile, *La dottrina platonica delle Idee numeri e Aristotele*,[64] which exploited the Platonic theory of the principles for the historical explanation of the Aristotelian one, then, in a later decade, with P. Wilpert's, *Zwei aristotelische Frühschriften über die Ideen-lehre*,[65] in which, on the one hand, he continued to retrace the lines that go from the oral doctrine of Plato to Aristotle and, on the other, he gave a new and more ample reconstruction to the "late doctrine of Plato" itself (Wilpert, among other things, took into consideration for the first time in a consistent manner the reports found in Sextus Empiricus, *Adversus mathematicos* 10.248 – 83; Appendix 3.12).

With the exception of H. Gomperz and the English scholar J. Burnet,[66] all the authors just mentioned limited the indirect tradition to the last period of Plato's life and, frequently, even to the last years of his life. Therefore, a fundamental distinction between the writings and the oral doctrines is not admitted, but they limit themselves to positing a late period for the oral doctrines, which would have prevented the publication of his final views. If, in this, they remain rooted in the developmental schema of Zeller and Hermann, however, it is, to register in general a clear advance in the positive evaluation of the indirect tradition, which arises from an accentuated interest in the philosophical content of the indirect tradition as well as its historical and philosophical implications.

The School of Tübingen and the New Method of Research Introduced by It

Schleiermacherianism became problematic and weakened by the re-evaluation and the growing interpretative deepening of the indirect tradition; however, in its substance, it succeeded again in preserving itself by means of the limitation of the unwritten doctrines to Plato's old age. Schleiermacherianism entered into a crisis for the first time when, beginning at the end of the 1950s, the so-called Tübingen School (H. Krämer, K. Gaiser) showed that the late dating of the indirect tradition was not sustainable and, with this, they shocked the foundations of the purported monopoly in favor of the literary works. They showed, in the first place, with detailed interpretations of the texts, that the self-testimonies of Plato, which from the *Seventh Letter* through the *Phaedrus* go on right to the cornerstone of Plato, the *Republic*, clearly place in the light the existence of a particular doctrine that ran parallel to the writings and was presented only orally.

The method that Krämer introduced in 1959 consisted in this. The fundamental statements found in the *Phaedrus* and the *Seventh Letter* must not only be evaluated in a very precise manner, as has not been done in the past, but the numerous indications of the "unwritten" in the ambit of the writings themselves likewise must be collected and interpreted in an integral manner and, consequently, the literary work of Plato, even in its particulars, combined in various ways with the indirect tradition.

The scholars of the School of Tübingen for the first time presented the two branches of the tradition in mutual relation, according to a precise plan, and made them converge in the reconstruction of a new complex picture of the philosophy of Plato. The methodological principle that served as their guide, in accord with the program of Robin, was that of putting to the test the capacity to clarify the reports handed down on the unwritten doctrines, applying them to the dialogues, but, at the same time, vice versa, to allow the scanty doxographic reports on the unwritten doctrines to speak in the light of the fullness of life and the richness of content of the dialogues. And thus, they achieve the possibility of a mutual integration and clarification, as well as a mutual verification and check on the two parts of the tradition. In this way the scholars of Tübingen tried to reconstruct in a historical and critical manner the coordinations provided by Plato himself and to ascertain and evaluate them in an historical and philosophical way. Thus, the problem of the systematic unity of Platonic philosophy is positioned in a new way, just as is the problem of its historical derivation. Krämer, in addition, in convergence with the criticism of C. J. De Vogel and W. D. Ross,[67] engaged in a detailed critique in reply to the criticism Cherniss directed against the indirect tradition.[68]

Let us take up the two self-testimonies of Plato contained in the *Phaedrus* and in the *Seventh Letter*. The first has already been treated in relation to the interpretation of the *Phaedrus* given by Schleiermacher.[69] The central part of the *Seventh Letter*, 34045 (Appendix 1.2), which goes back to the last years of the life of Plato, according to the interpretation of the School of Tübingen can be summarized in the following way.[70]

1. The so-called philosophical *excursus* of the *Seventh Letter*, 341-44 (Appendix 1.2), and its context, which because of its thematic complexity must be always treated as a whole and in connection with the entire *Letter*, does not develop a theory of knowledge, which is misunderstood sometimes in a mystical sense and sometimes in an agnostic sense, but rather develops a theory of teaching, learning, and philosophical communication. It lays out the difficulties and the limits, but also the *possibilities* for such communication as well.

2. The conception of Plato, founded on his personal experience, both positive and negative, tended to make this understandable; namely, that an effective communication, which guarantees an intelligent assimilation by those who understand, is possible only by going through a process of spiritual formation that lasts a long time and that is accomplished within the sphere of oral dialectic. The attempt to communicate through written texts and direct affirmations, not adequately prepared by means of gradual introduction and habituation, on the contrary, Plato maintained as ineffective. He, therefore, in his own case rejected it and even said clearly not to have composed even previously any written text about "the principles of reality" (τά περὶ φύσεως ἄκρα καὶ πρῶτα).

3. The object to which we make reference in communicative discourse enters into the means by which we communicate, and even in knowledge, only in an unfinished manner. This is true already for the objects of everyday life, which the *excursus* (342D; cf. Appendix 1.2) adduces as examples. But this is true in a much higher degree for the fundamental doctrines of philosophy (ἄκρα καὶ πρῶτα 344D; cf. Appendix 1.2),[71] which insofar as they are "abstrac-

tions," ultimate supersensibles,[72] "cannot be communicated as those other objects of our understanding" (341C; cf. Appendix 1.2). This, however, does not at all mean that such supreme objects of philosophical knowledge cannot be formulated in words. Rather, to them belongs, just as to all the objects of which the *excursus* speaks, a name (ὄνομα) and a definition (λόγος). Only in virtue of such instruments, again according to the *excursus*, is a communication in oral discourse, in general, possible. Therefore, because of their specific supersensible being—it could equally well be said, because of their higher degree of abstraction—the mediation, that is, the indirect and conditioned manner of communication, in these supreme objects is greater, even, than in the others. It is indeed this mediation that constrains us, for this reason, to use the methods of exercise and a long and continuous habituation, in the course of repeated face-to-face conversations. On the basis of this presupposition, Plato maintained that which is in question in the unwritten doctrines could also be said at any time, and it likewise could be put into writing at any time, but without any guarantee that it would be understood or assimilated and hence that it would produce true knowledge. To this subjective aspect, which consists in the risk of not being comprehended or being misunderstood, is added, on the side of the object, as in the *Phaedrus*, the argument of the "profanation" of the subject itself (341E, 344C-D; cf. Appendix 1.2). On these bases, consciously and with reflection, Plato did not want to write about the ultimate foundation of his philosophy. But, in the *Seventh Letter*, he has many times looked back at the successful oral process of communication of these subjects, within the circle of his followers (340C, 341A, 341C, 344B, 345 B; cf. Appendix 1.2).

4. There is no support for the thesis according to which Plato would have exempted his own dialogues in relation to the criticism of writing contained in the *Seventh Letter*. Against this thesis, instead, can be placed a whole series of facts and evidence. (*a*) The theory of understanding and teaching bound to "oraldiscourse," which is presented in the *excursus*, excludes every form of attempting to communicate through the written word (342A, 343A, 344C f.; cf. Appendix 1.2). (*b*) All future authors who should ever write about objects concerning what we have reasoned are condemned without restriction (341C1; cf. Appendix 1.2), without regard to the fact that they would simply, as Plato, use the artistic form of the dialogue. (*c*) The followers of Plato who were concerned with the oral teaching of the master, previously, according to Plato, had only "heard"

about his basic teachings, but never read about them (338D, 339E, 340B, 340C, 341A, 341B, 341C, 344D, 345A; consult in part Appendix 1.2); and with this agrees the fact that the aspirants before all, in the introductive try (πεῖρα, 340B ff.; consult Appendix 1.2), were put in a closer relation with the thing only by means of oral clarifications by Plato. (*d*) Numerous passages, in the dialogues of Plato, mostly in the culminating point of the exposition, hint at something further and beyond, which remains obscure, with an interruption and a heavily underlined silence.[73] (*e*) The *excursus* of the *Seventh Letter* converges with the criticism of writing contained in the *Phaedrus*, which posits as specific subject of the true philosopher something of "higher value" that is beyond the written word.[74] (*f*) Allusions are made to some central works of Plato himself, be it in the criticism of written work in the *Seventh Letter* (344C5; consult Appendix 1.2, which refers to the Platonic project of the *Laws* which is in the course of elaboration), be it in the criticism of the written word contained in the *Phaedrus* (276E2 f.; consult Appendix 1.1, which refers to the *Republic*).[75] (*g*) Aristotle expressly attests the existence of "the unwritten doctrines" of different content than the dialogues of Plato (τὰ ἄγραφα δόγματα, in *Physics* 209b15; Appendix 3.4), who for his part, in the *Seventh Letter*, states that he wishes to leave his basic doctrines unwritten. And there are still others. The exclusion of the dialogues from the criticism leveled at the written word cannot be made plausible by referring to the meaning of the Greek word σύγγραμμα as "treatise" used by Plato in this context (341C5, 344C4; consult Appendix 1.2). Actually, σύγγραμμα can occasionally include, as a generic meaning, even treatises and compendiums, but, considered in itself, it does not mean treatise, but simply a work of literary prose. In this sense, in the usage of Plato, the word occurs in the period of the *Seventh Letter*, as can be demonstrated, in opposition to works in verse,[76] and hence it includes all kinds of work in prose, and consequently, also the artistic dialogues of Plato. In addition, it cannot be maintained that the "insignificant allusion," according to which the scholars if they were endowed were in condition to find with the proper powers the basic doctrines of Plato (341E; consult Appendix 1.2), could refer also to the ideal reader of the dialogues consciously encoded by Plato. Against this supposition stands the fact that Plato, with this, referred to the oral teaching described before in the *Seventh Letter*,[77] and that searching in a purely intuitive manner further nexuses, starting only from the reading of the written work, is deprived of the necessary guarantee and foundation, which, as

Plato establishes, can be achieved only by means of a communion of long duration and living an appropriate life. In effect, the history of the influence of the Platonic corpus demonstrates *ex eventu* [after the fact] that it could never make the indirect tradition superfluous. Now, the literary dialogues of Plato are, indeed, primarily written works and only secondarily imitations of a true dialogue. Its psychagogic qualities, therefore, can be unfolded only from within and within the limits of the imperfections that are to be found in any written work, without achieving the higher dimension of the real conversation. In agreement with this, Plato, for good reason, beyond a general criticism of written work, did not develop any special theory of the literary dialogue and to this he did not, truly, concede a privileged position.

5. The *Seventh Letter* makes quite clear that the restricted circle of the followers, according to Plato's own judgment, has correctly understood his fundamental doctrines. This is demonstrated by going back to the numerous Platonic "testimonies," which were "much more competent" to make a judgment on the basic doctrines than Dionysius II of Syracuse, expressly criticized in the *Seventh Letter* (345B; consult Appendix 1.2).[78] It follows also from the fact that Plato describes the concluding noetic intuition of the object, in the process of communication, repeatedly on the basis of his own experience as a teacher (341C7 ff., 344B7 f.; consult Appendix 1.2).[79] With this, the indirect tradition is in principle authentically grounded, simply on the basis of the individual convictions of Plato himself. The theorizing of modern scholars about the supposed misunderstanding of the pupils for the most part loses its basis because of the testimony of the *Seventh Letter*.[80]

6. The nexus between that which Plato, due to the *Seventh Letter*, wanted to put aside voluntarily as unwritten and that which is expressed in the unwritten doctrine contained in the reports, is indicated by means of some hints in the text of the *Seventh Letter*. It is the question of τὰ περὶ φύσεως ἄκρα καὶ πρῶτα, that is, the principles of reality (344D; consult Appendix 1.2), and still more precisely, of the ἀλήθεια ἀρετῆς εἰς τὸ δυνατόν (καὶ) κακίας. Hence, it is the question of the ultimate truth about good and evil, which must be taken together (344A8 f.; consult Appendix 1.2). Here the Idea of the Good is undoubtedly implicit, and it is joined with an opposite negative principle, in a manner corresponding to the dualistic theory of the principles in the reports on the unwritten doctrines (for example, see Aristotle *Metaphysics* A.6; consult Ap-

pendix 3.9, where he speaks of the unity and the great-and-small as causes of good and evil).[81]

7. The basic unwritten doctrines, according to the information in the *Seventh Letter (345B, 341A f.; consult Appendix 1.2, 338C – E)*, *remain essentially constant, at least to begin from the spring of the year 366 BCE. That they arise from a period still prior to that which the Seventh Letter* (written about 353/2 BCE) by chance establishes for other reasons, is drawn from the *Phaedrus* (278B-D; consult Appendix 1.1), the redaction of which probably falls in a period of time determinable by means of the *Seventh Letter*. Now, since the criticism of the written word contained in the *Phaedrus* (which was probably composed toward the middle of the 360s), in its turn refers to the *Republic* (276E; consult Appendix 1.1, it refers to the *Republic* 376D and 501E), it follows that already by the period of the *Republic* (which falls about the middle of the 370s), with good reasons, the existence of an unwritten doctrine of the principles can be admitted, which is corroborated by the surprising self-restraint in the definition of the essence of the Good, expressed in the *Republic* (506D f.; consult Appendix 2.4, 509C; consult Appendix 2.5). These chronological clarifications compel a new rethinking also of the dialogues of the intermediate period in the light of the indirect tradition. Krämer, in addition, has shown that the indirect tradition itself does not in any way lend support for a late dating of the theory of the principles. Aristotle, in any case, is based on it as the position of Plato *simpliciter*, without confining it indeed to a late phase of Plato's life,[82] and as such, in addition, he compares it with the other specific positions of other Platonists, of Socrates, and the Presocratics. Nor can the late dating be drawn, indirectly, from the fact that it is handed down from the last generation of the followers of Plato. In fact, there existed a single and unique circle of followers of Plato, who kept together right up to the 370s and 380s BCE; that is, until about the time of the founding of the Platonic Academy.

The Convergence of the Researches of J. N. Findlay with the Acquisitions of the School of Tübingen

The School of Tübingen, with its interpretation of Plato, has tried to give an account, in numerous works, indeed of this state of things. In this—prescinding from a series of minor works of other authors—it has received confirmation chiefly from a book by he American philosopher J. N. Findlay.[83]

Findlay assumes a parallelism that runs between the written work and the unwritten doctrine and tries to confirm from an interpretive point of view the strict relation of one to the other for all periods of Platonic thought. Significant, from the point of view of the history of the researches with respect to the work of Findlay, putting aside his specific hermeneutic contribution, is the fact that it converges with the results of the School of Tübingen in an independent manner, since Findlay developed his position in the 1920s, and it was published only after a period of several decades. If, in this, H. Gomperz, the members of the School of Tübingen, and Findlay, wholly independent of one another, meet spontaneously in the assumption of an uninterrupted twofold line of Platonic philosophy, thus converging in their individual interpretations, then this means that what we have before us is a case of mutual and multiple confirmation, which depends on the power of the things studied. But in the measure in which the thesis of an unwritten theory of the principles with decisive value for the understanding of Plato's entire corpus gains in evidence and in power of persuasion, in the same measure Schleiermacherianism loses credibility and falls increasingly in doubt. The various defensive strategies that Schleiermacherianism has developed in Platonic studies within the last few decades, reflects this crisis in an eloquent manner and makes it still more manifest. Therefore, the next chapter will be dedicated chiefly to the criticism of these strategies.

4 On the Methodology and the Standards of Argument of Modern Schleiermacherianism

The unusually large divergences that emerged in the new research and that still exist in the judgment about the historicity, the quality, the range, and the philosophical relevance of the indirect tradition of Plato forces one inevitably to a series of methodological reflections, which must now be presented. Such reflections critically illuminate the concepts, the categories, the criteria, and the methods that are usually applied and, with this, in the measure possible, they give rise to a clarification or even produce a basic loosening up of the contrary positions. The problems concerning the philosophical nature and relevance of the indirect tradition will be treated in the Parts Two and Three of this study. Here we must bring into evidence some logical, methodological, epistemological, and hermeneutical perspectives that will contribute to the clarification of the more properly historical difficulties.

The Problem of Authenticity

The extremist criticism of the indirect tradition, which denies the historicity of a specific Platonic doctrine exposed only orally, has, little by little, differentiated the proper position supported on the hypothesis of misunderstandings and falsifications, beginning from Schlegel through Zeller to Cherniss, in ever increasing development. In fact, the plausibility of the derivation of the indirect tradition from the dialogues should be reinforced by means of an admission of numerous intermediate stages, by means of the discovery of the greatest possible number of passages of the dialogues allegedly assuming combinations among one another by the relators, and, finally, by means of the indications of analogous cases in which the pupils have presented the writings of Plato in a clearly forced and imprecise manner.

In effect, also here the old hermeneutic rule is valid,[1] according to which the burden of proof is with the objector and not with those who maintain the authenticity, which means that what is transmitted as authentic must be valued as such up to the point of adduced proof to the contrary. This basic principle is confirmed by the recent epistemological research supported on a more ample base.[2] On the other hand, the epistemological discussions on the principle of falsification of Popper that are found in Kuhn, Lakatos, Feyerabend, Sneed, Stegmüller, Naess, and in still others have recently been brought to the recognition of the fact that even within the ambit of the sciences in which laws flourish without exception, categorical falsifications of theories are achieved for the most part rarely and only over a long period of time. It must be concluded then that the chances of the historical and philological criticism of the authenticity of a written work and a document today necessitates an increasing self-criticism or, stated in another way, that the burden of proof considered objectively must respond to higher requirements, and, therefore, the chances of such falsification considerably increased. A rigorous argument, hence, is becoming more difficult than it was in the past.

To come back to our case, above all, isolated indications against the authenticity of the indirect Platonic tradition, unverifiable psychological motives, or purely possible considerations of doubt cannot be used as the basis of an adequate refutation. But it is no mistake that these attitudes are verified among extremist critics of the indirect tradition of Plato: they operate chiefly on the basis of pure abstract possibility, which cannot be supported by the necessary verifiable evidence and they cannot exclude in a categorical manner alternative explanations.[3] In this way they cannot be absolved from the *onus probandi* [burden of proof] with regard to what concerns the supposed inauthenticity of the indirect tradition of Plato. And this is also true for the analogical reasoning applied to the hilt by Zeller and Cherniss. Simply considered in itself—without further proof—it is not entirely sufficient to base the criticism of the authenticity of the indirect tradition, and it is still less sufficient as analogical reasoning *a minore ad maius* [from the lesser to the greater], as Zeller and Cherniss by preference apply it. If, for example, Aristotle and Xenocrates have isolated some individual passages of the dialogues, have interpreted in passing, or even were mistaken, transformed them in function of a different theoretical perspective, or reformulated them on the basis of their own terminology, then from this it is not possible to conclude in a necessary manner that they, by means of an erroneous interpretation of the dialogues, must have even invented the supreme principles of Platonic philosophy, which for decades have been at the center of the philosophical discussions in the Academy. This is a μετάβασις εἰς ἄλλο γένος, which weakens the analogical reasoning adduced. Moreover, the series of hypothetical intermediate passages subtly linked that is postulated by Cherniss, and that must fill up little by little the gap existing between the written work and the indirect tradition, is an abstract construction of an extremely fragile nature, which loses its demonstrative force in the particulars that it wishes to achieve on the whole. Actually, one can make appear as possible every kind of dependence by means of a number of intermediate passages augmentable at will; but each individual passage must be further supported by a specific proof, which, without exception, would be very difficult to adduce. The uncertainties of Cherniss and with them the vulnerability of his method find clear expression in the plurality of reasons by means of which he tries to explain the Aristotelian reports on the Platonic unwritten doctrines; according to the American scholar, in fact, historical influences on the interpretation of Plato on the part of Speusippus and Xenocrates must be conjoined to the tactic of an easy assimilation of Plato to these followers with a polemical goal that aimed to bring them together, and along with them the theoretical fitting together with the philosophical position of Aristotle himself. This is simply putting together a bunch of reasons in a hypothetical way, which are unverifiable, and hence are clearly inadequate to support such a heavy burden of proof [*onus probandi*].

The account of Cherniss is also futile in another respect: Aristotle always distinguishes very clearly between Plato and his followers (according to the fixed order, Plato, Speusippus, Xenocrates), without referring, in this respect, to the Platonic dialogues. Hence, Aristotle views Plato in a much more objective and independent manner with regard to the interpretation of the Academy than Cherniss presupposes. More precisely, Aristotle views Plato in a pre-Speusippean manner, whereas Xenocrates seems to view Plato frequently in a post-Speusippean manner,[4] with the consequence that the substance of the Aristotelian reports of the oral doctrines of Plato cannot be explained either by referring to the pupils or to the dialogues. But because even the presupposed fitting of Plato to his own theoretical position by Aristotle by itself is insufficient to explain the differences with the dialogues and at the same time the affinities to the Academics, the attempt to eliminate a particular doctrine of Plato placed within the Academy must necessarily be considered as unsuccessful. Cherniss, moreover, goes against the principle of coherence when he recognizes as authentic the reports of Aristotle on the followers of Plato, on which he bases his reconstruction, but not the reports of the same witness concerning Plato.[5] The "hypothesis"[6] of a derivation of the indirect tradition concerning Plato just as of the philosophy of the followers of Plato exclusively from the dialogues could in general arise notwithstanding the inconsistent character of the evidence only because of a presupposed prejudice in favor of the written works, which actually is understandable, but not justifiable from a purely scientific point of view.[7] This, as will clearly be seen in what follows, leads to a whole series of circular arguments and *petitiones principii* [begged questions] that are then found even in the philosophical and theoretical evaluation of the unwritten doctrine.

The Criterion of Contradiction

The criticism of the authenticity of the reports of the unwritten doctrines is frequently based on the existence of contradictions between such reports and the dialogues or within the reports themselves. In this the error is incurred of not distinguishing between simple opposition and authentic contradiction in which the terms completely exclude one another, that is, between the relation of mere contrariety and the relation of strict contradiction. Only the latter type of relation between terms that are incompatible and hence cannot coexist, obviously, can be relevant in the question of authenticity. Moreover, it is clear, right from the beginning, that by the way of contradiction only those inferences with respect to the problem of authenticity that are adequate and held within the limits of proper proportion in the order of their magnitude are justified. Individual contradictions, therefore, according to this rule, can touch only on the quality, not the data as such, of the existence of the tradition and the value of this fact as such. Even here, the criticism has often violated the principle of proportionality and opened the way to disproportionate conclusions (for example, Cherniss in the development of the presumed contradiction between the concept of the indivisible lines and the concept of the unit-points).[8] In general, the contradictions, in the historical ambit, do not annul the tradition, but rather constrain, by means of a more adequate critical analysis, to try to arrive at the authentic tradition. Moreover, in many cases, a more penetrating interpretation of the indirect tradition succeeded in the elimination of apparent contradictions, as for example, those that match the problems concerning the "intermediate" position of the mathematical entities in the reports of the unwritten doctrines and those in the *Republic* Books Six and Seven or in relation to those problems concerning the superordination or equality of the hierarchical ordering of Numbers and the Ideas, just as with respect to the relation between the indivisible lines, the unit-points and the great-and-small as their substrate.[9]

In other cases at the base of the arguments there is even an *ignoratio elenchi*, that is, an ignorance of the decisive point in dispute. Thus, for example, the "contradiction" between the unchangeability, unmixability, and indivisibility of the Ideas in the *Timaeus* and the *Philebus*, on the one hand, and, on the other, their "generation" by superordinated elements in the unwritten doctrines, is grounded in reality on a *quaternio terminorum* (fourth term). In fact, in the first case, the Ideas are distinct from what is corruptible and perceivable, without their constitution being a problem; in the second case, instead, the problem of the constitution and the principles of the Ideas is developed (also hinted at in the *Republic* 509B and in the *Parmenides*), which is located at a higher level and has as its object not a process of temporal generation but a logical analysis and structuring of the

Ideas.[10] These two problems are on two different levels and not comparable, consequently, they cannot in any way exclude one another. The same remarks are to be made with respect to the *Sophist* that has as examples the five supreme and coextensive genera of equal significance, which are incorrectly extrapolated and generalized and then placed in the camp against the privileged position that belongs to the One-Good, even if the *Sophist* clearly puts aside in the discussion the sphere of the principles.[11]

Nevertheless, two fundamental facts argue against an indiscriminate application of the criterion of contradiction. In the first place, the Platonic dialogues notoriously present numerous contradictions. In the second place, for the philosopher (and not only for the Hegelian philosopher) it is not strange that in philosophy there exist contrasts and contradictions that depend on the object about which the philosopher is concerned. An argument of a purely formal character always runs the danger of arguing without giving an account of the specific philosophical contents and consequently of drawing conclusions that are historically inadequate.[12] On the basis of these two facts, the contradictory character as such does not quite mean the absence of a Platonic character and an imitation on the part of a falsifier, just as, vice versa, the simple absence of contradiction, as such, cannot guarantee authenticity.

The Problem of the Doxographic Tradition

The indirect Platonic tradition cannot pretend to have the same evidential value as the direct tradition. It arouses a series of peculiar problems of a hermeneutical nature that intrinsically depend on the doxographical character of the evidence, on the concentration of the reports, and perhaps, also on the possible deformations of the unwritten doctrines.

First, however, we must again distinguish the problems relative to the comprehension (or lack of comprehension) of the philosophical content of the reports on the unwritten doctrines from those relative to the tradition of the reports themselves. But, with respect to the first point, the reports on the unwritten doctrines, in spite of their character as sketches can with difficulty be maintained as inferior to the dialogues. Even the dialogues, by reason of their technique of allusion and dissimulation, are incomplete, frequently difficult to understand, and present their own kind of ambiguity that depends on the hiddenness of Plato behind the characters of his dialogues. *The "hypomnematic" or recollective function of many dialogues affirmed in the* Phaedrus, *clearly presupposes a preceding activity of teaching, which is indeed also attested to by the doxographic reports. This type of preparation or relation of the written word to the spoken word is therefore precisely found in both branches of the tradition and combines them.* Dialogues and reports on the unwritten doctrines, then, must be questioned for their hidden implications and made to reveal themselves by similar hermeneutical means. In any case, it would be ingenuous to assume that the decisive hermeneutical problems are already resolved by reason of the complete preservation of the original texts.

On the other hand, in what concerns the specific problems of the intervening doxographic tradition, in the first place the following needs to be said. On the whole, they cannot be isolated from the problems of the ancient philosophical doxography in general, that is, of the doxography regarding the Presocratic philosophy, Socratic philosophy, and Hellenistic philosophy, and more generally, they cannot be isolated from the problems concerning the historical sciences on the whole that are founded chiefly on the reports of facts and events. Whoever maintains that historical philosophical research based on the doxographic reports has meaning— and this is commonly necessary to comprehend all the various historical nexuses—cannot consequently decide differently in the case of Plato. Actually the impression is often given that different criteria should be applied in the case of Plato than in other cases, evidently on the basis of a *petitio principii* (begging the question) coming from a prejudice of Schleiermacher who held that the true Plato was the literary Plato, in which case Plato's philosophy and writings coincide. Actually, in the case of Plato, the situation that is proper to the indirect tradition is essentially even more favorable than it is in the case of the Presocratics or the ancient Stoa, since with Plato it is a question chiefly of contemporary informants (Aristotle and Theophrastus) who were exposed to the verification of the Academic circle of the followers of Plato living at that time, and in fact the doxography can also be compared with the vast written work of Plato and can be tested on that basis. Therefore R. Mondolfo has placed the type of doxography accompanied by the original writings, in which he numbers Plato, beyond that represented by a purely doxographic tradition.[13] To this is added the fact that the Aristotelian reports regarding the circle of the followers of Plato are commonly accepted as valid without dissent.[14] Then, it is not licit to assume a different attitude toward the reports about Plato, without putting in danger the principle of consistency. Moreover, even if taking a critical position with respect to the doxography we must insist that it is not done with a skepticism of an aprioristic nature but it must be based on concrete specific demonstrations. The *onus probandi* (the burden of proof), then, rests fully absolved, only in the case of those who actually get insight into the real state of things, and in this way skepticism will become superfluous. Therefore, an initial skepticism opposed to the doxography cannot be maintained in the long run.

But, in the case of Plato, especially to be noted is the fact that the oral tradition is indirect, yet this is compensated by the fact that it expressly *has a preeminence with respect to the content of Plato's philosophy.* A different situation exists with respect to the majority of other authors,[15] for, in the case of the indirect tradition of Plato, it is not a question of some ancillary doctrine, since it is at the center of Platonic philosophy, that is, it concerns the *theory of principles,* and some lines of the structure of the system that is derived from it. Whoever wants to understand the historical Plato cannot in any way ignore the reports on the fundamental unwritten doctrines of this thinker nor could it be done if they were handed down in a manner much worse than they were in reality. If the correctness of the scientific method simply in itself requires the integration of all the materials in a general outline as complete as possible,[16] this is true in a more important respect in the case of a branch of the Platonic tradition that has so much weight because of its philosophical content. Therefore there is no other alternative than proceeding on the way indicated by the doxography as far as it is possible to go. How far it leads cannot be established before the fact, but only after having completed the whole journey. In this respect we must accept and tolerate not only the fact that the tradition is indirect, but at the same time, if need be, its scantiness and its gaps for the sake of the relevance of its philosophical content. In any case, it would be a grave error of method to use the same measure in determining the importance of the philosophical content and the kind of consistency and quality of the tradition itself and pretend to be able to pursue a relation of proportionality between both of them. To prescind from giving some minimal value to the tradition, below which one cannot proceed, it is not an issue here of a relation of dependence and correspondence but, on the contrary, rather the issue involves a relation of compensation. The relation between the high and indispensable value of the content of the indirect tradition and the imperfections of the form in which they have come down to us can be explained by this famous maxim of Aristotle's *De partibus animalium,* "*For although our grasp of eternal things is but slight,* nevertheless the joy which it brings is, by reason of their excellence and worth, greater than that of knowing all things that are here below" (1.5.644b31ff.).

The Value of the Self-Testimonies of Plato

The affirmations that Plato made in the *Phaedrus* and in the *Seventh Letter* and the hints to the "unsaid" in nearly all the more important dialogues,[17] by reason of their explicitness, have an absolute preeminence from the methodological standpoint with respect to all the extrapolations of a speculative character and to all the postulates of modern interpreters regarding the artistic form, the general plan, and the purposes of the Platonic written works. Nonetheless, they try again and again to explain the clarifications made by Plato himself, interpreting them in the sense of the theory of the dialogue of Schleiermacher and subordinating them to the autonomy of the literary works. In extreme cases this carries over even to simply ignoring the self-testimonies of Plato and right to the point of contradicting them. But it is absurd to defend the pretense of a monopoly in favor of the written works, rejecting out of hand the affirmations in this regard found in the written works, which Plato himself *has placed within these very works*, and thus refusing to take them seriously. This position is hardly consistent and becomes inevitably of such small consequence as to annul itself. This occurs, in a special way, in the attempt to apply the statements of the *Phaedrus* (consult *Appendix* 1.1) about the "playful" nature of the written work to themselves and in this way eliminating their value for all the other works. This attempt, however, breaks the type rule which states that second order statements cannot be treated as if they were first order statements, that means they cannot be applied to themselves, but second order statements can be applied only to first order statements. (The affirmation "Plato says that written work is play"—which is a second order statement—cannot be applied to itself and in this way transformed to mean, "Plato says that what he says of written work is play," but second order statements can be applied only to the affirmations within the written work—which are first order statements.) And this is even less admissible here insofar as it would be likewise to admit that Plato made statements only to destroy them *eo ipso* again, without, deriving by that fact consequences of some kind also for the rest of the written work. In the *Seventh Letter*, which serves the purposes of self-justification and is not on the same plane as the literary dialogues, the argument of the self-referential character of the affirmation is, evidently, completely out of place.[18]

In general, therefore, critics have not aimed at such audacious tactical strategies, but they try to weaken the statements of Plato, and by means of convenient reinterpretations, they try, in part, to reconcile them with the theory of the literary dialogue of Schleiermacher or, in part, to subject them to it.

A strategy of immunization in vogue consists in mitigating the criticism of the written work of Plato, interpolating into the simple distinction of Plato between written and oral dialectic a further distinction between scholastic systemic-dogmatic writing ("treatise," "compendium") and the living literary dialogue. In this way the literary and artistic dialogue would be exempted from the condemnation of written works, and in point of fact it would be put on the level of dialectical discourses. Plato, hence, according to this interpretation, would not have entirely criticized written work as written work, but, simply, the lack of the artistic and dialogical character of some written work; for the rest, however, he would not have established any differences of content between his own written work and his oral teaching. But the distinction postulated here in the wake of Schleiermacher is not found in Plato, just as no theory of the literary dialogue whether explicit or implicit is to be found.

In this context to speak of the "written work of the school," the "treatise" as the meanings that belong to the word σύγγραμμα (*Seventh Letter*, 341C, 344C; consult Appendix 1.2) is erroneous, because, in fact, this meaning from the lexicographical standpoint, as has been previously pointed out, is not attested to in Greek whether in the classical period or in succeeding periods. The term σύγγραμμα always occurs in the meaning of "written work"[19] or "work of literary prose" in opposition to poetic work (ποίημα)—as is documentable in Plato in the period of the *Seventh Letter* [20]—or, occasionally, in opposition to the nonliterary commentary (ὑπόμνημα).[21] The fact that, among others, here and there, sometimes, under the concept of σύγγραμμα understood in its generic extension treatises also can be subsumed in an exceptional way does not prove, naturally, anything about the generic concept itself, just as from the fact that some men are Schleiermacherians, the converse conclusion that man means "Schleiermacherian" does not follow. With this, the only apparent proof in favor of an implicit theory of the dialogue is eliminated.[22] Also to prescind from this, the criticism of written work contained in the *Seventh Letter* as well as in the *Phaedrus* is so radical and penetrating, that if Plato wished to exempt from it his own writings, he would have had to reorient them profoundly.[23] The attempt to neutralize the differences existing between written and oral dialectic by reducing them to a purely formal nature has in this way completely failed.

Erroneous interpretations imposed in this sense have been advanced for those passages in which the dialogues refer beyond themselves, to a "unsaid," if some critics did not even ignore them totally. Thus they may try to explain the incompleteness of the exposition concerning the Good in the *Republic* (506D-E; Appendix 2.4) with the presumed "ineffability" of the essence of the Good itself—the Romantic concept of the infinite of Schlegel continues to produce its effects!—even if Socrates, here, in a clear manner, intentionally avoids speaking about it, and according to this, in addition, in 509B, with the affirmation that the Good is beyond *ousia* (being), notwithstanding furnishes, in an exceptional way, a partial revelation. The concept of "ineffability" is not Platonic, since the *Seventh Letter*, which explains the meaning of this way of speaking that is encountered in the *Republic*, admits expressly for all subjects, even for the most elevated, instruments of communication (name and definition; the definition of the Good is postulated also in the *Republic* 534B-C). For this the Socratic manner of keeping silent cannot even be interpreted in an "ironic" sense, chiefly because it is limited by the precise pinpointing of Plato, especially by means of the expressions that refer unambiguously to the contingencies of the moment (the "now" of the "actual attempt"), and by the fact that it is found in numerous other passages in the *Republic*, [24] just as in the *Timaeus* [25]— belonging to the same trilogy—that do not refer to the Good, but to different subjects, and that oppose a panironic interpretation.

Characteristically, in the profoundly rooted pretense of a monopoly in favor of the written work, is the fact that the reviving of the indirect tradition is perceived by many scholars as a "reduction" and as a "depreciation" of the dialogues. Instead of seeing in it a positive amplification and deepening of the area of Platonic philosophy, they are indignant over the fact that it reorients what up to this time was understood, just as if someone were to see in the publication of the *Logic* of Hegel the depreciation of the *Phenomenology* of Hegel, or the art treasures known up to that time being depreciated by the rediscovery of the Venus of Milo.

The indignation, moreover, is incorrectly directed against the modern interpreters of Plato, since the determination of the hierarchical order existing between the unwritten doctrines and the written dialogues is based on what Plato himself wrote and, is completely comprehensible in its basic purpose. It touches chiefly the fact that the defenders of the indirect tradition are always charged with wanting to maintain a specific pretense of absoluteness in favor of the unwritten doctrine, that is, of wishing to eliminate the writings of Plato and wanting entirely to substitute the unwritten doctrines for them. Because this reproach is lacking in any basis (for the accused, in fact, instead are operating from the principle of the complementary coordination of both branches of the tradition),[26] it is characteristic and revelatory for the traditional way of thinking, that anything, so it seems, must be posited as an absolute; whether dialogues, or the unwritten doctrines; a third way of complementarity and synthesis is not, so it seems, conceivable. But it is clear that no logic in the world can support this paralogism (logical error), which is based on an erroneous transformation of a relation of contrariety into a relation of contradiction (that is, in the type of relation that is at the base of the principle "a third possibility is excluded"). However, the paralogism is explainable from the genetic standpoint. Schleiermacherianism evidently is essentially connected with a pretension to monopoly, which then, in the case of an alternative explanation, is transferred as something obvious to the indirect tradition.

A variant of the attempt to maintain the written work as self-sufficient and to protect it against a comparison with the indirect tradition is found in the affirmation that the dialogues would contain all that is essential. This view can be traced to Schleiermacher and, in part, Zeller. But this conception does not proceed only in the face of the self-testimonies of Plato, but also not in the face of the modern dispute about the authenticity and the dating of the indirect tradition. This controversy would be rendered superfluous and senseless, if the unwritten doctrine were, instead, in reality written and contained in the dialogues. But even the history of the influence of the dialogues shows *after the fact* that they were never in the condition to be the substitute for the indirect tradition. Platonism as a historical movement, rather, is divided into two basic currents that are distinguished according to whether they accepted in addition the doctrines of the indirect tradition (as occurs, for example, in Aristotle and in Neoplatonism, which are different in this respect from Hellenism and the modern age, beginning in the seventeenth century). The absence of equivalence between the two traditions even appears with respect to the *Parmenides*, whose metaphysical and constructive character and whose connection with a precise theory of the principles of Plato, without any preliminary "hypomnematic" knowledge of the indirect tradition, can be supposed only with difficulty, and even less so can be methodologically guaranteed in comparison with alternative interpretations.[27] For the modern investigator of Plato the experiment of discerning if the unwritten doctrine can be guessed at—if not directly confirmed—only by taking into account the dialogues, in any case, is no longer realizable, since such an investigation knows this doctrine in summary and from this knowledge there is no prescinding. Such an experiment, in addition, can be of no avail to the inquiry on Plato, granted that one is interested in such an inquiry on the philosophical content of Platonism and not in superficial controversies about the autonomy of particular sources. In fact, to reconstruct the most objective general outline possible, one must pay attention to the explicit affirmations and interpret the implicit affirmations in the light of the explicit ones.

Therefore, one can attribute only to the lack of philosophical interest the fact that Schleiermacherianism, in these recent periods, has tried to falsify even the self-testimonies of Plato, together with the criticism of the written work contained therein, changing them in a fallacious manner into a praise of the written work itself and into an indication for a hermeneutic approach to the dialogues.[28] The process of communication of long duration centered on the personal relation of the teacher and the student should be transferred to the exegesis of texts by means of an eclectic treatment of the texts themselves and by means of inaccurate translations; in addition, it should be suggested that Plato had professed a polyvalent theory of meaning for written work, and that this was likewise put into practice in the dialogues. The reader, by means of an intimate interaction with the text, proceeding little by little would gradually progress toward the most profound meaning of the written work itself, without needing to be taught through oral mediation. The unwritten doctrine of the principles, as such, would figure—and this is a reversal characteristic of Schleiermacherianism—only as a propaedeutic.

First, by means of this deadly hermeneutical leap, the self-testimonies of Plato are overturned and become their contrary. If it is true that the Platonic dialogue, as all written work, and perhaps also in a higher measure than the average, permits a comprehension that can be achieved little by little, and always more profoundly, then it is likewise true that the self-testimonies of Plato contained in the *Phaedrus* and in the *Seventh Letter* cannot be referred to this kind of work in any way. Rather, in Plato a theory of anagogic meaning of written work is lacking, just as a theory of the literary dialogue is lacking, in the sense claimed by Schleiermacher. All the specific connotations that can objectively be referred to the Platonic dialogues are, on the contrary, *subordinated* to the thesis of the existence of a *fundamental hiatus and hierarchical difference between written discourse and the oral discourse*, with which the self-testimonies of the *Phaedrus* and the *Seventh Letter* are exclusively concerned. For this reason Plato did not expressly treat as a theme those connotations in any part of his written work. In particular, the supposition, that the differences of content between the two branches of the tradition can also be overcome by means of an allegorical interpretation of the written works, this is refutable *after the fact*. The same goes for all other meanings (but which ones?) that should lead from the level of the literal meaning—and also beyond the level of the unwritten doctrine—to another dimension of differing content. (The polyvalence of the meaning of the text discovered by the most recent philosophical hermeneutics is referred to a different way of understanding, but no longer to a better or more elevated way of anagogic understanding).

Moreover, the hermeneutic theory attributed to Plato without foundation presupposes a relation with the literature that arises not until Hellenism. The "Socratic" Plato, instead, is still entirely dependent on the archaic conception of the primacy of the oral word, and his literary work is still prior to the structural changes of the Greek language into a literary phenomenon (R. Harder). The modern concept of the solitary reader and interpreter of written works, from the historical standpoint, hence in Plato, does not yet have any place. On the other hand, it is a surprising fact that this interpretation of Plato goes back to Neoplatonic allegories, which Schleiermacher, on the basis of the modern slogan "*sola scriptura* (scripture alone)," had abandoned. Now, instead, the absolute character of the literary dialogue is wanted to be maintained by renouncing its literal sense. And this, actually, is the spectacle of Schleiermacherianism that overturns itself, and that, to maintain the fiction of the self-sufficiency of the text, sacrifices with the autonomy of the text an acquisition of modern hermeneutics and one of the fundamental presuppositions of Schleiermacherianism itself.

To Write on the Unwritten Doctrines

Cherniss and his followers have insisted repeatedly on the apparent paradox that the original "unwritten" doctrines have been at some time fixed in writing and that only in this state they have been in a condition to begin a tradition that has endured many years. Thus their emphatic verdict is established that the indirect tradition of Plato—and hence also its modern historical treatment—in fairness to its author is illegitimate and, therefore, contradictory in itself.

We must first of all point out, for the sake of accuracy, that the prohibition of Plato presupposes the possibility that his fundamental doctrines can be written down and that he, on the other hand, conceded as possible, although certainly not as necessary, some of the hypomnematic notes (ὑπομνήματα) for the things already understood[29] (conforming to his theory of the *hypomnema* of the *Phaedrus*). The criticism of Plato centers only on the attempt of a direct written *communication*, if the factor of "orality" is eliminated with this, because, in his judgment, an authentic spiritual assimilation of the doctrine is guaranteed only by means of "orality." However, it is evident that this limits the legitimacy of the written work on the part of Plato, for an independent historical comprehension and for the philosophical interest of the scholarly historian once again can be only be a *subject* of historical inquiry and not a prior and theoretically binding principle. The wish to deduce the absolute prohibition of all possible scientific research from this principle would mean, on the contrary, to fall into a form of humanistic sentimentalism of a really overwhelming hermeneutic naïveté. Modern historians of philosophy certainly cannot accept or undoubtedly recognize as valid the Platonic theory of teaching and learning, of which they fully grasp the archaic quality, just as they are not able to adhere wholly to the philosophical position of Plato.[30] Such a theory could be renovated and reimposed in a theoretical manner only within the general sphere of a modern systematic theory of teaching and learning, which, however, then would be, practiced, not only, in Platonic research, but also, in general. To say it in another way, we people of today, after two millennia of experience with the culture of the written word, in regard to the Platonic method of teaching, find ourselves inevitably at a critical distance that cannot be overcome and that takes us as historians away from the Platonic norms concerned with the limitations of written work. The situation of Socrates and other philosophers who carried on their activity only orally (Pyrrho, Arcesilaus, Carneades, Ammonius) is instructive, for modern historians have at all times written about them without any hesitation. But, the thesis of the superiority of "oral discourse" maintained by Plato had its origin precisely in Socrates.

As, therefore, Plato's existential-communicative method of teaching is far removed from us and has become itself the object of historical research, it is, on the other hand, a datum, and with the help of the indirect tradition we can understand the writings of Plato and in addition to them the historical philosophical evolution from the Presocratics to Aristotle and then to Neoplatonism better than we could without them. Modern historical science, with respect to the actual state of things, not only has the possibility but the obligation of giving free rein to its actual understanding. And the understanding is justified by means of its actual realization. Seen from this standpoint, it is illegitimate, to refer to the fact that the basic Platonic doctrines originally were not written, to avoid from the beginning being concerned with them. And this is even more so for the Platonic theory of principles that has undoubtedly entered, in an irreversible manner, into the philosophical tradition through Neoplatonism and succeeding metaphysics. History can only reconstruct this process of reception in the particular cases after the fact. At the same time with this process of reception it becomes clear that ancient Platonism was already liberated from the Platonic limitations placed on the legitimacy of written work; and, with Neoplatonism, Plato's fundamental doctrines handed down by means of writing were renewed in a fruitful manner. Therefore today, one can hold on to the directing idea: the norm that an intelligent assimilation reenters into the presuppositions of a successful reception and reelaboration, and so much more, the more one tends to a systematic renovation of Platonism. This, evidently, could not in any case mean that one ought to return in general to the pristine state of the Platonic conditions of "orality," which would certainly be possible in different measures and in different grades.

Method and Ideology

The discussions of the last two decades have not always achieved that level which renders scholarly research meaningful and fruitful. The reason for this state of affairs, is on the one hand, the lack of philosophical interest, which can end in an aversion to facing questions concerning "the principles,"[31] as well as the violation of the duty to seek information, the fulfillment of which is part of the minimal conditions wherever there is scientific discussion. On the other hand, it must be noted that frequently the mixture of historical judgments about the doxographic data with the theoretical evaluations and modern theoretical criticism has damaged and ruined the work of the historical identification of the data. In this is verified—to use the terminology that is proper to the new philosophical hermeneutics—a kind of uncontrolled "fusion of horizons."

Furthermore, it must be remembered that the criticism of the philosophical content of the unwritten doctrines, which is in itself desirable, is not omnipotent, and cannot pretend to have some competence in resolving problems that concern the existence and authenticity of the tradition about which it is concerned. Because both, as experience shows, can be maintained as distinct, it is clear that one has to do so and that the second step cannot be accomplished before having completed the first. A similar methodological error also reoccurs, on a lower level, where pleasure and displeasure, the pleasurable and the not pleasurable, are more or less openly constructed as the criterion about what is historically true or false.[32]

In effect, the impression can scarcely be rejected that the myth of Schleiermacher about the self-sufficient literary dialogue has sometimes assumed even the character of a model of ideologically established research. In addition to this, a series of further preconceptions are solidified that, brought together, explain the strong emotional involvement and irritated anxiety, with which the defenders of Schleiermacherianism enter into the arena to fight the revival of the indirect tradition of Plato. These preconceptions are: (*a*) the aversion to a system that begins with Romanticism and goes from Schlegel onward to Kierkegaard and Nietzsche, reaching finally to the vitalistic and existentialistic philosophy of the twentieth century; (*b*) the discrediting of the oral tradition in the theological school of Tübingen, which has a way of also influencing the sphere of profane studies; (*c*) the dominant hermeneutics attached to the analysis of original and nonfragmentary literary texts, which is, in part irritated with, and in part indifferent to a supplementary doxographical tradition, (*d*) finally, reservations, which can be traced back to the republican-enlightenment criticism of Kant against the elitist esotericism of the Platonic *Seventh Letter*, in relation to the Platonic theory of principles which is presented there in a unified and hierarchized organization with a supposed totalitarianism contrary to the principles of equality and being open to the public.

The suspicion of totalitarianism mentioned (*d*) is, however, paradigmatic for the attempt to mix up a given ideological vision of reality with the problem regarding historical truth, instead of proceeding separately in a second step to measure the ascertained historical results in a critical way within the modern perspective and subject them to a theoretical scrutiny. Thus, the discussion about the theory of the principles of Plato is not at all the usual place for the defense of the commonwealth, because the political writings of Plato, if taken seriously at least in a certain measure, in this respect would have to be criticized to a much greater degree (the duality of the principles of the unwritten doctrine, in this regard, offers instead more ample room for freedom of choice). Also the absence of publicity, insofar as it is founded on the awareness of the responsibility for the thing that this doctrine treats, is in any case to evaluate, from the moral standpoint, in a rather positive way.[33]

A change of paradigm in science depends frequently, as we know beginning from T. S. Kuhn, from contingent motives and from extrascientific factors. In the research concerning Plato, for the moment, there are still strong antagonistic forces and difficulties that are opposed to a definitive overcoming of Schleiermacherianism.[34] However, the direction of Platonic research dedicated to the recovery and revival of the indirect tradition has strong arguments in its favor that justify such a change of paradigm, and precisely; the greater capacity for clarification and in general the greater fruitfulness that the new paradigm can bring to Platonic research, just as, more in general, for the history of ancient philosophy.

The followers of Schleiermacher must ponder at length on these rational arguments. At least, one must require that the emotional differences in the treatment of the two branches of the tradition and the frequent measuring by means of two weights and measures, recede in favor of considerations liberated from presuppositions. One who, without justification, commits in point of fact similar infractions against the principle of consistency, and, in the last analysis, against the principle of contradiction, must tolerate the questions, consequently, what kind of concepts of science one has and what kind of self-awareness as a scientist one possesses.

5 Conclusion: The Relation between the Direct and Indirect Platonic Tradition and the Significance of the Platonic Dialogues

The Structural Relations between the Direct and Indirect Tradition

The Platonic picture of the modern age is characterized by the decline of the allegorical method and the destruction of the Neoplatonic idea of system connected to it. The "system" that until that time was believed to be found expressed in the writings of Plato was removed by means of the principle of modern hermeneutics, on the basis of which the text of an author must be interpreted only by starting from it and consequently declined. For this reason, beginning from Leibniz, the question, How it is possible? notwithstanding to reduce the work of Plato to a system, becomes a dominant reason in the philosophical exegesis of Plato. With the falling apart of the Neoplatonic notion of system, however, the literary works of Plato, on the one hand, and the remains of the indirect tradition, which had been reabsorbed into the notion of system, on the other, for the first time beginning from antiquity were separated from one another again and thus a new coordination on an historical-critical basis was made necessary. This task of mediation between both branches of the tradition, since around the second half of the eighteenth century, has become the unique legitimate one from the scientific and historical-philosophical standpoint. However, in the meantime, it has been blocked for a century and a half by means of the invention on the part of Schleiermacher of the myth of the self-sufficient literary dialogue.

Schleiermacher has created the categories and some basic concepts on which the modern picture of Plato is based, developing his theory of the literary and artistic dialogue on the basis of the principle of the autonomy of the written work (*sola scriptura*). According to this theory, the idealized dialogical form of philosophical communication is not separable from its content and alone makes possible the spontaneous assimilation and understanding of it. The comprehension of the literary dialogue coincides, hence, in method and content, with the comprehension of Platonic philosophy itself, and, consequently, there is no room for a second branch of the tradition arising from the activity of oral teaching of Plato. The pretense of absoluteness that Schleiermacher had bound to the conception of the literary dialogue, however, in the course of the twentieth century, is shown increasingly to be insupportable; in fact, such a claim does not take seriously the Platonic doctrine of teaching and learning and the criticism of written work connected to it, and vice versa, at the same time it neglects the fact that Plato himself does not sketch in any way a theory of the literary dialogue, not even in terms of simple hints. If, in addition, the indirect Platonic tradition is deformed by Schleiermacher, as a *quantité négligeable* (negligible quantity), then the difference in weight given to the indirect tradition with respect to the direct tradition depends on hidden premises that are very specific and that belong to a metaphysics of art, which has its roots in the Idealistic philosophy of identity developed around the 1800s, and consequently, is to a large extent historically conditioned.[2] If these metaphysical and ontological premises are eliminated, then the literary dialogue is reduced to a series of didactic dispositions of Plato (as for example the apparent aporias, the digressions, the interruptions before the end of an argument and so on), which the critical attitude in relation to the written work cannot entirely overcome, but only modify, and especially not furnish any argument against the careful utilization of the reports on the unwritten doctrines that originated from the activity of the oral teaching of Plato.

The reorientation of the picture of Plato shaped by Schleiermacher, which is sketched in the research on Plato in the last decades, consists precisely in this state of affairs. It follows a *middle way* between the allegorical and Neoplatonic interpretation in vogue before the modern era and the literary modern interpretation. It does not abandon the unwritten doctrines, as the first, to antihistorical adaptations and theoretical transformations of Platonic philosophy, nor, as the second, make it coincide, in a reductive manner, with the corpus of the preserved written works. It instead re-establishes the indirect tradition with its proper weight and uses, in addition, the self-testimonies of Plato to produce a mediation between the two branches of the tradition.

In effect, Platonic research cannot be excused in the long run from the obligation to give an account of the twofold lines of the indirect and direct tradition and to give priority to their mutual clarification and their mutual corroboration. The arbitrary attempts, made in the wake of Schleiermacher, to eliminate or at the least neutralize the indirect tradition, as derived from the dialogues or arising from the late activity of Plato ("late lesson") have not achieved their aim and could not be in any condition to do so in the future, due to the conditions that exist in the Platonic tradition. Nor can inquiry into Plato that is aware and responsible any longer ignore in an artificial manner the indirect tradition and, hence, go contrary to the methodological principle of completion and integration of the *totality* of the documents and *all* the materials historically at our disposal. And this is the more inopportune, insofar as, by means of the acceptance of the indirect tradition, a whole series of perspectives indispensable for a better comprehension, a better explanation, and a better judgment about the written works and the philosophy of Plato is revealed. Here are these perspectives:

1. The self-testimonies of Plato, of themselves, allow for the possibility that to the uncertainties of the method connected to the "playful" *form* of the written work there likewise corresponds a lack of philosophical "seriousness" of the *content*. In any case, the question is open as to whether the literary dialogues in general are entitled to a documentary status as sources of Platonic philosophy, or if the *proprium* of the latter, which Plato maintained does not belong to the dialogues, is not placed at an incommensurable distance from them. The muddling of this issue is a consequence of Schleiermacherianism—in a certain sense its negative overturning—with which Platonic research has been weighed down for a long time, and so—puzzled by this—the reception of Plato from the side of theoretical philosophy, too. The entire literary legacy of Plato seemed to be restricted to something without foundation in the shadow of an elusive metaphilosophy, like the old and vague thesis already admitted that maintained the existence of a Platonic esotericism (a secret doctrine). On the contrary, the systematic rediscovery of the indirect tradition and the comparison of it with the direct tradition, before everything else, permits us to confirm on a methodologically secure basis *the essential connection that unites the content of the two traditions, and, with that, also the serious philosophical character of the literary work.* In the ambit of the activity of oral teaching, in which Plato—unlike in the dialogues in which Socrates is imitated—truly speaks in his own name, without concealing himself, "seriously," is the *Archimedean point*, beginning from which, as a foundation, the "philosophical seriousness" of the content of the dialogues can likewise be established and guaranteed. The indirect tradition, hence, is far from being used to disvalue the Platonic written works, on the contrary, it brings us, instead, to their reevaluation, insofar as it demonstrates that Plato spoke in his own voice even in the dialogues.

2. In addition, the knowledge of the indirect tradition puts within our grasp a criterion for the interpretation of Plato even in particular cases, leaving behind the equivocity of the dialogues, to establish certain priorities and to specify determinate elements that have a particular weight and emphasis. Therefore, when the reader of

Plato, especially the philosophical reader feels confused because he does not know specifically what persons of the dialogue truly represent Plato (one? which? none? all of them?), then the indirect tradition, on whose basis there is a precise and explicit taking of a position by Plato, on that condition furnishes us with useful and significant criteria. At least, it is present as an irreplaceable corrective and as an instrument of control reasonably suited for the interpretation of the written works.

3. Independent of the help that it can provide for the solution of controversial problems, the indirect tradition is also a fruitful hermeneutical instrument as well as an heuristic means for a better comprehension and for a more penetrating interpretation of the written works. From thence springs a new lucidity, a new explicitness and new conceptual understanding of the literary works, which, once again, is turned to the advantage of the philosophical understanding and theoretical elaboration of Plato.

4. For a reconstruction of the complex picture of Plato the indirect tradition carries a considerable increase and *increment of the philosophical content*, which amplifies in a significant manner, beyond the written works, the range of Platonic philosophy. It is correct to say it reveals a "new dimension" of Platonism,[3] the relevance of which we will treat in Parts Two and Three of this book. With this, Plato gains in a decisive manner as philosopher, without, however, losing anything as writer. Vice versa, by considering the literary works as self-sufficient, that is, absolutizing them, the writer has nothing to gain, while the philosopher has much to lose.

5. By being accessible through the indirect tradition the theory of the principles confers on Platonic philosophy a higher level of *unity*. This is so whether for all the dialogues and their respective thematic perspectives or for the individual phases of a possible evolution of Platonic thought, but it is also so with respect to the content, that is, for the plural nature of the Ideas. In the light of the theory of principles, the outlines of a *systematic philosophy* and even the contours of the construction of a system are presented, which achieves, in addition to a thematic increment, a new methodological characteristic for the philosophy of Plato as well.

6. Finally, the indirect tradition permits a new and more consistent location of the philosophy of Plato within the ambit of the development of the history of ancient philosophy. And this depends on the unity of this philosophy, supported by means of the indirect tradition, which enables us to make well-founded summary com-

parisons; and in a particular way it depends, also in regard to the content, on the theory of the principles, which in a visible way, historically, is to have a mediating function between Presocratic philosophy, on the one hand, and Aristotelianism and Neo-platonism, on the other. There also originates from the indirect tradition, vice versa, a vision of the profound consistency and continuity of the whole historical evolution of Greek philosophy itself.

The relations between the indirect and the direct traditions are not asymmetrical. Rather, they explain and clarify each other. This means, in regard to the indirect tradition, that, because of its higher level of abstraction and the fact that it is found within the doxographical tradition encapsulated in short sketches, it will present difficulties for anyone who wants to comprehend it in isolation, whereas one will understand it and it will become intelligible in terms of its purposes and relevance, as soon as one relates it to the written works and make them penetrate into it with all their riches. Therefore the dialogues, on their side, put at our disposal some criteria for the explanation of the indirect tradition. To this is added likewise the hermeneutic superiority of the written work, which is founded on a movement of thought developed in detail, while the indirect tradition is hardened into a block, and offers, so to say, petrified results. And these results have need of being loosened by means of the reconstruction of their argumentative origin, on the model of the dialectical method developed in the dialogues. In the resulting complexity hence there is a characteristic twofold direction and complementarity between the written work and the unwritten doctrine: contrary to the hermeneutical-methodological superiority of the written work and to the better quality of its tradition there goes the philosophical superiority of the unwritten theory of the principles that in any case involves, for its part, specific consequences for the standards of interpretation of the written work, in general and in particular. Hence, only by means of the mutual amplification, correction, and control of the written and unwritten work, there can be drawn little by little an historically based general vision of Platonic philosophy.

This is so for the thematic content as well as for the method. We have in the dialogues an incomparably richer source of material which is not in the reports of the oral doctrines. Perhaps Plato treated some themes only in the written works; in any case, most of the themes of the written works are not found in the indirect tradition (presumably there was a choice by our sources, using a criterion that revealed what is not documented in the dialogues and that hence was "unwritten"). Plato in addition, in the redaction of the written works, had to take into account especially a public constituted of readers who were not informed about the unwritten doctrines or only partially informed. All this confirms that the internal interpretation of the dialogues has its own right when compared with the indirect tradition, and that such an interpretation of the dialogues obviously cannot be substituted with the exclusive study of the unwritten doctrines.

The concept of the unwritten doctrine must be understood in a restricted sense, while that of the indirect tradition must be understood in a wide sense, that is, as such the latter is also to include some themes treated in the written works.[4] The two branches of the tradition, hence, are not only complementary, but in part also overlap and coincide. On the other hand, the unwritten doctrine does not coincide simply with the doctrine of the principles, but rather culminates in it.

Then, if the confines that divide the written work and the unwritten doctrine are understood in a rigorous manner, what results is that the technique of dissimulation that Plato practices in the dialogues consists not only in the omission of some parts of his doctrines but likewise, frequently, simply in the renunciation of any precise ultimate determination of the doctrines and in not making explicit their lines of connection. Notwithstanding this, the distance between the content of the written works and the unwritten ones due to the self-testimonies of Plato and the comparative data of the two branches of the tradition, is not traversable. This conclusion is methodologically based on the fact that the written work, in each of its forms, for Plato is inferior to the oral process involved in the spiritual formation of the soul of the philosopher over a long period of time; and because of this, it is not suitable to the communication of the basic doctrines. At the same time the written works risk that such doctrines will be misunderstood, and hence, that they will be treated in an improper manner. The literary and artistic dialogue as well cannot overcome these difficulties and remains necessarily on this side of the breach. And this is precisely so also for the *reflections* on the inferiority and on the playfulness of the written works;[5] also this reflection, in fact, cannot substitute for the long duration of the concrete oral process of teaching and learning that involves years and years, and hence in no way can recover in intuitive manner the ultimate results belonging to that process and still much less fix them by means of effective training in the certitude and in the security of knowledge and action as occurs instead within the ambit of oral dialectic.

The view of Schleiermacher, which in its sphere constitutes a referential standpoint, does not result in being negated by this understanding, but simply is relocated in its importance. In the first place, it is important to integrate the literary work of Plato in the full complexity of his whole philosophical activity and teaching and to turn anew to determining it in its function, considering it precisely in the vision of the whole. In fact, the problem of the legitimacy and purpose of the writing arises for Plato, if the primacy of the "oral" dimension is considered, in a different way and takes on likewise new possible responses. In the second place, moving from these premises, one must further explain the sense and the permanent significance of the form of the dialogue and the artistic form, which Schleiermacher was the first to rehabilitate and recognize in its function of communication. In this task of explanation can be subsumed and integrated the work of the followers of Schleiermacher (for example, J. Stenzel, P. Friedländer, R. Schaerer, V. Goldschmidt, H. Gundert, H. L. Sinaiko, S. Rosen, R. Burger and others),[6] who have tried to realize, by means of a concrete and detailed interpretation of the texts, the hermeneutical program of Schleiermacher himself, that is, they have tried to explain the form of the expression as part of the content itself.

The Significance of the Platonic Dialogue

The question What is the nature and significance of the Platonic dialogue? if taken from the standpoint of the unwritten doctrines—as, for other perspectives, if taken from the standpoint of the pre-Platonic tradition—is posited in a new way and its solution in a certain sense is already indicated. In fact, it assumes within itself the "Platonic problem" formulated by the research on Plato of the nineteenth century about the unity and interior articulation of the written work, which now broadens likewise into the wider question of the unity of the written work and the unwritten in Plato.

Schleiermacher had delineated the aim of the dialogues, in general, as philosophical communication in an exhortatory way. But this determination of the function of the dialogue must be differentiated and made more precise in the following way.

1. The self-testimony of Plato contained in the *Phaedrus* (consult Appendix 1.1) attributes a *hypomnematic* function to the writings; they must make reproducible and at the reader's disposal what has been achieved in the sphere of oral dialectic. This is so, in the first place, for the doctrinal dialogues beginning with the *Republic*; in effect, they offer, for members of the Academy and even also for Plato himself, a documentation that records, also in the exterior form, the original dialogue used in the teaching and, at the same time, refers again and again beyond itself to the highest fundamental doctrines, for which, due to the *Seventh Letter* (consult Appendix 1.2), one is not in need of commemorative instruments of this kind.[7]

2. The dialogues composed anteriorly that terminate frequently in an aporetic way have instead a chiefly *protreptic* and introductory function. This is guaranteed by numerous thematic reminiscences that go back to the preceding and contemporary literature, Sophis-

tic, Socratic, and rhetorical, of a type of propagandistic writings.[8]
Actually, the monograph of K. Gaiser[9] has also demonstrated that
in Plato in the *protreptic* introduction is always already included
likewise, in part, the educative conversion. The Platonic dialogues,
insofar as they act both protreptically and pedagogically, can begin
the practical exercise of the right way of living. They, therefore, in
addition to their protreptic function, also have a *propaedeutic* character and, so considered, constitute, in a certain measure, the more
external and basic circle in the educative work of the Platonic
Academy.[10]

3. The Platonic dialogues, in spite of their mimetic form, are not
   reports about colloquies that have actually happened historically.
   It is a matter rather of idealized fictional conversations, which have
   only the appearance of reality but which, for the rest, represent in
   an objective manner typical situations of both successful and unsuccessful communications, and to this is joined also a normative
   claim.[11] In this sense, in the dialogues in an implicit manner one can
   find a *normative* theory of the dialogue used in the course of
   teaching, of the argumentative and disputatious dialogue (R.
   Wiehl),[12] a theory that, as such, must react with a regulative and
   stabilizing function and in its turn also upon the discourses used
   in the course of the teaching and the discussions in the Platonic
   Academy. Such a theory modeled for the real dialogue would more
   strictly connect the written works to the oral activity of Plato than
   in the case of its (1) hypomnematic or (2) protreptic-propaedeutic
   functions, because in that way, the form of the dialogue and the
   artistic form would gain an important methodological function in
   the ambit of the "oral" dialogue itself. Naturally, such ideal
   schemas of the dialogue can only prepare for the concrete application to the real dialogue, but cannot substitute for it. The process
   of intellectual formation true and proper is bound in a way, and
   cannot be substituted, to its concrete actualization in the ambit of
   the development of the real dialogue.

4. Less easily documentable and concluded to only by analogy are
   those reasons as *representation* and *propaganda* in relation to the
   contemporary public and *influence on posterity*. In the first instance,
   Plato would have written his dialogues looking to the other
   Socratics or on the models of the discourses of Isocrates, in order
   not to leave unutilized this sphere of the discussion and of the
   influence in the competition concerned with *paideia* [culture and
   education]. In the second instance, instead, the reasoning of the
   Symposium about the spiritual procreation of the poet, the artist in

the representational arts, and the legislator[13] could be transferred
to the philosophical writer, who however in the *Symposium* is not
actually mentioned.

5. The communication purpose that is dominant in Schleiermacher,
   seems rather to be reduced to a lower rank in the self-testimonies
   of Plato; the *Phaedrus*, even, contests it. Nonetheless, for evident
   reasons, it cannot be totally absent and, as proof indirectly the
   reflections on the reach of the literary works, is at least taken into
   account by Plato. In effect, the protreptic-propaedeutic function of
   the writings implies already a certain level of communication,[14] just
   as, on the other hand, their hypomnematic role requires the possibility of communication with strangers for the oral dialectic. In
   this regard E. Schmalzriedt[15] developed a very promising thesis, on
   the basis of which he conceived the artistic form of the Platonic
   literary dialogue, like Schleiermacher, as an instrument that aids
   philosophical communication; at the same time, however, in a
   fruitful dialectical tension, he separates the artistic form of the
   dialogue from the unwritten oral doctrine, and together, he refers
   the artistic form to it. In this way Schmalzriedt overcame (by
   preserving and lifting up), in the Hegelian sense, Schleiermacher's
   own position. Schmalzriedt recognized that we, in the first place,
   encounter the writer Plato, who makes of a philosophical theme the
   occasion for a literary production, which is submitted to the laws
   of artistic creation. The intermediate ambit of the literature is thus
   the place of a veracious occurrence, which in a greater or lesser
   measure, brings the reader toward the central unwritten nucleus
   of Platonic philosophy, without, however, ever revealing it. The
   process of thought that the literary dialogues put in motion, therefore, is provisory and essentially inconclusive; it certainly has a
   philosophical character, but it is bound to literary means, and
   hence it is not in a condition to catch up and transmit the ultimate
   philosophical position of Plato, which is reserved for oral teaching.
   Schmalzriedt takes up hence the Platonic categories of
   "playfulness" and "seriousness" and connects them with those
   currents, derived from Attic tragedy, of "appearance" and "being,"
   not without reference to the Platonic distinctions between
   "opinion" (*doxa*) and "science" or "truth." The function in the
   sense of an aesthetic of the reception of the artistic dialogue, which
   Schleiermacher had concretized in the work of Plato, with this,
   properly understood in a specifically literary manner, is limited and
   distinct, as propaedeutic, from the decisive sphere of "orality." The
   dialectical procedure of Plato the writer gives way to a cognitive

process that achieves the end not already in the writings, but in the oral teaching activity of the Academy.

The artistic and literary dialogue, within the area of interest of Platonic philosophy, with this achieves in outline an authentic and genuine space, which gives room also to the legitimate intentions of Schleiermacher. The same is true likewise for the amplification and for the emphases that the followers of Schleiermacher have achieved in his observations (for example, R. Schaerer, changing of the view of the dialogues according to the partners in the dialogues; V. Goldschmidt, so-called sliding to the left, that is, deviations apparent from the chief lines of the dialogue; both similarly also in H. Gundert). For the rest the basic thesis of Schleiermacher, with respect to the analysis of the artistic dialogues of Plato in detail, in the meantime, has not been fundamentally surpassed.

This is true also for the conception of the polyvalence of the text maintained by the more recent philosophical hermeneutics, when it is applied to Plato. In the same way, also, the most recent discussions about the thematic dialogue, discourse, and dialectic have not yet achieved a systematic theory of the literary dialogue, which could be fruitful for Platonic research.[16]

PART TWO

The Philosophical Structure of the Platonic
Theory of the Principles,
Its Content and Its Historical Significance

6   *The Unified Structure of Platonic Philosophy*

The Theory of the Principles as the Ultimate Foundation that Goes Beyond the Theory of Ideas

Platonic philosophy[1] transmitted by the indirect tradition is presented as an etiology in the Presocratic sense, viz., as an inquiry into the ultimate causes, principles, and elements. In this kind of research the law dominates by which reality must be explained through principles that are the simplest and fewest in number as possible. The real pluralism of the theory of Ideas as a result was theoretically reoriented and methodologically surpassed on a higher level of reflection. The most important of the Aristotelian reports on the unwritten doctrines of Plato, contained in *Metaphysics* A 6.[2] clearly presents a twofold level of research of the foundations: as the Ideas are causes of all the remaining things, so the principles (ἀρχαί) are causes (αἰτίαι) and elements (στοιχεῖα) of the Ideas themselves. The theory of the principles, consequently, serves as the ultimate foundation that is beyond the theory of Ideas and includes them[3] and, guarantees a higher degree of unity to Platonic philosophy as a result. The difference that exists between the unwritten doctrines and the exposition of the central books of the *Republic* (Books Six and Seven), which allows a similar culmination of the world of Ideas to be recognized in the Idea of the Good, consists in the fact that in the former is found a more precise determination and description of the role of the Good as unity (ἔν) and as measure (μέτρον), and finally in the fact that the One-Good is opposed by a contrary principle of multiplicity (a principle of multiplication and gradation) equally original, not, however, with equal value and not of equal rank.

The Original Bipolarity of the Principles (Unity and Multiplicity)

Plato begins from the twofold nature of the two ultimate principles, beyond which a problem cannot be posed. Plato presupposes, therefore, that the totality of being cannot be deduced from a single principle without falling into the paradox of the self-duplication of the original One. The methodology of the Platonic theory of the principles, the remainder of which is otherwise lost for the most part, with respect to this point is still preserved: with the argument that the plurality of being postulates the admission of an opposing principle of multiplicity along with that of unity, Plato keeps his distance, in a special way, from the One-Whole of Parmenides and Eleaticism.[4]

The opposing principle of multiplicity was not conceived simply as the contrary opposed to unity, viz., as the essence of the plurality of beings, but as a strict contradictory, as not-unity, that is, as indeterminate and un-limited—and hence, also as divisible to infinity—principle and substrate of every individual multiplicity (ἄπειρον πλῆθος). This unlimitedness, in ad-dition, was understood in a twofold sense: as a continuum in the sense of an infinitely large (in modern terms: > 1), and, at the same time, oppositely, as a continuum in the sense of an infinitely small (in modern terms: < 1). With this universal "duality" of direction of the unlimited large-and-small (ἀόριστος δυάς of the μέγα-μικρόν, and also of the πολύ-ὀλίγον, summarily described also as ἄνισον), Plato, in the first place, manifestly aimed at the philosophical foundation of the mathematical doctrine of proportions and relations (1 : 1—2 : 1—3 : 1, etc., and vice versa 1 : 1—1 : 2—1 : 3, etc.),[5] but, beyond this, he tried to formulate a general principle of scales (μεῖζον-ἔλαττον, πλεῖον-μεῖον, μᾶλλον-ἧττον, etc.). Consequently, while the op-position between unity and notunity (multiplicity) is that of contradiction, that between the two aspects of the direction of the unlimited multiplicity (great-small) rather is of contrariety. And the structures of Platonic dialectic (diaeresis, synopsis, distinction of opposites) are founded on these relations. It is not a matter, therefore, simply of repeating the Presocratic doctrine of the opposites—for example the Pythagorean cosmogonical doctrine of the opposites—but rather of a reelaboration of it on the basis of a specifically Platonic dialectical method. On the other hand, the principles and their relations are still prior to determined being and to its determinations of identity and difference, similarity and dissimilarity, equality and ine-quality. Also the principles of contradiction and the excluded middle are established solely within the constitution of determined being. Therefore, in a strict sense, they can be valid for the highest principles themselves (One, Dyad) only in the prototypical sense and through analogy.

Being as a Mixture of Unity and Multiplicity

The cooperation of the two principles constitutes the structure of reality. Every being is essentially given from the cooperation of the two principles, and precisely from the determination, from the fixation and the limitation of the unlimited multiplicity—i.e., from the "equalization" between the two aspects of the great and the small—by means of unity as a principle of determination.[6] This "generation," naturally, is not to be understood as a temporal process, but rather as a metaphor to explain the analysis of the ontological structure; it has the aim of making understandable to the cognition that proceeds in a discursive manner, the structuring of being that is aprocessive and atemporal. Everything that is exists in the measure in which it is something limited, determined, distinct, identical, permanent, and insofar as it shares in the basic unity, which is a principle of every determination. Nothing is *something*, so far as it is not *one* something. But it can be, precisely, something and one and share in unity only because, at the same time, it shares in the contrary principle of unlimited multiplicity, and because of this, it is *another* with respect to unity itself. Being, therefore, is essentially *unity within multiplicity*. To that extent the role of the two principles is analogous to the Aristotelian distinction of formal and material principles.

Being is defined as that which is "generated" beginning from two principles by means of the limitation and determination of the material principle by the formal principle and that therefore in a certain way is like a mixture.[7] This is the core of Plato's *basic ontological conception*. Consequently, the same principles are not-being, but, insofar as they are constitutive of every being, they are *prior* to being and hence, unity as a principle of determination is *beyond* being, the material indeterminate principle as not-being is rather below being.[8] The concept of 'beyond being' is derived for the rest in a consistent way, from the admission of a multiplicity in being that corrected Eleaticism; if the Eleatic disjunction of unity and multiplicity is preserved, then this admission must inevitably push unity into a position beyond being.[9]

The Different Levels of the Constitution of Being

Plato has also pursued this fundamental ontological conception with respect to individual being, and he tried to put it to the test and confirm it, wherever he could, in the same way in which, for example, the Atomists tried to prove the soundness of their fundamental principles, viz., of the atoms and the void, with regard to all possible phenomena. In the unwritten doctrine, in the first place, the ideal and paradigmatic sphere of the universals in its precisely determined and well-ordered organization is analyzed. The structure of the ordering of the universals determined by the original unity constitutes a unitary whole, in which each member is to every other member in exactly determinable relations that can be expressed in mathematical relations, *logoi, analogiai* [10] (and this nexus constitutes the theoretical reason why Plato consequently already grounds the mathematical doctrine of proportions on the theoretical level of the principles). The theory of the *Idea-numbers* expresses especially the structure of the relations of the universals on a mathematical basis, and, consequently, by means of an ontological reduction, the universals are reduced to the series of the ideal numbers,[11] of which they participate in their determination and in their regularity. The ideal numbers, within the ambit of the universals, can therefore possess a privileged *status*, and because of this, they are presented as the first to be "generated" from the principles.[12] They play a role of mediation in the hierarchy of being between the principles and the rest of the Ideas, because they represent in paradigmatic form the characteristics of being, viz., limitation, determination, and order.

The Construction of Mathematical, Geometrical, and Stereometrical Realities

The basic ontological conception is manifested, in addition, in the construction of mathematical realities, and—in connection with this—in the internal structure at the base of the corporeal world; the unwritten doctrine constructs as many mathematical numbers as geometrical and stereometric figures, beginning from the "monads" (individual unities) and minimal magnitudes (the indivisible lines), which in their turn, are constituted by the limitation of the great-and-small by unity.[13] Also the elements of the corporeal world conceived stereometrically as regular polyhedrons (fire as a tetrahedron, water as an icosahedron, air as an octohedron, and earth as a cube), are reduced in a corresponding way, by means of the procedure of dimensional analysis, through surfaces and lines, to unitary-points (the indivisible lines),[14] as for the final unities of extension in themselves; they represent a derivative unity, which contains an additional multiplicity. The sphere of rational soul, which occupies a mediating position between the intelligible and extension, seems to be correlated with the dimension of surface.[15]

The Categorial Division and Its Significance

Sensible realities: the cosmos, natural objects, artifacts, the polis, and its virtue must be considered to have analogous structures. The unwritten doctrine in this respect offers a categorial division[16] between the *unrelated* and the *related*, being per se and relative being (καθ' αὐτὰ ὄντα - πρὸς ἕτερα ὄντα = ἐναντία - πρός τι: opposites and correlatives that correspond to the Aristotelian categories of quality and quantity), a prelude to the Aristotelian distinction between substance and accident, but which in Plato has the function of bringing every reality back to the theory of principles. While being in itself, substantial being, falls under unity, the relations (opposites and correlatives), according to their limited or their unlimited nature, go back through the categories of the equal (or equalized: ἴσον) or of the unequal (ἄνισον), respectively, to unity or to the contrary principle of the great-and-small. The basic ontological conception, therefore, is also operative here; at the same time, different degrees of the mixture of the two highest principles are manifested: according to which of the two principles predominates, a thing can be "equal" or "unequal," but insofar as it is a *determinate being*, it participates in both principles. The same can be said for the contrary pairs of *sameness* and *difference* (ταὐτόν – ἔτερον), of similarity and dissimilarity (ὅμοιον – ἀνόμοιον), of *rest* and *motion*, of *even* and *odd*, which Plato treated both in the late dialogues and in the unwritten doctrines, but in the latter in a more systematic manner, reducing each pair to the two highest principles.[17] All of these pairs of contraries share in both principles, however in such a way that sometimes one prevails and sometimes the other. Moreover, the same distinction in the degree of mixture of the two principles is at the base also of the relation between the intelligible world and the sensible world.

The Process of the Reduction to the Elements and the Process of Generalization (the Principles as Elements and Genera)

The *fundamental nexuses* that Plato in the unwritten doctrine, through the dialectical method, established between the individual spheres of being and the highest basic principles, as a result, are already becoming clearly visible. It is a question, substantially, of two different forms of thought that, moreover, complement each other but that, sometimes, also are in opposition or better in concurrence with one another: (1) *the process of reducing things to their elements*, based on the model of mathematics, which reduces everything, by means of always analyzing them into smaller and smaller parts, to those ultimate and simpler principles; this form of thinking is concerned chiefly with the reduction of the number series and the series of dimensions; (2) *the process of generalization*, of Socratic provenance, which rises from particular to always more general concepts; this form of thinking refers to the realm of the universals in the strict sense, and, especially, to the Meta-Ideas[18] mentioned earlier of identity, equality, similarity, and their contraries. These categorial concepts or concepts of reflection, as they would be called today, in the realm of the universals have a normative role like that of the Ideal Numbers. They are, to the principles, in the same relation in which species stand to genera, insofar as, for example, identity and similarity are species of unity, difference, and dissimilarity are species of multiplicity.[19] The categorial or *generalizing reduction* to which alone in the most recent research (beginning with the research of P. Wilpert) has been given a closer study, in the unwritten doctrine plays a role equal to that of the process of reducing things to their elements. It is necessary to take into account, therefore, Platonic *methodological pluralism*, in consequence of which the principles assume a twofold *status* both as *primary elements* and as *most general genera* (unity means, hence, the *most simple* as well as the *most universal*).[20] Plato, evidently, tried to grasp the totality of being by means of multiple convergent attempts, as much as possible without lacunae and gaps, and to guarantee, therefore, the greatest universality possible to the principles. (And such a *methodological pluralism* can be compared although only roughly with the pluralism of the perspectives that the dialogues present). The error, still quite rampant, that consists in maintaining that the theory of principles of Plato is of a "mathematical" nature and that unity is the number one, is amply refuted by the ideal character of the principles. In addition, the twofold function of the principles completely demonstrates that they are not in any way concepts that serve simply for the construction of the ideal mechanism of the numbers, and, hence, are not simply an appendix and a vehicle of the doctrine of the Idea-numbers, but are certainly meta-mathematical and universal principles.

The Regressive and Derivative Procedures
(*ratio cognoscendi* and *ratio essendi*)

The twofold nature of the methodological lines (*the process of reduction to the elements and the process of generalization*) is distinct from the *twofold direction of the process of argument* that moves in two contrary senses and that, on the basis of the information contained in numerous testimonies[21] on the unwritten doctrine of Plato, was manifestly essential. Plato worked with both the *reductive procedure*, starting from the lower to the higher according to the degrees of knowledge (this direction also notoriously predominates in the dialogues), and with the *derivative procedure*, descending from the higher to the lower, following the ordered hierarchical structure of being. This distinction between the order of knowledge (*ratio cognoscendi*) and the order of being (*ratio essendi*) is more familiar from the Aristotelian distinction, which marks the difference between things that are "prior for us" from things that are "prior in themselves," or also in modern terminology, the method of resolution and the method of composition, the analytic method and the synthetic method, the "heuristic nexus" and the "justificatory nexus" (H. Reichenbach).[22] The structure of the ordering of knowledge and that of being are included within the competence of the dialectical method in equal measure. Only that, in the first case, dialectic proceeds in a heuristic-introductory way, whereas, in the second way, it proceeds through division, definition, and demonstration. This is true both for the process of reduction *and deduction to and from the elements and for the process of reduction and deduction to and from the most general.*

The Four Levels of Reality, Their Relations, and Their
Internal Structures

The systematic compendium of the unwritten metaphysical doctrine of Plato involves a distinction of *four principal levels of reality* (because it is a question of the relation of an ontological structure, these levels clearly are not to be interpreted in a spatial sense). The level that we can call the lowest is made up of sensible objects in motion. The second level is made up of mathematical natures, which are intelligible and immutable, but that insofar as they are individuals still do not belong to the archetypical universals. On the third level are located the universals, which are not a multiplicity of individuals, but each is of an ideal uniqueness. The final level is composed of the principles that are above being; they are themselves of a purely universal character, and therefore can be grasped only by going through and beyond the remaining Ideas. These four levels, distinct according to precise ontological criteria (the criteria of immutability, universality, and simplicity), are further subdivided; for example, with the emergence of the primacy of the Meta-Ideas and the series of Ideal Numbers in the realm of the universals, or with the succession of arithmetic, geometry, stereometry, pure astronomy, musicology in the sphere of the mathematical entities,[23] to which the sphere of psychic realities (understood as mathematical form in motion) also belongs,[24] or with the distinction of the superlunary and the sublunary, bodies in eternal motion and bodies in corruptible motion in the sphere of sensible things.

In general, it is an ontological relation of derivation, in which the higher degrees always possess an ontological priority with respect to what is below them (πρότερον — ὕστερον φύσει),[25] and in which, to speak with Platonic terminology, the first can be or can be conceived without the second, the second cannot be or be thought without the first (συναναιρεῖν καὶ μὴ συναναιρεῖσθαι).[26] There exists, therefore, an asymmetrical relation of dependence that is not reversible, in which, however, the higher level is only the necessary condition but not the sufficient condition for the succeeding ones. In fact, the Dyad of the great-and-small plays a fundamental role on all the levels as a material principle, but without a further grounding of its differentiation for the individual spheres of being; the categorial *novum*, hence, is not explained. Nevertheless, the concepts of function and relation taught by Plato and employed in a technical terminological sense by him, show that he tended to a general coherent and consistent plan. The theory of the principles therefore guarantees the unity of the system and its theoretical structure.[27]

The Doctrine of the Principles as the Foundation of All the Spheres of Being and the Doctrine of a Universal Science

The theory of the principles was intended by Plato as a final foundation of all the spheres of being and reality and their related sciences, to the extent they were then developed. The principles therefore were prior to and had in a similar degree the function of the *highest genera* within all these spheres:

that of mathematics, logic, physics, or ethico-politics, without being sub-jected to particular specifications. This is also true for the fundamental conception of being that is derived from them; that is, of being as a mixture of unity and multiplicity, something limited and determined, even if such a conception could be represented as differently specified according to different aspects within diverse spheres of being. The *polyvalent role* of the principles, which was revealed previously on the basis of their twofold role both as generic (that is, as "genera") and as elementary (that is, as "elements"), can therefore be further unfolded in the elements and in the concepts of special genera, which belong to each of the levels. In effect, the single levels (οὐσίαι, γένη, φύσεις) are determined by means of *special principles*:[28] the monad (for numbers), circular movement and rectilinear movement (for all the forms of motion),[29] the temporal unity of the 'now' (that is, the νῦν for time), and so on.[30] This is connected with the fact that all the construction at the same time is the structure of the doctrine of a universal science.

This is valid not only for pure mathematics, which is presented in the tripartition of arithmetic-geometry-astronomy (movements of the heaven and of the stars), but also for the starting points of the "physics" present in Plato (to use the term that Xenocrates and Aristotle will apply) in the structuring of the corporal world to begin with the series of the dimensions, and finally, to begin with numbers. The same is true for the smallest interval in music (a quarter tone), for the sounds in the spoken language, for the letters in writing. Aristotle, following Plato, formulated this maxim, "the first measure is the principle, in fact that which is the principle of knowledge for each class of things, is the first measure of what is within that sphere; hence, the one is the principle of knowledge within each sphere of things."[31] The elements, therefore, are not only the principles of being, but also principles of knowledge of whatever is within their sphere of things. The derivatives are comprehensible only if the elements and the principles are previously grasped.

The elements and the principles, however, in turn are derivatives and copies of the original and fundamental measure, viz., of unity itself at different levels; point, circular movement, unity of time, and so on are monads or unities that reflect the original unity of the principle of being according to the levels of different degrees of materiality. Toward the original unity and between them precisely there is a relation of mathemati-cal proportionality (*logoi, analogiai*), according to the relation of subtraction and addition understood ontologically (ἀφαίρεσις-πρόσθεσις) and accord-ing to the relation of prior and posterior (πρότερον-ὕστερον) and likewise according to the relation on the basis of which that which is dependent can be destroyed without in any way destroying that on which it depends (συναναιρεῖν καὶ μὴ συναναιρεῖσθαι). To give an example, arithmetical unity is a point without position (μονὰς στιγμὴ ἄθετος), but, vice versa, also the point, viz., the indivisible line, is a unity having position (στιγμὴ μονὰς θέσιν ἔχουσα).[32] Extension enters into play as connoted by all the geometrical entities, when one passes from arithmetic to geometry, by addition (πρόσθεσις) to number, or it is eliminated (ἀφαίρεσις), when from geometry one goes back to arithmetic.

From all this it is clear that we find here a tendency toward a universal philosophical doctrine of science and toward a science of foundations at least of mathematical sciences, but ideally also of all the sciences in general, and precisely we find at bottom a tendency toward a philosophical doctrine of the sciences grounded by a universal axiomatic system and methodology. Note, for example, that in the doctrine of the proportions, in the doctrine of the irrationals and of the regular polyhedrons, Euclid was grounded in the Platonic Academy and that the Academy represents a decisive stage in the development of Greek mathematics.[33] The science of nature and the historical sciences in the modern sense, nevertheless, are considered only in the measure in which they have foundations determined in a rule-like manner, which, hence, are conceived ontologically (thus, for example, the biology in the work of Speusippus, *On Similarities;*[34] instead, the theory of the political constitution and the theory of *technai* [knowledges] seems to be treated by Plato only in the dialogues; the indirect tradition, in any case, does not offer any indications in this respect).

In general, the unwritten doctrine makes clear that the founder of classical metaphysics, much more than was previously acknowledged, stood at the summit of the science of his time. This results clearly in the fruition, and simultaneously, in the foundation of basic concepts and models of mathematical construction (the foundation of the doctrine of proportions) and medicine (more-less, excess-defect) already on the level of principles. The trait of a certain vagueness in world-view that accompanied Platonism throughout the centuries is eliminated by means of the unwritten doctrines and is here replaced by a concreteness that can be of notable advantage in the critical reception and reinterpretation in a theoretical way of Plato today.[35]

The Axiological Significance of the Theory of Principles and the First Formulation of the Theory of the Transcendentals

The theory of the principles of Plato and the related basic ontological conception, however, are not yet complete. The unwritten doctrine, according to the information contained in the writings of some followers, was delivered in the Academy with the title *On the Good* (περὶ τοῦ ἀγαθοῦ). In this it is manifest, just as from the preeminence given to "orality," that Plato, even reaching back to the Presocratic problematic, did not believe that he had stepped outside the limits of what Socrates had started.[36] The Good, according to the perspective of the order of knowledge (ratio cognoscendi), was more precisely determined as the One;[37] according to the perspective of the structure and order of being (ratio essendi), it is presented as a functional aspect of the One.[38] The same is true for the principle contrary to the One, which is specified as the cause of evil or directly as evil (κακόν). The equalization of unity and the good becomes clear through the explication of the unity within the arrangement of being: unity as a principle produces order (τάξις) and stability (ἠρεμία)[39] in that which is conditioned; and precisely, first in the (ideal) numbers and then in the virtues (ἀρεταί) of man that participate in number, and analogously also in the characteristics belonging to the cosmos. The character of order that belongs to each good thing is based, thus, on the limitation of multiplicity produced by unity; order is limited multiplicity (ὡρισμένον) and, so to speak, is unity in multiplicity; it is, in addition, like the ontological prius—as for example the fundamental measure of a sphere of things—that which is more knowable.[40] In place of the unity in multiplicity can also come the "mean" and the "equilibrium" between the extremes of the too much or the too little; this is a precision of the axiological structure worked in relation to the twofold direction of the contrary principle.[41] The mean is conceived, likewise, as limited and hence as a kind of unified being.[42]

From this it is clear that the basic ontological conception of Plato at the same time possesses an axiological significance; everything that exists, in the measure in which it is limited and determined by the One is not only being and knowable but, at the same time, is endowed with values (good and beautiful: καλόν).[43] With this Plato is revealed as the precursor of the medieval doctrine of the transcendentals (ens, unum, bonum, verum convertuntur; omne ens est bonum [being, unity, good, and truth are convertible; all being is good]).[44] However, he grounded it on a unitary conception of being, which is rooted in his theory of the principles. The fundamental concept that functions as a mediation between the various aspects is that of limit. And with it are also given its formal determinations: accuracy, distinction, identity, stability, symmetry, harmony, proportion, validity, security. These formal determinations are structured under the ontological, epistemological, and axiological aspect as essence and entity (οὐσία, ὄν), cognizibility (and truth), and value (goodness, beauty, and similars), which are equal and original to one another; each being, in the measure in which it is, is always, at the same time, likewise good and knowable (true). But it is in the measure in which, insofar as it is limited, it approximates the status of the original unity. And, with this, the general ontological structure of Plato is completed.

The Operational Polyvalence of the Principles

The elaboration of the basic ontological conception of Plato by the axiological aspect brings us more fully into the comprehension of the theory of principles and in a special way to unity as the principle of being, knowledge, and value. Also what is revealed here, again, is an operational polyvalence and a plurality of aspects, which can emerge in the explication (*explicatio*) of the principle in the conditioned in different measures but which in the principle itself are together yet unseparated in the sense of being folded together (*complicatio*). Plato has tried to give an account of this state of things in the determination of the definition of the principle. The dialectical-discursive grasp of the principles, in which dialectic culminates, requires such a definition (λόγος), because it prepares and guides intellectual intuition (νόησις).[45] Plato, then, so far as it is possible to conclude, proceeding from different evidence,[46] has defined unity as "*measure*" (μέτρον), and, more precisely, as the "most accurate measure" (ἀκριβέστατον μέτρον). In this, on the one hand, consists the meaning, which is connected to the form of thought proceeding toward the elements, of unity as a fundamental element and as a measure of a multiplicity is derived from it and measured by it; on the other hand, this measure is distinct and separated from every other kind of unity by reason of its great exactitude, viz., by reason of the supreme indivisibility, simplicity, and immutability of the basic principle. Plato, however, beyond the fundamental meaning concerning the process of reduction to the elements and its epistemological implications, has structurally combined with the concept of measure, in a consciously ambiguous manner, as well the meanings of *limit* and *norm*. With that the operational polyvalence was clearly indicated in both its ontological and in its axiological aspect. The definition of the contrary principle, then, clearly follows by means of the privation of the essential connotations of the primary principle (ἀ-όριστον, ἄ-μετρον).

The definition of unity as "measure" is not intended as a regular definition, reached through the subsumption of a species in a genus. Plato was well aware that the ultimate principles cannot be defined and proven properly by beginning from prior genera.[47] In this case the definition rather is understood as a bipolar relation and, in this sense, structurally referring to that which is conditioned by it ("*measure of a multiplicity*").[48] Plato, then, defines the principle not by beginning *from above*, but, in a certain sense, by way of compensation, by beginning *from below*, viz., beginning from that which is derived. This corresponds to the procedure of the "circular demonstration" professed by some members of the Academy[49] and evidently has been discussed in detail there.[50] The reversal of the direction of the regular definition can be supported in Plato in the context of the procedure of the reduction to elements already at the time of the *Meno*.[51] Also for the theory of principles the dialectical definition of unity is not empty or negative; introduced into the world, unity is manifested as "norm" and "measure" of every being. Unity in its relations with the world is the highest measure of being, goodness (*arete*), and truth, and because of this, precisely as measure, is referred to the world. The concept of unity as measure expresses, therefore, the correlation between being and the first principle. And insofar as it functions as an intermediate between them, it summarizes in itself the basic ontological conception of Plato. By means of it Plato brings the principle of the world into the world, explicating it and developing it in its character as foundation and grounding. This concept guarantees the diverse character of the principle of the world in its pure unity, and at the same time, it becomes fruitful for the foundation of each individual being: this concept of measure, by means of mediating pure unity with the being-one of being in all its aspects, shows that unity is the fundamental categorial constitutive of each being. On this basis, the dialectical discursive edifice, in a certain way the system of the Platonic science of being, is established that, in its purposes, contains in itself objects and methods for all possible sciences.

It is, in addition, instructive to observe that owing to the conditions of such a structure of being, for Plato the problem of a mediation between ontology and axiology, mathematics and politics, theory and praxis, etc., can in no way be posited, because, so to speak, it is already resolved from the start.[52] Under the axiom *omne ens est bonum* (every being is good), no science is axiologically indifferent (in fact, the mathematical sciences are "noble"), and it is inconceivable that there is a good which is not ontologically grounded and, hence, is not rooted in the very essence of things. In particular, therefore, the theory of the principles must no longer furnish a mediation between *being* and *value* (ὄν and ἀγαθόν), but must simply explicate the isomorphism of the regional structures of being and fill up the differences remaining (for example, to show logical identity, mathematical equality, physical immobility, political unity having among them an analogical relation and being mutually reflected). Notwithstanding all the dialectic of distinction, which Plato brings to bear against Eleaticism and the Sophists, on the level of the treatment of the principles the synoptic-unifying moment in a quite evident manner predominates in him. By reason of this polyvalent generality of the theory of the principles not yet specified and apparently formal and empty, the difficulty of "communicating it like other objects" is well explained.[53] The highest grade of abstraction of the principles, actually, demands a gradual introduction by a long process of learning so that it can be assimilated in an intelligible and clear manner.

The fact that the theory of the principles is an "unwritten doctrine" and that for its communication a theory and a peculiar and complicated praxis of teaching and learning has been created, acquires, in such a manner, a precise systematic foundation. Without training, long practical apprenticeship, and secure familiarity, the understanding of the doctrine of the principles could not be fulfilled in that highest noetic intuition, which alone guarantees its real comprehension and interior assimilation. The amazement of modern critics about the "abstract aridity" and the "empty schematism" of the unwritten doctrine is nothing other than the confirmation of the assessment that Plato himself had made about the realistic chances of its communicability and consequently of the didactic measures adopted by him.

The Dialectical Method

The *concept of the dialectical method* correctly understood really links the schemata of the unwritten doctrine preserved by the doxographers with the dialogues of Plato. The ascent within the synoptic process to the most general by going to ever higher hypotheses, which belongs to dialectic, reaches its unconditioned conclusion (ἀνυπόθετον) only with the principles that are the most general genera (the highest genera of all the Meta-Ideas). And if it is true, in addition, that dialectic by virtue of its definition treats of the opposites, [54] it is likewise true that the division and the reduplication of the reality in opposites achieves its conclusion only in the unwritten doctrines. The schemata of *generalized* opposites referred to by the indirect tradition are therefore an eminent expression of the dialectical method, and are more so by the fact that they reduce all individual pairs of opposites to the same basic opposition of the primary principles that first grounds and makes possible all contrariety and thereby also all dialectic. Because, finally, dialectic in its content is linked to the sphere of the universals, which include the Idea-numbers, the ideal Numbers and the principles as *basicelements*, even the form of thought concerning the *process of reduction to the elements* falls into the legitimate sphere of competence of the dialectical method. [55] Therefore, the relation of part (element) and whole (the complex) belongs in a clear manner to the principal themes of Academic dialectic. [56] The unwritten doctrine, due to all this, contains the consequent fulfillment and completion of Platonic dialectic, which in the theory of principles and in the grounding nexuses relative to it is forced up to the ultimate limits of its objective possibilities. This is true independently of the fact that the doxographic tradition only furnishes the systematic results, whereas the argumentative genesis must be reconstructed with the help of the procedure of thought contained in the dialogues in a detailed manner.

reconstructed with the help of the procedure of thought contained in the dialogues in a detailed manner.

Although the written work presents the philosophy of Plato always under a determined aspect, on a specific literary level, and not in its ultimate stage, there emerges from the unwritten doctrine, instead, the theoretic construction in all its unity. A new base for the systematic-theoretical interpretation of the philosophy of Plato, as a result, is achieved and it places in a new light the problem of its interior theoretical connections. It is clear, hence, that the theoretical construction of the philosophy of Plato must be considered in general as much more pregnant, sophisticated, and logically consistent than what the written works, at first glance, tend to suggest. The interior continuity and coherence of the unwritten doctrine moreover circumscribes a unified area of theoretical interest within which are placed certain unshakable criteria both for the interpretation of the dialogues and for the appraisal of the Platonic philosophical position in its totality.

The Type of System and the Type of Theory that Belong to Platonic Philosophy

The *type of system* constituted by Platonic philosophy can be further defined in a more precise manner. It is a form of system that develops by grounding structures both hierarchically graduated and differentiated and that, in this respect, is expressed by means of generative metaphors. In this regard the system cannot be spoken of as involving a deductive and logically derivative method in the strict sense (in particular it cannot be spoken of as an "emanationism"). This depends on the fact that the relation between principle and the principled is not conceived in a radical manner, which would be necessary, so instead of furnishing the necessary and sufficient conditions, it provides only the necessary conditions.

The *type of theory* constituted by Platonic philosophy, nonetheless, is determined, also in the light of the unwritten doctrine, by a dialectic of the universal essences. But, in particular, at the same time, a methodological pluralism is present in the formation of the Platonic theory that seems to be structural.

The Claim of Validity of the Platonic Systematic

The *claim of validity* of the systematic of Platonic philosophy must be considered by making a series of distinctions. The dogmatic claim of a definitive validity of the unwritten doctrines and the claim that they were in no need of any revision is barely implied; this can be drawn from the dynamic concept of *philo*-sophy (understood in its strong sense),[57] just as from the divergencies of the pupils, both in relation to Plato and in relation to one another, which were tolerated in the Academy. Also the claim of exhausting the totality of the philosophical content probably is not implied either; this project was maintained as rather elastic and flexible and was fundamentally open to amplification both as a whole and in its details. Therefore it can be said to be a nondogmatic but heuristic project and is in its details even on the programmatic level an outline, and hence an open system; not, however, surely, of an antisystemic kind, full of fragments of theories, without any specific connections. Instead it certainly ought to be conceived in terms of its tendency to be a holistic, coherent, and consistent project. This is provided by the theory of the principles, by the elaboration of the general concepts of relation and function,[58] and likewise by the agreement of all the followers with the aim of constructing a system. Therefore, in the evaluation of these issues the viewpoints of the degrees of coherence of the doctrine and its degrees of validity are quite distinct.

7   *The Relation of the Unwritten Doctrines to the Dialogues*

The Problem of the Evolution of the Philosophy of Plato

To begin with Zeller, the indirect Platonic tradition has been held as something marginal for the purposes of comprehending the philosophy of Plato, especially because it was located at the end of an evolutionary arc of the philosophy of Plato. But the decisive self-testimonies of Plato contained in the *Seventh Letter* and in the *Phaedrus,*[1] that are enlarged by a dense network of references in the dialogues, falsify this hypothesis, just as it is falsified by the fact that the system of the principles is understood by Aristotle and Theophrastus and evidently also by the other followers of Plato as the undoubtedly true and proper philosophical position of Plato. And because the criticism made against the written works in the *Phaedrus* also involves the *Republic,* the theory of the principles extends backwards with much probability up to the period of that masterpiece of Plato and, hence, *up to the intermediate period in the composition of the written works.* In comparison to this explicit result the method of the scholars working from the evolutionary hypothesis to interpret the succession of the dialogues as an evolution of the thought of Plato, without explicit indications from the side of Plato himself, cannot be supported.

First, this method, considered in itself, has been always highly problematic, because, to achieve a stringent and convincing result, it would be necessary to exclude in a definitive manner reasons that are in contrast with it, that is to say, reasons of a protreptic-didactic nature, systematic reasons, or reasons concerning the specific literary genre of the various writings (the *Republic* as a political writing!), reasons of an artistic-compositive nature, or pragmatic-economic nature. As a matter of fact, however, the upholders of the evolutionary method have almost never taken into consideration the possibility of the just mentioned alternative explanations and, on the contrary, they have applied extrinsically to the writings the evolutionary thesis as though it were obvious and hence completely acritically, as if it were a necessary presupposition from the very beginning.[2] And in this a disastrous tendency to transform functional aspects of Platonic philosophy into positions representing the spiritual biography of Plato is evident. The fundamental principle, which at first glance is presented as a critical principle and in appearance free from presuppositions, according to which one would have in any case to attribute to Plato only the level of

awareness that is expressed little by little in the various dialogues taken into
consideration, respectively, however, could claim validity only if Plato had
definitively wished to show the totality of his philosophy in *every one* of his
writings. Only then the "progressive development" could be drawn from
the differences between one writing and another, achieved by way of
subtracting the old from the new. But this necessary condition for the
application of the genetic principle cannot have a place, simply by reason
of the thematic differences of the individual written works.

The correct estimation of the indirect tradition forces us in a peremptory
manner to abandon once and for all this type of simplistic evolutionary
interpretation. Neither, consequently, can the attempt to link Plato indissolub-
ly to the writings on the basis of the argument ex silentio (from silence) be
accepted, since his self-testimonies, together with the various allusions in the
written works, prove that Plato completely avoided expressing a determined
basic position for a rather long period of time. These observations are confirmed
by common knowledge based on the fact that most of the great philosophers,
of whose biography we possess a complete overview, have conceived the
essential foundations of their own philosophy between thirty and forty
years of age.[3] Owing to these circumstances the question of the evolution
of the philosopher Plato (not the writer) can be faced only with caution and
only on the basis of new critically based criteria, if one wishes to have any
probability of success. Especially, it is certain, first, that from the succession
of the *literary expositions* contained in the dialogues any direct conclusions
cannot be drawn for the origin and evolution of the *philosophical thought*.[4]
The following three open questions are connected to this issue: (1) Up to
what point can the indirect tradition be followed back to the beginning of
Plato's thought? (2) Is the consistency of the fundamental position concerning the theory of the principles compatible with an evolution in its details,
which, nevertheless, on the basis of appropriate criteria, can be recovered
from the dialogues? (3) Is there evidence which permits us to conclude to a
development of the unwritten doctrine itself?

1. It cannot be overlooked that in the notion of the *noble* in the-
   Symposium and in the *primary friend* (πρῶτον φίλον) of the *Lysis* are
   analogous correspondences or at the least prefigurations of the *Idea
   of the Good*, and that there is also evidence that proves that Plato
   early in his career must have been concerned with Eleaticism,[5] that
   he, owing to the report of the *Parmenides*, has interpreted it in a
   henological sense; that is, in function of the category of unity. In
   addition, significant allusions to an "unspoken" are present in the
   Protagoras and in the *Meno*.[6] The common knowledge that the most
   productive period, for philosophers, falls in their forties, and their
   fundamental conceptions, perhaps also prior to their forties, holds also

in this case. Moreover, there is evidence that proves that the philosophical conceptions of Plato arose at a date much earlier than the works in which they are presented for the first time, which means that there exists a kind of lag between the written and the oral statements, which, once again, limits the value of the works as expressions of an evolutionary span of time.[7] From these considerations, in sum, a conclusion in favor of an early dating of the theory of the principles can be drawn, conclusions that can claim to have a certain probability, even if they are not confirmed in quite the same way as for the period of the *Republic*.

2. From the theoretical standpoint, the metaphysical and ontological position at bottom concerning the principles certainly left room for a change in the particulars. It is, therefore, incorrect, on the basis of the indirect tradition in general to try to draw a rigid picture of Platonic philosophy, which excludes every form of genetic inquiry.[8] Certainly, in any particular case one needs special evidence of decisive weight that would thereby impose a genetic solution. It is not correct, first of all, to interpret any allusions or simple remarks as "programmatic" (viz., as announcing a program to be carried out afterward), and, hence, to undoubtedly understand as the point of departure for a successive evolution of the thought. For this there would have to be excluded in a solid manner, as was made clear earlier, rivaling economic and compositional reasons, or even reasons of a more important nature, like the general renunciation to fix certain doctrines in writing. Moreover, in many of these cases, the connection with the system of the principles is easily recognizable, as for example in the analogy of the divided line contained in the *Republic* or in the central part of the *Timaeus*. In addition to this, it is necessary to account for a growing convergence between the activity of teaching and the written work, which is expressed also in the doctrinal form of the late dialogues; the growth of the school, in fact, seems to have been accompanied by a shifting of the boundaries between oral teaching and written works that took on an increasing "hypomnematic function."[9] Hasty genetic explanations that do not take all this into consideration are out of place. The evolution, here, is less in the doctrine than in the relation between the written works and the oral teaching of the school.

3. For the evolution of the unwritten doctrine itself there is a report of Aristotle in this respect, which however does not concern the theory of principles and which is not clear in its context as to what time it should be dated.[10] Moreover, an evolution of Plato in the doctrine professed orally within the Academy is difficult to verify,

since no other reports have come down to us nor do the dialogues offer criteria that give us any confidence in the matter. The difference between the earliest and the late concept of virtue together with the scientific presuppositions of the period (Eudoxus) still suggests as a possible hypothesis that the conception of the principle opposed to unity (the material principle), understood as the great-and-small, belongs only to a relatively late period.[11]

The self-testimonies of Plato and the preeminent role that our informants give to the unwritten doctrine guarantee in any case an ample duration during which there is a chronological parallelism of the two branches of the tradition. From here is born the task of testing by means of particular interpretations the complementary relations of one tradition to the other and to profit therefrom with a better comprehension of the texts and also of Platonic philosophy in its totality.[12]

The *Republic*

In this respect, the written work of Plato on the *Republic* plays a philosophic and hermeneutic key function.[13] This masterpiece of Plato is in an especially close relation with the unwritten doctrine. (*a*) The *Republic* was composed and published more than a decade after the presumed foundation of the Academy, and for this reason has to be seen, as at that time, against the background of the Academy. (*b*) It, in addition, culminates in the revelation of the "Good itself" (in the Sixth and Seventh Books), and under the title *Concerning the Good* (περὶ τοῦ ἀγαθοῦ) Plato has presented his unwritten doctrine in the Academy. (*c*) The statement of the *Phaedrus* (276E) delimits precisely the *Republic* from the unwritten doctrine and establishes, in such a way, mediately, a relation between both of them.[14] (*d*) The explicit testimonies contained in the text of the *Republic* itself about the intentions of Plato to be silent about certain things, which in part regard the essence of the Good itself, in part the mathematical disciplines and the essence of the soul are added to this.[15] (*e*) The series of similes in the central part of the *Republic* (the similes of the sun, of the divided line, and the cave) belong as is widely known to the most dense and important philosophical parts in the literary works of Plato, but arouse difficult questions because the material is presented in an incomplete way through images. (*f*) The *Republic* belongs to the intermediate phase of the activity of Plato the writer and, at the same time, takes up the thematic of the first works. Hence, if this fundamental work of Plato can be placed in relation to the unwritten doctrines, then from this arise consequences of vast importance for the remaining works of Plato and even more so for the later works.

With respect to the attempts at explanation often quite speculative of the traditional interpretation, the interpretation grounded on the indirect tradition, first of all, has the advantage of being able to support historical materials and criteria. It, in addition, can demonstrate its own validity, by reason of not having solely proposed individual isolated explanations, but making comprehensible *all* the functions and *all* the connotations of the Good in a complete manner, and without there remaining nothing having need of further explanation, and because—and this is a decisive criterion for its correctness—it does this in a unitary manner beginning from *one* common foundation of explanation.

The traditional explanation exclusively linked to the text of the *Republic* is far from such a solution—also in hypothetical form—and, instead, stirs up numerous aporias; in what way the Good as *cause* (αἰτία) of *being* (οὐσία) and *truth* (ἀλήθεια) *ought to be* understood remains especially unexplained. Perhaps still more obscure and enigmatic is the relation of the Good to mathematical objects, which ought to be traced to the principle (ἀρχή) of the Good, to be grasped by means of noetic intuition. (For this reason, in the past some authors such as F. M. Cornford, H. W. B. Joseph and W. D. Ross brought in the unwritten doctrines (ἄγραφα δόγματα) to explain the simile of the divided line). Then, the ascent to the Good connected to this and the definition of the essence (λόγος τῆς οὐσίας) of the Good itself, which is an indispensable presupposition (534B-C) for its noetic comprehension, remain inaccessible. But also the way in which the Good itself must be a foundation of each virtue and the structures of the order linked to justice and temperance (for example, 500C, 506A, 540A) is still vague and incomprehensible.

Only from the statement that the Good is "beyond being" (509B) it is assumed to be drawn philosophical significance by interpreting the Good itself on the basis of the *Phaedo* 97C-D as final cause, for the sake of which all the rest exists. But this interpretation is not correct for many reasons; the analogy with the sun, which is in the cosmos unequivocally as an efficient cause and not a final cause, likewise imposes the assumption for the Good of a function that, if not for generation, still serves for the conservation of the Ideas and not just for their justification.[16] To this points not only the text of the *Republic*, 509B, but likewise the fact that the Good in the *Republic*, throughout, even in the restricted axiological sphere (506A; 517C), is presented as an *efficient cause* and not as a final cause. The presumed parallel of *Phaedo* 97C/D leads, on the other side, into error, because in it is treated an anthropomorphic planning (cosmologico-demiurgic or technico-practical) that belongs to a sphere wholly different from the sphere of the ideal. The Good in itself, in the *Republic*, instead, is in no way a human or existential Good, as that of the *Phaedo* and the *Philebus*, but a universal and metaphysical Good.[17] Moreover, this attempt at explanation of *Republic* 509B has always remained isolated and cannot be placed into relationship with the other characteristics of the Good, that are problematical for the traditional interpretation.

The fact that Plato, in the *Republic*, in a very clear manner abstained from determining the essence of the Good (τί ποτ ᾽ ἐστὶ τἀγαθόν, 506D; consult Appendix 2.3) needs to be carefully considered and that, on the other side, all the *connotations* and all the *functions* that are proper to the Good must be derived from this *essence that is held as hidden*,[18] and therefore, can be understood only in conformity to it. In regard to this one can guess that the multiplicity and the heterogeneity of the functions of the Good hint at the fact that the very essence of the Good itself is at a grade of universality higher than the specific aspect of the Good as such. This supposition is reinforced by the fact that within the written works are axiological aspects of the highest Idea, that are different with respect to the Good and thus only an aspect is placed in the light by the Good (the noble in itself in the *Symposium,* the πρῶτον φίλον [primary friend] in the *Lysis*). Therefore, it is necessary to bring back the Good to a more general concept, which as a condition substantiates also its epistemological and ontological functions and those of the theoretical foundation of the sciences (of mathematics!), in conjunction with those of the axiological.

Prior to everything, however, the axiological function of the Good itself in relation to its hidden implications needs to be determined. If it can be shown that even this goes beyond the nature of the Good as such, then *a fortiori* the same can also be concluded about the remaining functions. The multiplicity of the political and psychological discussions of the *Republic* have as their center the concept of *order* (κόσμος, τάξις; consult *Gorgias*) in the State and the soul. The concept of order is rooted in the Idea of the Good (506A, 517C, 540A) that from the axiological standpoint, is, precisely, the principle of all order. The principle of order cannot, however, be itself ordered, but must be the grounding of the order, which unites in a unity the parts of a whole. To this is referred the fact that, in the *Republic*, the concepts of order and unity frequently alternate; the supreme norm of the ideal State is consistently indicated in this: that it must be *one* and not many.[19] But also the individual man must be unitary in himself,[20] and also be concerned with only *one* profession, to be *one*, and to make, consequently, one State.[21] The Good itself, hence, acts as the foundation and the source of order (that is, of unity in the multiplicity!) as well as of unity. It is easy to understand, therefore, that the *essence (τί ἐστιν) of the Good,* which Plato, in the *Republic* abstains from revealing, *consists in unity itself.* This exactly corresponds to the determination of the Good as unity found in the reports about the unwritten doctrines. It corresponds, in the second place, to the axiology of the unwritten doctrine, on the basis of which the One-Good produces in general, by means of the limitation of multiplicity, order (τάξις, τεταγμένον), and stability (ἠρεμία).[22] To this, in the third place, is joined the fact that the fundamental role of number, which in the reports on the unwritten doctrines mediates unity and order,[23] is present already in the *Republic*, if the numerical relations hidden in the so-called number of the marriages of the *Republic* Book Eight, are referred in a correct manner to the theory of the ideal State and to the arrangement of life corresponding to it.[24] The number, hence, already in the design of the ideal State of the *Republic*, has a theoretical significance similar to that which it has in the late works and in the unwritten doctrines. Altogether, hence, it is possible to refer some fundamental doctrines of Plato in the *Republic*, and precisely the concept of the well-ordered and proportioned State and man, that are both specified by their order (κόσμος, τάξις), to their deeper foundational and ontological nexuses. Plato presents these structures, for the first time, in a phenomenological manner and with them carries as concrete evidence the presence of the original unity in the One-Being of individual beings. These modes of order and proportion reproduce, in their individual one-being, the unity of the principle in the world of multiplicity.[25] Discovering these connections, Plato refers, before everything else, the moral virtues of human beings (justice and temperance) that had become problematic, to their proper being and tries, with this, to recover from the crisis of the Greek *polis* on the ontological level and to conceptually overcome it.

To the concept of order are also combined wisdom, and knowledge (ἐπιστήμη, γνῶσις) more precisely, the cognitive power of the soul (δύναμις τοῦ γιγνώσκειν) that is produced as "goodlike" (ἀγαθοειδής), by the cause (αἰτία) of the Good (508E). The rational soul (νοῦς), to which allusion is made here, in the unwritten doctrine, actually, on the basis of its mode of intuitive and holistic cognition, is taken in parallel with the One.[26] Considered more deeply, order, proportion, and symmetry[27] of the spiritual nature of the rational soul, whose numerical determination emerges clearly in the *Timaeus*, but that is already present on the evident basis of the numerous allusions found in the *Republic*.[28] Insofar as it is a mathematically organized structure, the rational soul depends on certain characteristics of *order* that makes it capable of recognizing the identical in an identical way. The *areté* (virtue) of the soul, therefore, consists likewise in the acquisition of the greatest unity that is possible to it, which is grounded on the One-Good, and to that extent is "agathoid" (henoid!).[29]

The introduction of the Good as the *foundation* of knowledge is separated from the identification of the Good with the knowledge (φρόνησις) that we meet with in the Socratics and that is surpassed by it.[30] The following affirmation about the Good as principle of *Being* (509B) is introduced in parallel to the determination of the Good as an epistemological principle and represents a continuation, evoked by means of the simile of the sun, which amplifies and completes the doctrine, to which there is allusion in the simile of the sun in the *Republic*. It is, hence, evident that the two functions of the Good about which we argued are grounded in a similar way. On the other hand, the further function of the "Good" as foundation of *truth* and *cognizability* is also connected in the most strict manner with its fundamental nature for the power of knowing (in fact, both are "agathoid"). A really basic unitary concept that corresponds to the different functions is confirmed by the fundamental ontological conception of the unwritten doctrine that follows from the theory of the principles: by means of the *limitation* and *determination* of an indeterminate substrate on the part of *unity*, not only virtue (order in the State and soul, and so on), but also essence (οὐσία) and truth (ἀλήθεια) is given and characterized by formal connotations such as determination, accuracy, distinction, identity, consistency, stability, and similar ones, all of which are modes of one-being in the multiplicity and, as such, are imitations of the basic unity. In the essence, this is shown to be true, once again, by the fact that all the individual Ideas, in the *Republic* as in the dialogues closest to it (*Parmenides*, *Phaedo*), are characterized in a marked manner as *unities*.[31] Essence, truth (ἀλήθεια: the state of that which is not hidden, that which is unveiled), the power of knowing, and in general, virtue (order) are here understood in the sense of the doctrine of the transcendentals (which will be expressly formulated only in succeeding periods), as different aspects of the same structure of being, that are constituted by the basic unity with a single hallmark, and among which, therefore, exists a kind of reciprocal implication (following upon one another reciprocally [*antakoluthie*]).[32] A fundamental level of reflection, which undoubtedly *precedes* the individual aspects (the ontological, epistemological, and axiological) is achieved as a result and, which simply because of this, can ground them in a basic and unitary way. Above all, by considering things in the way that we have indicated, there are no longer any aporias, obstacles, or unexplained residues, as instead, inevitably happens in the typical traditional exegesis.

In addition, the interpretation maintained here is confirmed with respect to the *status* "beyond being" (ἐπέκεινα τῆς οὐσίας), which the *Republic*, 509B, assigns to the Good to differentiate it from all the other Ideas and which is difficult to understand. It, as we have already seen, in the context of the simile of the sun cannot be explained from the teleological standpoint, but neither can it be tied in a general way to the Presocratic tradition, to which such distinctions are still substantially extraneous. On the contrary, the whole ontological context of the Ideas in the *Republic*—beginning from the introduction of the theory of Ideas in the Fifth Book—seems to show clearly the taking of a position in relation to the Eleatic doctrine of Being, which Plato, according to the statement of the Parmenides, following Zeno, had interpreted in a henological sense; that is, focused on the concept of unity. Actually, the doxography of the indirect tradition places the theory of the principles also in connection with the Eleatic disjunction of unity and multiplicity and joins, in this respect, the superessentiality of unity with the assumption of an opposed principle and with the multiplicity of being derived from it.[33] Decisive in this regard was evidently the displacement of the concept of being from unity to multiplicity, and this displacement, holding firm the Eleatic disjunction of unity and multiplicity, pushed, in a coherent manner, the unity to a position "beyond being." But this historical origin of the problem includes, together with the Eleatic-Zenonian disjunction of unity and multiplicity, the consequence that what is beyond being in the *Republic*, in regard to its essence, can be only pure unity (τὸ ἕν). The validity of the unwritten doctrine of the principles, for the purpose of understanding the masterpiece of Plato, hence, once again can be ascertained independently and guaranteed by starting from another side, precisely, from what has historically preceded it.[34]

On this basis also the remaining problems can be resolved: *the simile of the divided line*[35] is about the final foundation of the axioms and concepts of mathematics by means of their reduction to the Good as a foundation (ἀρχή) that "is no longer simply a postulate" (ἀνυπόθετος), just as their consequent derivation from the principle, both of which are pursued by means of the dialectical method. At the same time supreme entities directly connected to the principle (τὰ ἐκείνης ἐχόμενα, 511B;[36] consult the stars in the simile of 516A8, 532A4) also are assumed, which in the dialectical ascent evidently develop as mediations between the mathematical entities and their Ideas and the highest principle. It is not erroneous if the Meta-Ideas of identity and diversity, equality and inequality, similarity and dissimilarity , even and odd are recognized here that emerge in a clearer manner in the later dialogues and that in the sphere of the unwritten doctrine, in the perspective of an ultimate *generalizing* synopsis, are subordinated to the principles as to their *highest genera*. The examples of the simile of the divided line confirm this: the pair of odd and even (510C4) belongs itself to the sphere of the most universal genera, or, at least, is treated on the same level; the three genera of angles (510C4 f.)—acute, right, and obtuse—in the successive Platonic tradition are entirely subordinated to equality (right angle as a limited, that is presented solely in one form) or to inequality (acute and obtuse angles with unlimited variations multiplied according to the more or less) and, consequently, are indirectly subordinated to the highest principles.[37] The two contrary forms of movement toward the highest and toward the lowest correspond, then, to the distinction between the order of cognition and the order of being in the unwritten doctrine. Once again the elevated degree of universality, in order not to say the elevated degree of "abstraction" of the principles, seems to be revealed with its functional polyvalence, also in the grounding epistemological nexuses, in which in virtue of their polyvalence the principles[38] can be exercised further in different ways.

By means of the simile of the divided line the dialectical ascent to the Idea of the Good itself is alluded to, which the Seventh Book of the *Republic* limits again to sketching but does not specify in its individual passages. The dialectical ascent, as it can be traced from what is said up to this point, goes on toward the totality of the Meta-Ideas, continuing to the simple unity of the basic principle, which with an act of dialectical-synoptic "abstraction" comes to be separated from them and placed as such as highest genus. Actually, the formulation of the "abstraction" of the Good is found in the passage of the *Republic* that goes further there than all the others and that joins with this the postulate of the definition of the Good (διορίσασθαι τῷ λόγῳ[39] ἀπό τῶν ἄλλων πάντων ἀφελὼν τὴν τοῦ ἀγαθοῦ ἰδέαν, 534B). The noetic understanding of the Good depends according to the context on this dialectical definition and hence the entire carrying out of the ideal of the State and of the science of the *Republic*. Plato, therefore, could not have postulated it gratuitously, but already at the time of the *Republic*, insofar as his dialectic is concerned, he must have been quite clear about it.

If that is so, the indirect tradition furnishes the definition (λόγος) of the One-Good as "measure" (the most exact one), in the multiple meanings of criterion, norm, and limit, and evidently conceived as a synthesis of the ontological, epistemological, and axiological functions of the principle. It is therefore important that Book Six of the *Republic*, on the occasion of the introduction of the Good itself, alludes to a perfect measure (μέτρον τέλειον) of the greatest accuracy, which must be absolutely taken into consideration (504B5-C3; E13).[40] It must be concluded that the definition of the Good transmitted by the indirect tradition had been achieved by Plato by the time of the *Republic*, and that, in this work, it is presupposed. Plato, in conformity with the theory of teaching and learning in the *Phaedrus* and in the *Seventh Letter* has avoided displaying it directly in the *Republic*, because it could be understood with the corresponding adequate intellectual intuition only at the end of an apprenticeship and a process of dialectical formation that lasted whole decades. The definition of the Good, hence, insofar as it is the fundamental and culminating point of the *paideia* of the Academy, must be reserved for the sphere of "orality" of the unwritten doctrine.

In this way, all the essential connotations of the Good itself, in the *Republic*, are led back, in a convergent way, to the theory of principles of the unwritten doctrine and, beginning from it, are explained in a unitary way.

Moreover, to prescind from the explicit reservations Plato made in this regard in the work, it is not sound to conjecture that our philosopher first posited here only in a programmatic manner all the problems connected to the thematic of the Good, and left them open in an aporetic manner, and only much later, thanks to extraordinary circumstances, was suddenly able to resolve everything with a single fundamental concept. It is more likely, instead, to suppose that Plato was not at all able to pose the problems in a thus unified manner, if he did not have readily available a unitary solution of them. Moreover, Plato, even in his later written works, never reveals the whole conceptual complexity of his philosophic thought; in fact, it emerges only from the indirect tradition. It is hence evident that Plato abstains from unveiling this conceptual complexity for essential reasons, and therefore even in the *Republic* as well; in fact, in conformity with the educational process that endures over entire decades as foreseen in the *Republic*, to entirely comprehend it one needed a long training in the Platonic Academy. In any case, in summary, it can be maintained that, at the present state of our knowledge, the unwritten doctrine depends on recognition of the background of thought professed within the Academy, if we get an approach to the comprehension of the fundamental parts of the Platonic masterpiece, viz., of the *Republic*, or persist in not comprehending it.

More difficult, instead, is the question concerning the role of the principle contrary to the Good, which in the *Republic* in contrast to the Good is not even manifested in a veiled form, as well as the question which concerns the theory of the Idea-numbers, for which, in the same way, in the *Republic* there is no secure point of support and that according to Aristotle, does not belong to the earliest phase of the theory of Ideas.[41] It is instead evident that Plato in this political work—just as in general in the preceding work of a protreptic nature—did not think it advisable to reveal the opposition of the principles, in which the world of Ideas must necessarily be coinvolved. However, the simile of the sun permits us to conclude that to the function of the Good as principle of being must correspond a material substrate, just as to the generative function of life proper to the Sun the earth is subjected (509B).[42] To which is added that the pairs of the highest genera, which also in their negative forms (the even and unequal that are structured according to the more-and-less) have an ideal character (note the image of the "stars" in the simile of the cave), are brought back to a common contrary principle of the negative series, to which principle this series is chiefly reduced.

Finally, let us note that because Plato did not develop in detail the theory of Ideas, consequently the question of their numerical structuring remains in the background, just as *diaeresis, synagoge,* and the doctrine of the definition also do (perhaps a hint is contained in 500C4).

The *Phaedo* and the *Symposium*

If central parts of the Platonic masterpiece, beginning from the Archimedean point of the unwritten doctrine, can be understood better and little by little deciphered, analogous results can be expected also for the works of the intermediate period that are nearest to the *Republic*, as the *Symposium* and the *Phaedo*, even if taking into account their relatively slender theoretical burden and their inferior degree of explicitness. While the last proof of the *Phaedo* (101D5 ff.) alludes to a procedure for graduated hypotheses, which formally points to the *Republic*, Books Six and Seven, a procedure that continues to the extreme limits attainable by man (107B5 ff.; consult Appendix 2.3), the discourse of Diotima brings to light even more in the *Symposium*. This discourse, just as the whole of this work, is under the definition of the *concept of virtue*, in which the more restricted aspect of the beautiful (καλὸν) emerges. As a kind of virtue, beauty is a form of order and proportion,[43] viz., a form of unity in multiplicity. The fact that the Idea of the Good, in the *Republic*, not only produces beauty (506A, 517C), but in itself possesses the highest beauty (508E f.) corresponds to this; which means that insofar as it is the principle of each individual concrete beautiful thing, as of every good thing, at the same time it is also beauty itself. Things being this way, also behind the limited standpoint of the discourse of Diotima is to be expected a general ontological conception joined to the doctrine of the principles. This emerges above all in the role that belongs to the "noble" sciences, through which the ascent to beauty in itself is carried out and which are referred to ὄντα (210C f.). Further the definition of *Eros* as a tendency toward a lasting possession of the Good proceeds in the same direction: the string of generations imitates, in the world of becoming, the form of being of the universals, of the Ideas, and in this way guarantees, in a rough manner, the identity[44] and permanence, viz., the greatest unity[45] in time.

Further, the good is seen as the specific virtue, viz., as that which possesses intrinsic ability and certainty with the characteristics of stability and order (209A7 f.). *Eros*, hence, is the innate tendency of being toward essence and toward substantial stability, and finally, the tendency to achieve the identity and unitary character in the highest degree possible. The self-fulfillment of being in the acts of physical and spiritual generation makes use of beauty as an important manifestation of the unity and essence of all things, which appear as order (proportion and harmony, and so on). If beauty itself is only an aspect of the Good, and Good itself an aspect of unity, then the *Symposium*, just as the *Republic*, is located within the dimensions of a single conception of being understood as the limitation of multiplicity by means of unity, which brings together all the individual themes (a tendency toward permanence and perdurance of the Good by means of beauty) and joins one to the other. This evidently is based on the same point of "undifferentiation" between ontology and axiology, to which we have already made allusions, based on the conception of the "transcendentals" of the *Republic*, Book Six and the unwritten doctrine. The epistemological aspect, unlike the *Republic*, does not emerge in its own meaning, however; it is implicitly present in the sciences that prepare for the highest science of beauty, or that—considered according to the order of being—depend on it.

The *Parmenides*

From this nexus among the writings of the period of the *Republic* and the unwritten doctrine of Plato emerge a fortiori criteria that impose an outline on the later works, beginning from the *Parmenides*. This dialogue, in spite of its historical (Eleatic-Zenonian) and formal-methodological overlay, can be interpreted in a more adequate way by connecting it to some specific, fundamental aspects of the theory of the principles and especially by linking it to the foundation of the duality of the principles themselves. In particular, the part of the dialogue that discusses the hypotheses applies the Zenonian method for examining hypotheses to the Eleatic-Zenonian disjunction of unity and multiplicity and achieves the formulation of eight pathways the combination of multiple perspectives (unity-disunity in the sense of the many; being — not being; related — unrelated).

The first path shows that a solitary unity in the Eleatic sense (Cornford) excludes cognitive relations and hence every form of predication (Plato refers here to the criticism of Gorgias, but formulates it in a new way with the dialectical method; consult *Sophist* 243 ff.).

The second pathway destroys the unity monistically conceived in a dialectical manner, placing being together with unity and representing unity, for this reason, as multiple and consequently as predicable (the deduction of the number series must not be conceived as dogmatically binding, but as an ad hoc argument (evidence brought forward especially to shore up an otherwise weak reasoning). The universal predicability of contrary predicates remains without the precision of the principle of contradiction—it appears only in the *Sophist*—for the purpose of completing the ironic self-destruction of Eleaticism (the One-Being itself is contradictory!), but already leads to the theory of Ideas.

The third pathway (157B – 160B) is theoretically central; for the first time it clearly separates unity (now understood in an unequivocal manner as Idea) from the not-one in the sense of the many and leads to the discovery of the fundamental dual structure, which remains binding throughout the succeeding pathways; the relation between the many and the one, then, is determined by a relationship of participation of the other (understood in its structure of divisibility to infinity) in the one, by which there is delineated a differentiation of the concept of unity (unity in itself—the totality of the other; consult Sophist 245B—the individual part).

The fourth path offers an *apagogic* confirmation of the third, by eliminating, together with the relation of participation, the predicability of the other (insofar, as a contrary to the first pathway is also present, only that there the One was seen as solitary and not just as isolated, that is, as in the first pathway, multiplicity, unlike in the fourth path, is not yet explained).

After paths one through three have shown, contrary to Eleaticism, the necessity of multiplicity, the fifth to the eighth, on the contrary, prove in an *apagogic* manner the necessity of unity (supposing that the many are, but that the one is not), and as a result, this time, the thesis of the anti-Eleatics (Gorgias, the Sophists, Anaxagoras, and the Atomists) is shown to be false.[46]

The series of hypotheses, therefore, in its totality by means of dialectic leads to a result that introduces an intermediate solution between that of the monists (the Eleatic thesis of a unique One-Whole) and that of the Pluralists. Linguistically, epistemologically, and ontologically a universal dualistic structure is established in which unity is placed in a relation to multiplicity and vice versa in the sense of a relation of mutual implication, a structure according to which everything whatever it appears to be is a mixture of unity and multiplicity. In this, undoubtedly, there was given, for the initiated, a historical self-clarification and justification of the Platonic theory of the principles in relation to Eleaticism, which here is subjected to a radical internal critique and to a transformation (in conformity with the Academic reports of Speusippus = *Test. Plat.* 50 and Aristotle *Met.* N 1089a2 ff.). At the same time, debates in the Academy that are reflected in the introductory part of the *Parmenides* about the problem of participation (with the alternative: *chorismus* [separation] without mediation or similarity with regress to infinity) are fundamentally clarified with the presentation of a general structure of being (participation of the other in unity).

It would, however, be quite erroneous to turn the allusions about the theory of the principles of Plato contained in the *Parmenides* against the unwritten doctrine, by maintaining that this dialogue makes the indirect tradition superfluous. Rather, the *Parmenides*, as the history of its interpretation up to our own day attests, is constructed in its make-up, in its form, and in its choice of its themes in such a manner that the systematic nexus that is behind and the relation with the thematic of the other works, for example the relation with the concept of virtue, becomes not really clear. The *Parmenides*, therefore, in accord with the self-testimony of the *Phaedrus*, with respect to the aspects of the doctrine of the principles touched on in it, does not have a function of communication, but it has at most an hypomnematic role. In fact, without a previous knowledge of the indirect tradition, it is not possible to derive a properly Platonic constructive position and even less possible to derive a complete theory of the principles, trying to guess it from the "dialectical play" and polemic of the *Parmenides*, let alone to confirm it in comparison with alternative interpretations or against the suspicion of philosophical unreliability suggested by the *Seventh Letter*. On the contrary, the indirect tradition permits us not only to obtain, with an earlier dating, a relatively independent chronology from the succession of the dialogues that belongs to the totality of the nexuses of the Platonic system, but also to verify *the philosophical relevance* of the written work and hence also of the *Parmenides* through the connection with the authentic doctrine professed by Plato within the Academy. The discussion contained in the second part of the *Parmenides*, viz., in the part concerned with the hypotheses, does not even make partially superfluous the indirect tradition, but on the contrary presupposes it, precisely for the aspects noted here, in its holding good for the written work. In addition, note that even the hypomnematic function of the dialogue, for the initiated reader who already has a knowledge of the doctrine, is truly limited. If it is true that, here, one calls to mind some special problems (the duality of the principles, the relation of participation, the relation of the mixture, and hence the solution of the problem of *metexis*),[47] it is therefore likewise true that there remains outside of the limited perspective of the *Parmenides* the nucleus of Platonic philosophy, that is to say, the complete explanation of the structure of being, which includes also the axiological aspect and which, hence, corresponds to the later theory of the transcendentals, with the definition that is proper to it of the One-Good as "the most exact measure." And just as this central point is outside, viz., of the nondifferentiation of ontology and axiology, so also an outline of the hierarchical structure of being with the connected twofold dialectical movement of the categorial (or generalizing) type and of the process toward the elements type is missing. For these basic doctrines, therefore, the *Parmenides* does not even have an hypomnematic value. It is maintained, therefore, within the limits indicated by the self-testimonies of Plato in the *Phaedrus* and the *Seventh Letter*, according to which, for the philosopher, there is "something of greater value" in comparison with a written work,[48] and according to which, in particular, "the highest and first principles of all things" must remain reserved for the "spoken word," because, otherwise, they would become unintelligible or erroneously understood and, hence, treated in an inadequate manner. In a significant manner Plato avoided revealing the structure of being even in the simile of the sun of the *Republic* and did not ever reveal it in its totality, not even in the late works.

The Dialogues Later than the *Parmenides*: the *Sophist,*
Timaeus, Philebus, Statesman, and the *Laws*

The dialogues that follow, complete the outline of the *Parmenides* or thematically amplify it, presenting sometimes, in the particulars, clarifications that support one another. As the *Parmenides*, so also the *Sophist* determines the doctrine of Ideas in the manner of historical self-clarification in the comparison with Eleaticism, the Sophists, and the Socratics, but on a much more particular level and concerning in rather minor measure the level of the principles. The dialogue substitutes the opposition of contrariety (of content) between being and not-being by means of the opposition of the contradictories (formal) and absolute not-being by means of the more general conception of relationship given by difference (alteriety). With the aid of the principle of contradiction, more precisely stated, specific types of compatibility (participation) and noncompatibility arise and, in particular, the logical possibility of multiple participations among the Ideas themselves is demonstrated. Predication is not identification, but subsumption. In this context the false judgment can be explained as the erroneous interpretation of a relationship of being and distinguished by means of precise criteria from the true judgment.

An explanation of such a kind obtained by dialectical means is certainly of the greatest importance for the foundation and the self-constitution of dialectic and logic, but it would be totally erroneous to want to find in the *Sophist*, for this reason, also the highest position of the philosophy of Plato, as frequently happens, making reference to succeeding forms of first philosophy. Methodological reflection, conducted on the model of the five Meta-Ideas (especially of Being, Identity, and Diversity), includes, actually, some fundamental concepts of dialectic, but leaves aside both the thematic of the ontological constitution in the form in which it is presented in the *Parmenides* and in the indirect tradition, and the axiological-moral aspect of dialectic. That, however, the preliminary logical clarification is accomplished in the function of a philosophic-moral dialectic culminating in the ascent to the Good, which in the *Sophist* itself is not developed and which corresponds instead to the program in the *Republic*, is to be drawn from the allusions of 226A ff. and the presence of Socrates, as well as from the projected *Philosopher*, and it is confirmed in the *Statesman*, which follows the *Sophist*, and especially by the *Seventh Letter*. On the other hand, a characteristic passage in which Plato says he wishes to maintain silence about certain things (254C; Appendix 2.7) maintains in obscurity the essence of being and not-being in an eloquent manner, that is further emphasized, if the projected *Philosopher* is considered, which ought to have contained the positive presentation and which Plato never put down in writing.

The rules of participation of the *Sophist* cannot therefore be extrapolated and referred to the theory of the principles, which in this dialogue is not treated, and for example, placed in the list against the thesis of the superessentiality of the Good explicitly formulated in the *Republic* 509B. The limited perspective of the *Sophist* is to be arranged rather, in its turn, in the general area of interest of the Platonic theory of being and of the principles in different ways, which we will indicate.

1. All the Meta-Ideas, that are treated here as champions of a "choice" (254C; Appendix 2.7, 255E1), already presuppose the limitation of the contrary principle by means of the One. Also the Idea of difference is already a limited Idea and determined in an univocal way, which, differing in respect to the λόγος ἀόριστος of the unlimited duality of the great-and-small, indicates only a determined relationship.[49]

2. The pairs of Meta-Ideas, by means of the categorial reduction—in the completion of the dialectical ascent hinted at in the *Republic* and developed in the unwritten doctrine—fall back under the principles as under their supreme genera. It follows that the principles, for example, by means of their species of identity and difference are at the same time determinable and not determinable. The One-Good, hence, does not participate, properly, in identity and difference except analogously.[50]

3. The same goes for the Idea of Being. It participates in identity and difference and both principles because being is defined as that which is constituted by both principles, and hence, as a mixture of both;[51] the principles themselves, therefore, precisely for this reason, are not being, but *are prior to all being*. And because, in addition, being also always has an axiological aspect—as it has an aspect of truth—so unity itself like the principle of being and the good itself do not have a relation of participation (that belongs only among the various Ideas), but are equal in essence.

The *Sophist* analyzes, therefore, the function of some concepts referring to the structure and arrangement of the sphere of the universals, but offers, with this, only an analysis complementary to the foundations of the ontological constitution of it, viz., with respect to the theory of the principles of the unwritten doctrine. The particular point of view of the *Sophist*, hence, is perfectly compatible with the synoptic dialectic and with the hierarchical structure of the *Republic* Books Six and Seven and the indirect tradition, if it is maintained as such and not absolutized in an unjustifiable way.

The axiological and teleological aspect of the structure of being that is largely obscured in the *Parmenides* and in the *Sophist* is developed in an increasing way in the succeeding dialogues, *Statesman, Timaeus, Philebus,* even if only for a limited region, in reference to the cosmos and to the good of man. The furthest reaching of all is the end of the *Philebus* (64B ff.), with an analysis of the "limited" human good, based on quantitative and limiting, qualitative and virtue-connected, epistemological and ontological aspects. This analysis converges with the more fundamental allusions contained in the simile of the sun in the *Republic,* which in an equal way are directed to the Good, in the sphere of interest of the unwritten conception of being, and in the reciprocal connections of the transcendentals. Moreover, the *Timaeus,* on the one hand, and the *Philebus* and the *Statesman,* on the other, complete one another in the sense that by means of a series of typical formulas in which Plato speaks of wanting to abstain from saying certain things, they refer to the dimensional reduction (the process toward the elements) and to the categorial (the process of generalization) of the indirect tradition.

So the central part of the *Timaeus,* which reduces by simplifying the corporeal world to a few elementary geometrical data—two types of triangular figures—gives further allusions (48C; Appendix 2.9; 53D; Appendix 3.10) to "even higher ἀρχαί," which with further simplification concern the smallest elements of extension (indivisible lines) and also the ideal figures and the ideal numbers, which emerge in the indirect tradition. The significance of these nexuses, for the purposes of the cosmological and physical deduction of Plato from a few ultimate principles and in general to bridge the gap between the different ambits of being, is enucleated in a convincing manner by Robin, Stenzel, Gaiser, and von Weizsäcker.[52] In addition, Aristotle expressly puts in relation to space (χώρα), understood as the ultimate material substrate of the cosmology of the *Timaeus,* the great-and-small of the unwritten doctrine.[53] Beyond these controllable connections it is possible to trace the greater part of the analyses in the *Timaeus* to the fundamental antagonism, but also to the cooperation and to the "mixture" of *unity* and *multiplicity,* viz., in the ultimate analysis, to the basic ontological conception of the unwritten doctrine. The two kinds of triangles (right-angled, isosceles; equilateral divided into two), out of which the corporeal world is formed, characterized by means of the greatest simplicity, symmetry, harmony, and equilibrium, and consequently have the character of unity.[54] But the cosmos also is a whole (ἕν, ὅλον), which, with its spherical form, presents a degree of symmetry equally elevated and in the rotational movement joins rest and motion. The soul is a mixture of an indivisible element and a divisible one, that are carried back, just as identity and difference in knowledge (and in this way is there a reference to the *Sophist*), to unity and multiplicity. As an intermediate between the corporeal-divisible and the incorporeal-indivisible the soul, consequently, is specified as an essence having the nature of a surface, which hence comes to be in an analogical way with the elementary surfaces of the corporeal world and, like these, leads to an ontological-dimensional hierarchy, the analogical relations of which the indirect tradition explains in a detailed manner.[55] Also in virtue of its numerical structure, the soul is a unity in multiplicity. And the functional forms of unity (in addition to the material realities) as analogy and proportionality (which also contain the medium: 30C) are also unities in multiplicity.[56] Also the sphere of the movement of the stars that is central in the *Timaeus*, just as it is hinted in the *Republic* Book Seven, was treated in the ambit of the unwritten doctrine and placed at the service of the theory of the principles.[57]

The *Philebus*, in its introductory exposition of the fundamental concepts, presents a kind of theory of the principles of a cosmological character (23C ff.),[58] which with the concepts of limit and unlimitedness goes back to the third path of the *Parmenides*, while with the concept of the mixture and the demiurgic cause, just as with the general axiological orientation, it echoes the *Timaeus*. This dialogue, in addition, presents precisions by differentiations of the not-limited on the basis of the degrees of the more and less and similars. This corresponds to the special categorial series of the indirect tradition with the division of the contraries and the correlatives into limited and not-limited and with their reduction to unity itself and to the great-and-small by means of the concepts of the equal and unequal.

This process of reductive generalizing is already hinted at in a recognizable manner in the central part of the *Statesman*, when, on the basis of the measure, viz., of the just measure determined in relation to the more and the less, the demonstration is announced (never carried out then in the written works) of the exact in itself, viz., of the absolutely exact; that is, of the most exact measure (284D1 f.; Appendix 2.8). Since the multiple "technological," ethical-anthropological, and dialectical-methodological analyses of the *Statesman* culminate in the concept of the just measure (284E; Appendix 2.8), this dialogue is located fully within the categorial reduction—here only just begun—just as the central part of the *Timaeus* is located within the dimensional reduction.

Within this systematic sphere of interest, which leads, in the ultimate analysis, to the theory of the universal principles, can be arranged in the same manner the principal parts of the *Philebus*, as well as ample parts of the *Laws*,[59] especially the theory of the so-called mixed constitution, understood as a mean between extremes, developed in the *Laws*.[60] The end of the *Philebus* shows that the "just measure" is, in any case—like the structure of the order that it presupposes[61] and specifies—being, good, and cognizable in the highest measure.[62] And this is like a kind of monadic equilibrium between too little and too much, which represents a mode of one-being derived from the original unity.

Allusions to Some Dialogues of the First Phase

With this choice of dialogues shedding light on the middle and late phases of the literary activity of Plato, we can conclude here. But some of the dialogues of the first phase also offer equally persuasive occasions that presuppose an unwritten doctrine of the principles. Thus, the *Lysis*, has the notion of the supreme Idea of a "primary friend" (πρῶτον φίλον), which corresponds to Beauty itself and the Good itself; the *Protagoras*, has a concluding allusion to the art of normative measure (357B; Appendix 2.1), which anticipates the *Statesman* and refers to it; and especially, the *Meno* which already many times, in a certain way, is seen to have references to the Academy and which with the allusions to degrees of being (procedure through hypotheses) and with the convergence between the mathematical world and the axiological—moral world, seems to refer on the whole to basic ontological conceptions of Plato.[63] However, since, in the present context, it is sufficient to reveal the fundamental relationship between the written and the unwritten word in Plato, it is superfluous to give a complete exposition of all the individual examples, which, at any rate, here could not be treated in detail.

Conclusions

Instead it is more important to reflect by way of summary on the relationship of thematic complementarity between the doctrine of the dialogues and the unwritten doctrine of the principles and to draw some conclusions. This relation is not present right from the beginning in a unitary manner. Although in the dialogues of the first period and the intermediate period through the *Republic*, the practical aspect of philosophy dominates with the ethico-political themes and the more properly theoretical problems of "first philosophy" and "metaphysics" remain largely reserved to the "oral," the relation is made more complicated in the late works, that are understood always in a more hypomnematic manner; just as in the *Parmenides* and the *Sophist* are found treatises about the problems of first philosophy, that are referred to the structure of the sphere of the universals in its totality, without being limited, as the *Statesman*, the *Philebus*, and the *Timaeus*, to regional sections of reality. But in any case it remains simply true also here, notwithstanding what has been said in the *Parmenides* and the *Sophist*, that the basic ontological foundations are developed in a complete manner, and in their intrinsic relations and with the grounding nexuses that reduce to them, only in the sphere of "orality." And if the undifferentiation between ontology and ethics is at the base of Platonic philosophy in its totality and in each of its expressions, the structure of being emerges in an explicit manner only in the foundations of the unwritten doctrines. The same is true for the complete development of all the categorial Meta-Ideas and for their deduction from the theory of the principles.

This peculiar carrying out of the dialectic—viz., the arrangement of the Meta-Ideas with the One-Good itself following the ways of knowledge as well as that of being[64]—Plato in the dialogues (*Republic, Parmenides, Sophist,* and *Statesman*)[65] has always traced only on the programmatic level or only in simple allusions made to it, but it was never carried out to completion. The fact that the ultimate and decisive synopsis that takes up the themes of the *Parmenides* and the *Sophist*, on the one hand, and the *Republic*, the *Symposium*, and *Statesman*, on the other, must appear to still be absent from the written work, as is demonstrated by the repeated reference to the (unwritten) dialogue entitled *The Philosopher*, which beyond the written works refers to the unwritten doctrine of the Academy.[66]

Theoretical abstraction, hence, is carried to a more advanced level in the discussions held within the circle of the Academy than in the dialogues,[67] while the philosophy of politics and ethics, as well as cosmology, seem rather to be found in the written works.[68] This, however, must not be misunderstood, as though the elevation to a theoretical level of the unwritten doctrine were to imply a renunciation of praxis: the dialogical moment and the spiritual assimilation, the existential choice of the type of life to be lived, the normative concept of truth, which mutually conjoins knowledge, the form of life and action, and, ultimately, the political activity of the members of the Platonic Academy—all this in the *Seventh Letter* still is postulated as essential just for the activity of oral teaching. And whereas these Socratic elements cannot indicate any difference between the written works and the unwritten (*On the Good!*), the claim to political domination of Platonic philosophy, on the contrary, by starting from the plain of the theory of principles is also theoretically grounded. The cogently developed theory of the Whole consistently announces not, indeed, unconditional, yet nonetheless far-reaching, claims of power.[69]

Moreover, with respect to the difference between the written work and the unwritten the fact is significant that in the indirect tradition there exists an approximate equilibrium between the order of knowledge and the order of being whereas in the written works the order of knowledge on the whole strongly predominates.[70] But it is only within the sphere of the unwritten doctrine that the order of knowledge is brought to completion—in form, degree, and implication.

8 The Place of the Theory of the Principles in the History of Ancient Philosophy

Some consequences of an historical-philosophical character of vast importance emerge from the renovated global perspective that embraces the whole Plato. In fact, elements of continuity and consistent developments that confirm in a mediate manner the new picture of Plato emerge by proceeding chronologically both backwards and forwards with regard to Plato in every respect.

Relations with the Presocratics and Socrates

In the first place, concerning the relations of Plato with the prior history of philosophy,[1] it becomes clear that the ontological theme in its totality and the metaphysical problem of Plato himself are determined through the Presocratic speculations concerning the principles, in which both the Eleatic and the Pythagorean tradition are combined. Plato joined the theory of permanent being, taking it on the level to which it had carried the Presocratics, with the Sophistic-Socratic problem of the conduct of life and the *polis*. The consideration of the Whole must be utilized in a normative manner to determine the order of human life, and on the other hand, this must be grounded in a more profound manner, precisely by moving from the consideration of the Whole. The concepts of principle and political problems, Parmenides and Solon, Pythagoras and Socrates are fused so intimately, in Plato, that indeed in the mutual intertwining of the two aspects in the Platonic concept of philosophy something quite important is grasped. In the history of ancient ontology, therefore, there is no break, while, instead, until today they posit with Socrates and Plato a caesura and a radically new position, whereby the classical philosophy of the fourth century BCE seemed to be almost something floating on air, without substrate and without historical foundation.

In the background of Presocratic speculation concerning the *arché* [2] in addition the religious and theological tradition is to be recognized as tending toward monotheism of a supreme, all enveloping deity, which was followed, as was correctly said, by the Platonic theory of principles, just as the mutual influence also of theory and praxis in Plato can lead back, among other things, to the religious unity between myth and the practices of cult and rites.[3]

In particular the indirect tradition, and similarly the *Parmenides*, also shows that Plato, with the disjunction of unity and multiplicity, placed himself primarily in the wake of Eleaticism—interpreted with Zeno in the henological sense—but still radically separated from it by the rehabilitation of multiplicity (which would lead, on the one hand, to the admission of a principle of multiplicity and, on the other, to the separation from the multiplicity of beings of a purely superessential unity).[4] However, the conception of the contrary principle as a principle of undetermined degrees (more-and-less, great-and-small) also comes principally from Presocratic speculation beginning with the Milesians through the Eleatics to Plato,[5]— and for this reason Aristotle distinguished him from the Pythagoreans,[6]— whereas the conceptual material of mathematical and medical abstraction (excess-defect) is accepted probably only in a secondary way; to these the tradition of the ancient Greek ethics of the measure is added, for example in the form which Democritus had given to it.[7] The basic ontological conception of Plato—limitation and determination of the indeterminate material substrate (of the great-and-small) by means of unity as principle of determination ("measure" and "limit")—reflects, the generative model of Pythagoreanism (limit and unlimited as constitutive principles of axiological importance). The connection of the ontological and axiological aspects, however, is already rooted in the prephilosophical notion of virtue (which in an implicit manner is also consistently conceived ontologically), whereas the connection with the epistemological aspects is grounded, once again, in the Eleatic connection of the problem of being with the problem of truth, and in addition, in a prephilosophical veridical conception of being.

On the whole, the theory of the principles of Plato presents a novel and very complex type of solution to the basic problem of Presocratic philosophy; that is to say, about the relation of *unity* and *multiplicity*. The reply of Plato to this problem is actually passed through Eleaticism, but is not exhausted in the dualism of a schema of two worlds, in which *aletheia* and *doxa* of the Eleatics approach one another and compenetrate one another to some degree. Plato overcame Eleaticism and the whole ancient tradition and corrected it, moving it to a still more profound base in the perspective of the inquiry into the principles, conceiving the two worlds of *aletheia* and *doxa* beginning from a unitary structure of being, which is constituted by the principles of pure unity and pure multiplicity.[8]

The position of the problem by the Presocratics, with the inclusion of the Eleatics, comes, thus, to be elevated to a higher level of metaphysical reflection, and the theme unity-multiplicity is formulated in a more general and novel manner. (The unity is understood in the twofold sense of universality and simplicity.)[9] This transformation of the traditional thematic is made possible and carried out through the new instrument of the *dialectical method*.

Dialectic is originally an inheritance from the Sophists, developed by Protagoras and Gorgias on the basis of Eleatic starting-points and transformed into a critical method turning against the very same Eleatic speculation on being from the perspective of common sense, with the conscious insistence on the pluralistic world of phenomena and opinion, and having as its goal that of conquering the adversary in argument. Socrates imprinted on dialectic a decisive turn, referring it to that unique goal which until that moment was obscured, precisely to the person of the interlocutor in the dialogue himself. Moving the person to reexplain himself, dialectic evoked the concern for the virtue of the person's soul, whereas provoking an existential turbulence, and hence, a basic concern for the truth, which breaks the Sophistic eristic and prepares for the return to the Presocratics with Plato. The metaphysics of Plato, considered from this point of view, is presented as a conscious critical renovation of Presocratic thought by the reform of the position proper to a finite dialectic, because an up-to-date renovation of Presocratic thought, after the Sophistic, was possible from the historical-philosophical standpoint only on this level.[10] What this means is that the methodological position of Plato contains from the start a bottleneck, in consequence of which it is constituted as something more and at the same time less with respect to the primitive form of the old ontology. Something less, because it is developed from the position of finite dialectic, hence in a certain way it began from below, something more because one's own soul or, to speak in modern terms, the "self," with its unconditioned interest in the truth is necessarily included and it is not methodologically possible to eliminate it. Without the engagement of the whole human person it is not possible to penetrate into Platonic philosophy. Socratic dialectic, therefore, holds together all the theoretical approaches of Plato up to the last phase of his philosophy. And because the Socratic moment opens in a new way the path to the problem of being and the principles, it is also methodologically an irrevocable and decisive moment.[11] Therefore, with Platonic philosophy we have to do, more precisely, with an amplification of the Socratic-dialectical approach, which rises to the level of the Presocratic philosophy without ever bursting the original approach itself.

Beginning from this point we finally understand the great synthesis in which Plato located the Sophistic-Socratic problem of the conduct of life with the Presocratic thematic of the principle, and we grasp the point of the "theoretical undifferentiation" between ethics and ontology, which his philosophy throughout assumed. All this is reflected in the polyvalence of the theory of the principles—of which the title *On the Good* already constitutes evidence—which works unitarily in the sense of the foundation of being, of science, and of action, and also is reflected in the corresponding conception of being, in which the ontological, epistemological, and axiological moments are inseparably compenetrated. From here is derived above all—with an extension in universality of the Socratic unity of knowledge and action—the consistent mutual correlation of theory and praxis, together with the ontological foundation of the postulated political rule of philosophers. In the philosophical approach of Plato, no essential area of the theory can remain without consequences for the ends of the constitution of the ordering of human life; in particular, every theory—not only that which is specifically political—can be transformed into political praxis. This mediation must be guaranteed on the highest level and rationally founded by means of the theory of the principles.

If, therefore, it is true that Platonic philosophy contains the claim to the critical reflection on the praxis supported by the Socratic spirit, then it is still likewise true that the fusion with the Presocratic tradition produces a robust enrichment of content within the original framework, which leads to a new dimension. It is manifested in the polemical discussion of Plato with the Sophists, but also with the Socratic schools. This controversy, in its nucleus, is a dispute about principles, to which the Platonic affirmation of God as measure of all things, which is directed against Protagoras, gives a particularly important significance.[12] In a more special sense Plato conducts such a controversy also against the Presocratics, when he tries to deepen in a dialectical-noetic sense the speculations about the principles that were handed down or, when, as in the case of the Eleatics, he tries to break up the monism of being into a pluralistic and dualistic sense and hence to make the concept of being fruitful for the first time for the purpose of explaining the world. In these basic theoretical positions of Plato concerning the principles must be recognized the foundation of the classical period of Greek philosophy, which also includes Aristotelianism, and, then, the later Neoplatonic tradition associated with it.

Inevitably this is also joined to the problem whether the general doctrine of Plato concerning the Ideas had been determined by a theory of the principles right from its beginnings, or only afterwards, when reflection on the doctrine of the Ideas was already existent and because of the difficulties internal to it, Plato turned again to the Presocratic speculation on the principle. This problem cannot be resolved in a secure manner either in one sense or the other, for lack of adequate evidence.[13] What is certain is that the doctrine of the Ideas conceived ontologically presupposes in every one of its aspects Eleaticism and that, considering the function of the principle of the Good itself in the *Republic* and its corresponding analogies in the first dialogues (the *Symposium* and the *Lysis*),[14] only with difficulty would anyone succeed in indicating a moment in which Plato could have moved from a general doctrine of the Ideas to the theory of the principles. Therefore, the most plausible solution, at least on the hypothetical level, viz., without alleging the claim of the support of a decisive proof, is again in maintaining that the return of Plato to the Presocratics did not take place through a series of successive stages but was carried out from the beginning with the process of transformation and correction of the Eleatic approach in the theory of the principles, by virtue of which the admission of a multiplicity of beings within it was structurally justified. Already J. Stenzel[15] had recognized the analogy between the sensible *eidos* and the transcendent *eidos* and based on it his deduction of the theory of Ideas from the theory of the arete-*eidos*. Actually, the early Plato, on occasion, used *eidos* and *kosmos* as synonyms.[16] It can be therefore assumed that the Idea also, as the individual *arete*, is *order* (*kosmos*), and thereby, *unity in multiplicity* (μονοειδές), but in perfect fashion. The same goes, in an analogous manner, for the Ideal Numbers and for the geometric figures. If Plato, hence, from the start understood ethico-political realities on the basis of their organized structures, which, further, for epistemological reasons have need of the existence of proportion and order in themselves (i.e., of the Ideas), then it is clear that the relation with the fundamental ontological conception handed down—what is limited and ordered depends on unity—is imposed also from the theoretical standpoint for both things, viz., for *arete* and for its Idea. And this is the more so, insofar as Plato interpreted Eleaticism from the start in the sense of its later followers Zeno and Melissus, that is, in a henological sense. Therefore, a conception of the *arete-eidos* independent from a single foundation of being probably never existed. This explanation has the advantage of not leaving methodologically unprotected the theory of Ideas beginning from Eleaticism within the Eleatic disjunction of unity and multiplicity, whereas the evolutionary explanation must presuppose a series of *aporias* that Plato would have overcome only little by little.[17] On the basis of the interpretation favored here, the traditional Idealism of Plato, viz., the distinction of the two worlds, would all along be brought rather under a conception of the principles oriented in general to the Presocratics, and by this become structurally as well as ontologically more comprehensible.

But the discovery both of the realm of the universals and its internal organization and, finally, the delimitation of pure unity itself as its common ground is an achievement of dialectical method. Plato, in this way, has not simply adapted the conceptually analytic analysis of the universal principle—the principle is the One considered according to number, continuity, time, and scale—taken from the ancient tradition, and in particular from the

Eleatic, but he has brought the theory of the principles with a new cogency and strictness into discursive—both in their generalizing and in their reduction to the elements mode—nexuses of foundation. He derives the polyvalent structure of the principles, in addition, from the supreme degree of abstraction achieved by dialectical means.

Precisely against this background of the pre-Platonic speculation concerning the principles, the contribution made by Plato is clear with its more ample statement, achieved by means of a process of dialectic generalization. It is clear in addition that Plato has not only purified critically the sphere of the principles from its sensible analogies that still persisted in Eleaticism and has placed it in the sphere of the purely conceptual, but he has also taken it upward, by means of a restriction and an essentializing criticism, to an absolute ultimate and to a hypertranscendence that is continued by the approach of negative theology. Indeed, in Plato, the explanation of the world in its totality must be achieved just according to this way.[18] The ultimate metaphysical explanation, in the incisive formulation given by Plato—that is, that the extreme transcendence of the principles is, *precisely because of this*, the most comprehensive explanation of the universe—, has determined in a decisive manner the successive history of thought up to the twentieth century.

Relations with Aristotle

With respect to the position of Platonic philosophy in comparison with the succeeding history of ancient philosophy, note that, without the complete inclusion of the Platonic indirect tradition, it is impossible to make a useful reconstruction of the relations and a reasonable limitation of the confines that divide Plato from Aristotelianism and from Neoplatonism. Aristotle little by little becomes more and more comprehensible by beginning from the doctrine professed by Plato within the Academy (different from the written works of the same): in first philosophy and physics, in ethics and politics, in the *Organon* and finally even in his biological writings. Aristotle is Platonic in a surprising measure, as soon as he is compared to the whole Plato. Certainly, in doing this, we see also with new clarity that Aristotle abandoned the methodological orientation of Plato with respect to the Socratic dialectic and the mathematical sciences, and that, in addition, between Plato and Aristotle are the ancient pupils of the Platonic Academy.

In particular,[19] the clarifying power of the unwritten doctrine of Plato is shown chiefly in the first philosophy of Aristotle, and in the first place, in relation to the most difficult and greatest problem, viz., the problem of the unity of the object of metaphysics. The determination of first philosophy understood as theology and together as the universal science of being concerned with all spheres of being (οὐσίαι), *because* it is first and concerns the πρώτη οὐσία (*Met.* E 1; K 7), becomes more comprehensible if it is considered within the historical background of the Platonic-Academic theory of the principles and the reality derived therefrom and, in a particular way, in the method at play in its process of reduction to the elements.[20] Certainly, Aristotle is separated in a decisive manner from the mechanism of the generative process of the philosophy of the elements, oriented in the sense of their mathematical construction. However, the exegesis of Aristotle based on internal criticism (G. Reale and others) has shown that in Aristotle the principle on the basis of which the levels of being are distinguished is also that of the series (the relationship of ἐφεξῆς).[21] In this serial relationship an ontological nexus is preserved, although in a weakened form, by which from the "priority" of the highest sphere of the principles follows its universality in a logically necessary manner. (In fact, in the "series," the first member is always the most universal). On the basis of this agreement, which arises in the admission of differing types of matter for each sphere of being,[22] scholars (P. Merlan, H. Wagner, H. Happ, and others) have grasped in an ever increasing measure the knowledge of the original intentions of Aristotle.[23]

But also the general direction of the thought of first philosophy, with its analytic-regressive procedure—Aristotle also maintains, from a terminological standpoint, the position of the problem about the "elements" (*Met.* Γ 1; E 1; Λ 4-5)—beginning from accidental being through *ousia* in general until finally achieving the πρώτη οὐσία [G. Reale] and with the deduction in the direction opposed to this, which remains on the programmatic level (*Met.* A 2; E 1; K 7), is also oriented according to the twofold methodological direction of the order of knowledge (structured from low to high) and of the order of being (structured from high to low), which is proper to the unwritten systematic of Plato. The Aristotelian distinction of that which is more knowable in itself and that which is more knowable to us immediately accepts this twofold procedure, maintaining firmly the point of departure in sensible substances (*Met.* ZHΘ; Λ 1—5; *Phys.* A 1, and so on).

The "Copernican" revolution of the Aristotelian ontology towards the ἄτομον (ἔνυλον) εἶδος (*infima species*), just as, for a certain period of time, toward the individual (*Cat.* 5, and so on) actually, is not of Platonic origin, but has arisen and develops in the Academy through aporias internal to the system deriving from the methodological pluralism of Plato. As the attempts at solution by his predecessors, which in part (Speusippus) lead to the early Aristotle, and in part (Xenocrates) to the late Aristotle, so also the Aristotelian conception of the problem of the universals, with the displacement of the ontological importance in favor of the lowest universals, is a consequence of the growing predominance of the form of thought that moves toward the elements over that which moves toward the general. This predominance carried over to the primacy of the ousiological criterion of simplicity and indivisibility with respect to that of universality and by this forced a transformation of the sphere of the universals toward the individual by a process toward the elements and hence an ontological weakening of the higher universal. The Aristotelian doctrine of the *eidos*, consequently, presents itself, considered historically, as the ultimate consequence and the conclusive result of a re-organization of the structure of the genera in the sense of process toward the elements (not, note, as a result of a process of mathematization). The problematic that results from the unwritten systematic of Plato, culminating in the operational polyvalence of the theory of the principles, and from the matter of conflict latent in it, has become, hence, determining for the basic position of the Aristotelian ontology.

But also the not generalizing structures of first philosophy and ethics, which Aristotle carried into the arena against the theory of Ideas, and precisely analogy and the πρὸς ἕν relation, are not as originally Aristotelian as the comparison with only the Platonic dialogues might suggest. In fact both go back, again, to the central structure of the thought pattern that is a reduction to the elements, viz., to the series, which in Plato and in the Academy is not, in its turn, generalizable. Aristotle, therefore, argues here against the doctrine of the Ideas with arguments internal to Platonism. In particular, it is undoubtedly clear that analogy in its strictly mathematical form represents a special case of the series, that is to say, a series of progressive relations. The πρὸς ἕν relation (which in the Middle Ages was called the analogy of attribution and is today also called the focal meaning [G. E. L. Owen]) is obtained, on the one hand, by means of a choice of a significant homonymy on the example of the paronymy within the diaeretic system already developed in the Academy concerning expressions having multiple meanings (πολλαχῶς λεγόμενα).[24] On the other hand, considered from the standpoint of methodology, it is represented as a weakened and mutilated form of the series (not generalizable), in which the members that make it up are all immediately referred to the first and that, precisely for this reason, acquires the widest range of applicability.[25]

The method of the distinction of the meanings, which continuously serves the analysis of being of the first philosophy of Aristotle, when it explains the multiplicity of the meanings of the words ὄν, οὐσία, or ἀρχή, is of dialectical origin. It is in a strict relationship with the distinction between linguistic expressions (ὄνομα) and the determination of the essence (λόγος) found in Platonic dialectic and as such has been, consequently, systematically fixed in the Academy with a systematic listing of the different types (synonymy, homonymy, polyonymy, paronymy, and heteronymy); and Aristotle touched on this typology. Also from the standpoint of content, the analysis of being is oriented on the basis of Academic starting points, which Aristotle critically transformed or amplified. This is of value chiefly for the dualistic theory of the principles, which Aristotle, at first, transforms into a doctrine of three principles (*eidos-hyle-steresis*), using the introduction of matter as a mediating substrate (or, more exactly, disassociating the contrary principle in matter and privation; *Met.* Λ 10; N 2; as well as Γ 2; *Phys.* A 7—9), and then completed using the addition of the movent cause and the final cause, in the doctrine of the four causes (*Met.* Λ 3—5; Δ 2; *Phys.* B 3; privation is eliminated). In this is manifested a transformation of the universal ontological theory of the principles of Plato and the Academy,[26] which takes on a cosmological emphasis in an increasing measure and—in a corresponding measure to a change in the doctrine of the *eidos*—*is specified in a regional sense.*[27] *In an analogous manner the doctrine of the categories of Aristotle is to be understood as an improvement on the Platonic division of being into being in itself and being relative to another,*[28] *to which the Categories* already referred with a continuous comparison and that already contained a systematic distinction between fundamental beings and their properties. To prescind from further differentiations of relative and dependent beings, the progress is, here, in the fact that Aristotle radicalizes the distinction by desubstantializing definitively, in the course of the categorial transformation, dependent being, to which in Platonism correspond still largely ideal paradigms.[29] Without doubt, Aristotle achieves the greatest originality in the modal analysis (that is founded equally on distinctions of the signified); however, also for this the method of the process to the elements of the Academy (and more generally of the mathematicians) offers, at least, some corresponding terminological analogies worthy of consideration.[30]

Moreover, the two other disciplines that follow first philosophy, practical philosophy and physics (including biology), are under the influence of the conception of being of Plato based on the theory of the principles. The determination of moral virtue as the just mean between excess and defect, just as the theory of the mixed constitution (*Politics* Γ, E, Z; consult *Rhet.* A 4) goes back not only to the *Statesman* and the *Laws* but, from the terminological and categorial standpoints (doctrine of the contraries), also to the axiological starting points of the indirect tradition.[31] This is confirmed in a precise manner by the principle, connected to this, of order according to the more or less, excess and defect, which plays a central role in the Aristotelian zoology and in the botany of Theophrastus, and which, throughout the fundamental reports contained in the first book of the *Physics* concerning the Platonic concept of the great-and-small, is possible to follow back to its origins in the unwritten doctrine.[32]

In what concerns the history of philosophy, from these statements,[33] the following is achieved: that presumed new attempts, presumed antitheses, breaks, and misinterpretations, which must be undoubtedly postulated if one is limited to a onesided comparison between the Plato of the dialogues and Aristotle, instead, are to be resolved in developments having a continuous nature and that, now, on the basis of what exists in common between the two philosophers, the real choices and decisions produced by Aristotle can be finally judged, in their full scope and implications. From this follows another result: that many things which in the vision of a restricted consideration seem in part to be facts of a "phenomenological" immediacy and in part a theoretical presupposition in reality depend on the philosophic problematic and the level of reflection and argumentation developed previously by Platonism, and that Aristotle's originality consists, instead, often in shadings and limited accentuations, which have a precise goal and importance.[34]

In addition, it is possible, on these bases, to attempt to establish a determined summary and a new characterization, grounded and improved, of the relations between Aristotelianism and Platonism. In this regard three fundamental differences between Aristotle and Plato come to mind.

1. The elimination of mathematical quanta in Platonism, viz., the separation of the mathematicizing nature proper to the form of thinking that reduces things to elements, and, in general, the abandonment of the role of mathematics as the sphere of the inquiry capable of furnishing the heuristic model of confirming and verifying metaphysics. In positive terms this means the emancipation and pure representation of the qualitative and the teleological moment in all the spheres of interest. Eliminating from Platonic speculation the mathematicizing and quantitative moment, Aristotle still maintained thereof a form of logical reduction, which thus achieved a new qualitative connection and teleological determination.[35] For this reason the relationship of Aristotle concerning the method of reduction to the elements is ambivalent: he accepts the speculative content and is essentially influenced by the problematic aroused by this method, but he rejects its mathematical substance.

2. The Platonic dialectic, which was of a Socratic character, in Aristotle no longer has any place. Dialectic in Aristotle is reduced to the level of an *organon*, and precisely to the level of a formal method having heuristic goals, but without a specific philosophical content, which passed chiefly to "first philosophy." Both, dialectic and first philosophy in Aristotle are ethically and politically neutralized and objectivized and therefore no longer constitute the Socratic

"bottleneck" of the Platonic approach, which had constituted the moment of mediation and integration of the philosophy of Plato. Hence, again, a Presocratic way of comprehending the world (not by chance does he turn to figures like Democritus and Anaxagoras) penetrates into the philosophical conception of Aristotle. With respect to Plato, Aristotle supports a compact theory of *physis*, which prescinds from reflection on the self that philosophizes. This is the reason why theoretical and practical philosophy, in Aristotle, are kept apart or, to say it in a positive way, theoretical philosophy is disenfranchised from the ethico-political bond and left free in its pure autonomy and self-sufficiency. From the metaphysical standpoint and from the standpoint of the theory of principles, this means that the structure of being peculiar to Plato is critically overcome by Aristotle and that the point of the "lack of differentiation" between ontology and axiology is left alone;[36] consequently, a theory of the polyvalence of the principles of a Platonic type, for Aristotle, is acceptable, in any case, only with notable restrictions.[37]

3. By means of the dialectical method Plato was in condition not only to renovate the position of the problems of the Presocratics, but also to reformulate them in a more incisive manner. The further consequence of the abandonment of the universal ontological dialectic of the Platonic type consists in the critical self-limitation with which Aristotelian first philosophy consciously renounced the fundamental metaphysical problems concerning the unity and essence of being and limited itself to an inventory and the division of the different meanings of being and its elements. Aristotle did not tend to reinterpret the totality of being in a radical manner, like Plato, starting from the unity of the principle, viz., he did not tend to perform an ontological deduction beginning from ultimate principles. Instead, in the place of the problem about the relationship between these primary principles and being, the problem about the order and succession of being itself is substituted, and the method of synoptic generalizing is resolved in that of the analysis; the intent to go back to the ultimate foundation is replaced by the procedure of the distinction and differentiation of the levels. The Aristotelian concept of science, therefore, is distant from the metaphysical doctrine of Plato and it is proximate to, in a certain measure, that of the particular sciences (not mathematical). The position of the problem concerning the theory of the principles of a Platonic type, both in a reductive sense and in a generalizing sense, hence, is definitively abandoned and leaves in its place solutions that have minor

demands, but that are also less risky. Seen in this positive perspective, this means that the fecund form of thought of the analyses of the various aspects of the real for the first time is seen completely with Aristotle.[38]

Relations with Hellenism and with Neoplatonism

Whereas Aristotelianism as a critically revisited Platonism remains still linked, in the greater part of its problems, to the foundations of the philosophy of Plato, the philosophies of Hellenism are located fundamentally in another tradition, the Presocratic and Socratic. However, the Hellenistic period is mediately influenced by some descendants of the system of Plato, which in the course of the disputes of the Garden and the Stoa with the Academy and with the Peripatos, by way of adaptations, imitations, analogies, or through reasons of competition, enter in a more or less marginal manner in the late schools. Examples of an acceptance of this kind, frequently mediated and refracted in a variety of ways, are offered by the Epicurean theory of the *minima*, the crypto-ontological characteristics of the Hellenistic concepts of virtue and *eudaemonia* (limitation, no degrees, beyond time, and so on), or the exploitation in the techniques of argument and formal dialectic of the principle of degrees (the great-and-small); for example, in the argument of the sorites, the division of being, the trope of the relatives contrary to being itself, or the aporetic of the New Academy.[39]

On the contrary, in the sphere of the new research (Robin, Dodds, Merlan, De Vogel, Krämer, Hager, and Szlezák), by means of the doctrine of the unwritten principles and systematic of Plato, in an ever increasing measure emerges an approach between Plato and Neoplatonism. The continuity of the tradition, in this regard, in part goes back to the ancient Academy[40] and to its pseudo-morphosis in Neo-Pythagoreanism or to its doxographic reelaboration, which, however, in Plotinus, unlike late Neoplatonists, is recognizable only with difficulty; instead, the Aristotelian reports on the unwritten doctrine enjoy in Plotinus a remarkable and not unrecognizable role.[41] Two things, especially, connect the indirect tradition of Plato with Neoplatonism. The conception of the One beyond being; and the plurality of the levels of being. Other themes are added such as the central position of the ideal numbers or the dimensional ontology of bodies, but have lost their theoretical power. The specific traits of Neoplatonism, that are revealed in this background with greater precision, are the limitation of the Socratic approach, which leads to the elimination of politics from philosophy; the transformation of the dualism of the principles into a more radical monism, therefore confronting the problems avoided by Plato, in consequence of which unity is made to issue the contrary principle from itself and which is immediately connected with the concept of "emanation"; the more complete dynamic animation and spiritualization of the whole system (Bréhier).[42] On the whole, however, the peculiar historical influence of the unwritten philosophy of Plato was exercised less on Aristotle than on Neoplatonism, which—oriented in a more conservative manner in a Platonic sense—has transmitted fundamental concepts of the metaphysics of Plato to the medieval and modern tradition.

If the history of ancient speculation concerning the principles is considered in its totality, the Platonic theory of the principles constitutes the central terminus in the process of mediation between the Presocratics, on the one hand, and Aristotelianism and Neoplatonism, on the other. And with this is achieved not only a greater understanding of the continuity, coherence, and consistency of the evolution of thought, but also a most important criterion for the evaluation of the philosophical teaching of Plato. Whoever tries to discredit the unwritten theory of the principles, by maintaining their negligible value in comparison with the dialogues—one of the current strategies of Schleiermacherianism—must furnish a well-founded response to questions about the position he intends to take, consequently, in respect to the metaphysical tradition that Plato has taken from the Presocratics and that through Plato has been passed on to Neoplatonism and thence to the West.

Part Three

The Philosophical Implications of the Platonic Theory
of the Principles and
Viewpoints for Its Interpretation

9 *The Theory of the Principles in the Light of Analytic Philosophy*

The Platonic conception of the principles and its system, no matter how much in metaphysical dress, claims to make contributions of a methodological and epistemological character. The theoretical status of such a conception can be analyzed according to modern standpoints of a linguistic, logical, and epistemological nature and hence, can be taken in relation to contemporary theoretical positions and their relevant discussions. In the work of comparison, the arguments and methodology, in part, in the measure in which they are only implicit in the reports of the unwritten doctrines, can be reconstructed on the basis of circumstantial evidence and in part, instead, must be amplified by means of reflections that proceed beyond this.

Analysis of the Platonic Theory of the Principles from the Linguistic Viewpoint

The linguistic presuppositions of the Platonic theory of the principles, just as the presuppositions that take into account the problem of being and the thematic of the universals, in general, lead to certain particularities in the syntax of the Greek language; for example, the possibility of changing adjectives, participles, and infinitives into substantives by means of the definite article, and the abstraction of classes, made possible precisely by this.[1] In this, Plato like Aristotle and Hegel but unlike the Stoa and modern thought after Frege, was oriented not toward propositional logic but toward predicate logic and in the theory of Ideas developed indeed an *ontology of predicates* (an ontology of classes, names, terms, "concepts").[2] With the categorial distinction between predicates that do not refer to others (which are in se and per se) and predicates that refer to others (*relatives*), Plato, like Aristotle, was left to be guided by language.[3] However, in this, the fact that the Ideas of things, that is, the classes of things that are in themselves and through themselves were hierarchically subordinated, was decisive, while the properties, as for example qualities and in addition relations and functions, in the hierarchy of being were located more on a higher level, and the greater level of universality they had, the higher up they were. For this reason the concepts of categorial reflection, as Meta-Ideas and "supreme genera," are beyond the Ideas of things; the principles of unity and duality (the great-and-small), hence, insofar as they are the most general Meta-predicates coinvolved in every predication, are, at the same time, the highest categories of the widest universality and power of being. The theory of the principles, hence, insofar as it is a logic of the highest kind of predicates, is a theory of the most general categories,[4] from which more particular categories can be derived and, further, also propositional axioms.

On the other hand, the function of the principles also as "elements" and ultimate structural aspects of being (στοιχεῖα) can be reconstructed by beginning from common language. The relation here in question between the part and the whole, elements and complexity, goes back to the corresponding activities, actions, and procedures of connection, to synthesis and analysis, which are operative not only in every process of production but likewise in the processes of thought. The "generative" trait proper to the construction of the Platonic system is not by chance grounded in representations characterized by the *method of reduction to elements*. From the linguistic standpoint, at the base of this methodological procedure is a *narrative aspect*, a structure of recounting in the form of a "story," that describes in what way many constitutive parts (elements) of the same kind are aligned one after the other and summarized in a whole of greater magnitude, with the repetition of the same process many times over.[5] Those who, by enumerating, embrace with a glance the whole series, either produce it themselves by means of the repetition of a plurality of similar acts, or, at the least, they call it to mind in a successive way for themselves, or ("re-counting"!) to others.

In this respect, for Plato, exemplary models are constituted by the number series of arithmetical numbers, or the geometrical and stereometrical series of lines, surfaces, and solids, which in modern times would be expressed by means of recursive definitions, because they are always constituted by identical elements, just as by their ideal paradigms (viz., the ideal numbers, the ideal magnitudes). In their systematic function these series appear only in the context of the *reductive* method of the unwritten doctrine. In the Platonic allegorizing about the "generation" of atemporal entities nothing other is expressed than the discursive scanning act to comprehend the theoretic structure of the arrangement of being according to scales. The figurative language is referred, however, evidently to a prephilosophical use of language. Moreover, on the level of the theory of Ideas, the element in itself as essence of the class, principle, and measure of all the individual elements and moments of the series, is drawn by means of a process of *generalizing* and it is hypostatized in the *primary elements* of the theory of the principles.

The general schema of thought, however, which the *reductive* method supports, originally, in its linguistic substrate in colloquial language, is always linked to a narrative structure made by propositions and repetitions of propositions, which describe acts and "steps" always new of the same type. In this regard, it is here on the basis of a higher linguistic structure with respect to the simple *generalizing* of the analysis of predicates: it is not a question of simple parts of propositions, but of forms of propositions, and, precisely, transphrastic systems of propositions of an iterative character (that is, of a plurality of propositions of the same kind that are repeated many times). The same is valid for a whole set of other fundamental concepts of Platonic philosophy oriented to an hierarchical arrangement or to a process of division: πρῶτον (πρότερον-ὕστερον !), *arché, anhypotheton, atomon,* and *minimum* (ἐλάχιστον).

The reflection on language which Plato used in the *Cratylus*, assigned to philosophical dialectic and to *noesis* the role of conceptual purification, which must straighten out the language that is positively constituted in two different directions; by means of the distinction of meanings, viz., by means of the discovery of the equivocities (homonymies) through *diaeresis* and definition, and vice versa, in the attempt to overcome linguistic pluralism in the widest signification of synonymy (then it was said to be polyonymy), helping the unitary concept to emerge.[6] If in the first case the issue is to eliminate the ambiguities by means of a statement of the difference of things in contrast to the deceptive identity of the word, in the second case it is instead a question of the elimination of the ambiguity by means of the evidence of the identity of the thing in contrast to the deceptive multiplicity of the linguistic statement. Dialectic as a universal semantics[7] undertakes, therefore, the function of the regulation of language, with the purpose of bettering the referential relation and with an undeniable tendency to fix terminologically language itself,[8] which, consequently, proceeds in the direction of an universal ideal language (*characteristica universalis*). Dialectic, to determine in a new way the relation of unity and multiplicity in language and thought, possesses an ontological importance and is, at the same time, in a normative relationship with the theory of the principles, which in the ultimate analysis grounds identity and difference and, hence also the possibility of a criticism of language. Because, on the other hand, the theory of the principles itself depends on language, it is possible to apply the methods of linguistic criticism of dialectic especially in view of an adequate conception of the principles and, hence, it turns out to be a self-grounding of dialectic. In this regard three positions are of particular importance.

1. It is necessary to state the difference of the signified, by unmasking the equivocations between the derived copies and the original

models (particular significations, general significations, and significations referring to the principles) and by learning to draw forth
from language the more universal significations by means of training in the process of abstraction (for example, by means of the
distinction of the unity in itself from sensible ones, from that of
mathematics and logic). The categorial distinction (which prepares
for the Aristotelian one), between being in itself and relative being
is also in the service of the theory of the principles, while the
distinction of types of propositions (*is* in the existential, copulative, veridical, and identity use) is not expressly made a topic of
consideration by Plato.

2. Vice versa, Plato was guided by language, when interpreting in the
   sense of the univocal (in the vocabulary of the time: *synonymy*),
   following a procedure of synoptic *generalization*, cognate significations having the same linguistic substrate, with the aim, in this way,
   of guaranteeing to the doctrine of the principles the greatest
   universality possible[9] (unity as "highest genus" and as "ultimate
   element,"[10] defined as "measure" in the threefold sense of the *unity
   of measure, norm,* and *limit*).

3. On the other hand, Plato, starting from his theory of the principles,
   tried to interpret as synonymies (in the language of those days to
   be *polyonymies*) the linguistically distinct character of unity, goodness (virtue), truth, and being (essence) and to refer them to a
   fundamental structure consisting in *being limited* and *determined*
   that is strictly connected with the definition of unity itself as
   "measure." Plato wants, evidently, to proceed more basically on the
   way of philosophical semantics, which is nothing more than an
   aspect of dialectic, and to define the terms *good, being, one,* and *truth,*
   notwithstanding differences of *intensional* connotations, as identical in their *extension*, precisely by means of the common *logos* of
   "that which is limited and determined from the original One." The
   prephilosophical linguistic use again furnished startingpoints in
   the sense that some connotations could favor this approach.[11]

On the whole, therefore, Plato, who in polemical contexts shows himself
to be rather a dialectician of distinction, in the heart of his philosophy, on
the contrary, shows himself to be not so much an analytic dialectician but
a synthesizing dialectician who proceeds with a synthetic-unifying method
and who also orients his criticism of language, in the last respect, toward
identifying mediations (for him the discovery of synonymy is more important than the discovery of homonymy). The fact that this attitude, notwithstanding the categorial and modal differences of Aristotelianism,
managed to survive up to the twentieth century with the formulation of the

problem concerning "Being" posited in a univocal manner depends on Plato and Porphyry. Porphyry, in fact, had given the Platonic *Unity itself* a clearer determination through designating it by the infinitive of the verb *"to be"* used as a substantive with the definite article, making it something actual and setting it in contrast with that which is.[12] Actually, the theory of the principles of Plato shows, more than all the rest of Platonic philosophy, that in notable measure Plato has philosophized starting from language and with language, but with the aim of proceeding beyond language.[13] The theory of the principles as the ultimate condition of the possibility of the nonequivocity and clear-cut linguistic and semantic correlations grounds, as a result, also the possibility of a universal ideal language critically purified from the philosophical standpoint and produces, because of its normative role within the ambit of praxis, the concrete carrying out of such a language.

Analysis of the Platonic Theory of the Principles from the Methodological-Logical Standpoint

From the *methodological standpoint*, Plato has distinguished for the first time in general a "heuristic nexus" and a "justificatory nexus" between the analytic and synthetic procedure (H. Reichenbach), albeit with a metaphysical and essentialistic intent. The mathematical sciences, in this, serve as a model chiefly with the arrangement of the series, the regularities of which Plato, on analogy with the modern recursive definitions, tried to interpret in terms of "generation," beginning from the elements themselves of the same kind, and in terms of asymmetry (irreversibility).

Starting points for a general set theory are found instead, at best, in the original structure of the material indeterminate principle of the great-and-small (as principle of multiplicity and degrees), prior to the specification of number and magnitude. On the other hand, the Platonic conception of the structure of being excluded an infinite in act,[14] just as it excluded the continuum, which was abandoned in favor of an ontology of the minima.

The organization of the sphere of the universals, which exploited the concept of the mathematical logos ("relation," "analogy" in the sense of equality of relationship, "proportion"),[15] as a system of relations exactly quantifiable (the theory of the Idea-numbers), used relations of equivalence (symmetrical relations), homomorphisms and isomorphisms, like the transitivity and asymmetry of numerical sets.[16] In this organization the ordering of the series, just as all derived systems of relations or as the Euclidization of geometry,[17] perhaps started by Plato, was understood and ontologically grounded as a limitation of multiplicity by means of unity.

Plato interpreted the rigorous relational structure of the sphere of the universals in the sense of an ontological primacy of Ideal Numbers. But only the successive *elementarizing* interpretation of the structure of the genera, which was given in the Platonic Academy, led to a weakening and falling away from the *generalizing* (viz., universalizing) form of thought by means of a conception, which understood the *universals as totalities divisible*[18] *into elements*, and with this anticipated, in a certain sense, the modern nominalistic interpretation of the universals (in Goodman and in others, classes are conceived as individual sums and wholes).[19] In this context elements of a class can also be spoken of, in the modern sense, whereas the concepts of element and *reduction* to the first elements, in general, in Plato and in Aristotle do not have anything to do with the theory of the universals and its method, but, usually, are in contrast with it (consult for example, Aristotle, *Met.* B 3).

The twofold function of the principles, understood as the *most general genera* and as *primary elements*, which corresponds to the twofoldness of the *generalizing* and *reductive* method, can be considered in relation chiefly with the distinction of Frege between signification (unitary) and sense (which depends on context).[20] The relation, in which the two *senses* of the principles (as highest genera and as primary elements) appear at first as logically incompatible, however, is to be understood in a more precise manner by reason of the ideal character of the principles also in their function as primary elements. In fact, the "reduction" of the ideal principled (in the first place of the Ideal Numbers, which by reason of their ideal status are not susceptible of arithmetical operations and are not comparable) by means of ideal principles is intended only as an improper formulation for expressing a constitutive relation, in virtue of which the ideal principled, like every being, is derived from the cooperation of unity as a formal principle and multiplicity as a material principle. The distinction between that which is a "deductive" principle, by means of which every being participates in unity and multiplicity, and the "constitutive" principle is not, hence, so great as to lead to the impossibility of their reconciliation. Actually, in the Ancient Academy it was marked a conflict only if the two types of consideration resulted in a contrast *under the same respect* or if the principles themselves risked being taken under more universal genera.

Moreover, the strictly logical conception of mathematics, to which Plato in the *Republic* seems to adhere with the subordination of mathematics to dialectic, may receive, in the light of the indirect tradition, some limitations. However, to insert mathematical models in the dialectic itself did not modify its specificity and competence, just as it did not modify the ideality of its objects, while, vice versa, the *Republic* (509B) and similarly the *Parmenides* (especially in the third hypothesis) also hint at a constitution of the universals.

Plato knew well that the ultimate principles and elements cannot be defined and demonstrated in the usual way.[21] On the other hand, he had joined the noetic comprehension of the principles to the condition of the capacity to give a definition (λόγος τῆς οὐσίας) of them.[22] Actually, there are some starting points on the basis of which it can be asserted that Plato did not affirm, as Aristotle did, the indemonstrability of the principles,[23] but that he rather took account of their peculiar status by a procedure that is comparable to the modern notion of *implicit definition*. The so-called trilemma of Fries, to which Aristotle already refers in the *Posterior Analytics* 1.3 (consult *Posterior Analytics* 1.8) and that goes back to the discussions in the Platonic Academy, quotes, among other things, the *circular proof*, which was maintained in the Academy, as can be documented, for example, in the case of the mathematician Menaechmus.[24] But it is believed that implicit definition can already be found in the mathematician Eudoxus, who collaborated with Plato.[25] Plato himself has now evidently tried to determine the principles, in demonstration and in definition, beginning from that which is principled. Thus unity is defined by him as "measure" (μέτρον) in relation to a subordinate multiplicity, viz., in the sense of a bipolar relation.[26] Such "definitions" actually had their origin in the mathematical sphere, and it can be shown that they are already present in the early Plato.[27] To deduce unity as (the most accurate) measure from a universal genus of "measure," which would suppress the character as principle of unity and would lead to an infinite regress, on the contrary, was excluded for what concerns the principle together with the exclusion of the infinite regress itself (we will immediately address the infinite regress argument and the "third man"); all the individual "measures" were rather to be determined by the reduction to the "most accurate" measure, viz., to the measure, which involves the absolute absence of parts and change, and hence to the fundamental and prototypical measure of the principle.

Moreover, Plato did not further analyze the polyvalent sense contained in the definition ("measure" as "unity of measure," "limit," and "norm"), but he has consciously maintained it as such in view of the interdependence and unitary foundation of ontological, epistemological, and axiological aspects. The definition of the principle contrary to the one (the principle of multiplicity and indeterminate degrees) was instead obtained by negation of the connotations of unity. On the whole, the Platonic claim of coming to an ultimate foundation is to be seen on the basis of this presupposition of the limited capacity of dialectic, which must go around the impasse by means of "circular" definitions of some concepts. However, the clarity of intellectual intuition (*noesis*) must come to the assistance of dialectic, bringing it positively to completion and exercising a controlling function.[28]

As a definition that starts from superordinated genera[29] was not possible for the principles, so it was not possible, in the strict sense, to admit the validity of the highest logical principles for them (the principle of contradiction, of the excluded middle, and so on), because the principles had to precede logic and first constitute it. Actually, the sphere of logic presupposes limitation and determination, just as the being to which it belongs, while the great-and-small is unlimited and unity is limiting (viz., precedes the limitation). The most general logical propositional principles, like the principle of contradiction[30] and the excluded middle,[31] presuppose, speaking in a more accurate manner, the metaphysical principles as prior, because identity and difference, on the one hand, imply multiplicity and, on the other, can be conceived and defined solely on the basis of the principle of determination. Insofar as, in addition, identity and difference fall under the principles as highest genera, these are, in the sense of trivalued logic, at the same time determinable and indeterminable by means of their species and hence involve, in this respect, undifferentiation.[32] In addition, the enunciation of the principle of contradiction, which repeatedly makes use of the concept of identity under different aspects, in the view of an ontology of "concepts," is presented as derived and principled.

The same may be said for the logical status of the principles in general; so it seems evident that the fundamental opposition between unity and duality (in the sense of not-unity) is determined as an opposition of contradictoriness, while the fundamental opposition between the aspects of duality (the great-and-small) is determined as the opposition of contrariety. These determinations, however, cannot be conceived except in a prototypical manner[33] and by analogy,[34] just as the principles can participate only by *analogy* in identity and difference.[35]

On the other hand, the principles, by means of their function as being the most general genera (schema of genera-species), by their mutual limitation as opposites and by their dialectical-definitional determination, are inevitably in a logical connection. The dilemma is resolved, probably, by specifying the "analogical" relationship that exists between the principles and the principled in the sense of the successive distinction between *complicatio* and *explicatio*, by giving significance to the logical determinations for the principles only *implicitly* and for the principled *explicitly*. The logical determinations can be formulated with their full sense only on the level of the principled.

The Third Man Argument in the Light of Recent Research

The argument of the *regress to infinity* (traditionally called the *third man argument*), referred to already by Plato in the *Parmenides* and employed against the doctrine of the Ideas, can be placed in analogical relationship with the antinomian traits of modern set theory and, therefore, under the rubric of self-predication as has been incessantly discussed in the last rubric of self-predication as has been incessantly discussed in the last decades (by Vlastos and others).[36] Actually, the supposed regress to infinity, which deprives the Ideas of their function as principles in relation to particular things, presupposes the self-application of the Idea in the form of self-predication (for example, the noble in itself is noble), which seems to carry it to the same level as particular things, and—on the basis of the further presupposition of the separation of the bearer of the quality and the foundation of the quality—carries to a new, "third" occurrence, in which the Idea on its side participates, and so on. The self-inclusion in the self-predication corresponds, here, in a certain sense, for example, to the formulation of the antinomy of Russell, according to which the set of all sets does not include itself (by definition) and at the same time includes itself (as a totality). The ancient formulation of the problem is distinguished from this Russellian one by the fact that it emphasizes not logical inconsistency but the further ontological consequences that are in the infinite regress.

In the context of recent research, however, the placing of the argument of the infinite regress and self-predication in relation to the theory of the principles of Plato is neglected, although both manifest their whole importance only in this context.

1. Not only certain spheres of species and genera of being, but *all* beings are in a relation of participation with respect to the principles.
2. The other Ideas as they are unities (monads and henads) have a relationship of special affinity to unity itself, which invites a further regress in the direction of a third, or fourth unity, and so on.
3. The theory of the principles, as the Aristotelian polemic demonstrates,[37] in addition, is exposed to an analogous regress, which reduces "unity" and "duality," by means of a regular deduction, to the genera of "number," "relation," and such.

The argument of the regress to infinity and its presupposition, self-predication, therefore, can be examined, for the purpose of justification, on the basis of the theory of the principles, in a sense, so to say, *prototypical*. In this regard the fact is important and decisive that not only the Academy but Plato himself [38] previously had expressly established the principle—which in the more recent research, as it seems, is not taken into consideration, too—according to which the members of a series and a hierarchy, that are among themselves in an ontological relationship of prior and posterior (πρότερον-ὕστερον), cannot have any Idea in common and hence cannot be susceptible of further *generalization*. This axiom, which maintains the preeminence of the difference between the grades of being and the levels of the hierarchies with respect to a formal equalization, corresponds, in its nucleus, to Russell's theory of types and to the *complements* connected to the modern arguments about antinomies. It does not exclude only the possibility of putting on the same level the Ideas and particular things, but in a more radical manner excludes the possibility of putting on the same level principles and principled—whether Ideas (that are intelligible principled) or individual things (that are sensible principled)—and therefore excludes the regress to infinity connected to it.[39] In addition, the axiom prevents a fortiori that derived genera, belonging themselves to the principled, as "relation" and such, by overturning the hierarchical order of being can be put above the principles (consult, what was said earlier on this point in 3). Independent of the theory of types, which guards the different levels of being against their being leveled, the axiom we discussed contains likewise a rule of separation,[40] which, in the case of conflict, reserves the primacy to the *reductive* method in relation to the *generalizing* method, for the purpose of guaranteeing to the *reductive* series together with their generative nexus all their theoretical weight.[41]

The permanent self-reference of the principles—unity is itself one, duality itself is dual, just as the noble itself is noble—in agreement with the theory of types, is of a different kind with respect to the relationship of participation expressed in the predication of individual things. The principles, therefore, like all the Ideas, but in a prototypical form, have a relationship precisely of participation with themselves, but not with another that ground them. With modern language this can be expressed by means of the semantic distinction of different types of predication (which, evidently, Plato did not have at his disposal);[42] in the case of the Ideas and in a preeminent manner in the case of the principles the *is* means identity and is not used as a copula as in the case of individuals. The principles, however, are elevated still beyond the other Ideas, because they, unlike the other Ideas, in a very strict sense admit, in general, *only* the self-predication of identity.

The Platonic Theory of the Principles as a Philosophical Axiomatic

Euclid distinguished in the first book, as is known, definitions, postulates, and axioms. Aristotle distinguished definitions, suppositions (hypotheses or enunciations of existence), and axioms;[43] and the follower of Plato, Speusippus, seems to have distinguished (indemonstrable) axioms and (demonstrable) theorems.[44] The term ἀξίωμα has been placed in relation, not without reason, with the dialectical disputes of the Academy.[45] Kurt von Fritz, then, has shown the plausibility[46] of the fact that the distinctions in Euclid and Aristotle, with respect to their content, in part are more ancient, but that the terminological distinctions would still have been incomplete.

In particular, at the time of Plato, the postulates and the axioms circulated only under the form and denomination of the term *definition*.[47]

Now mathematics functioned for the philosophy of Plato, and in a special way for the theory of the principles and for the unwritten systematic, from the formal and content standpoint as a model (this goes chiefly for the process of *reduction*, among others characterized by analysis and synthesis, for the formation of the series, for the conception of an ideal of exactness, and for the conception of the theory of Idea-numbers and final definitions); on the other hand, the axiomatization of Greek mathematics was further promoted through Platonic philosophy[48] and, precisely, not without relation for the theory of the metaphysical principles, of the highest "concepts" from which further propositions could be deduced through "definitions," especially those that stand at the basis of the mathematical sciences, as hinted at in the Sixth Book of the *Republic*, in the simile of the divided line.[49] In this strict interweaving of dialectic and mathematics, it seems obvious that Plato not only tried to provide a philosophical foundation for mathematics with his theory of the principles, for example with the theory of the proportions of Eudoxus,[50] but also that, with reference to mathematics, he has structured his own theory in its totality as a philosophical axiomatic and, hence, he developed it in a prevalently definitional system of principles and theorems. In proof of this, here are some supporting points.

1. Aristotle professed an axiomatic philosophy of the most general logical propositions, which, as ultimate foundation of demonstration, are beyond the axioms of the particular sciences (for this, the principle of contradiction is understood as "principle of all the other axioms").[51] Now these propositions belong, according to the Platonic conception, to the sphere of dialectic.

2. W. Schwabe, in his monograph on the concept of "element" (στοιχεῖον), has shown the plausibility [52] that the subjective signification of this word in the sense of "assumption," "fundamental proposition," occurs for the first time in Plato and it refers especially to definitions and postulates (suppositions).[53] In such a way, the relation between the theory of principles (with στοιχεῖα) and a (definitional) system of propositions seems to be established also from the terminological standpoint. This agrees likewise with the reflection that an ontology of predicates and "concepts," of the kind that Plato had, worked less with names than with relations of concepts, which are manifested chiefly in definitions (λόγοι).

3. To indicate that which Plato did not put into writing the summary denomination of ἄγραφα δόγματα was commonly used.[54] And with *dogmata* were understood not just mere "opinions" or

"views," but, rather, "doctrinal propositions." That, in any case, they were conceived as a system of propositions, in addition, is suggested by the Platonic term, close to this, of judgment (δόξα),[55] just as it is suggested by the formulation of the *Seventh Letter*, according to which the unwritten doctrines are enclosed in some concise formulas (ἐν βραχυτάτοις).[56]

In the light of these circumstances, the attempt at reconstruction of the unwritten doctrines of Plato as an axiomatic system of definitions or at least—conforming to the requirements of logic and modern epistemology—at representation of them in this way, is well justified.[57]

The first place in the philosophical axiomatic of Plato is obtained undoubtedly by the axiom of the principles that could also be called Plato's *universal formula*. It establishes, in the form of a definition of being, that *everything that is is constituted by means of the synergic action of a constant and a variable* and, precisely, of *unity* and *multiplicity*. The multiplicity, more accurately, is here understood as infinite greatness and infinite smallness ($\rightarrow \infty$ and $\rightarrow 0$), and by reason of this twofoldness of direction is called likewise indeterminate *duality*. The *universal formula* in equating being with the relationship of the two principles, expresses in a structural form the same thing which in general was expressed in the form of a generative model:[58]

$$E(x) = \bigwedge_x (x \in U \wedge x \in \hat{U})$$

(9.1)

The relation of the principles that are at the basis of every being can be specified by the definition of unity as "measure" (μέτρον) and, more accurately, in a prototypical manner as the most accurate measure (ἀκριβέστατον μέτρον, sc., πλῆθους). It specifies the definition in equation (9.1) in different ways: unity is referred to the unlimited multiplicity as its limiting principle (μέτρον in the ontological sense of limit), but at the same time it is referred also to the so limited multiplicity as absolute ("most accurate") unity of measure of it (in the epistemological sense) and as its absolute norm (in the axiological sense):

$$\bigwedge_{u_i} (u_i \in U)$$

(9.2)

The multiplicity of the meanings of the concept of measure contained in proposition (9.2) is explicated in the proposition that establishes the coextension of *unitariety* (limitation), *being, truth,* and *value* (goodness, nobleness, and so on). It corresponds to the proposition about the convertibility of the transcendentals belonging to medieval scholastics (*ens, unum, bonum, verum convertuntur*), with which, moreover, turns up, along with the principle of contradiction, on occasion as a metaphysical *axiom*.[59] The proposition, with the aid of the modern sign of equivalence, can be expressed in the following way:[60]

$$\bigwedge_x (E (x) \leftrightarrow B (x) \leftrightarrow V (x) \leftrightarrow u (x))$$

(9.3)

A further group of theorems can be derived from the axioms developed hitherto and chiefly from the basal axiom (9.1). This is the case in the first place, for the proposition not expressly handed down to us but clearly derivable, according to which every being is constituted by means of unity and multiplicity in such a way that either unity or multiplicity prevails. From this "axiom of prevalence" all the fundamental concepts of dialectic can be deduced, the fundamental logical principles, just as the principle of an hierarchical arrangement of being:[61]

$$\bigwedge_x \left[(u (x) > \hat{u} (x)) \;>\!\!-\!\!< (u (x) < \hat{u} (x)) \right]$$

(9.4)

From here follow, in the first place, the pairs of concepts of the categorial reflection, which represent the different modes of the predominance of unity or plurality (identity-diversity, equality-inequality, similarity-dissimilarity, being-in-itself relative-being, and others). On the basis of the concept of identity, then, the principle of contradiction can explicitly be formulated and, in addition, also the principle of the excluded third, while the concept of diversity embraces in itself the different forms of opposition (contrariety and contradictoriness):

$$\rightarrow (A \wedge \rightarrow A)$$

(9.5a)

$$A \vee \rightarrow A$$

(9.5b)

In a corresponding manner, the Meta-Ideas of equality and of inequality ground the special axioms of equality proper to the mathematical sciences,[62] just as the Meta-Ideas of rest and movement are represented as fundamental concepts of cosmology, astronomy, and physics.

The axiom of prevalence, however, shows its full importance only when the two modes of predominance are both referred to each other in degrees and in ontological hierarchies and, thus, are further differentiated each in itself by means of a scale. This is the well known Platonic distinction of ontological priority and posteriority (πρότερον—ὕστερον φύσει), which determines the whole construction of the arrangement of being right down to the particulars—first of all the difference between the intelligible and the sensible world—to which are connected the rules of transitivity, asymmetry, and hence onesided dependence (συναναιρεῖν καὶ μὴ συναναιρεῖσθαι):[63]

$$\bigwedge_{a \vee b} ([a, b] \in R) \Rightarrow \rightarrow ([b, a] \in R)$$

(9.6)

That which is ontologically "prior," with respect to what is ontologically "posterior," in conformity with proposition), is always distinguished by means of a greater quantity of unity. This also holds for the degrees of unity of the method of generalizing as well as for those of the reductive method. If there it is a question of a developing unity in the sense of identity, as for example, in the series ταὐτόν [sameness], viz., ἐν ἀριθμῷ-εἴδει-γένει-ἀναλογία, here it is a question, instead, of a growing unity in the sense of simplicity (as, for example, in the succession of the dimensions of body-surface-line-element of lines). Above all, the dialectical concepts of the construction of the arrangement of being are achieved in this way, as universal (genera and species)-particular, or part-whole (element-totality), which means that they are involved in propositions (9.4) and (9.6).[64] For all both types of method—that of generalizing just as that of the reduction—are valid, then, the rule developed in connection with proposition (9.6), which prevents the members of a hierarchical succession from further generalization and which, in the first case, is presented as a "theory of types," in the second case, instead, is presented rather as a rule of separation:[65]

$$(a, b) \in R$$

$$\rightarrow \bigvee_{a'} (a \in a' \wedge b \in a')$$

(9.7)

The fundamental propositions of Plato's theoretical construction, from what is still given and can be drawn from the tradition, with (9.1)–(9.7), are almost completed and determined in their intimate connection. Perhaps Plato made a distinction between *axioms* (9.1)–(9.3) and *theorems* (9.4)–(9.7) on the basis of the different mode by which they are proven: for the most on the basis of the different mode by which they are proven: for the most general propositions, in fact, could be treated only by a "demonstration" or preliminary argument and not by a deductive proof. Aristotle, in this case, would then have expressed in a more accentuated way the indemonstrability of the axioms and, at the same time, he would have in a novel way specified the concept of the axiom within regions of being and in the sense proper to the special sciences. Only the highest logical principles were maintained by Aristotle to be supergeneric and, as such, seem to have been derived from the general axiomatic theory of the Platonic dialectic.[66] The idea, however, that Aristotle would have been the first to draw up a general doctrine of science of the axiomatic type,[67] must certainly be abandoned. It is based on insufficient information, and precisely on the ignorance of the theory of the principles of Plato, which contains in itself all the connotations of an axiomatic foundation of philosophy and consequently all the sciences in their totality.[68]

The philosophy of Plato, therefore, on the basis of the fundamental positions of the unwritten doctrines, can be presented just like a *metaphysica more geometrico demonstrata* [a metaphysics using demonstration patterned on geometry, that is, a deductive model], in a unitary and binding form; in addition, it can be compared with modern axiomatic systems. In this, it is indisputable that the new development of post-Hilbertian axiomatic, with the definitive abandonment of the conviction of the existence of supreme and evident propositions, with the *deontologization* and the *formalization*—the propositional forms fixed axiomatically no longer contain truth value—from antiquity is far off and has gone its own, quite different path. Also the formal criterion of the absence of contradiction (consistency) does not have any comparable role in Plato. On the other hand, to the ancient and also to the Platonic less sophisticated axiomatic, the problem of the *application* that accompanies the highly formalized systems of the modern age, cannot yet be placed.

To prescind from such differences between ancient axiomatic and modern axiomatic, the essentialistic and metaphysical approach of Plato, as such, in the light of analytic philosophy poses particular problems. This holds not only for the deduction, which on the basis of the modern conceptions, appears defective—in fact, the principles furnish only the *necessary* conditions, not, the *sufficient* conditions, to explain what is derived from them—, but it also holds still more so for the synoptic procedure of confounding, viz., of unifying everything heterogeneously signified on the level of the principles, and it also holds for the tendency, really often exaggerated but which unfortunately is not to be excluded, toward the naturalistic fallacy (viz., for the tendency to derive the "ought" from the "is"), which was denounced by Hume and with respect to Plato, in another form, chiefly by Moore. The ever-increasing criticism of the ideal of an ultimate foundation removes Plato also from modern theory of science. Instead, other currents of contemporary philosophy, in this regard, are considerably closer to Platonism, first, among all, the tradition of transcendental philosophy, and we will be concerned with these in the next chapter.

10 The Theory of the Principles in the Light of Transcendental Philosophy

The Comparison between Platonism and Criticism Made by the School of Marburg

Modern transcendental philosophy since Kant's "Copernican revolution" reflects "critically" on the cognitive consciousness as on the authentic foundation ("the subject") and from such a standpoint tries to construct metaphysics and ontology in a new way. In this operation, however, the thematic of the foundation, the principles, and the categories of the old metaphysics is adapted and largely transformed on the basis of the approach of the problematic of subjectivity. Pointing out the way here, even before Aristotle, was the Platonic tradition that was carried on through Christian Neoplatonism and Leibniz to Kant. The criticism has been transformed, consequently, not without good reason, into a new Idealism; and it is not by chance that one of the masterpieces of the neo-Kantianism of Marburg is devoted to the *Doctrine of the Ideas of Plato*. Natorp has clearly recognized the theme of the ultimate foundation in the series of similes of the Sixth and Seventh Books of the *Republic*;[1] he, in addition, has interpreted the indirect tradition and defended it against the criticism of Aristotle.[2] On the other hand, Natorp followed throughout the hypothesis maintained by Zeller of the late dating of the doctrines contained in the reports on the unwritten doctrines, which, consequently, remain unused for the purposes of the explanation chiefly of the *Republic*. In addition, Natorp interpreted the Doctrine of the Ideas, beginning from the start, in a modern way, viz., as laws of thought posited by thought itself—the Idea of the Good is understood, consequently, as the "law of laws"[3]—and therefore, not recognizing the differences, lost also the possibility of observing the real points of contact and affinity between Platonism and the criticism of transcendental philosophy.[4]

The Further Perspectives Opened by the School of Tübingen: The Role of the Transcendental Foundation to the Platonic Principles

It is necessary to re-examine the relation between the Platonic transcendental ultimate foundations, considering that the basic statements of Book

Six of the *Republic*, which in this dialogue are maintained at a level that seems to be chiefly programmatic, can be determined and concretely specified in their peculiar intention precisely by means of the unwritten theory of the principles. If it is true that the problem of the transcendental philosophy turns around the conditions of the possibility of knowledge, then it is also true that an objectivistic ontology, that is, one not grounded in the theory of the subject, can contain some transcendental aspects. Already the theory of the universals, which is included in the Platonic theory of the Ideas, can be interpreted in a transcendental sense from the epistemological standpoint, insofar as it makes possible, explains, and guarantees the knowability of sensible things. The transcendental foundation tends, however, always toward unification in a supreme principle or in an ultimate set of principles. And to this, in Plato, corresponds in a first moment the explicit function of the "Good in itself" as principle of truth and knowledge (*Republic* 508E f.; 509B6). The "Good in itself," in the measure in which it confers knowability to the Ideas and indirectly to sensible things, implies an aspect of transcendentality, by virtue of which, along with its functions of grounding essence and goodness, it has also the transcendental function of grounding that makes possible the knowledge of all things. This formal characterization, however, as is known, in the *Republic* is not perfectly comprehensible in its intrinsic meaning. But the issue is clarified, if one also takes into consideration the unwritten theory of the principles, which is wholly explicit, with its determination of the Good as unity and fundamental unity of measure. The transcendental relation is then specified in the sense that "that which is the principle of our knowledge for each kind of thing, is the first measure of each kind of thing," and in the sense that "consequently, the principle of the knowable is always unity."[5] There is for each area, therefore, and furthermore for the totality of being, a transcendental point of reference, by virtue of which we can know all that which can be referred to it. This principle that guarantees knowability is not only unitary from the formal viewpoint, but it is so also from the standpoint of content, insofar as it is defined as the (absolute) unity in itself. And as such, it guarantees the structure and order of being, and it communicates, in addition, to each individual being unity, limitation, and determination. But the "the object of knowledge is in a higher degree that which is determined and ordered than that which is contrary to this,"[6] because to it belongs essentially consistency, identity, and distinction. Without the knowledge of the principles and first elements (ἄκρα, πρῶτα, στοιχεῖα), it is, hence, impossible, in the strict sense, that anything else can be known.[7] On the other hand, determination and limitation presuppose (unlimited) multiplicity, which, indeed, not directly as the principle of determination, but nevertheless, indirectly as its material substrate can be recognized as the condition of truth and knowledge. Therefore, Plato's theory of the principles shows a correlative character also in the transcendental perspective quite similar to contemporary transcendental philosophy which takes into account the correlative nature of the highest principles (for example, H. Wagner, subject-object, as previously Natorp and A. Görland; H. Holz, unity and multiplicity).[8] The theory of the principles, therefore, is also taken altogether as a transcendental foundation, from which the structural conditions of objective knowledge can be deduced. These conditions, however, are not limited only to the objects of each possible experience in space and time, but include likewise the sphere of the ideal and the intelligible perceived a priori.[9]

Starting Points Concerning the Theory of the Subject in Plato and Their Limits

The theory of the consciousness, conceived in terms of mind [*nous*] and soul [*psyché*], in this framework is allowed to enter in an objective manner, without leading to a theory of the "subject" in a criticalistic sense. Therefore, in Platonic philosophy there are starting points for a philosophy of consciouness as well as of transcendental philosophy, but there is no theory of consciouness qua transcendental philosophy (or vice versa), except on a subordinated and derived level: the unity and the order of the rational soul is a condition of its capacity to know, which, as such, also corresponds to the unity and determination of the object.[10] Objectively speaking, this, in a certain way, constitutes an anticipation of the transcendental unity and identity of the apperception of Kant, but in Plato it remains subordinated.[11] In fact, the identity and unity of thought, in their turn, have their transcendental justification in the metaphysical theory of the principles, without, as happens vice versa in criticism, the category of unity being conceived as dependent on transcendental apperception.[12] Therefore, the theory of the subject and the concept of the transcendental grounding in Plato and modern philosophy are between them in a relation of inverse inclusion, with different emphasis. In fact, transcendental philosophy, understood in the wide sense, in modern philosophy is approximately identical with the philosophy of the subject. This difference stands out still more clearly against the background of a marked likeness in the content. In addition, this makes comprehensible the fact that the correlation between subject-object in Plato cannot yet appear on the level of the principles as in modern transcendental philosophy; therefore, the theory of the principles, instead, so to speak, is limited to the sphere of the object. On the other hand, a transcendental philosophy consistently subject-based, moreover, would have to integrate the starting points for transcendental grounding in Platonic metaphysics and hence, interpret it as an unconscious dogmatic projection of the conditions proper to the subject. Unity in itself, then, must be deduced from the simplicity and identity[13] of the finite self-conscious-ness, just as the principle of multiplicity must be referred to the plurality relative to it.[14]

The Problem of the Justification of the Validity of Knowledge in Transcendental Philosophy and Plato

Transcendental philosophy does not coincide *simpliciter* with the theory of the validity of knowledge. In fact the conditions of every possible knowledge can be sought without inquiring into the validity of the cogni-tive truth claim and the means of which knowledge avails itself. Neverthe-less in Kant, the pure concepts of the intellect (the categories), as the transcendental conditions of every possible experience, are themselves justified in the transcendental deduction and thus their legitimacy and their objective validity are tested. Now, it is certainly accurate to state that the question of the validity of knowledge in this form, which belongs to the Kantian critical attitude, could not be positioned thus in Plato. However, the dialectical method of Plato has passed through the skepticism and (partial) agnosticism of the Sophists;[15] it operates, therefore, in whatever measure, on a comparatively dogmatic basis, yet in an analogous situation. For this reason, for Plato, the ultimate grounding in an "unconditioned" (ἀνυπόθετον) unity, dialectically ascertained and verified through the evidence of intellectual intuition, has such a central theoretical role. The "certainty" that the dialectical procedure achieves in the "principle"[16] as such, can be compared to the modern problem of the validity of knowledge in Kant; as in Kant the unity of self-consciousness guarantees the validity of the categories, but also the arrangement of the plurality achieved by the same categories—even in what concerns the relation of the categories among themselves[17]—so, in another manner, in Plato the unity in itself as unconditioned guarantees the character of truth chiefly of the categorial Meta-Ideas and the Ideal Numbers, which rule the organization of the intelligibles, and, indirectly, the character of truth of the intelligibles them-selves.[18] In this, both the classes of the Meta-Ideas (supreme categories and Ideal Numbers), insofar as species of unity, are directly referred to the unity of the basic principle.

The Theory of the Constitution of Reality in Kant and in Plato

In the more recent studies on Kant, the justifiable tendency can be noted of separating the theory of the constitution of objects from the question of the validity of knowledge and treating the latter as a matter of preference.[19]

Actually, the transcendental problem about the conditions of knowledge and its validity can also be maintained without a further ontological hypothesis, according to which consciousness imposes on the phenomena its regularity and even constitutes them by means of its spontaneity. The indications of the rebirth of a new critical realism in some contemporary authors seem to increase the affinities with precritical philosophy, but, in the case of Plato, it is more instructive to put in relation his theory of the constitution of reality bound to the metaphysical theory of the principles with that belonging to the Kantian critical attitude. The hint in the *Republic* (509B), that the Ideas (and indirectly, sensible things) receive their being from the "Good itself," just as in the sensible cosmos living beings receive it from the sun, in the unwritten systematic again becomes further specified in the sense that pure unity is posited in the unlimited measure and limit, and, consequently, differentiation, (self)-identity, essence, permanence, enduring consistency; pure unity grounds, in sum, the defining characteristics of substantiality. But unity also grounds all the species of determined relations and connections in the branches of being, which are at the base of judgment and proposition.[20] Being, therefore, is defined, in general, as that which is constituted by means of limitation and determination of (unlimited) multiplicity on the part of unity; and to this corresponds the fact that the principles themselves, insofar as they are constitutive of being, can be considered not as being, but must be considered as prior to being (beyond or beneath it).

If in this distinction between the formal determinations of being and the realities constituted by means of them there is an analogy between Platonic theory and the modern theory of the constitution of reality, this holds in a more complete way if the relation of the two theories with the transcendental standpoint is considered: in Plato, in the the determination of being, the ontological, epistemological, and veridical (concerning validity) aspects are given directly and originally on the same level; in Kant, the theory of the constitution demonstrates the regularity and objective validity of the series of the categories drawn from the theory of judgment and, hence, works toward the goal of guaranteeing the validity of knowledge.[21]

But the two theories are focused in different ways: whereas the theory of the constitution in Kant reinforces the weight of the central reflections on the problem of the theoretical validity of knowledge, in Plato the superior ontological aspect grounds the transcendental one, the concept of the constitution, however, carries, here, substantially beyond the latter issue.The process of the constitution of reality, in Plato, is conceived primarily as the structuring of reality starting at its highest principles, in which the relation between the principle and the principled is seen in a stricter manner than that in a proper deductive process of the genera-species kind. This relation has a transcendental aspect, but it is not resolved into it.

Moreover, the metaphor of "generation," which illustrates the grounding nexus, in Plato does not have any temporal meaning, just as it does not have one in the theory of the constitution of being in Kant. (The Ideas as entities free from every form of process can be represented , at best, as perduring in being, but cannot be represented as brought to being, viz., as generated.) The metaphor of "generation" should rather—and in this, Plato again gets nearer somewhat superficially to Kant— evoke the spontaneity for understanding through successive discursive achievement in the contemplator, who, as a finite being in contrast to the all-encompassing *intuitus* of an *intellectus divinus*, has need of such a successive display.[22] Another important difference between the theory of the Platonic constitution and the modern one is in the fact that, in Kant, the multiplicity of the things constituted is explained as function of a theory of the principles, but not that of the constituents (viz., the series of purely categorial concepts of the intellect). In Plato, on the contrary, the concepts of categorial reflection (the Meta-Ideas) in their multiplicity are deduced from the (unlimited) multiplicity (of the great-and-small) as from their material substrate. In this regard in the conception of the constitution of reality Plato outlines a metaphysical plurality of degrees; the structural correlative of unity and multiplicity in its grounding function emerges at the same time on the level of the theory of the principles.

The Progressive Procedure and the Regressive Procedure in Kant and in Plato

Kant, in *Untersuchung über die Deutlichkeit der Grundsätze* (1764) (*Researches on the Clarity of the Principles*), defined the difference in the philosophical method to that of mathematics as analytical-regressive and in some of his critical works he followed this procedure in the exterior representation as well.[23] W. Röd has pointed out the importance of the analytical method for modern philosophy from the seventeenth century onwards and placed it in relation with the modern sciences of nature.[24] Instead, the limits of the confines traced by Kant between philosophy and mathematics is connected more easily to Plato's problematization of mathematics contained in the *Republic* (Book Six, at the end), and it futher can be tied to the Platonic distinction between analytic *ratio cognoscendi* and the synthetic *ratio essendi*. Actually, the Kant of the critical period moved from the foundation so achieved, and placed synthesis beside analysis and progression alongside regression. The progression for transcendental philosophy is even constitutive, if it wishes to be something more than a mere metatheory; in fact, the discussion about the reception of Kant on the part of analytical philosophy has demonstrated that a simple ascent in a descriptive manner to the conditions that make knowledge possible leaves open and unresolved the problem of the validity of knowledge (for example, in the early Strawson).[25] In this regard, a methodological affinity exists between Platonism and transcendental philosophy: also in Plato the principles are at first discovered by, and drawn from, the analytical-regressive procedure, and only afterwards does the progressive-synthetic deduction follow the principled beginning from the principles.[26] In addition, both in Kant and in Plato, a linearity of the development of thought is to be noted, which, in Kant, from the unity of the self-consciousness throughout the deduction of the categories leads to the axioms, and in Plato, from the principles through the categorial Meta-Ideas and the Ideal Numbers leads to the remaining universals and the sensibles.[27]

The Conception of System in the Unwritten Doctrines of Plato and Its Relation with the Modern and Transcendental Conception

This arouses the question of if and at what point, in Plato, a concept of system in its actual meaning, which has been developed in modern times, is present. M. Heidegger has replied to the question in a decisively negative manner, and explained the concept of system that is handed down, on the basis of the pressure exercised by the problem of the certitude of knowledge characteristic of the modern period, which would have led to the peculiar conception of a "system" of certain knowledge obtained in an *a priori* way.[28] Now, a situation in antiquity comparable to this one in the modern period has not certainly existed; however, other reasons, such as the soteriological problem of the conduct of life that is secure in Hellenism (Stoicism as well as Epicureanism) or the dogmatic needs in late antiquity (as, for example, Proclus), have resulted analogously in the construction of systems. Therefore, a more specific solution must be looked into also in the case of Plato that takes account of the fact that already Plato—and not only, the modern period, as Heidegger supposes[29]—allowed for the introduction of starting points of a philosophy *more geometrico demonstrata* [as axioms] and connected to this a conception of reality as totally knowable and available. If, therefore, the specifically accentuated modern concept of system that involves absolute self-consciousness is yet missing certainly in all antiquity and in Plato, existing analogies can still be recovered, like both the methods, as well as the types of structures of the theories. The method of regression and progression, which proceeds in opposite directions, like linearity, together with the elements structurally linked to them, connects Plato's philosophy with modern transcendental philosophy.

On the basis of these common features in Plato, therefore also, a *systematic* can be legitimately spoken about,30 even if, in its purpose and other features which characterize it, it is differentiated from the typically modern systematic. This difference is revealed, for example, in the fact that the regression and progression, notwithstanding the dialectical method that comprehends it, also leaves room for a pluralism of the particular spheres of interest and their special methods (*generalization-reductionism*), a pluralism that also has its downfall in the operational polyvalence of the theory of the principles.[31] The addition of further realms and special methods is generally possible in this open systematic, from which consequently, the possibility of modifications on the level of the theory of the principles also is not excluded. A certain preeminence of the method of regression with respect to progression is manifested in this, the methodological peculiarities of which latter, moreover, it is hardly possible to reconstruct in detail.[32] On the other hand, in Plato, the concept of grounding is not yet defined on the basis of the principle of sufficient reason, arising from the Christian doctrine of creation *ex nihilo* and formulated for the first time by Leibniz.[33] Therefore, to Plato the distinction between cause and effect, reason and consequence is still extraneous. The Platonic systematic and its theory of basic principles almost throughout, offers therefore, only the necessary conditions and not the sufficient ones, conditions that, usually, do not at all explain being in a determined mode of things derived from it but their existence only in an incomplete manner. Only a few essential ontological determinations can be deduced in the strict sense from the Platonic theory of the principles. The Platonic claim of furnishing an ultimate foundation does not exclude, therefore, a weak point in the deduction and a *deficit* in the explanation. However, the distance with respect to transcendental philosophy, on this point, is not entirely untraversable: the deduction of the content of the categories and judgment in general from self-consciousness remained, for Kant, on an aporetic-programmatic level,[34] just as, it seems, for Plato the generation of Ideal Numbers from the first principles remained on an aporetic-programmatic level. In other words, in an analogous manner, the transcendental unity of apperception offers only necessary conditions, but not sufficient ones in the sense of the requirements of the principle of sufficient reason, for the explanation of the unity of judgment and the series of the categories.[35] In addition, in Kant, unlike Plato, the formal mediation between the unity of self-consciousness and the plurality of thoughts already is problematic. New attempts at reconstruction have therefore postulated, following the theory of the self of phenomenology (and the developments of the same, for example in R. Hönigswald and W. Cramer), for the identity of pure apperception having a purely logical rigor, passages almost temporal, which aim at making the connection of the multiple contents of the representations with the unity of self-consciousness comprehensible and which must be controlled specifically by means of the categories.[36] But, as a result, the multiplicity is already made to enter into the unity of self-consciousness as such, the identity of which is understood as the determination of relation-ship and comparison of the data of consciousness. Independent of various theoretical problems that arise, a re-Platonization is announced here, by considering the issue from the historical point of view, insofar as the theoretical correlativity of the principles of unity and multiplicity is again carried into effect purely on the level of a theoretical position strictly grounded on subjectivity.

Conclusion: Historical Antecedents of Transcendental Philosophy in Platonic Ontology

Transcendental philosophy cannot deny its historical antecedents in the metaphysics of the Platonic tradition. In the light of the theory of the principles and the unwritten systematic of Plato, the affinities appear to be even closer (for example, the ultimate grounding by means of a unifying principle, the detailed linear stressing of regression and progression, the theory of the constitution), while Neoplatonism, from a certain viewpoint, functions historically as a mediator, but in other points, methodologically, is inferior to both (for example, in the correlativity of the principles and the rigor of the dialectical deduction employed by original Platonism).

Owing to all of these things, the possibility is offered, with the aid of conceptions furnished by transcendental philosophy, in part to restore, in part to complete, by way of reconstruction and specific differentiation, the methodology and topic of arguments of Platonism, which in its details are lost for the most part. The analogy is presented much more easily, when the transcendental philosophy relies on the distinctions of later metaphysics and first philosophy. Thus it is, for example, in the attempt to interpret the fundamental nexus existing between the principles and the principled, at the same time, also as a relation of explication.[37] This relation of explication in transcendental philosophy includes a modification of the relation be-tween the principle and the principled conceived by Plato as strictly asym-metrical,[38] since now the level of the principled is a necessary condition (but not a sufficient one) for the explication of the principles.[39]

A self-grounding of the principle, which Platonism recognizes beginning from Plotinus,[40] by reason of the convertibility of the ground and the grounded *in* the principle, considered from the transcendental viewpoint, implies its self-application; viz., implies that the principle supports the same conditions of knowledge for itself that it posits for other things.[41] With this the problems, posed by analytic philosophy, of self-predication and the predication of identity in Plato converge, which in the preceding we have seen must be applied to the theory of the principles.[42] In the concrete this means, in the present context, that the principle of determination is veridical and knowable for the reason that it is itself not only determining, but—as pure unity—also determined par excellence.[43] The same holds for the contrary principle of indeterminate and unlimited multiplicity, that, as it grounds indirectly the truth of each relationship and every totality, just so itself is *per eminentiam* veridical and knowable,[44] because transcendentally conditioned by itself, that is, by multiplicity.

In the conviction that the ultimate foundations in the strict sense are possible only with a type of circular proof, the contemporary transcendental philosophy meets with Plato, but also with Aristotle and his dialectical "demonstration" or elenchic-apagogical proof of the principle of contradiction.[45] However, such an elenchic "demonstration" represents only a special significant case of the general dialectical "demonstration" of the principles beginning with the principled, which—formally belonging to the circular type of proof [46]—had a genuine place in the regressive procedure in the sphere of interest of the unwritten systematic of Plato.

11 *The Theory of the Principles in the Light of Hegelianism*

A Comparison of the Platonic Theory of the Principles and Hegel's Logic

The well-known preference, based on an actual affinity of content,[1] that Hegel evidenced for Neoplatonism in the sphere of ancient philosophy, on the one hand, and the historical relation, on the other, between Neoplatonism and the indirect Platonic tradition, which has been studied in detail in the twentieth century,[2] suggests in ever-increasing way that an opportunity for establishing the relations that exist between the unwritten theory of the principles of Plato and the position of Hegelianism, has now arrived. A first important attempt has already been made by J. N. Findlay,[3] who has not limited his inquiry to Hegel and also introduced into the argument his own theoretical convictions.

A comparison of the unwritten theory of the principles and the systematic of Plato especially with the *Logic* of Hegel is appropriate, because Hegel himself in the *Logic* of Jena also has integrated in a fruitful manner into his own speculative dialectic Platonic dialogues, for example, the *Parmenides* and the *Philebus*, as well as the *Sophist*, dialogues that stand closest to the unwritten doctrines (you find in Hegel the concepts of unity-multiplicity, determination-indetermination, limitation-nonlimitation; that is, πέρας-ἄπειρον, a proportion that includes definition and division).[4] Also, later Hegel praised the *Parmenides*, saying that it was "the most famous masterpiece of Platonic dialectic," and he connected it with his own logic of being, just as he connected the *Sophist* with his logic of essence.[5] In addition, Hegel had knowledge of some important reports of the unwritten doctrines handed down through the indirect tradition (Aristotle, *Met.* A 6; Sext. Emp., *Adv. math.* 10.248 ff.; *LCL* 3:331, 333; and others) whose philosophical meaning he judged to be just as valuable and which he likewise tried to put in relation to his own speculative position.[6] Hegel also was aware that between the direct and indirect Platonic tradition is a difference in degree of explication, which he took in relation with his distinction between "representation" and "concept"—these are mixed between them in the dialogues, while in the oral doctrine the concept predominates—and also with the conception of the "systematic."[7] Hegel, however, did not make a systematic use of the testimonies, since the first collection, edited by Brandis, was published only in the last decade of his life (1823).

From a historical standpoint Hegel interpreted the late dialogues of Plato, wrongfully, as having a speculative character, viz., on the basis of the identity of identity and nonidentity; and, in addition, he interpreted the *Sophist* and the *Philebus* in terms of his own system, but inverted the valuation they had in Plato, understanding them as a progress and con-cretization compared to the abstraction of the *Parmenides*.[8] On the other hand, Hegel did not find in Plato the explicit formulation of the systematic synthesis of the contraries as a negation of negation, the subjectivity of the concept, and the systematic development of concepts, which in Plato would be substituted by means of "exterior reflection," which is based still on prephilosophical representations and on a pure comparison of them.[9] A unified and consistent utilization of the indirect tradition, which permits recognition of the undoubtedly present outlines of a systematic linear progression in the sphere of the unwritten Platonic doctrine, however would have led Hegel necessarily, on the final point, to a different evalua-tion of Plato.

The philosophy of Hegel can be understood as a following out and deepening of Platonic-Neoplatonic philosophy, filtered through the modern transcendental philosophy; and this is evident chiefly in the unity of the dialectical method and ontology, in the realism of the universals of an essentialistic character, in the threefold distinction of levels: (1) of the principles (viz., of the absolute), (2) of the logical transcendental principled, and (3) of the real principled things, just as in its declared scope of renovat-ing the old metaphysics on the basis of Kantian criticism.[10] The advancement of the *Phenomenology of the Spirit* to absolute knowledge, the explanation of this in the categories of the Logic and their extrinsicizing emanationism in nature and in history recalls the twofold ordering of the contrary direction of the ways of knowledge and being in Plato and Platonism.[11] However, the fundamental traditional schema, in Hegel, is radically changed in its direc-tion; and, in part, it is even overturned into its contrary: the schema of the ordering of being of the *Logic*, in Hegel, goes not toward the lower, but from the lower to the higher, and only at the end, with an increasing enrichment and a concretization of the basic empty and abstract categories, leads to the absolute. In other words, it presents a parallel with respect to the process and the ordering of knowledge of the *Phenomenology*, insofar as the progress, in a strict sense, is a return to the principle of the absolute Idea, as to that which is first in itself. The traditional opposition of the direction of the ontological and the epistemological process is thus overcome and the ordering of being has achieved a greater weight, because, to speak in this way, it continues the process of ascent.

The Aristotelianizing turn of Hegel is revealed again when the pure *logos* of the *Logic*, through the reduplication of the subject-object of the finite consciousness, mediates once again with itself and in this way, by reflecting, becomes aware of the identity of the subject-object implicit in it. Only in the absolute Spirit, viz., in the absolute reflection of philosophy, does the Absolute return to itself and is it fulfilled, knowing itself as the perfect identity of subject and object. In the Absolute, which as a result is ultimate but in itself is first, the principle and end of the total process are joined together in a circle. Absolute knowledge recognizes that all the degrees and all the objects are only moments and abstractions of itself that absolute knowledge is carrying out in itself.

One of the consequences of this philosophy of consciousness, which develops the theoretical approach of subjectivity proper to transcendental philosophy, consists in the fact that the sphere of the *logos*, of the pure categories, culminates in a logic of the concept that is still extraneous to ancient metaphysics and that historically is connected to the transcendental apperception of Kant. Another consequence lies in the fact that the supreme categories of being of traditional metaphysics have lost their autonomy and are reduced to mere abstractions and moments of a concrete absolute. Thus, in Hegel, the principles and the Meta-Ideas of Platonism, so to speak unity-multiplicity, being-nonbeing, equal-unequal, more-less, appear as mere abstractions,[12] which must be carried out by further development of thought and achieve their concretization in the real world turned "upside down."[13] Not the degree of universality, but interior richness and the fullness of the category determines their range in the sphere of being. Pure unity in itself, therefore, as in Plato, cannot claim to have a grounding function on the transcendental or ontological level, but it remains, as pure multiplicity or pure indetermination or as being and nonbeing (nothing), referred structurally to the absolute Idea as to the richest form of the concept and, finally, to absolute knowledge.[14] Platonism, hence, can represent itself in its content within Hegelianism, but as a result receives, in consequence of the criticism of Hegel, a different function insofar as it is included in a more ample context, while considered in itself it remains abstract.[15] According to Hegel, a relation of inclusiveness exists between the philosophies of Plato and Hegel, which, however, in its details is developed further into a relation of explication and specification.

In addition, Hegel, by conceiving the Absolute not as a super-mundane stage but as a concrete totality, escapes from the difficulties of Plato and ancient metaphysics, viz., to have to deduct logic from the Absolute and nonetheless, in the development of the process of knowledge, to have logic apply to the process. Hegel did not ground his logic on a level different from it, but he carried it out in the concrete together with the structuring of the whole of knowledge.[16]

On the other hand, Hegel is grouped with Plato and differs from Kant, by the fact that the finite subjectivity is placed within the sphere of interest of the absolute validity of an absolute (divine) Subjectivity—of the absolute Idea—and by that supports the requirement of further transcendental criticism. Hegel's objective Idealism like Plato's maintains a position that transcends the subject critically and as a result distinguishes the dimension of the principles from that of contingent facticity (empirical subjectivity).[17] The finite subject, consequently, also in the Hegelian outline focused on subjectivity, is deduced and explained in a way comparable to that of Plato.[18] Certainly the total nexus, in Hegel, is once more overextended in a subjectivistic sense, since, secretly, the Spirit, in general, is found everywhere always on the way that takes it back to itself.

Identity and Difference in Hegel and the Unwritten Doctrines of Plato

Moreover, if we try to be more specific about the theory of the principles of Plato in the system of Hegel, then we enter into the issue, above all, concerning the categories of identity and difference. We find that Hegel treated them in the logic of essence and conceived them as reflexive forms, which are nearer to the absolute ground, of being and nothing,[19] from which—as from categories which are the most general and most empty— the conceptual development of logic starts. But being is also represented by Hegel as unity.[20] Moreover as, historically considered, the infinitive form "to be," actually, used as a substantive with the definite article, represents a Neoplatonic interpretation of the Platonic "unity itself."[21] In accord with such a conception and supported by the Platonic *Parmenides*,[22] in the writings of the period of Jena, Hegel had specified the Absolute still as the identity of unity and multiplicity. In the succeeding *Logic* this is replaced, instead, by the determination of the Absolute as the identity of identity and nonidentity or as the unity of being diverse and nondiverse.[23] Conforming to this, Hegel also interprets the unity and duality of the indirect Platonic tradition in the sense of identity and indetermination and reveals their cooperation, relationship, and opposition in each individual being.[24]

In the speculative formula of Hegel concerning unity or the identity of identity and nonidentity, unity, however, is always conceived dialectically in itself, since on the level of the synthesis also there is no unity without difference just as there is no difference without identity. The identity of identity and nonidentity is therefore, at the same time, the nonidentity of identity and nonidentity. This means that in Hegel, as in Plato, the conception has to be made with a correlativity of the supreme categories, which are reciprocally implied in one another.[25]

The speculative dialectic of this correlation, which makes the correlatives inseparable from each other not only really but also conceptually is new with respect to Plato. This speculative dialectic is rooted in the subjectivistic approach of Hegel and, in consequence, becomes reflected only at the end of the logic of the concept, in summary fashion, in association with the free "I" as the true infinite and in the context of the Absolute Idea. While Plato maintains only the thesis of a mixture of the supreme contraries and therefore maintains the validity of the principle of contradiction,[26] Hegel instead goes beyond Plato in a conscious manner, by making the opposites pass into one another (in the logic of being) by the suspension of the principle of contradiction, or (in the logic of essence) by making them appear in their contrary, or (in the logic of the concept) making them continue one into the other.[27] The position of pure identity and pure difference is considered instead by Hegel as a consequence of the extrinsic reflection and, hence, as an abstraction of the intellect.[28]

The Platonic theory of the principles and of the categorial Meta-Ideas, in this perspective, appears as the product of a "philosophy of reflection" that is arrested at the contraries without working out their ultimate synthesis. The Platonic theory of the principles and categorial Meta-Ideas, hence, after a first metaphysical abstraction of the most universal categories, falls into a second abstraction, by not placing these categories in a sufficient mutual relation and, hence, arresting them prematurely in an "extrinsic" reflection limited to placing them in a mere comparison. Only distantly comparable to that of Hegel is Plato's intention in conceiving the principles by including synoptically in them different functional aspects.[29] Such an intention is not motivated by the dialectical viewpoint, just as the conception of the *coincidentia oppositorum* (the identification of opposites) in the absolute One is not, which from Proclus through Nicholas of Cusa went on to Spinoza and Schelling and which, in the ultimate analysis, is resolved into an undifferentiated stasis.

On the contrary, Hegel's interest is focused on the speculative conception of the movement of the concept, with which he assumes a position unmistakably intermediate between the dialectic of distinctions proper to the Platonic theory of the principles and the basic monism of the Neoplatonic tradition. But Hegel agrees with Plato against the Neoplatonists, insofar as he shows in detail the dual fundamental structure likewise in the principled, in which however, the implications and the completion of Hegel is lacking in Plato. For the rest, from the theoretical standpoint, both are consistent Plato, from his viewpoint, by following the generalizing method, places unity above identity, and Hegel, on the contrary, gives the preeminence to the more concrete and determined identity with respect to unity.[30]

A further important difference between Plato and Hegel consists in the fact that, in Plato, the principle contrary to the One grounds plurality and difference (being diverse) in the most general sense, while in Hegel, conforming to the principle of Spinoza *omnis determinatio est negatio* (all determination is negation), the *determined* negation (the *non*identity!) emerges into the foreground in a more specific way. The criticism of Hegel coming from neo-Kantianism (for example, by H. Rickert and W. Flach),[31] which proposes a softening of the principle of negation in favor of a more general *heterology* (an account of otherness), could appeal not only to the *Sophist* of Plato but in a more fundamental way also to his theory of principles. Consequently, the Platonic concept of determination belongs to a more universal level than that of Hegel, even if "limitation" also can be interpreted as a negative separation (*per negationem* [through negation]) from an infinite[32] (from the contrary unlimited principle). The nexus between the single steps of the determination is shaped, in the Platonic theory of the constitution of things, as a succession of diverse degrees and levels of a mixture, in which unity and multiplicity compenetrate each other "successively" not as in Hegel, like a spiral process that moves toward itself.

Lastly, it is instructive to show that, in comparison with Plato, Hegel has begun a change of emphasis in the relation between unity and multiplicity, identity and difference,[33] a change that is further reinforced by the young Hegelians and by other thinkers of the twentieth century (for example, Heidegger, Adorno, and still others).[34] It tends to emphasize, evidently in opposition to monism proper to the Neoplatonic-Christian tradition, difference and nonidentity in a more marked manner than unity and identity, while in Plato unity is considered, in an unequivocal manner, to be privileged.[35]

The Linear Progression and Nexuses of the System in Plato and Hegel

Against the comparison between Hegel and Plato in the preceding pages, it could seem possible to object that such a comparison could be sustained without bringing to bear the unwritten doctrine of the principles, simply by referring to the *Parmenides*, a dialogue with which Hegel expressly associated himself. However, in our attempt, we rather propose a comparison between the position of the whole of Plato with Hegelianism and to make it thus enter into an actual living philosophical debate and not, on the contrary, a reconstruction, once again, of the influence historically exercised by the Platonic writings or even to integrate it by means of the discovery of forgotten relations between the indirect tradition, Neoplatonism and Hegelianism. But chiefly, to take this into consideration,[36] viz., that only on the basis of a knowledge of the indirect tradition, we can be in a condition to place the *Parmenides* in relation to its proper position among Platonic works in an authentic and incontrovertible manner and, in particular, interpreting it on the basis of the Platonic theory of the principles. In addition, only the indirect tradition offers the possibility of referring the allusions and hints from the *Parmenides* to a more ample theoretical context, in terms of content and chronological development, and, in this way, to build bridges to the other dialogues like the *Sophist* and the *Republic*. For both reasons, the attempt to make a comparison between the whole position of the historical Plato with a contemporary position like Hegelianism—and the same would be true of the comparison with transcendental philosophy made in the preceding chapter—even for all the points which we have treated in the preceding pages cannot renounce a knowledge of the indirect tradition, which found some expression in the *Parmenides* or in other dialogues.

In a much greater measure and in an entirely unequivocal way this holds for those parts of the indirect tradition which have not entered into the written works of Plato, and which, hence, remained in this sense really unwritten. Therefore, we propose to compare these doctrines with Hegelianism in the remaining part of this chapter.

The supposition of Hegel according to which Plato "in his oral arguments proceeded also in a systematic manner" and thetic-"dogmatic,"[37] is confirmed on the basis of the serial structure of the processes of reduction and linear deductions spoken about in the reports that have come down to us on the unwritten doctrines. In these series, in fact, are present a movement of progression and a movement of regression in the contrary sense, which in essential points prefigure metaphysically the concept of foundation and explanation and the analytico-synthetic procedure of the new Idealism and in particular of Hegel. Plato has fixed in a thematic manner the linearity of the process of the formation of the series and the hierarchical structure[38] and he has likewise expressed its regularity also from the terminological standpoint (the relation of ontological priority and posteriority was understood as an asymmetrical but transitive relation; the non-reciprocity of dependence was specified as a relation of "being destroyed together with that which is destroyed and not being destroyed together with that which is destroyed"). And even if the procedure of Plato is not perfectly unilinear as that of Hegel and continues according to different lines of force—the relations between genus and species, and part and whole constitute, in any case, separate lines—the tendency in Plato to systemize is, notwithstanding, here, effectively undeniable. It is clear, hence, that the mixture and the interweaving of the Ideas, which are presented in dialogues like the *Sophist* and the *Parmenides*, do not represent the last word of Plato on the theme of first philosophy, but simply show some parts of a much more ample context. The analogy with the development of the concept of Hegel, in truth, carries far beyond. The reproach of "exterior reflection" made by Hegel against the dialogues of Plato and especially the *Parmenides*, viz., the absence of the interior development of the concept, can therefore be fully refuted, or at least restricted, precisely on the basis of the unwritten systematic of Plato, by taking into account, naturally, that it is not yet a question of the speculative nexuses in the Hegelian sense, insofar as in Plato the conception of the synthesis of contraries is lacking. In any case Plato was not satisfied, as the dialogues leave us instead to believe, with a non-mediated comparison of the conceptual determinations, but he undoubtedly carried through the logical connection of the categories in a systematic arrangement, in which each category is deduced and grounded by the corresponding place that theoretically belongs to it within the system. This holds, above all, for the progression that is proper to the structure of the order of being, which, with the "generation" and constitution of the individual areas of being together with their categories and beginning from the principles, offers a distant, not a speculative, correspondence (insofar as, as we have already said, the moment of synthesis is lacking) of the development of the concept of Hegelian logic. And in this realm some of the categorial entities already appear that have an essential role both in the logic of being and in Hegel's logic of essence, as we will see further on.[39]

In what measure Plato aimed at a methodic and argumentative specificity of the progressive *ratio essendi* (the order of being), can be drawn from the reports on the unwritten doctrines with sufficient clarity.[40] Plato, as Hegel, always proceeds from the more simple to the more complex and the more concrete, and in this process, little by little, the negative principle—the unlimited duality (Plato), the nothing in the form of the nonidentity and the determinate negation (Hegel)—penetrates by degrees into being and changes it, converting it to new forms.[41] And as Hegel conceives the movement of the concept of the *Logic*, to begin at the logic of being through the logic of the essence up to the logic of the concept, as an increase by degrees of the relation and the interior reflection of the categories up to the moment of self-reference of the Subjectivity itself,[42] thus also Plato instituted his special doctrine of the categories, ordering it by reason of the increasing degrees of relation,[43] which from a prevalence of unity leads to a prevalence of multiplicity, and consequently, but in this contrary to Hegel, proceeding in the sense of an ontological diminution, while in Hegel they proceed in the sense of an ontological augmentation.

The "progression" proper to the order of being, grounds, in Plato, the "regression" proper to the order of knowledge. The order of knowledge follows, in its process of structuring, in the direction opposite to the order of being, and in this process the ontological grounding nexus, step by step and degree by degree—without discontinuous jumps—in the long way of learning, must be gained by work and interior assimilation in successive stages. The specifically Platonic theory of teaching and learning, which Plato developed programmatically in the *Phaedrus* (consult Appendix 1.1) and in the *Seventh Letter* (consult Appendix 1.2) and applied in outline in the projected education course in the *Republic*, therefore, in point of fact, is to be referred to the context that is the founding nexus of the unwritten doctrine and only by means of this assumes a precise concretization; it explains, at the same time, that and why this systematic must remain unwritten. In Hegel, there is a theoretical correspondence of this in the way of the "experience of consciousness," of which the *Phenomenology of the Spirit* speaks, which "mediates" the common consciousness[44] with absolute knowledge through a series of provisional but necessary degrees of "phenomenal" consciousness.

The display of absolute knowledge in the *Logic*,[45] itself, however, in Hegel—to prescind from inverting the importance of the start and goal—is undoubtedly a key indicator of the modern philosophy of subjectivity, to which at best, in Plato, only the weak analogical correspondence of the metaphor of the "generation" of the deduced entities can be compared;[46] with the proviso that the "self-movement of concepts" in Plato cannot be spoken of, just as an ultimate identity of subject-object cannot be stated. Common to Hegel and Plato is the structural linking of the cognitive consciousness to a non-interchangeable succession of categorial determinations, which it must first pass through successive stages to grasp the Absolute—the sphere of the principles, the absolute Idea. In Hegel, however, the foundation of the succession is in the succession itself, whereas in Plato the foundation of the succession must be looked for, afterward, in the *ratio essendi* of the order and structure of being. In overcoming this distinction, once again, a progress achieved by Hegelianism in comparison to the ancient metaphysics ought to be acknowledged.

The Coherence Theory of Truth in Plato and in Hegel

The nexus of the system becomes relevant, in Hegel, for the concept of truth and validity, which is gauged on the basis of a theory of coherence; in fact for Hegel "truth is the whole," the totality. The whole, however, is only the essence that is completed by its development, in which each individual thing has its justification only as a moment of the whole.[47] The coherence of the totality is guaranteed by the dialectical method, which leads, by the constant fundamental figure (the triad of thesis, antithesis, and synthesis), to a "circle of circles" or spiral of spirals, in which the Absolute, insofar as it is in itself the first, at the same time, is also the result. Now the unwritten systematic of Plato allows a glimpse, at least in a regional way, of starting points of a theory of truth based on the criterion of coherence comparable to that of Hegel and precisely in the attempt to organize the sphere of the universals in an accurate manner by means of mathematical relations and proportions (the theory of Idea-numbers). This conception, intensely discussed and further developed in the Platonic Academy, understood universals and categories in a totalizing manner as a system of relations, in which each member with respect to each other member is in a determinate relation that is expressible accurately and quantitatively and in which each part in the sum of its relations mirrors the whole. The order of the whole is primarily a product of unity itself, which, as such, limits and determines the unlimited material substrate in a complete way. The Platonic dialectic follows up this rigorous determination of the relations and, in doing this, unfolds the mathematical importance of the traditional concept of *logos* ("ratio") and exploits it epistemologically.[48]

This conception, considered from the standpoint of content, for Hegelianism is certainly not acceptable, since Hegel had developed his speculative dialectic in antithesis to a static and rigid mathematical identity. (Hegel, consequently, wanted to eliminate from the Platonic dialectic the Pythagorean elements he found there, also those found in the reports on the unwritten doctrines, and he wanted to subordinate them as merely "symbolic"[49] to the true and proper dialectic, understood in the categorial sense and hence interpretable in a speculative sense). Nonetheless, both Plato and Hegel conceive the sphere of "logic,"[50] of first philosophy, as a totality, in which the truth of every part dialectically is realizable and conditioned by the function that each of them develops within the ambit of the whole. Therefore, the theoretical aspect of validity and the justification of the Platonic theory of the principles[51] achieves its full development only in the theory of the Idea-numbers. Moreover, the theory of the principles itself is part of the theory of the coherence of reality and truth, insofar as it functions as final terminus of a process of "regression" and as the point of departure of a process of "progression," and can be carried on in total clarity only by a passage through all the principled.[52]

Concluding Remarks with Special Regard to the Concept of Measure in Plato and Hegel

If the unwritten systematic of Plato is compared with the *Logic* of Hegel in detail, then it can be seen that almost none of the categories of Plato are not likewise represented in the system of the categories of Hegel. The program of the "science of logic," which summarizes and re-elaborates the traditional metaphysics, therefore, is also completed in respect to the general position of Plato. In this regard it is instructive that the reductive component of the unwritten systematic and theory of the principles of Plato (the mathematical component together with the system of the dimensions,[53] the concepts of finite and infinite, one and many,[54] and similars) is confined to the logic of being, as somewhat primitive and abstract. Hegel, with this judgment, agreed with Aristotle and his criticism of Pythagoreanism and Platonism. Still, the relation of the part with the whole reenters into the logic of essence, in which also the greater part of the Platonic Meta-Ideas (identity and difference along with opposition, equality and inequality) find their place as determinations of the reflection.[55] The relation of genera-species and definition—Hegel did not accept both of them without reservation— belongs in the logic of the concept, which, however, follows post-Aristotelian traditions with the distinction concept-judgment-syllogism.

More important is the fact that in the category of measure is found preserved at least a part of the fundamental conception of Plato, which also historically is joined to our philosopher (especially to the *Philebus*). According to Hegel the measure is the unity of quantity and quality—and here enters into play also the axiological moment[56]—which referred the one to the other and reciprocally mediated, lead to the form of reflection of being in the essence.[57]

In this systematic key position, the category of the measure has a function of mediation, in the course of the development of the concepts, between the abstract fundamental concepts of the logic of being and the richer categories of reflection of the logic of essence. This can be easily placed in parallel with the Platonic outline that mediates the sphere of the principles with each individual entity and according to which the limited (quantitative) is, at the same time, good, being (essence!)[58] and knowable. Also the epistemological moment, as in Plato, is present in Hegel, who, in this context, manifestly takes his starting point from the ambit of that which we today call the exact sciences.[59]

In addition, the fact that the measure, in its relation to itself, is conceived as a relation of measure and precisely as an aggregate of relations of particular measures equally rejoins Hegel to Plato.[60] Certainly, that which, in Plato, was at the center itself of his general philosophical position, in Hegel, is instead reduced to an individual moment inserted in a more ample categorial nexus. But in this way the phenomenal content that was still proper to the Platonic outline, in the Hegelian *Logic* is "taken away yet preserved" (*aufgehoben*).

12   *The Theory of the Principles in the Light of Phenomenology and the Philosophy of Heidegger*

Contacts and Divergences between Platonism and Phenomenology

The general affinity between Platonism and Phenomenology has been noted repeatedly by scholars, both from the historical and the systematic standpoints.[1] The eidetic reduction within the intuitive vision of the essence leads to "Platonism"; only the phenomenological reduction leads to a genuine conceptualism, whereas the transcendental reduction leads to the theory of the grounding subject. However, different from transcendental philosophy in the context of the phenomenological reduction the fact that in the phenomenal *noemata* the world in its contents is retained is still Platonic. On the other hand, Phenomenology differs again from Platonism because unlike transcendental philosophy and ancient metaphysics, it reveals an absence of an ultimate foundation, that is not counterbalanced by the Husserlian *Egology*, which tends to facticity [empirical subjectivity].[2]

Vice versa, Plato draws nearest to Phenomenology, when in a purely hypothetical way, he leads back the Idea to a *noema* understood in a conceptualistic sense,[3] or at least when a psychic *noema*, which is closer to the Idea itself than other "reproductions" of a linguistic or a physical nature corresponds to the Idea.[4] Naturally, in Plato no phenomenological reduction is present. But such a *noema* of the soul corresponds also to the theory of the principles,[5] which interests us in the present context. And connected to this consideration is the problem how far the theory of the principles and, in general, the theory of categorial concepts of reflection of Plato can be reconstructed on the level of Phenomenology and if starting points in this direction can be found in Husserl. Indeed, this is the case.

The Theory of the Principles in the Pre-phenomenological Phase of Husserl

Already in his psychologistic prephenomenological phase, Husserl—in his doctoral dissertation *Über den Begriff der Zahl* (1887) (*Concerning the Concept of Number*) and chiefly in his volume *Philosophie der Arithmetik* (1891) (*Philosophy of Arithmetic*)—presented and interpreted the concepts of one, multiplicity, and plurality, along with "something," as the most universal and emptiest of content of all concepts and characterized them as categories.[6] They originate by the reflection on psychic acts—Husserl speaks already here of "interest" and of "awareness," which produces unification[7]—and can be illustrated only in a context of this kind—going back to psychic phenomena from which they are abstracted—but they cannot be defined.[8] In identity and difference, just as in equality and inequality, Husserl found concepts of relations, similar to these whereby the accurate comprehension of inequality presupposes the knowledge of the more and the less.[9] The analysis of the concept of the one leads to the distinction of the number one and unity as totality or the togetherness of a multiplicity, which, as such, is not properly the antithesis of multiplicity. These correspond to the derived forms of unity in Plato, while the original metaphysical unity at the base of all forms of unity, in a significant way is not discussed as a topic in Husserl. The distinctions of the neo-Kantian Rickert,[10] which contrast the All-One from what is one in logic (the antithesis of which is the diverse) go further here.

The Theory of the Principles in the Phenomenological Writings of Husserl

In his successive phenomenological writings Husserl, then, collects these fundamental categorial concepts, first of all unity and multiplicity (plurality, variety), in a more ample systematic context. Husserl distinguishes the material concepts (species of every type) from general categories, having universal extension, and within these, further, the formal categories of meaning (concept, judgment, syllogism, etc.) from the formal categories of object (object, state, unity, multiplicity, plurality, relation, to which likewise belong identity, equality, and similarity; being and not-being, whole-part, and such).[11] In doing so, unity and multiplicity are distinguished with respect to other concepts by the fact that they, in the sphere of the pure (philosophical) doctrine of multiplicity (set theory), projected in the final chapter of the first volume of the Logical Inquiries, have a central function and are a model for other spheres. In addition, totality, equality, as well as identity are, in comparison with the category of unity, in a complex relation, in the context of which, however, unity emerges as that which is most universal and most extended.[12] In this respect, in Husserl, one notices a correspondence to the Platonic hierarchy of the principles, of the Meta-Ideas, and the Ideas of things. However, Husserl, in general, has not distinguished the categories of the object in a hierarchical manner, but, in their totality, he has treated them in a paratactic manner, even if unity and multiplicity always belong to the most important categories.

   Moreover, Husserl, beginning with the sixth of the Logical Inquiries, turns against the theory of the abstraction of the categories which he had professed previously, and substituted for it the doctrine of the categorial intuition, which constitutes a corresponding analogy with respect to sensorial intuition and grounds a particular and higher sphere of objects. And in this—on the conceptualistic level of Phenomenology—he returns to "Platonism" and its noetic intuition, also formulated on the basis of the analogy with sensible intuition.[13] Unity, plurality, and identity have here an exemplary significance.[14] The application of these categories in the phenomenological description is varied. There are different degrees of unity of the constitution of things, which are mutually conditioned; viz., are grounded on each other.[15] The unity of the *eidos* or of that which is manifested, hence, always is in correlation with the difference or the infinite multiplicity of its manifestations.[16]

Moreover, there are degrees of the universal, which culminate in the most general categories and through which knowledge must go by successive stages in a gradual ascent.[17] Also in this way, the *generalizing* order of knowledge that belongs to Platonism is preserved wholly from the formal, and partially from the content standpoints.

The inquiry concerning the area of the ultimate universal and most abstract essences is the main task of phenomenological philosophy that aspires to be a fundamental *mathesis universalis*, which includes in itself both logic and mathematical set theory. Also this program—just in the joining of mathematics and logic expressly and thoroughly discussed—can be analogically compared with Platonism and, in particular, with the Platonic theory of the principles, on condition that one considers the different type of thetic-metaphysical orientation that belongs to the latter. If this is taken away, then, Phenomenology can even be considered as a reductive form of Platonism and that is so in a degree still higher than transcendental philosophy, which is much more formalized.

The Platonic Theory of the Principles and Heideggerian Ontology

The phenomenological starting point of the existentialistic ontology of Heidegger can justify the treatment of such a philosophy in this chapter immediately following the phenomenology of Husserl. Although the philosophy of Heidegger, including its terminological detail, is presented as a project antithetical to the first philosophy of Aristotle, the *univocal* concept of being of Heidegger is not of Aristotelian provenance (since Aristotle professed an homonymous conception of being) but Neoplatonic. Also the ontological difference between Being and the existent stems from the Neoplatonic tradition[18] and not from the Aristotelian or even from the Presocratic ones, to whom Heidegger for other reasons —in opposition to idealistic subjectivity—tried to return. But Being was conceived in

Neoplatonism (for the first time by Porphyry) as an explanation of Platonic unity itself[19] and, therefore, in all the succeeding span of the history of philosophy can be referred to the Platonic theory of the principles not only historically but—at least analogically—also theoretically. On the other side, in Heidegger, the conception according to which Being and Not-Being (Nothing) are two aspects of the meaning of the same thing is not Platonic, but Neoplatonic (and also Hegelian, but Hegel was not the first to maintain it).[20] Being, moreover, in Heidegger, after his passing through the position of transcendental subjectivity, no longer is "separable" from the "being-there" (*Dasein*) of man and hence is no longer conceived in a metaphysical manner.[21] Consequently, the ontological difference also receives a new and unusual meaning that separates it from the analogical relationship of principles and the principled in Platonic and Neoplatonic metaphysics.

Being, however, also in Heidegger has an essentially unifying meaning: in contrast to the conception of transcendental subjectivity of modern philosophy, Heidegger, in his later years, conceived Being (*Ereignis*, event) as the original mediator between subject and object, the "I" and the world and as capable of producing identity and "belongingness" (of the one to the other).[22] Being is the unitary area of interest in which the I and the world naturally meet. Unity has here achieved a still more radical and universal meaning than it had in the objectivistic metaphysics of Platonism, because it is not limited to being based on the world of objects, but, in a more general manner, it also grounds the relation of the world with the comprehending subject, as it had been made a problem throughout the modern philosophy of subjectivity. Notwithstanding, in Plato, as in this, there is an analogical correspondence, which is purely in the limits of precritical and objectivistic metaphysics prefiguring the concept of a mediation of subject and object; in fact, the simile of the sun in the *Republic*, understood in the light of the explications of the theory of the principles, shows that knower and known can have a mutual correspondence because both participate equally in the unifying power of unity itself.[23] From this viewpoint, unity itself reciprocally mediates knower and known in a unified relationship, which relation (just as each of the correlatives) is itself determined by unity itself. Therefore, the unity of Being for Heidegger, having passed through idealistic subjectivity, approaches anew the unity of subject and object analogically ascending, which in the Presocratics was present in a still naive manner and which in Plato instead was expressly and thoroughly discussed and hypostatized in unity itself, understood as a metaphysical entity. Heidegger himself, however, did not take account of the historical relationship of his conception of Being with that of Plato, because he did not take the indirect Platonic tradition into consideration and has not really made even Neoplatonism his own.[24]

Instead, Heidegger is furthest from Plato insofar as he conceived Being as time, that is, as becoming, as movement, as destiny that allots itself differently from time to time. As Being is dialectically presented also as Not-Being (Nothing), thus unity—Platonically considered—passes into duality and multiplicity. Not only the duality of the sensible world and the intelligible world but also the wider duality of the principles on the basis of this Heideggerian position is definitely rejected: the Being of Heidegger, actually, can be compared with the Platonic sphere of the principles only considered as a whole.

Part Four

Conclusions:
Illusion of Plato or Agony of Schleiermacherianism?

On the Problem of the Theoretical Evaluation of the Unwritten Doctrines

The New Total Picture of Plato

The relationship between the written work and the unwritten doctrine, outlined in the conclusion of Part One (Chapter 5) of this book, has been confirmed, conceptually defined, and emphasized in the Parts Two and Three. Only if the indirect and direct Platonic traditions are placed in a precise reciprocal correlation do the essential traits again emerge of that total perspective of the thought of Plato that was canonical in the fourth century BCE for Plato himself, for all the members of the Academy, and for some contemporary initiates.

So it is demonstrated (in Part Two, Chapter 7), (1) that the two branches of the tradition do not run parallel to each other without any relationship between them but, on the contrary, have a reciprocal relationship that is programmed by Plato in a precise manner and that is possible to reconstruct from the historical philosophical standpoint; (2) that these two branches of the tradition are in agreement and partly coincide, partly complete one another. It is a question, on the whole, of a relationship of "explication," in virtue of which the unwritten doctrine develops *in extenso* and, in addition, places in a unitary perspective that which in the dialogues is mentioned only through allusions or outlined in a summary fashion.

In the measure to which the two traditions coincide, the role of the indirect tradition guarantees with its explicit affirmations the philosophical seriousness of the direct literary tradition, which in itself is problematic because of the Platonic self-testimonies that limit the value of the written works and because of the imitation of Socrates that is a prominent feature of the dialogues and seems to obscure the position that is specific to Plato.

In the measure in which, then, the two traditions stand in a complementary relationship, the unwritten doctrine offers an authentic widening and enrichment that goes beyond the content of the dialogues and that, therefore, cannot be eliminated as negligible. In particular, the indirect tradition is hence to furnish the concrete accomplishment of the program in the dialogues is always outlined that only in a very concise way (as for example in the *Republic*) or maintained chiefly on the propaedeutic and provisory level with the indication of only some limited examples (as for example in the *Parmenides* and the *Sophist*), in other words, the program of bringing to complete fulfillment in a concrete and detailed manner the dialectical method and continuing it to its final conclusion in the synoptic vision of the Good itself. To this aim it was necessary to lead back to a common point of convergence dialogues like the *Republic* and the *Symposium*,[1] on the one hand, and the *Parmenides* and the *Sophist*, on the other. And that a claimed convergence of themes for Plato himself, different from what is presented in the dialogues, did not only constitute a programmatic approach, but that in the sphere of orality such convergence, instead always has been carried out, is sufficiently demonstrated by the chronology which is drawn from the self-testimonies contained in the *Seventh Letter* and in the *Phaedrus*. The systematic unification proper to the unwritten doctrine, therefore, cannot be limited by recourse to developmental theses relegating it to the final phase of Plato's philosophical activity. Consequently, this explicitly and thoroughly discussed unification elevates Platonic philosophy to a higher level of metaphysical reflection, insofar as it develops a unitary foundational and explanatory nexus and culminates in a theory of universal principles.

A more elevated grade of coherence of this theme, however, does not necessarily mean the dogmatic impossibility of its revision. On the other hand, the unwritten doctrine is able to eliminate these traits of theoretical and doctrinal indetermination that have accompanied Platonism over the centuries and substitute for such an indetermination a concreteness and specificity of philosophical content that can be a notable advantage for the critical reception and the theoretical reinterpretation of Plato by contemporary philosophy. In this sense the fundamental ontological determinations that are deduced from the theory of the principles or the strict relations existing with fundamental concepts and models of constructions from medicine and mathematics, which are extended to the sphere of the principles (as the ontological foundation of the doctrine of the proportions, the normative means between excess and defect, and others), acquire a specific theoretical relevance.

Independent of the contributions made by the theory of the principles to the effect of systematic unification and theoretical grounding, the indirect tradition of the unwritten doctrine *makes possible a better philosophical-comprehension of the Platonic dialogues themselves*, as happens, for example, when, contrary to the impasse that is verified in the interpretation of certain central parts of Books Six and Seven of the *Republic*, a historically grounded unitary solution can be adduced.

In this respect it is demonstrated that the indirect tradition not only completes the written work in an extrinsic and contingent manner but that this work, far from enjoying a full independence in the decisive questions is structurally dependent on the "relief"[2] that comes from it. In addition, the indirect tradition *acts as a kind of control and furnishes criteria for deciding between possible interpretations of the dialogues,* which are often ambiguous, as for example, in the case of the *Parmenides,* or *it functions as a corrective,* as in the case of the *Sophist,* whose strongly specialized themes can only with difficulty be inserted in the outline of the Platonic dialectic that is traced in the *Republic.*

But also to prescind from the just summarized evident assistance that the indirect tradition is capable of furnishing, from the methodological viewpoint it is not admissable, whatever the reasons are—skepticism in respect to the tradition, purist-literary prejudices, or preferences based on one's own philosophical position—simply to abandon the indirect tradition and put it aside without using it. If one part of the tradition is eliminated, the mutilated position thus created is truly acritical and unscientific, since it furnishes a fragmentary and one-sided, and hence an erroneous picture, of the historical position of Plato, certainly leading to fallacious conclusions.[3]

Moreover, the total position of Plato grounded on the theory of the principles, on the one hand, which mediates historically the philosophy of the Presocratics and, on the other hand, that of Aristotle and the Neoplatonists, can be inserted with a greater number of consequences than the theory of the Ideas and its pluralism in the area of the historical development of ancient philosophy, which, for its part, in virtue of this becomes more coherent and more continuous, as can be seen in the Chapter 8. In particular, Plato in his own theory of the principles has accepted the basic thought of the Presocratics about the "principle," and he has posed the traditional problem of the relation of the *one and the many* in a more radical manner with the assistance of the dialectical method. He has also pursued its solution in a more rigorous and more coherent manner than his predecessors. Many reasons contribute to the thesis that the general theory of the Ideas, constructed on the basis of a radically reinterpreted Eleaticism, would have been grounded from the start on the basis of a theory of principles. Moreover, the hermeneutical fertility and capacity for clarification of the unwritten theory of the principles and systematic furnishes the best results not only applied to the Platonic dialogues, but, in many ways, when applied to the philosophy of Aristotle and to Neoplatonism that more or less indirectly are connected to the unwritten doctrine of Plato.

The Relations between the New Total Picture of Plato and the Principal Currents of Contemporary Philosophy

In addition to this, in Part Three, it is demonstrated that the Platonic theory prefigures different philosophical positions both succeeding and still current. The choice is limited in this regard (by waiving the treatment of the rich history of its influence on Neoplatonism, the Middle Ages, and the modern age) to some basic contemporary positions, chiefly to show the possibility of realizing a theoretical exploitation or reelaboration and critical reception of Platonic philosophy as a whole in the context of contemporary philosophy. In doing this, a plurality of references in many different directions spontaneously arises, from analytic philosophy to transcendental philosophy, from speculative dialectic to phenomenology and existentialism.

In the *analytic approach* the Platonic theory of the principles is presented as corresponding with modern attempts to determine the foundations of science, which, in its turn, can be analyzed by the modern tools of epistemology, logic, and linguistics and which it is possible to represent and reconstruct as an axiomatic system of propositions. In particular, in this regard, in the unwritten doctrine of Plato instructive parallels are encountered with the modern attempts at a *mathesis universalis* (universal formal science), or also with respect to the theme of the reduction of the corporeal world to incorporeal mathematical structures, or further with respect to the problematic of discontinuity and the elementary quanta that have been treated precisely in the unwritten systematic. In addition, analogies are encountered with the modern problem of the antinomies, which Plato, owing to the indications of the indirect tradition, tried to resolve with a kind of solution that prefigured the Russellian "theory of types."

Still closer is the affinity to *modern Idealism*, whose *transcendental problem about the principles of knowledge* is presented as a renewal of the theme of the foundation according to the perspective of the theory of subjectivity; the theme that commenced with Plato for the first time and to which the transcendental purview also belonged. Especially viewed in this way, the theory of the principles of Plato is the first theory to have taken up as a philosophical principle unity itself in all its aspects—transcendental, ontological, axiological, linguistic, epistemological, and noetic—and to have developed and accomplished it *in linear progression* in all the individual spheres of being and knowledge. Plato, therefore, not only developed a formal grounding structure that unifies with new rigor and confidence, but, within it, he thoroughly discussed unity itself, once again from the standpoint of the philosophical content and not only from the formal standpoint, as the highest grounding category. At the same time Plato posited a principle of multiplicity and degrees as an additional condition to explain the grounding function of unity.

The metaphysical theory of the principles of Plato prefigures, hence, the unity of transcendental apperception of Kant, just as it prefigures the absolute identity interspersed by the nonidentity of the Idealism of Hegel, or the fundamental formal categories of the objects of unity and plurality in the *Phenomenology of Husserl*, as well as the position of the *Being of Heidegger* that mediates "being-there" and the world and unifies subject and object. Already in Plato, the concept of being is treated in view of the problem of the principles and the constitution of reality. In addition, from unity and multiplicity is deduced a series of supreme categories. The relationship of reciprocal implication of the principles in the unwritten systematic of Plato corresponds to the principle of correlativeness of contemporary transcendental philosophy. In a particular way, then, the unwritten systematic of Plato joins with Hegelianism in the conception of the *linearity* of the grounding nexus in the descending and ascending sense, which, instead, in the writings of Plato is not carried out (as in the *Republic*) or is apparently substituted by paratactic relationships (as in the *Parmenides* and *Sophist*).

The reinterpretation of such affinities within the modern perspective, of which we have furnished the most important examples, better presuppositions are created with respect to the past for the theoretical reception and for the critical reelaboration of the philosophy of Plato in its totality in the sphere of contemporary philosophy. On the other hand, the multiplicity of the possible relationships, which are referred to strongly divergent currents of thought between themselves, demonstrates that the unwritten theory of the principles and systematic of Plato cannot be bound to a single current of contemporary thought and to its interest in its own historical self-legitimization. The reacquisition of the indirect tradition of Plato and its reevaluation *is not on the same level as a particular interpretation of Plato guided by a particular and one-sided theoretical interest, but it precedes all the interpretations of this type,* changing, so to speak, and enriching in a more profound dimension the objective data of the tradition concerning Platonic philosophy, on the basis of which such theoretical interpretations can be elaborated and grounded. The new historico-doxographical discovery of the indirect tradition of Plato, therefore, does not presuppose any particular contemporary interpretation of Plato, but, on the contrary, *it remains open and alone prepares a new sphere for a whole series of possible interpretations of Plato and hermeneutic perspectives theoretically aimed at.* In fact, the doctrine of the principles can be interpreted as much in the sense of analytic philosophy as in the sense of Transcendental philosophy, or Phenomenology, or Structuralism, or even Marxist philosophy, without its historical existence and importance for Platonic philosophy becoming dependent on one of these perspectives.

Therefore, it is a grave error to want to affix the picture of Plato, reconstructed by the School of Tübingen, to the philosophy of Heidegger or that of N. Hartmann, as though the representation of Platonism proposed by it were comprehensible in its philosophical content only on the basis of the theoretical presuppositions of one or the other philosopher.[4] Certainly, it is possible to trace parallels towards both of these philosophers, and in the past the School of Tübingen has also traced them, in part with the intent of espousing Platonism, in part with a purely didactic intent,[5] while today the interest generally is turned rather to analytical interpretation or that of neo-Hegelians because the spirit of the epoch has changed. However, the theme of the principles, being, and the categories cannot in any way be considered as a *proprium* precisely of these philosophers, just as the thesis of the existence of an hierarchy of levels of being in Plato cannot in any way be drawn from the analysis of the levels of being proper to Hartmann. Ontology begins notoriously with Parmenides; categorial analysis from the terminological viewpoint begins with Aristotle, but from the point of view of conceptual content, it begins precisely with Plato himself and with the Platonic Academy, and since Kant almost all noted philosophers have outlined a theory of the categories in the most varied forms. It is not possible, in addition, to join to Heidegger the fundamental problematic, if one does not want to make the Presocratics depend on Heidegger. And the conception of the hierarchical degrees of being can only anachronistically be made to connect with Boutroux or with Hartmann; viz., only by forgetting Neoplatonism, which had been prepared by the Platonic Academy. The single question that is meaningful for those competent in the matter long since has been this one: in what measure ought we admit as already present for ancient Platonism a hierarchical structure of reality corresponding to that proper to Neoplatonism? (Hence, whoever calls Hartmann in defense simply has no familiarity with the centuries of Neoplatonism.[6])

Against all attempts of this kind to discredit the indirect tradition, contrary to the dialogues, by the link between it and a particular if possible bygone form of philosophy most possibly no longer present, one ought instead to maintain as a factual datum that *the indirect Platonic tradition leaves room for numerous hermeneutical perspectives no less than the written works*, and that it can arouse an interest in different epochs in totally different ways. And on the basis of what has been said thus far, this must be maintained as valid likewise for the future. In this *hermeneutic fertility* it is possible to recognize the importance of the philosophical nucleus and conceptual range of the first order in the indirect Platonic tradition.

The Systematic Evaluation of the Theory
of the Principles of Plato

The solution to the problem of the systematic evaluation of the philosophical content of the indirect Platonic tradition on the basis of what has been stated, in a certain respect, already is predetermined. We will be occupied in the pages that follow with coming to a conclusion on the issue. In particular, we will evaluate the relevance of the philosophical contribution of Plato, which concerns his theory of the principles, for explaining the dialogues and the Platonic philosophy in its totality and its relevance in the contemporary theoretical debates.

In doing this, it is absolutely indispensable to separate the critical reinterpretation conducted within a modern philosophical position (which is necessary for any history of philosophy that does not resolve into mere historicism) from a precise preliminary and historical reconstruction, which, especially, has to consider the movement of thought belonging to the past and measure it on the basis of the requirements internal to it. Where this distinction of the two phases of work is not made or the historical reconstruction is omitted, there is a danger that strange elements are inserted in the interpretation and evaluation and that all becomes leveled.[7] In addition, a critical self-vigilance and awareness is necessary to avoid the excessive transformation of the history of philosophy—in this case Platonic research—in the area of the battle of modern polemics in part, of a merely theoretical nature. The critical and philosophical evaluation, finally, is always linked to a particular position and particular interests, which, naturally, lead to different conclusions, according to which of the different positions are used as starting points.

No scholar, therefore, can pass a judgment on the value of a philosophy of antiquity in the name of philosophy *simpliciter*, nor even in the name of the philosophy of his or her own period.[8]

Strangely, instead, in the discussions in our days about the Platonic theory of the principles, examples of careless and simplistic approaches of this kind are met in which the criticism neglects the preliminary question of the internal evaluation of Platonic philosophy; viz., it is not concerned with any particular theoretical reasons proper to it and with its historical influence, and in addition, does not reflect on the idiosyncrasies of its own critical position.[9] To be more precise then, mostly modern scholars surreptitiously tend to produce a demetaphysicalization of Plato, which, however, is fundamentally nonspecific, since the position of the dialogues, understood in an adequate historical manner, is opposed to it no less than the theory of the principles.

Thus, for example, some (G. Patzig) find the theory of the principles "inaccessible," "bizarre," and "abstract" because it does not satisfy the neopositivistic postulate of the concreteness of principles (a *contradictio in adjecto*). However, the doctrine of Ideas of the dialogues, which contrary to the doctrine of the principles is valued highly, from the nominalistic viewpoint is no less contestable than that contained in the doctrines of the indirect tradition; prescinding from the fact that the historical contribution of Plato has been precisely that of overcoming the archaic mode of thought of the Greeks, still conditioned by the concreteness of their imaginations, and of proceeding, beyond Parmenides, to the conquest of a form of conceptuality, without which the level of theorizing of the succeeding epochs—including that which is proper to formal logic—would not have been possible (J. Stenzel).[10]

The same thing is true for the ethico-pragmatic restrictions of the Idea of the Good reduced to a rule of action in individual cases (W. Wieland).[11] Also in this case, a demetaphysicalization of Plato furtively performed, to which the unwritten Platonic doctrine of the principles is clearly opposed, but which, in addition, cannot be argued historically even on the basis of the dialogues, because the dialogues also do not justify such a restriction. Actually, we find here basically a paradigmatic case of an incorrect methodological procedure, which consists in wishing to make the second move (the insertion of an ancient author in a modern theoretical context) before making the first move (that is, before entering into the spirit of the movement of thought of the past, to successively go on to criticism) and, hence, in the historical estrangement of the author, by unduly leveling him.[12]

Against such an attempt to put in a false light the Platonic theory of the principles by not sufficiently explicit premises, it is necessary to keep firmly in mind that it would be necessary either to demonstrate in general the inconsistency of the question of the foundation just as it emerges from the problematic of the principles proper to antiquity and from its medieval and modern successors, or to show *in extenso* (at length) that especially the Platonic theory of the principles is unlike the others through its inadequacy. But hitherto, in the context of Platonic research, neither the one nor the other has been done. In this regard it is worth noting that it would be very difficult to isolate the Platonic solution, within a theoretical and historically continuous outline, from the preceding and following thematic of the principles.

A similar lack of historical sense also betrays the attempt to project the aversion of Hegel against mathematics, which is grounded on speculative presuppositions, onto the position of Plato, which is founded instead on presuppositions not at all speculative, and, on the basis of it, to declare that the theory of the Idea-numbers and finally the theory of the principles are not philosophical or to deny their authenticity. But the discussion on the foundations of mathematics, contained in Books Six and Seven of the *Republic*, which is placed on a quite different basis, cannot in any way be taken into consideration in the sense of the speculative criticism of mathematical identity of the Hegelian type. In this case, it is necessary that it be recognized, instead, that the possibilities of verifying the position of Hegel, in comparison with the history of philosophy, are limited, and that in particular mathematics was not at all considered as not philosophical by Plato, just as it is not correct to project onto Plato the position of Hegel, taken in respect to the logic of genus-species, which—together with Aristotelian syllogistic—after a two millennium process of assimilation and appropriation, Hegel for the first time judged banal, while, in their times, these doctrines constituted a revolutionary and hard-earned achievement. The attempt to institute a difference of value between the Platonic direct tradition and the indirect, therefore, also in this perspective is destined to failure.[13]

Moreover, the Platonic theory of the principles, as has been demonstrated, through its historical influence, reaches right up to contemporary positions, both from the formal standpoint (the thematic of the foundation) and, in part, from the standpoint of content (the problematic of unity-multiplicity and correlation). At least there are, in several important contemporary philosophical positions, some analogical correspondences strictly akin to the Platonic doctrine of the principles. The same thing is true for other characteristics of Platonic philosophy (as, for example, for the methodological procedure of progression and regression, for linearity, for the problematic of the coherence theory of truth, and still others). On this depends the fact that leading representatives of modern philosophy (G. W. F. Hegel, A. N. Whitehead, T. W. Adorno, K. R. Popper, C. F. von Weizsäcker, J. N. Findlay, and others),[14] in what concerns systematic questions of philosophy, have taken into consideration and critically discussed in a fecund manner the indirect Platonic tradition. In such a way, the Platonic theory of the principles in different historical periods, many times through a series of different standpoints, has been made to enter advantageously into living philosophical argument. If, for example, philosophical interest in the first part of the century was determined chiefly by neo-Kantianism and the new ontology, the center of interest has since instead shifted to the problematic of analytic philosophy (Whitehead, Popper, Annas, and others), to neo-Hegelianism (Adorno, Findlay and others), or also to the philosophy of nature (von Weizsäcker).[15]

This emphasizes the factual datum which would by now be obvious in contemporary hermeneutics, that in what concerns the possibility of its comprehension and the various chances of its being carried out, the indirect Platonic tradition, far from being joined to a determined philosophical position, chiefly linked with the past, on the contrary, from the standpoint of hermeneutics, is no less polyvalent than the direct tradition. And is this not only pointed out, it is likewise demonstrated that the indiscriminate reproof of the presumed lack of success and even the harmfulness of the indirect tradition for the purposes of modern theoreticians (G. Patzig) or

that of philosophical irrelevance (W. Wieland) in reality are wholly unjustifiable. Such reproaches are based rather on an absence of information and
the enduring refusal of scholars to go into the philosophical problems of
the unwritten doctrine, even at a surface level,[16] notwithstanding that it
presents itself in a privileged way for a comparison with the modern theory
of science and the epistemological inquiries into its foundations.[17]

On the basis of this situation a difference in treatment between the two
traditions is evident, which goes against the principle of coherence and falls
victim to "begging the question" in favor of the literary work of Plato.[18]
Actually, the campaign of discrimination and devaluation turned against
the indirect tradition of Plato, begun in a significant way by F. Schlegel,[19] is
revealed to be nothing other than a form of Schleiermacherian strategy,
which comes into play as an *ultima ratio* (final reason), whenever the specific
historico-philological competence is lacking or whenever other strategies
are exhausted, so the criticism of the authenticity of the indirect tradition
or its chronological isolation and the reduction of the unwritten doctrines
to the final phase of the philosophical evolution of Plato. (The fact that in
the twentieth century the strategy of devaluation of the indirect tradition
has been carried out within the sphere of Platonic studies only after the
thesis of the late dating of the indirect tradition had been demonstrated as
fictitious and, consequently, had to be rejected is particularly suggestive
and revealing.)

The dominant interest, which acts in the strategy and the tactics of
philosophical discrimination, reflected in the categorical verdicts and in the
crude obstructionist attempts, is inserted seamlessly into the fundamental
conception of Schleiermacherianism of the literary Plato. It is an attempt at
self-defense of the philosophical hermeneuticism feeling compromised if an
indirect tradition mediating between the original texts and Plato himself is
inserted and that, precisely for this reason, clings in a much more intran-
sigent manner to the original texts. In fact, since the degree of indetermination and liberty of the Platonic texts is limited by the corrective of the
indirect tradition, the clarifications that come from the indirect tradition
consequently are perceived as rather disturbing. The theoretical discussion
and argument of the dialogues conjured in this context, in reality, is carried
out largely with the exclusion of some central parts of the texts, since they
cannot be understood in any way, as for example, the simile of the sun or
the divided line found in the *Republic*. However, there is a propensity to
accept this and tolerate the difficulties, if they do not also deliberately
misuse the enigmatic character of such texts for the purpose of recovering
from them a point of support for a transformation of their significance into
a modernistic and historically unmediated setting.

Curiously, hermeneuticism, with its tendency to be based solely on the original literary texts and make them available for any theoretical interpretation whatsoever, goes against the fundamental principle of the philological hermeneutical tradition, according to which a vision of the totality of an author, historically well founded, is carried out solely in an holistic way in the hermeneutical circle that gathers *all* the parts of a *whole* preserved by the tradition. And this principle, in the case of Plato, cannot be limited to the literary works, by an arbitrary restriction, just as it cannot be done in the case of Democritus,[20] but must be applied with its widest signification also to the indirect tradition. In the contrary case the result remains mutilated and fragmentary, and because of its uncertainty, contains in itself a grave risk of errors.

The orientation toward the position of Schleiermacher becomes entirely evident in those scholars (W. Wieland, J. Mittelstrass)[21] who deny the necessary theoretical level of the indirect tradition, appealing to criteria of the irrenouncability of the philosophical dialogical character proper to Plato. The mistakes committed in these cases are twofold: (1) The relevance of the content, which is precisely that of the theory of the principles, is not distinguished from the contingent and casual form in which it is presented in the indirect tradition that reports it, and, instead, comes to depend on this.[22] (2) Vice versa, they ignore the methodological difference between the literary dialogue and the real colloquy and confound one with the other in a crude manner. Both these positions, the absence of distinctions of form and content and the absence of distinctions between the oral and written form, at their core, are of genuine Schleiermacherian extraction, but not, certainly, of Platonic extraction.[23] Of all that is contrary to the Platonic spirit, then, the prize goes to the reasoning on the basis of which the contingency linked to the situation in which the indirect tradition has come down to us is considered also as belonging to its philosophical content and, hence, the results of the Platonic method, by absolutizing the method itself, become irrelevant.

The reproach of the absence of philosophical interest here, evidently, goes against philosophical Schleiermacherianism. This reasoning, in addition, shares a conceptual error that further exacerbates the situation and that this position overturns itself: it does not grasp that, on the basis of the methodological premises of Plato, the literary works of Plato also must, in any case, be transformed and taken back to oral conversation[24] and that, then, a corresponding reconstruction also must be possible, in principle, for the indirect tradition.

But the most absurd consequence of Schleiermacherianism which justly exposes it to the most grave reproach, is that it must admit the improbable theses that Plato's theory of the principles (1) not only has remained, in general, much below the intellectual level of the dialogues, but that (2) in this circumstance Plato has been deceived in such a total way that he incurred in inverting the real relation of values in the evaluation of his own position. But the admission that Plato has been deceived in such a grave way, implies that Plato was a thinker so gravely lacking in the capacity of discrimination and judgment, as, in general, could be admitted only for a very poor philosopher. But, before accepting a judgment of this kind, it is necessary to be clearly aware that in reality, without foundation and with fatal consequences, the judgment of Schleiermacher is posited over and above that of *Plato himself*, and likewise above the judgment *of Platonism*, which is manifested wherever in the history of the influence of Plato both traditions were present together.

The insufficient evaluation of the theory of the principles and of the system of Plato, maintained by some in good faith and by others in bad faith, is based not so much on arguments as on an insufficiency of knowledge or as in the case of some philologists, on a philosophical incompetence or as in the case of philosophical opponents, on a repudiation that is contrary to what they know well and, hence, in bad faith, of a great philosophical tradition the determining influence of which has reached right up to the present day.[25]

APPENDICES

1. The "Self-Testimonies" of Plato

1. Plato, *Phaedrus* 274B6–278E3

Socrates: What we have left is the subject of propriety and impropriety in *writing*: **247B**
in what way, when it is done, it will be done acceptably, and in what way
improperly. True?

Phaedrus: Yes.

Socrates: So do you know how you will most gratify god in relation to speaking,
whether actually speaking, or talking about it?

Phaedrus: Not at all; do you?

Socrates: I can tell you, at least, something I have heard from those who came before **C**
us; they alone know the truth of it. But if we were to find it out for ourselves, would
we care any longer at all about what mere men happen to think?

Phaedrus: An absurd question; tell me what you say you have heard.

Socrates: Well then, what I heard was that there was at Naucratis in Egypt one of
the ancient gods of that country, the one to whom the sacred bird they call the ibis
belongs; the divinity's own name was Theuth. The story was that he was the first **D**
to discover number and calculation, and geometry and astronomy, and also games
of draughts and dice; and, to cap it all, letters. King of all Egypt at that time was
Thamus—all of it, that is, that surrounds the great city of the upper region which
the Greeks call Egyptian Thebes; Thamus they call Ammon. Theuth came to him
and displayed his technical inventions, saying that they should be passed on to the
rest of the Egyptians; and Thamus asked what benefit each brought. As Theuth
went through them, Thamus criticized or praised whatever he seemed to be getting
right or wrong. The story goes that Thamus expressed many views to Theuth about **E**
each science, both for and against; it would take a long time to go through them in
detail, but when it came to the subject of letters, Theuth said 'But this study, King
Thamus, will make the Egyptians wiser and improve their memory; what I have
discovered is an elixir of memory and wisdom.' Thamus replied 'Most scientific
Theuth, one man has the ability to beget the elements of a science, but it belongs
to a different person to be able to judge what measure of harm and benefit it
contains for those who are going to make use of it; so now you, as the father of
letters, have been led by your affection for them to describe them as having the **275A**
opposite of their real effect. For your invention will produce forgetfulness in the
souls of those who have learned it, through lack of practice at using their memory,
as through reliance on writing they are reminded from outside by alien marks, not
from inside, themselves by themselves: you have discovered an elixir not of
memory but of *reminding*. To your students you give an appearance of wisdom, not
the reality of it; having heard much, in the absence of teaching, they will appear to

know much when for the most part they know nothing, and they will be difficult
to get along with, because they have acquired the appearance of wisdom instead   **B**
of wisdom itself.

Phaedrus: Socrates, you easily make up stories from Egypt or from anywhere else
you like.

Socrates: Well, my friend, those at the sanctuary of Zeus of Dodona said that words
of an oak were the first prophetic utterances. So the men of those days, because
they were not wise like you moderns, were content because of their simplicity to
listen to oak and rock, provided only that they said what was true; but for you,
Phaedrus, perhaps it makes a difference who the speaker is and where he comes   **C**
from: you don't just consider whether what he says is right or not.

Phaedrus: You rightly rebuke me, and it seems to me to be as the Theban says about
letters.

Socrates: So the man who thinks that he has left behind him a science in writing,
and in his turn the man who receives it from him in the belief that anything clear
or certain will result from what is written down, would be full of simplicity and
would be really ignorant of Ammon's prophetic utterance, in thinking that written
words were anything more than a *reminder* to the man who knows the subjects to   **D**
which the things written relate.

Phaedrus: Quite right.

Socrates: Yes, Phaedrus, because I think writing has this strange feature, which
makes it like painting. The offspring of painting stand there as if alive, but if you
ask them something, they preserve a quite solemn silence. Similarly with written
words: you might think that they spoke as if they had some thought in their heads,
but if you ever ask them about any of the things they say out of a desire to learn,
they point to just one thing, the same each time. *And when once it is written, every
composition is trundled about everywhere in the same way, in the presence both of those who*   **E**
*know about the subject and of those who have nothing at all to do with it, and it does not
know how to address those it should address and not those it should not. When it is ill-treated
and unjustly abused, it always needs its father to help it; for it is incapable of defending or
helping itself.*

Phaedrus: You're quite right about that too.

Socrates: Well then, do we see another way of speaking, a legitimate brother of this   **27(**
one? Do we see both how it comes into being and how much better and more
capable it is from its birth?

Phaedrus: Which is this, and how does it come into being, as you put it?

Socrates: The one that is written together with knowledge *in the soul of the learner,
capable of defending itself, and knowing how to speak and keep silent in relation to the people
it should.*

Phaedrus: You mean the living and animate speech of the man who knows, of
which written speech would rightly be called a kind of phantom.

Socrates: Absolutely. Then tell me this: the sensible farmer who had some seeds he
cared about and wanted to bear fruit - would he sow them with *serious* purpose

during the summer in some garden of Adonis, and delight in watching it becoming **B**
beautiful within *eight days*, or would he do that for the sake of *amusement* on a
feast-day, when he did it at all; whereas for the purposes *about which he was in earnest*,
he would make use of the science of farming and sow them in appropriate soil,
being content if what he sowed reached maturity *in the eighth month*?

Phaedrus: Just so, I think, Socrates: he would do the one sort of thing in *earnest*, the **C**
other in the other way, the way you say.

Socrates: And are we to say that the man who has knowledge about what is just,
fine and *good* has a less sensible attitude towards his seeds than the farmer?

Phaedrus: Certainly not.

Socrates: In that case he will not be in *earnest* about writing them in water - black
water, sowing them through a pen with words which are *incapable of speaking in
their own support, and incapable of adequately teaching what is true*.

Phaedrus: It certainly isn't likely.

Socrates: No, it isn't; but his gardens of letters, it seems, he will sow and write for **D**
amusement, when he does write, laying up a store of *reminders both for himself*, when
he 'reaches a forgetful old age', *and for anyone who is following the same track*, and he
will be pleased as he watches their tender growth; and when others resort to other
sorts of amusements, watering themselves with drinking-parties and the other
things which go along with these, then he, it seems, will spend his time *amusing*
himself with the things I say, instead of these.

Phaedrus: A very fine form of *amusement* it is you're talking of, Socrates, in contrast **E**
with a mean one—that of the man who is able to *amuse* himself with words, *telling
stories about justice and the other subjects you speak of*.

Socrates: Yes, Phaedrus, just so; but I think it is far finer if one is in *earnest* about
them; when a man makes *use of the science of dialectic*, and taking a fitting soul plants
and sows in it words accompanied by knowledge, which are *able to help themselves* **277A**
and the man who planted them, and are not without fruit but contain a seed, from
which others grow in other soils, capable of rendering it for ever immortal, and
making the one who has it *as happy as it is possible for a man to be*.

Phaedrus: This is indeed still finer.

Socrates: Then now, Phaedrus, we can decide those other issues, since we have
agreed about these.

Phaedrus: What are they?

Socrates: The ones we wanted to look into, which brought us to our present
conclusion: how we were to weigh up the reproach aimed at Lysias about his
writing of speeches, and speeches themselves, which were written scientifically and **B**
which not. Well then, what is scientific and what is unscientific seems to me to have
been demonstrated in fair measure.

Phaedrus: I thought so; but remind me again how.

Socrates: Until a man knows the truth about each of the things about which he
speaks or writes, and becomes capable of defining the whole by itself and, having

defined it, knows how to cut it up again according to its forms until it can no longer be cut; and until he has reached an understanding of the nature of soul along the same lines, discovering the form that fits each nature, and so arranges and orders his speech, offering a complex soul complex speeches containing all the modes, and simple speeches to a simple soul—not before then will he be capable of pursuing the making of speeches as a whole in a scientific way, to the degree that its nature allows, whether for the purposes of teaching or persuading, as the whole of our previous argument has indicated. **C**

Phaedrus: Absolutely; that was just about how it appeared to us.

Socrates: And what about the matter of its being fine or shameful to give speeches **D** and write them, and the circumstances under which it would rightly be called a disgrace or not? Hasn't what we said a little earlier shown it?

Phaedrus: What are you referring to?

Socrates: Hasn't it shown that whether Lysias or anyone else ever wrote or writes in the future either for private purposes, or publicly, in the course of proposing laws, so writing a political composition, and thinks there is any great certainty or clarity in it, then it is a reproach to its writer, whether anyone says so or not; for to be ignorant, whether awake or asleep, about what is just and unjust and *bad* and **E** *good* cannot truly escape being a matter of reproach, even if the whole mass of the people applauds it.

Phaedrus: No indeed.

Socrates: But the man who thinks that there is necessarily *much* that is merely for *amusement in a written speech* on any subject, and that none has ever yet been written, whether in verse or in prose, which is worth *much serious* attention—or indeed spoken, in the way that rhapsodes speak theirs, to produce conviction *without questioning or teaching*, but that the best of them have really been a way of **278.** *reminding people who know*; who thinks that clearness and completeness and *seriousness* exist only in those things that are *taught* about what is just and fine and *good*, and are said for the purpose of someone's *learning* from them, and genuinely written in the soul; who thinks that speeches of that kind should be said to be as it were his legitimate sons, first of all the one within him, *if it is found and contained there*, and in second place any offspring and brothers of this one that have sprung up simultaneously, as they should, in other souls of other men; and who says **B** goodbye to the other kinds—this is likely to be the sort of man, Phaedrus, that you and I would pray that we both might come to be.

Phaedrus: Quite definitely I wish and pray for what you say.

Socrates: So now we have had due amusement from the subject of speaking; and as for you, go and tell Lysias that we two came down to the spring and the sacred place of the Nymphs and listened to speeches (*logoi*) that instructed us to tell this to Lysias and anyone else who composes speeches (*logoi*), and to Homer and anyone **C** else in their turn who has composed verses, whether without music or to be sung, and thirdly to Solon and whoever writes compositions in the form of political speeches, which he calls laws: *if he has composed these things knowing how the truth is, able to help his composition when rendering account of its subjects, and with the capacity,* *when speaking in his own person, to show that what he has written is of little worth, then such a man ought not to derive his title from these, and be called after them, but rather from those things in which he is seriously engaged.* **D**

Phaedrus: What are the titles you assign him, then?

Socrates: To call him wise seems to me to be too much, and to be fitting only in the case of a god; *to call him either a lover of wisdom—a philosopher—or something like that would both fit him more and be in better taste.*

Phaedrus: And not at all inappropriate.

Socrates: On the other hand, then, *the man who does not possess things of more value than the things he composed or wrote*, turning them upside down over a long period of time, sticking them together and taking them apart—him, I think, *you'll rightly* **E** *call a poet or author of speeches or writer of laws?*

Phaedrus: Of course.

2. Plato, *Epistle* VII 340B1-345C3

When I arrived, I thought my first task was to prove whether Dionysius was really **340B** on fire with philosophy, or whether the many reports that came to Athens were without foundation. Now there is a certain way of putting this to the test, a dignified way and quite appropriate to tyrants, especially to those whose heads are full of half-understood reports, which I saw at once upon my arrival was particularly the case with Dionysius. You must picture to such men the extent of the *undertaking,* describing what sort of inquiry it is, with how many difficulties it is beset, and how much labor it involves. For anyone who *hears* this, who is a true **C** lover of wisdom, with the divine quality that makes him akin to it and worthy of pursuing it, thinks that he has *heard* of a marvellous quest that he must at once enter upon with all earnestness, or life is not worth living; and from that time forth he pushes himself and urges on his *leader* without ceasing, until he has reached the end of the journey or has become capable of doing without a *guide* and finding the way himself. This is the state of mind in which such a man lives; whatever his **D** occupation may be, above everything and always he holds fast to philosophy and to the daily discipline that best makes him apt at learning and remembering, and capable of reasoning soberly with himself; while for the opposite way of living he has a persistent hatred. Those who are really not philosophers but have only a coating of opinions, like men whose bodies are tanned by the sun, when they see how much learning is required, and how great the labor, and how orderly their daily lives must be to suit *the subject* they are pursuing, conclude that the task is too **E** difficult for their powers; and rightly so, for they are not equipped for this pursuit. But some of them persuade themselves that they have already *heard* enough about **341A** *the whole thing* and need make no further effort. Now this is a clear and infallible test to apply to those who love ease and are incapable of strenuous labor, for none of them can ever blame his *teacher,* but only himself, if he is unable to put forth the efforts that the *task* demands.

It was in this fashion that I then *spoke* to Dionysius. I did not *explain* everything to him, nor did he ask me to, for he claimed to have already a sufficient knowledge of **B** many and even the most important points because of what he had *heard others say* about them. Later, I hear, he *wrote* a book *on the matters we talked about*, putting it forward as his own teaching, not what he had *learned* from me. Whether this is true I do not know. I know that certain others also have written *on these same matters*; but who they are they themselves do not know. So much at least I can affirm with confidence about *any who have written or propose to write* on these questions, pretend-   C ing to a knowledge of the problems with which I am concerned, whether they claim to have *learned* from me or from others or to have made their discoveries for themselves: it is impossible, in my opinion, that they can have understood anything at all about the subject. *There is no writing of mine about these matters, nor will there ever be one.* For this knowledge is not something that can be communicated in words like other objects of learning; but *after long-continued intercourse between teacher and pupil, in joint pursuit of the subject*, suddenly, like light flashing forth when a fire is   D kindled, it is born in the soul and straightway nourishes itself. And this too I know: if these matters are to be expounded at all in books or lectures, they would best come from me. Certainly I am harmed not least of all if they are misrepresented. *If I thought they should be put into written words and could be communicated adequately for the multitude, what nobler work could I have done in my life than to compose something of such great benefit to mankind and bring to light the nature of things for all to see?* But I do not think that the attempt at communication of these subjects would be of any   E benefit to men, except to a few, i.e., to those who could with a little guidance discover the truth by themselves. Of the rest, some would be filled with an ill-founded and quite unbecoming disdain, and some with an exaggerated and foolish elation, as if they had learned something grand.

Let me go into these matters at somewhat greater length, for perhaps what I am   342 saying will become clearer when I have done so. There is *a true doctrine that confutes anyone who has presumed to write anything whatever on such subjects, a doctrine that I have often before expounded*, but it seems that it must now be said again. For every real being, there are three things that are necessary if knowledge of it is to be acquired: first, the *name*; second, the *definition*; third, the image; knowledge comes fourth, and in the fifth place we must put the object itself, the knowable and truly   B real being. To understand what this means, take a particular example, and think of all other objects as analogous to it. There is something called a circle, and its name is this very word we have just used. Second, there is its definition, composed of nouns and verbs. "The figure whose extremities are everywhere equally distant from its center" is the definition of precisely that to which the names "round," "circumference," and "circle" apply. Third is what we draw or rub out, what is   C turned or destroyed; but the circle itself to which they all refer remains unaffected, because it is different from them. In the fourth place are knowledge (ἐπιστήμη), reason (νοῦς), and right opinion (which are in our minds, not in words or bodily shapes, and therefore must be taken together as something distinct both from the circle itself and from the three things previously mentioned); of these, reason is   D nearest the fifth in kinship and likeness, while the others are further away. The same thing is true of straight-lined as well as of circular figures; of color; of the *good*, the beautiful, the just; of body in general, whether artificial or natural; of fire, water, and all the elements; of all living beings and qualities of souls; of all actions and affections. For in each case, whoever does not somehow grasp the four things   E mentioned will never fully attain knowledge of the fifth.

These things, moreover, because of the weakness of language, are just as much concerned with making clear the particular property (τὸ ποῖόν τι) of each object as the being (τὸ ὄν) of it. On this account no sensible man will venture to express his deepest thoughts in words, *especially in a form that is unchangeable, as is true of written outlines.* Let us go back and study again the illustration just given. Every circle that we make or draw in common life is full of characteristics that contradict the "fifth," for it everywhere touches a straight line, while the circle itself, we say, has in it not the slightest element belonging to a contrary nature. And we say that their names are by no means fixed; there is no reason why what we call *circles* might not be called *straight lines,* and the straight lines "circles," and their natures will be none the less fixed despite this exchange of names. Indeed the same thing is true of the definition: since it is a combination of nouns and verbs, there is nothing surely fixed about it. Much more might be said to show that each of these four instruments is unclear, but the most important point is what I said earlier: that of the two objects of search-the particular quality (τὸ ποῖόν τι) and the being (τὸ ὄν) of an object-the soul seeks to know not the quality but the essence (τὸ τί), whereas each of these four instruments presents to the soul, in discourse and in examples, what it is not seeking, and thus makes it easy to refute by sense perception anything that may be said or pointed out, and fills everyone, so to speak, with perplexity and confusion. Now in those matters in which, because of our defective training, we are not accustomed to look for truth but are satisfied with the first image suggested to us, we can ask and answer without making ourselves *ridiculous* to one another, being proficient in manipulating and testing these four instruments. But when it is "the fifth" about which we are compeled to answer questions or to make explanations, then anyone who wishes to refute has the advantage and can make *the propounder of a doctrine, whether in writing or speaking or in answering questions, seem to most of his listeners completely ignorant* of the matter on which he is trying to speak or write. Those who are listening sometimes do not realize that it is not the mind of the speaker or writer which is being refuted, but these four instruments mentioned, each of which is by nature defective.

By *the repeated use of all these instruments, ascending and descending to each in turn, it is barely possible for knowledge to be engendered of an object naturally good, in a man naturally good;* but if his nature is defective, as is that of most men, for the acquisition of knowledge and the so-called virtues, and if the qualities he has have been corrupted, then not even Lynceus could make such a man see. In short, neither quickness nor learning nor a good memory can make a man see when his nature is not akin to the object, for this knowledge never takes root in an alien nature; so that no man who is not naturally inclined and akin to justice and all other forms of excellence, even though he may be quick at learning and remembering this and that and other things, nor any man who, though akin to justice, is slow at learning and forgetful, will ever attain *the truth as far as it is attainable about virtue nor about vice, either, for these must be learned together, just as the truth and error about any part of being must be learned together, through long and earnest labor,* as I said at the beginning. Only when all of these things—*names, definitions,* and visual and other perceptions—have been rubbed against one another and tested, pupil and teacher *asking and answering questions* in good will and without envy—only then, *when reason and knowledge are at the very extremity of human effort, can they illuminate the nature of any object.*

For this reason anyone who is seriously studying high matters will be the last to write about them and thus expose his thought to the envy and criticism of men. What I have said comes, in short, to this: whenever we see a book, whether the laws of a legislator or a composition of any other type, we can be sure that if the author is really serious, this book does not contain his best thoughts; they are stored away with the fairest of his possessions. And if he has committed these *serious thoughts* to writing, it is because men, not the gods, "have taken his wits away."

C

D

To anyone who has followed this discourse and digression it will be clear that if Dionysius or anyone else—whether more or less able than he—has written concerning the first and highest principles of nature, he has not properly heard or *learned* anything of what he has written about; *otherwise he would have respected these principles as I do, and would not have dared to give them this discordant and unseemly publicity. Nor can he have written them down for the sake of remembrance; for there is no danger of their being forgotten if the soul has once grasped them, since they are contained in the briefest of formulas.* If he wrote them, it was from unworthy ambition, either to have them regarded as his own ideas, or to show that he had participated in an *education* of which he was unworthy if he loved only the reputation that would come from having shared in it. Now if Dionysius did indeed come to understand these matters from our single *conversation*, how that happened, "God wot," as the Thebans say. For as I said, I *went through the matter* with him once only, never afterwards. Whoever cares to understand the course of subsequent events should consider why it was that we did not go over the matter *a second or a third time, or even oftener.* Was it that Dionysius, after this one *hearing*, thought he understood well enough and really did understand, either because he had already found these principles himself or had previously *learned* them from others? Or did he think that what I said was of not value? Or, a third possibility, did he realize that this teaching was beyond him, and that truly he would not be able to live in constant pursuit of virtue and wisdom? *If he thought my teachings of no value he contradicts many witnesses who say the opposite and who are probably much more capable judges of such matters than Dionysius.* And if he had already discovered or learned these doctrines and regarded them as fitted for educating a liberal mind, how—unless he is a very strange creature indeed—could he have so lightly brought ignominy upon their teacher and guardian? But this is what he did, as I shall now tell you.

E

345

B

C

2. The References of the Platonic Writings to Selected Unwritten Doctrines

1. Plato, *Protagoras* 356E8-357C1

What would save our life? Would it not be knowledge; a knowledge of measure- **356E8**
ment, since the art here is concerned with excess and defect, and of numeration, as **357A**
it has to do with odd and even? People would admit this, would they not?

Protagoras agreed that they would.

Well then, my friends, since we have found that the salvation of our life depends **B**
on making a right choice of pleasure and pain—of the more and the fewer, the
greater and smaller, and the nearer and the remoter—is it not evident, in the first
place, that it is *measurement* because it is a study of *excess and defect and equality in
relation to each other*?

This must needs be so.

And being measurement, I presume it must be an art or science?

They will assent to this.

Well, the nature of this art or science we shall consider some other time; but the mere fact
of its being a science *will suffice* for the proof which Protagoras and I are required **C**
to give in answer to the question you have put to us.

2. Plato, *Meno* 76E3-77B1

Socrates: It is an answer in the high poetic style, Meno, and so more agreeable to **76E3**
you than that about *figure*.

Meno: Yes, it is.

Socrates: But yet, son of Alexidemus, I am inclined to think the other was the better
of the two; and I believe you also would prefer it, if you were not compelled, as you
were saying yesterday, *to go away before the mysteries*, and could stay awhile and *be
initiated*.

Meno: But I should stay, Socrates, if you would give me *many* such answers. **77A**

Socrates: Well then, I will spare no endeavour, both for your sake and for my own,
to continue in that style; *but I fear I may not succeed in saying many such things.* But
come now, you in your turn must try and fulfil your promise by telling me what
virtue is in a general way; and you must stop producing *a plural from the singular*,
as the wags say whenever one breaks something, but leave virtue whole and
sound, and tell me what it is. The pattern you have now got from me. **B**

3. Plato, *Phaedo* 107B4-10

"Not only that, Simmias," said Socrates, "but our *first assumptions* ought to be more   107B4
carefully examined, even though they seem to you to be certain. And if you analyse
them completely, *you will,* I think, *follow and agree with the argument, so far as it is
possible for man to do so. And if this is made clear, you will seek no farther.*"

"That is true," he said.

4. Plato, *Republic* 506D2-507A2

'Now, by heavens, Socrates,' said Glaucon, 'don't stop as if you were at the end.   506D2
We shall be quite content if you discuss the good in the same way as you have
discussed justice, and temperance, and the other virtues.'

" 'Well, yes, my friend,' I said, 'I shall be quite content myself. But I am afraid that
I shall not manage it, and if I have the courage to try, my awkwardness will be
laughed at. But, my very good friends, *let us leave for the moment the question of what*   E
*the good itself actually is. To reach what is now in my mind seems too ambitious for our
present attempt.* But I am ready to state what seems to me to be an offspring of the
good, and extremely like it, if the proposal pleases you; if not, I will leave it alone.'

'Please state it,' he said, '*and you will render your account of the parent another time.*'

'I wish,' I said, 'I could pay and you could collect the parent sum, and I did not have   507A
to put you off with the increase like this time.' "

5. *Plato, Republic* 509C1-11

"Glaucon said very comically, 'By Apollo, a miraculous transcendence.'   509C

'Well,' I said, 'it is your fault, you compelled me to say *what I think* about it.'

'Don't stop, please,' he said, 'or at any rate complete the simile of the sun if you
have still anything to say.'

'Yes,' I said, '*I still have many things to say.*'

'Well, don't omit the smallest thing,' he said.

'I fancy,' I said, 'that *I shall omit much.* But nevertheless I shall not, if I can help it,
omit anything *which can be brought forward at present.*'

'Do not,' he said."

6. Plato, *Parmenides* 136D4-E3

Pythodorus said that Zeno answered with a smile: "Let us ask it of Parmenides   136D4
himself, Socrates; for there is a great deal in what he says, and perhaps you do not
see how heavy a task you are imposing upon him. If there were more of us, it would
not be fair to ask it of him; *for it is not suitable for him to speak on such subjects before
many,* especially at his age; *for the many do not know that except by this devious passage*   E
through all things the mind cannot attain to the truth.

7. Plato, *Sophist* 254B7-D3

Eleatic Stranger: Since, therefore, we are agreed that some of the classes will mingle 254B7
with one another, and others will not, and some will mingle with few and others
with many, and that there is nothing to hinder some from mingling universally
with all, let us next proceed with our discussion by investigating, not all the forms C
or ideas, lest we become confused among so many, but *some only, selecting them from
those that are considered the most important*; let us first consider their several natures,
then what their power of mingling with one another is, and so, *if we cannot grasp
being and not-being with perfect clearness, we shall at any rate not fail to reason fully about
them, so far as the method of our present inquiry permits.* Let us in this way see whether
it is, after all, permitted us to say that not-being really is, although not being, and D
yet come off unscathed.

Theaetetus: Yes; that is the proper thing for us to do.

8. Plato, *Statesman* 284A1-E8

Eleatic Stranger: If we assert that the greater has no relation to anything except the 284A1
less, it will never have any relation to *the standard of the mean*, will it?

Young Socrates: No.

Eleatic Stranger: Will not this doctrine destroy the arts and their works one and all,
and do away also with statesmanship, which we are now trying to define, and with
weaving, which we did define? For all these are doubtless careful about excess and
deficiency in relation to the standard of the mean; they regard them not as non-ex-
istent, but as real difficulties in actual practice, and it is in this way, when they B
preserve *the standard of the mean*, that all their works are good and beautiful.

Young Socrates: Certainly.

Eleatic Stranger: And if we do away with the art of statesmanship, our subsequent
search for the kingly art will be hopeless, will it not?

Young Socrates: Certainly.

Eleatic Stranger: Then just as in the case of the sophist we forced the conclusion
that not-being exists, since that was the point at which we had lost our hold of the
argument, so now we must force this second conclusion, that the greater and the
less are to be measured in relation, not only *to one another*, but also *to the establishment* C
of the standard of the mean, must we not? For if this is not admitted, neither the
statesman nor any other man who has knowledge of practical affairs can be said
without any doubt to exist.

Young Socrates: Then we must by all means do now the same that we did then.

Eleatic Stranger: This, Socrates, is a still greater task than that was; and yet we
remember how long that took us; but it is perfectly fair to make about them some
such assumption as this.

Young Socrates: As what?

Eleatic Stranger: *That sometime we shall need this principle of the mean for the demonstra-* D
tion of the exact itself. But our belief that the demonstration is *for our present purpose*

good and *sufficient* is, in my opinion, magnificently supported by this argument—that we must believe that all the arts alike exist and that the greater and the less are measured in relation not only *to one another* but also *to the establishment of the standard of the mean.* For if this exists, they exist also, and if they exist, it exists also, but neither can ever exist if the other does not.

Young Socrates: That is quite right. But what comes next?   E

Eleatic Stranger: We should evidently divide the *science of measurement* into two parts in accordance with what has been said. One part comprises all the arts which measure number, length, depth, breadth, and thickness in relation to their opposites; *the other comprises those which measure them in relation to the moderate, the fitting, the opportune, the needful, and all the other standards that are situated in the mean between the extremes.*

9. Plato, *Timaeus* 48C2-E1

For the present, however, let our procedure be as follows. *We shall not now expound*   48C
the principle of all things—or their principles, or whatever term we use concerning
them; and that solely *for this reason, that it is difficult for us to explain our views while
keeping to our present method of exposition.* You, therefore, ought not to suppose that
I should expound them, while as for me—I should never be able to convince myself
that I should be right in attempting to undertake *so great a task.* Strictly adhering,   D
then, to what we previously affirmed, the import of the "likely" account, I will essay
(as I did before) to give as "likely" an exposition as any other (nay, more so),
regarding both particular things and the totality of things from the very beginning.   E

10. Plato, *Timaeus* 53C4-D7

In the first place, then, it is plain I presume to everyone that fire and earth and water   53C
and air are solid bodies; and the form of a body, in every case, possesses depth also.
Further, it is absolutely necessary that depth should be bounded by a plane surface;
and the rectilinear plane is composed of triangles. Now all triangles *derive their origin
from two triangles,* each having one angle right and the others acute; and the one of   D
these triangles has on each side half a right angle marked off by equal sides, while
the other has the right angle divided into unequal parts by unequal sides. These
we lay down as the *principles* of fire and all the other bodies, proceeding according
to a method in which the probable is combined with the necessary; *but the principles
which are still higher than these are knows only to God and the man who is dear to God.*

11. Plato, *Laws* 894A1-5

And what is the condition which must occur in everything to bring about genera-   894A
tion? Obviously whenever a *starting-principle receiving increase comes to the second
change, and from this to the next, and on coming to the third* admits of perception by
percipients.

3. The Chief Reports of the Unwritten Doctrines (Testimonia Platonica)

(a) Testimonies to the Existence of the Unwritten Doctrines

1. Aristoxenus, *The Elements of Harmony* II (pp. 39-40 Da Rios = *Test. Plat.* 7 Gaiser)

Aristotle was wont to relate that most of those who heard Plato's Discourse (ἀκρόασις) *On the Good* had the following experience. Each came thinking he would be told something about one of the recognized human goods, such as Wealth, Health or Strength, or, in sum, some marvelous Happiness. But when it appeared that Plato was to talk *on Mathematics and Numbers and Geometry and Astronomy*, leading up to the statement that there exists *a Good, a Unity* (ὅτι ἀγαθόν ἐστιν, ἕν), they were overwhelmed by the paradox of the whole matter. Some then thought little of the whole thing and others even reproved it.

39

40

2. Simplicius on Aristotle's *Physics*, 187a12 (pp.151, 6-19 Diels = *Test. Plat.* 8 Gaiser)

Alexander says that '*according to Plato the One and the Indefinite Dyad, which he spoke of as Great and Small, are the Principles of all things and even of the Forms themselves. So Aristotle reports also in his books On the Good*'. One might also have got this from Speusippus and Xenocrates and the others *who attended Plato's course on the Good. For all of them wrote down and preserved his opinion and say that he made use of these same Principles.* It is very likely that Plato made the One and the Indefinite Dyad the Principles of all things, since this was the doctrine of the Pythagoreans whom Plato followed at many points. And Plato made the Indefinite Dyad a Principle of the Ideas also, calling it Great and Small to signify Matter....

187a12

3. Simplicius on Aristotle's *Physics* 202b36 (pp. 453, 22-30 Diels = *Test. Plat.* 23B Gaiser)

Plato denies that the Ideas are beyond the Heavens, since they are not located in space at all, but he asserts none the less that there is an Infinite Element both in sensible things and in the Ideas. They say that Plato made *the One* and *the Indefinite Dyad the Principles* also of sensible things *in his discourses on the Good* but he located the Indefinite Dyad in the noetic realm too, saying it infinite and made the Great and Small into Principles there, saying they were the Infinite. *Aristotle and Heracleides and Hestiaeus and other fellows of Plato were present at these discourses and wrote down Plato's enigmatic utterances.*

202b36

4. Aristotle, *Physics* IV 2.209 b 11-17 (*Test. Plat.* 54 A Gaiser)

This is why Plato, in the *Timaeus*, identifies 'matter' and 'room,' because 'room' and   **209b11**
'the receptive-of-determination' are one and the same thing. His account of the
'receptive' *differs* in the Timaeus and *in what are known as his Unwritten Doctrines*,   **15**
but he is consistent in asserting the identity of 'place' and 'room.' Thus, whereas
everyone asserts the reality of 'place,' only Plato has so much as attempted to tell
us what it is.

5. Aristotle, *Physics* IV 2.209b33-210a2

At which point we may remark parenthetically that Plato ought to tell us why the   **209b33**
Ideas and Numbers have no locality or place, if 'place' is indeed the 'receptive   **35**
factor,'—and this *whether the said receptive factor is 'the great and small'* or (as he writes   **210a**
in the *Timaeus*) 'matter.'

(b) The Whole of the Doctrine, with the Theory of the Dimensions and the Categories

6. Aristotle, *Nicomachean Ethics* I 4.1095a30-b3 (*Test. Plat.* 10 Gaiser)

Let us not fail to notice, however, that there is a difference between *arguments from*   **1095a30**
and those to the first principles. For *Plato, too, was right in raising this question and asking,*
as he used to do, if the way starts from or goes to the first principles. There is a difference,
as there is in a race-course between the course from the judges to the turning-point   **b**
and the way back. For, while we must begin with what is known, things are objects
of knowledge in two senses—some to us, some in an absolute sense.

7. Aristotle, *Metaphysics* Δ 11,1018b37-1019a4 (*Test. Plat.* 33a Gaiser)

The attributes of prior things are called prior, e.g., straightness is prior to smooth-   **1018b37**
ness; for one is an attribute of a line as such, and the other of a surface.   **1019a**

Some things then are called *prior and posterior* in this sense, *others in respect of nature*
and substance, i.e., those which can be without other things, while the others cannot be
without them,—a distinction which Plato used.

8. Theophrastus, Metaphysics 6a15-b17 (Test. Plat. 30 Gaiser)

But at any rate, starting from this first principle or these first principles, one might   **6a15**
demand (and presumable also from any other first principles that may be assumed)
that they should go straight on to give an account of the successive derivatives, and
not proceed to a certain point and then stop; for this is the part of a competent and   **20**
sensible man, to do what Archytas once said Eurytus did as he arranged certain
pebbles; he said (according to Archytas) that this is in fact the number of man, and
this of horse, and this of something else. But now most philosophers go to a certain
point and then stop, as those do also *who set up the One and the indefinite dyad*; for   **25**
after generating *numbers* and *planes* and *solids* they leave out almost everything else,
except to the extent of just touching on them and making this much, and only this

much, plain, that *some things proceed from the indefinite dyad, e.g., place, the void, and* **6b**
the infinite, and others from the numbers and the One, e.g., soul and certain other things;
and they generate simultaneously time and the heavens and several other things,
but of the heavens and the remaining things in the universe they make no further
mention; and similarly the school of Speusippus does not do so, nor does any of **5**
the other philosophers except Xenocrates; for he does somehow assign everything
its place in the universe, alike objects of sense, objects of reason and mathematical
objects, and divine things as well. And Hestiaeus too tries, up to a point, and does
not speak, in the way we have described, only about the first principles. *Now Plato* **10**
in reducing things to the ruling principles might seem to be treating of the other things in
linking them up with the Ideas, and these with the numbers, and in proceeding from the
numbers to the ruling principles, and then, following the order of generation, down as far as **15**
the things we have named; but the others treat of the ruling principles only. And some
even find the truth of things only in these; for they concentrate reality entirely in
the ruling principles.

9. Aristotle, *Metaphysics* A 6.987a29-988a17 *(Test. Plat.* 22 A Gaiser)

After the systems we have named came the philosophy of *Plato,* which in most **987a29**
respects followed these thinkers, but had peculiarities that distinguished it from **30**
the philosophy of the Italians. For, having in his youth first become familiar with
Cratylus and with the Heraclitean doctrines (that all sensible things are ever in a
state of flux and there is no knowledge about them), these views he held even in **987b**
later years. Socrates, however, was busying himself about ethical matters and
neglecting the world of nature as a whole but seeking the universal in these ethical
matters, and fixed thought for the first time on definitions; Plato accepted his
teaching, but held that the problem applied not to sensible things but to entities of **5**
another kind—for this reason, that the common definition could not be a definition
of any sensible thing, as they were always changing. Things of this other sort, then,
he called Ideas, and sensible things, he said, were all named after these, and in virtue
of a relation to these; for the many existed by participation in the Ideas that have
the same name as they. Only the name 'participation' was new; for the **10**
Pythagoreans say that things exist by 'imitation' of numbers, and Plato says they
exist by participation, changing the name. But what the participation or the imitation of the Forms could be they left an open question.

Further, *besides sensible things and Forms he says there are the objects of mathematics, which*
occupy an intermediate position, differing from sensible things in being eternal and **15**
unchangeable, from Forms in that there are many alike, while the Form itself is in
each case unique.

Since the Forms were the causes of all other things, he thought their elements were the
elements of all things. As matter, the great and the small were principles; as essential reality, **20**
the One; for from the great and the small, by participation in the One, come the Forms, esp.
the Numbers.

But he agreed with the Pythagoreans in saying that the One is substance and not
a predicate of something else; and in saying that the Numbers are the causes of the **25**
reality of other things he agreed with them; but *positing a dyad and constructing the*
infinite out of great and small, instead of treating the infinite as one, is peculiar to him; and

so is his view that *the Numbers exist apart from sensible things*, while they say that the things themselves are Numbers, and do not place *the objects of mathematics between Forms and sensible things*. His divergence from the Pythagoreans in making the One   **30** and Numbers separate from things, and his introduction of the Forms, were *due to his inquiries in the region of pure discourse* (for the earlier thinkers had no tincture of dialectic), and his making the other entity besides the One a dyad was due to the belief that the numbers, except those which were prime, could be neatly produced out of the dyad as out of some plastic material. (Yet what happens is the contrary;   **988a** the theory is not a reasonable one. For they make many things out of the matter, and the form generates only once, but what we observe is that one table is made from one matter, while the man who applies the form, though he is one, makes many tables. And the relation of the male to the female is similar; for the latter is   **5** impregnated by one copulation, but the male impregnates many females; yet these are analogues of those first principles.)

Plato, then, declared himself thus on the points in question; it is evident from what has been said that he has used only two causes, that of the essence and the material cause *(for the Forms are the causes of the essence of all other things, and the One is the cause*   **10** *of the essence of the Forms); and it is evident what the underlying matter is, of which the Forms are predicated in the case of sensible things, and the One in the case of Forms, viz., that this is a dyad, the great and the small. Further, he has assigned the cause of good and*   **15** *that of evil to the elements, one to each of the two,* as we say some of his predecessors sought to do, e.g., Empedocles and Anaxagoras.

10. Alexander of Aphrodisias on Aristotle's *Metaphysics*, 987b 33 (pp. 55, 20-56, 35 Hayduck = *Test. Plat.* 22B Gaiser)

Plato and the Pythagoreans made Numbers the Principles of things, since they   **55,20** thought that *what comes first and is uncompounded is a Principle*, and since *Surfaces come before Bodies*—things that are simpler than other things and that are not destroyed by the destruction of the latter, have a natural precedence over those other things—and since *Lines* by parity of reasoning come before Surfaces, and *Points* before Lines. What the mathematicians call Points they called Units   **25** (μονάδες), things wholly incomposite and preceded by nothing. But Units are *Numbers,* and Numbers are therefore the Primary entities. And since for Plato the Forms are primary and the Ideas come before everything that is relative to them,   **56,1** and owes its being to them—their existence he tried to prove in many ways—he said the Forms were Numbers. For if a simple Nature comes before what is relative to it, and nothing comes before Number, the Forms must be Numbers. *He accordingly identified the Principles of Number with Principles of the Forms,* and made *Unity*   **5** *the universal Principle of everything.*

The Forms are the Principles of other things, and since they are Numbers, their Principles are the Principles of Number. *These Principles he said were Unity and the Dyad.* And since in Numbers we meet with Unity and with what surpasses Unity, and since this last is Many and Few, the origin of what surpasses Unity lies in the latter, and he made this the Principle of the Many and Few. The Dyad comes first   **10** besides the One, containing both the Much and the Little in itself. For the Double is much, and the Half little, and both are contained in the Dyad. And the Dyad is opposed to the One, being divided, whereas the One is undivided.

Plato also tried to show that the Equal and Unequal were universal Principles both of 15
self-existent things and the opposites, for he tried to reduce everything to these as being most
simple. He connected Equality with the Unit, and Inequality with Excess and Defect. For
Inequality is to be found both in the *Great and the Small*, in what surpasses and falls
short. For this reason he spoke of the Dyad as indefinite, as being as such deter-   20
mined neither to what exceeds nor to what is exceeded, but as being indefinite and
unbounded.

When limited by the One, the Indefinite Dyad became the Numerical Dyad. For this Dyad
was one Eidos, and the first of the Numbers. Its Principles were the Exceeding and
the Exceeded, since both Double and Half are present in the first Dyad. The Double
and Half are Exceeding and Exceeded respectively, but the Exceeding and Exceeded are not as yet Double and Half, and are therefore Principles of the Double.   25
And since, when bounded, *the Exceeding and Exceeded become Double and Half* (for
these are not indefinite any more than the Triple and the Third, or the Quadruple
and the Quarter, or any other case of definite Excess), it must be *the nature of Unity*
which effects this bounding (each thing being one since it is this definite thing). The Elements   30
of the Numerical Dyad are therefore the One and the Great and Small. But this Dyad is
the first Number, and so these are the Elements of the Dyad (and of every Number).
Such, more or less, are the reasons why Plato made Unity and *the Dyad the Principles*
of the Numbers and of all things, as Aristotle tells us in the books *On the Good.*   35

11. Simplicius on Aristotle's *Physics* 202b36 (pp. 453,30-455,11 Diels = *Test. Plat.* 23 B Gaiser)

And Porphyry, expounding their reports, has this to say about them in his writing   453,30
on the *Philebus*:

'Plato made *the More and the Less*, and the Strong and the Mild, of the nature of the
Infinite. For, wherever they are present, and become *intensified or reduced*, they do
not stand still nor set bounds to what shares in them, but progress into the
indefinitely Infinite. The same is true of the *Greater and Smaller*, or, as Plato call them,   35
the *Great and Small*.

'Let us take a *limited magnitude* like a cubit and divide it into two parts, leaving the
one half-cubit undivided, and dividing the other and adding it bit by bit to the   454,1
undivided portion: we shall then have two parts of the cubit, one proceedingly
infinitely towards increased Smallness, and one towards increased Bigness. For we
shall never reach the Indivisible by such partial division, since a cubit is continuous,
and a continuum always divides into divisibles. This gapless segmentation reveals   5
a certain Infinite Nature locked up in the cubit, or rather more than one such
Nature, the one proceeding towards the Great, the other towards the Small. In these
the *Indefinite Dyad* shows up as constituted by a quantum (μονάς) which tends
towards the Great and a quantum which tends towards the Small.

'*These properties are found both in continuous bodies and in Numbers.* The first Number
is the even Number Two, and in the nature of the Even both Double and Half are   10
embraced, the Double being in excess and the Half in defect. Excess and Defect are

therefore present in the Even. The Dyad is the first among even Numbers, but *in itself it is indefinite, and receives bounds by participating in Unity. For the Dyad is limited in so far as it becomes a single form. Unity and Dyad are therefore the Elements of Number,* 15 *the one limiting and formative, the other indefinite in its Excess and Defect.'*

This Porphyry says nearly literally, setting forth in order the enigmatic utterances made at the seminar (συνουσίᾳ) *On the Good,* (by Plato), and perhaps because these were in accord with what was written down in the *Philebus.*

And *Alexander* himself confessing to take from the statements of Plato in his talks 20 *On the Good,* as reported by Aristotle and the other friends of Plato, has written as follows:

'Plato was in quest of the *Principles* of real things and considered that *Number* came before all other things in nature, for the limits of Lines are *Points, which are Units having position,* and without Lines one can have neither *Surfaces* nor *Solids,* whereas 25 Number can exist without these. Since then Number came before all other things in nature, he thought it to be the Principle of all, and the Principles of the first Number to be the Principles of all Numbers. *But the first Number is the Dyad, whose Principles he said were the One and the Great and Small.* For being a Dyad, it holds both Multitude and Fewness in itself. In so far as there is Doubleness in it, it includes 30 Multitude—for the Double is a case of Multitude and Excess and Magnitude—and in so far as Halfness is in it, it includes Fewness. Excess and Defect and the Great and the Small are accordingly in it. But, inasmuch as each of its parts is a Unit, and it itself is one single form of Duality, it shares in Unity. He therefore said that the One and the Great and Small were the Principles of the Dyad. He called it the Indefinite Dyad in so far as it shared in the Great and Small, or the Greater and 35 Smaller, and so was more or less. For these go on expanding or contracting 455, unceasingly, and in progression towards the indefinitely infinite. Since then the Dyad is the first of the Numbers, and Its Principles are the One and the Great and Small, these are the Principles of all Number. *But Numbers are the Elements of all other things. So that the Principles of all things are the One and the Great and Small (or Indefinite* 5 *Dyad).* And each of the Numbers, to the extent that it is this definite single Number, shares in Unity, but to the extent that it is divided and is a multitude, in the Indefinite Dyad. Plato also said that *the Ideas* were Numbers, and therefore plausible made *the Principles of Number be the Principles of the Ideas.* But he said the Dyad was of the nature of the Infinite, since neither the Great and Small nor the Greater and Smaller have bounds, but involve the More and Less, which go on to infinity.' 10

12. Sextus Empiricus, *Against the mathematicians*, X 248-283 (*Test. Plat.* 32 Gaiser)

Since the number also is one of the things linked closely with time—seeing that the 248 measurement of time (as, for instance, of hours and days and months, and years as well) does not take place without numeration,—after the investigation of the latter which we have now completed we consider that it is well for us to give an orderly discussion of the former; and that the more so because the most learned of the Physicists have attributed so great a potency to numbers as to deem them the principles and elements of all things. These men are Pythagoras of Samos and his

school. For they say that those who are genuinely philosophizing are like those **249**
who work at language. Now the latter first examine the *words* (for language is
composed of words); and since words are formed from the *syllables*, they scrutinize
the syllables first; and as syllables are resolved into the *elements* of written speech,
they investigate these first; so likewise the true physicists, as the Pythagoreans say, **250**
when investigating the Universe, ought in the first place to inquire *what are the
elements into which the Universe can be resolved.*—Now to assert that the principle of
all things is apparent is contrary to physical science; for every apparent thing must
be composed of non-apparents, and what is composed of things is not a principle,
but rather the component of that compound is a principle. Hence one ought not to **251**
say that the apparent things are principles of all things, but the components of the
apparent things, and these are no longer apparent.—Thus they assumed the
principles of existing things to be non-evident and non-apparent, yet they did not **252**
do so with one consent. For those who declared that atoms or homoeomeries or
molecules or, in general, intelligible bodies are the principles of all existing things
proved partly right, but partly went wrong. For in so far as they consider the **253**
principles to be non-evident, their procedure is correct, but in so far as they assume
them to be corporeal they go wrong. For just as the intelligible and non-evident
bodies precede the sensible bodies, so the incorporeals ought to be the principles
of the intelligible bodies. And logically so: for just as the elements of a word are not
words, so also *the elements of bodies are not bodies*; but they must be either bodies or
incorporeals; certainly, then, they are incorporeals.—Moreover, it is not admissible **254**
to say that it is a property of atoms to be eternal, and that on this account they can
be the principles of all things although they are corporeal. For, in the first place,
those who assert that homoeomeries or molecules or minimals and indivisibles are
elements assign to them an eternal existence, so that the atoms are no more elements
than they. Next, let it be granted that the atoms are in very truth eternal; yet, just **255**
as those who allow that the Universe is ingenerable and eternal seek none the less,
in theory, for the principles which first composed it, so also we—as those Physical
philosophers, the Pythagoreans, say—examine theoretically the problem as to what
are the components of these eternal bodies perceptible by the reason. Their components, then, are either bodies or incorporeals. And we will not say that they are **256**
bodies, since then we should have to say that the components of these also are
bodies, and, as the conception thus proceeds ad infinitum, that the Whole is
without beginning. It only remains, therefore, to declare that the intelligible bodies **257**
are composed of incorporeals; and this, too, Epicurus acknowledged, when he said
that "body is conceived by means of a combination of form and magnitude and
resistance and weight."

Well then, it is plain from what has been said that *the principles* of the bodies **258**
perceptible by reason *must be incorporeal.* But if certain incorporeals exist before the
bodies, these are not already of necessity elements of existing things and primary
principles. For see how *the Ideas, which are incorporeal, exist before the bodies, according
to Plato, and everything which becomes becomes because of its relation to them; yet they are
not principles of existing things since each Idea taken separately is said to be a unit, but two
or three or four when taken in conjunction with one or more others, so that there is something
which transcends their substance, namely number, by participation in which the terms one
or two or three or a still higher number than these is predicated of them.* **259**

The *solid forms* also, which are of an incorporeal nature, are conceived before bodies; but they, again, are not principles of all things, for the *plane forms* precede them in conception, since out of these the solid are composed. Yet, indeed, one should not posit the plane forms either as elements of existing things, for each of   **260** these likewise is composed of prior things*namely lines—and lines have numbers* already pre-conceived, inasmuch as the compound of three lines is called a triangle and that of four a quadrangle. And since the simple line is not conceived apart from number but, as drawn from a point to a point, involves the number two, and *all the numbers themselves fall under the One* (for the two is a single two, and the three is   **261** one particular thing, a three, and the ten is one sum of number), Pythagoras, moved by these considerations, declared that the *One is the principle of existing things, by participation in which each of the existing things is termed one*; and this when conceived in its self-identity is conceived as One, but when, in its otherness, it is added to itself it creates the *"Indefinite Dyad,"* so-called because it is not itself any one of the numbered and definite dyads but they all are conceived as dyads through their participation in it, just as they try to prove in the case of the monad. There are, then,   **262** *two principles of existing things, the First One, by participation in which all the numbered ones are conceived as ones, and also the Indefinite Dyad, by participation in which the definite dyads are dyads.*

And that these are in very truth the principles of all things the Pythagoreans teach   **263** in a variety of ways.

Of *existing things* some, they say, are conceived *absolutely*, some by way of *contrariety*, some *relatively. Absolute*, then, are those which subsist of themselves and in com-   **264** plete independence, such as man, horse, plant, earth, water, air, fire; for each of these is regarded absolutely and not in respect of its relation to something else. And *contraries* are all those which are regarded in respect of their contrariety one to another, such as good and evil, just and unjust, advantageous and disad- vantageous, holy and unholy, pious and impious, in motion and at rest, and all other things similar to these. And *relatives* are the things conceived as standing in   **265** a relation to something else, such as right and left, above and below, double and half; for right is conceived as standing in relation to left, and left also as standing in relation to right, and below as related to above, and above as related to below; and similarly in the other cases.—And they say that things conceived as contraries differ   **266** from relatives. For in the case of *contraries the destruction of the one is the generation of the other*, as in the case of health and disease, of motion and rest; for the generation of disease is the removal of health and the generation of health is the removal of disease, and the existence of motion is the destruction of rest and the generation of rest the removal of motion. And the same account holds also in the case of pain and painlessness, of good and evil, and in general of all things that are of opposite natures. But *relatives* have the property both of *co-existence and of co-destruction one*   **267** *with the other*; for there is no right unless a left also exists, nor a double unless the half also, whereof it is the double, pre-exists.—Furthermore, in the case of *opposites*,   **268** as a universal rule, *no intermediate state is conceived*, as for instance in the cases of health and disease, life and death, motion and rest; for there is nothing between healthiness and illness, and between living and being dead, or again between moving and resting. But in the case of *relatives there is a middle state; for the equal* (let us say) *will be between the greater and the smaller*, these being relatives; *and so likewise* *the adequate between the more and the less, and the harmonious between the high and the deep.*—So then, as there are these three classes—the self-existent things, those 269 conceived as in opposition, and also those conceived as relatives,*above all these there must stand of necessity a certain genus, and it must exist first for the reason that every genus must exist before the particulars classed under it. When it, then, is abolished all the particulars are abolished along with it, but when the particular is abolished the genus is not also done away with;* for the former depends on the latter, and not conversely.—Thus the disciples of the Pythagoreans postulated *the One as the supreme genus* of the things 270 conceived as self-existent. For even as this is self-existent, so also each of the absolute things is one and is conceived by itself.

But of the opposites *the equal and the unequal* are, they said, the principles and hold 271 the rank of genus; for in them is seen the nature of all the opposites,—that of rest, for instance, in equality (*for it does not admit of the more and the less*), and that of motion in inequality (*for it does admit of the more and the less*). So too the natural in equality 272 (for they defined it a summit not to be surpassed), but the unnatural in inequality (for it admits they said, of the more and less). The same account holds also in the case of health and disease, and of straightness and crookedness. The relatives, however, are classed under *the genus of excess and defect*; thus great and greater, 273 much and more, high and higher are conceived by way of excess; but small and smaller, few and fewer, low and lower by way of defect.—But since self-existents 274 and opposites and relatives, which are genera, are found to be subordinate to other genera—namely, the One, and equality and inequality, and excess and defect,—let us consider whether these genera also can be referred back to others. *Equality*, then, 275 *is brought under the One* (for the One first of all is equal to itself), but *inequality is seen in excess and defect*; for things of which the one exceeds and the other is exceeded are unequal. But *both excess and defect are ranked under the head of the Indefinite Dyad*, since in fact the primary excess and defect is in two things, that which exceeds and that which is exceeded. *Thus as the highest principles of all things there have emerged the* 276 *primary One and the Indefinite Dyad*; and from these, they say, spring both *the numerical one and the numerical two*,—the one from the primary One, and the two from the One and the Indefinite Dyad. For the two is twice the one, and when the two did not as yet exist among the numbers neither did the twice exist amongst them, but it was taken from the Indefinite Dyad, and in this way the numerical two sprang from it and the One. And in the same way *the rest of the numbers* were 277 constructed from these, *the One always limiting and the Indefinite Dyad generating two and extending the numbers to an infinite amount*.—Hence they say that, of these principles, the One holds the position of the efficient cause and the Dyad that of the passive matter; and just as they have constructed the numbers composed of these, so also they have built up *the Universe* and all things in the Universe.

Thus the *point*, for example, is ranked under the head of the One; for as the One is 278 an indivisible thing, so also is the point; and just as the One is a principle in numbers, so too the point is a principle in lines. So that the point comes under the head of the One, but the *line* is regarded as belonging to the class of the Dyad; for both the Dyad and the line are conceived by way of transition.—And again: the 279 length without breadth conceived as lying between two points is a line. So then, the line will belong to the Dyad class, but the *plane* to the Triad since it is not merely regarded as length, as was the Dyad, but has also taken to itself a third dimension,

breadth. Also when three points are set down, two at an interval opposite to each other, and a third midway in the line formed from the two, but at a different interval, a plane is constructed. And the *solid form and the body*, as also the pyramid, are classed under the Tetrad. For when the three points are placed, as I said before,   280
and another point is placed upon them from above, there is constructed the pyramidal form of the solid body; for it now possesses the three dimensions length, breadth, and depth.—But some assert that the body is constructed from one point;   281
for this point when it has flowed produces the line, and the line when it has flowed makes the plane, and this when it has moved towards depth generates the body which has three dimensions. But this view of the later Pythagoreans differs from   282
that of the earlier ones. For these latter *formed the numbers from two principles, the One and the Indefinite Dyad, and then, from the numbers, the points and the lines and both the plane and the solid forms*; but the former build up all of them from a single point. For from this the line is produced, and from the line the plane, and from this the body.

This, however, is the way in which the solid forms are constructed, with the   283
numbers leading; and, finally, from these <solids> the sensibles are composed, *earth and water and air and fire*, and *the Universe* at large; and it, they declare (holding fast once more to the numbers), is ordered *according to harmony*, since it is in numbers that the ratios reside of those symphonies which make up the perfect harmony,— namely, the Fourth and the Fifth and the Octave of which the first lies in the ratio 4:3, the second in the ratio 3:2, the third in that of 2:1.

13. Simplicius on Aristotle's *Physics* A 9.192 a 3 (pp. 247, 30-248, 15 Diels = *Test. Plat.* 31 Gaiser)

As Aristotle often mentions that Plato called matter the great-and-small, people   247,3
must know that Porphyry communicates that Dercyllides in the eleventh book of his "Philosophy of Plato", where he speaks about matter, quotes a passage of *Hermodorus*, the disciple of Plato's, from his book about Plato, from which appears that Plato admitted matter in the sense of the infinite and indeterminate, and that   35
he showed this by means of things which admit of a more and less, to which belongs   248,1
also the great and small. First, namely, he says: "Plato says that of all things certain things exist *by themselves*, such as man and horse, and others with *a relation to other things*. Of this last group some have a relation *to a counterpart* such as good and bad, and others simply to *something else*. And of these (the whole last group) some are limited, others undetermined." He continues: "And all that is called great with   5
relation to small, has *the more and less* in it. For it is possible to be greater and smaller ad infinitum, and in the same way also broader and narrower, heavier and lighter and all such things will go on ad infinitum. But *things like the equal and the permanent and the arranged do not contain the more and less; their opposites, however, do.* For "unequal" admits of a difference of degree, and so does "moving" and   10
"unarranged". Consequently of both last-mentioned groups of pairs all contain accepted the more and less, except the unitary member of the series. Hence such a thing (that admits of the more and less) must be called unstable, formless, unlimited and non-being, because being is denied of it. And to such a thing it neither belongs to be a principle nor to be an essence, but it is rather proper to it to move in a certain   15
disorder and undecidedness."

14. Aristotle, *Metaphysics* Γ 2.1003b33-1004a2 (*Test. Plat.* 39 A Gaiser)

All this being so, there must be exactly as many *species* of being as *of unity*. And to investigate the essence of these is the work of a science which is generically one—I mean, for instance, the discussion of *the same* and *the similar* and *the other concepts of this sort* (and their counterparts); and nearly all *contraries* may be *referred* to this *origin*; let us take them as having been investigated in the *'Selection of Contraries'*.

15. Alexander of Aphrodisias on Aristotle's *Metaphysics* Γ 1003b33-1004a2 (pp. 250, 13-20 Hayduck = *Test. Plat.* 39 B Gaiser)

He makes a Principle out of the opposition of *the One* and what is contrary to it, i.e., *Multitude*. The same is a sense of oneness, the other a Multitude and multitudinous. Similarly, the Like and the Equal falls under Unity, the Unlike and the Unequal under Multitude. In order that we may know how almost all Opposites lead back to Unity and Multitude as their Principles, he refers us to his *List of Opposites*, the List in which he especially dealt with them. *He talked of such a list also in the Second Book of his* On the Good. [250,13 / 15 / 20]

16. Aristotle, *Metaphysics* Γ 2.1004b27-1005a2 (*Test. Plat.* 40 A Gaiser)

Further, in the list of contraries one of the two columns is privative, and *all contraries are reducible* to being and non-being, and *to unity and plurality, as for instance rest belongs to unity and movement to plurality*. And nearly all thinkers agree that being and substance are composed of contraries; at least all name contraries as their first principles—some name odd and even, some hot and cold, some limit and the unlimited, some love and strife. And *all the others as well are evidently reducible to unity and plurality (this reduction we must take for granted)*, and the principles stated by other thinkers *fall entirely under these as their genera*. [1047b27 / 30 / 1050a]

17. Alexander of Aphrodisias on Aristotle's *Metaphysics* Γ 1004b27–1005a2 (pp. 262, 18 f. Hayduck = *Test. Plat.* 40 B Gaiser)

By talking of such a reduction, he is again referring us to what he proved *in the Second Book of On the Good*.

18. Aristotle, *Metaphysics* I 3.1054a20-32 (*Test. Plat.* 41 A Gaiser)

The one and *the many* are opposed in several ways, of which one is the opposition of the one and plurality as indivisible and divisible; for that which is either divided or divisible is called a plurality, and that which is indivisible or not divided is called one. Now since opposition is of four kinds, and one of these two terms is privative in meaning, they must be contraries, and neither contradictory nor correlative in meaning. And the one derives its name and its explanation from its contrary, the indivisible from the divisible, because plurality and the divisible is more perceptible than the indivisible, so that in definition plurality is prior to the indivisible, because of the conditions of perception. [1054a20 / 25]

To the one belong, as we indicated graphically in our *Distinction of the Contraries, the*   30
same and the like and the equal, and to plurality belong the other and the unlike and the
unequal.

19. Pseudo-Alexander Aphrodisias on Aristotle's *Metaphysics* 1054a20-32 (pp. 615, 14-17 Hayduck = *Test. Plat.* 41 B Gaiser)

Aristotle performed this division in his books *On the Good*, as we have said elsewhere, reducing all Opposites to Multitude and the One: *the Same, Like and Equal*
to the One, and the Different, Unlike and Unequal to Multitude.   15

20. Aristotle, *Metaphysics* K 3,1061a10-15 (*Test. Plat.* 42 A Gaiser)

And since everything that is may be referred to something single and common, *each*   106
of the contrarieties also may be referred to the first differences and contrarieties of being,
whether the first differences of being *are plurality and unity*, or likeness and unlike-
ness, or some other differences; let these be taken as already discussed.   15

21. Pseudo-Alexander Aphrodisias on Aristotle's *Metaphysics* 1061a10-15 (pp. 642,29 – 643,3 Hayduck = *Test. Plat.* 42 B Gaiser)

Like the categories beside the substance (as are quantum, quale, where and the   642
rest), because they are affections or states of the substance, are referred to the   30
substance and in virtue of this are called to be, so also each of all contrarieties:
warmth-chilness, dryness-humidity, *equality-unequality* and all the others are to be
referred to the first differences and contrarieties of being and to be called contrarieties according to them. For like the categories are related to substance, so the   35
contrarieties are related to the first contrariety of being. But the categories are and
are called to be in virtue of the substance. Consequently, also the contrarieties are
to be called contrarieties in virtue of the first contrariety. But, says Aristotle, these   643
first contrarieties of being, if they are *plurality* and the *One* or *similarity* and
dissimilarity or others, have been already considered elsewhere. *In fact, which these*
are he has said in his book with the title On the Good.

22. Aristotle, *Nicomachean Ethics* A 4.1096a17-19

The men who introduced this doctrine (of the Forms) did not posit Ideas of classes
within which they recognized priority and posteriority; this is the reason why they
also did not maintain the existence of an Idea embracing all numbers.

23. Aristotle, *Eudemian Ethics* A 8.1218 a 1-8

Further, in things having a natural succession, a prior and a posterior, there is no   121
common element beyond, and, further, separable from, them, for then there would
be something prior to the first. For the common and separable element would be
prior, because with its destruction the first would be destroyed as well; e.g., if the
double is the first of the multiples, then the universal multiple cannot be separable,   5
for it would be prior to the double.

(c) Axiology

24. Aristotle, *Metaphysics* N 4.1091b13-15 (*Test. Plat.* 51 Gaiser)

Of those who maintain the existence of the unchangeable substances some say *the One itself is the good itself;* but they thought its substance lay mainly in its oneness.

25. Aristotle, *Eudemian Ethics* A 8.1218a15-28

But we should show the nature of the good per se in the opposite way to that now 1218a15
used. For now from what is not agreed to possess the good they demonstrate the
things admitted to be good, e.g., from numbers they demonstrate that *justice* and
health are goods, *for they are arrangements and numbers, and it is assumed that goodness
is a property of numbers and units because unity is the good itself.* But they ought, from 20
what are admitted to be goods, e.g., *health, strength,* and *temperance,* to demonstrate
that beauty is present even more in the changeless; for all these things in the
sensible world are *order and rest;* but if so, then the changeless is still more beautiful,
for it has these attributes still more. And it is a bold way to demonstrate *that unity
is the good per se* to say that *numbers* aim at it; for no one says distinctly how they do 25
so, but the saying is altogether too unqualified. And how can one suppose that
there is desire where there is no life?

26. Iamblichus, *Protrepticus* 6.37, 26 – 39, 8 Pistelli (Aristotle, *Protrepticus* fr.32-36 Düring = *Test. Plat.* 34 Gaiser)

It is easy to show that we are capable of acquiring the sciences that deal with the 37,26
just and the expedient and also those that deal with nature and the rest of reality. 38,1

The *prior* is always *more knowable* than the posterior, and that which is by nature
better more knowable than that which is worse. For knowledge is more concerned 5
with things that are *defined* and *ordered* than with their *contraries,* and more with
causes than effects. *Now good things are more defined and ordered than evil things,* just
as a good man is more defined and ordered than a bad man; there must be the same
difference. Besides, *things that are prior are causes, more than things that are posterior;* 10
*for if the former are removed, the things that have their being from them are removed, lines
if numbers are removed, planes if lines are removed, solids if planes are removed, the so-called
'syllables' if the letters are removed.*

Therefore if soul is better than body (being by nature more able to command), and 15
there are arts and sciences concerned with the body, namely medicine and gym-
nastics (for we reckon these as sciences and say that some people possess them),
clearly with regard to the soul too and its virtues there is a care and an art, and we
can acquire it, since we can do this even with regard to things of which our 20
ignorance is greater and knowledge is harder to come by.

So too with regard to nature; it is far *more necessary to have knowledge of the causes and
elements than of things posterior to them; for the latter are not among the highest realities,
and the first principles do not arise from them, but from and through the first principles all* 39,1
other things manifestly proceed and are constituted.

Whether it be fire or air or number or other natures that are the *causes and principles*   5
of other things, *if we are ignorant of them we cannot know any of the other things*; for
how could one recognize speech if one did not know the syllables, or know these
if we knew none of the letters?

27. Aristotelian Divisions, Diogenes Laertius III 108-109; nr.32, pp.39 – 41 Mutschmann (*Test. Plat.* 43 Gaiser)

Of existing things some are *absolute* and some are called *relative*. Things said to exist   39a
absolutely are those which need nothing else to explain them, as man, horse, and
all other animals. For none of these gains by explanation. To those which are called   40a
relative belong all which stand in need of some explanation, as that which is greater
than something or quicker than something, or more beautiful and the like. For *the*
greater implies a less, and the quicker is quicker than something. Thus existing things   41a
are either absolute or relative. *And in this way*, according to Aristotle, *Plato used to*
divide the primary entities also.

28. Aristotelian Divisions, Codex Marcianus 67, pp. 39-40 Mutschmann (*Test. Plat.* 43 Gaiser)

Of existing things some are *absolute for themselves*, and some are *relative to something*   39b
else. Now, absolute things for themselves are for example house, dress, gold and
everything that simply exists and not because it is necessarily another thing.
Relatives are for example the double and the knowledge, because the *double is relative*   40b
to the half and knowledge is relative to something other (which is not knowledge).

29. Aristotelian Divisions, Codex Marcianus 68, pp. 65-66 Mutschmann (*Test. Plat.* 44 a Gaiser)

Contraries are divided as follows: *Of some things there exists a contrary, of others not.*   65
For of gold and man and dress and the like there is no contrary, but of virtue and
good and warm there exists a contrary. For to the good is contrary the evil, to virtue
vice, to the warm the cold. Now, of the contraries themselves some do have a mean,
others do not. For between good and evil there exists a mean, but between motion
and rest there is no mean, because it is necessary that everything either is in motion   66
or in rest. Also between life and death there is no mean, because everything
susceptible to life either is living or dead.—The *contraries* themselves we call in *three*
senses: either as the *evil* is contrary to the *good*, for example injustice to justice or
self-indulgence to temperance and the like; or as the *neutral* is contrary to the *neutral*
(i.e., the neither good nor evil to the neither good nor evil, for example the white
is contrary to the black and the light is contrary to the heavy), for none of these is
either good or evil. But as *evil* to the *evil* is contrary the *excess* to the *defect* and what
we call *according to excess and defect*, for example the excessively being cooled (to the
excessively being warmed)—these are called in the sense of excess—and the defective in warm to the defective in cold, because also these are contraries, viz., in the
sense of defect.

30. Aristotelian Divisions, Diogenes Laertius III 104-105 (nr. 27, pp. 34-35 Mutschmann = *Test. Plat.* 44 b Gaiser)

Contraries are divided into *three* species. For instance, we say that *goods* are contrary to *evils*, as justice to injustice, wisdom to folly, and the like. Again, *evils* are contrary to *evils*, *prodigality* is contrary to *niggardliness*, and to be unjustly tortured is the contrary of being justly tortured, and so with similar evils. Again, heavy is the contrary of light, quick of slow, black of white, and these pairs are contraries, while they are *neither good nor evil*. Thus, of contraries, some are opposed as goods to evils, others as evils to evils, and others, as things which are neither good nor evil, are opposed to one another.

34a

35a

31. Aristotelian Divisions, Codex Marcianus 23 (pp.34-35 Mutschmann = *Test. Plat.* 44 b Gaiser)

Contraries are divided into three species. For some of them are contrary as good to evil, for example health to disease and beauty to ugliness, and the like. Others are contrary as neutral to neutral (i.e., neither good nor evil to neither good nor evil), for example whiteness to blackness and lightness to heaviness, and the like. And still others are *contrary as what is to be avoided to what is to be avoided, for example prodigality to niggardliness* and warmth to chilness and thinness to thickness, and the like.

34b

35b

Notes

Chapter 1

1. *Platons Werke von F. Schleiermacher*, I 1 (Berlin, 1804), I 2 (1805), II 1 (1805), II 2 (1807), II 3 (1809), III 1 (1828). The Introduction of (1804) will be cited according to the first edition; the second edition of (1817) has identical page numbers. (The reader will find this Introduction also reproduced in K. Gaiser, *Das Platonbild. Zehn Beiträge zum Platonverständnis* (Hildesheim, 1969), pp. 1-32, which places the pagination of the third edition of 1855 in parentheses.)

2. *Ueber die verschiedenen Methoden des Uebersezens* (1813), in *Sämmtliche Werke*, III 2 (1838), pp. 207-45 (with reference to Plato, pp. 240ff.).

3. Introduction, p. 38 (Gaiser, p. 24).

4. In the Introduction, p. 16 (Gaiser, p. 10) we read: "thus every proposition can be correctly understood only in the place in which it is found and in the context and within the limits within which Plato has placed it." Consult also page 15 (Gaiser, p. 9), in which the importance of "the context" of every proposition is emphasized as well as the connection of each proposition with the context. This concept is also pointed out in the Introduction to the *Parmenides* (I 2, p. 91 [p. 89^2]): "so that, when we wish to judge whether the doctrines which they attributed (sc., to Plato) truly are his or are not, it is necessary to evaluate every statement on the basis of the place it occupies, and in the context in which it is found."

5. Consult the judgment of H. von Stein, *Sieben Bücher zur Geschichte des Platonismus*, vol. III (Göttingen, 1875), pp. 360f., 364.

6. *Sämmtliche Werke*, III 4,1: *Geschichte der Philosophie, aus Schleiermachers handschriftlichem Nachlasse*, ed. H. Ritter (Berlin, 1839), pp. 97-111.

7. The supposition of Schleiermacher according to which Plato would have been able to achieve his general plan, precociously conceived, exactly in the span of time alloted to him, is problematic already at its very inception.

8. Introduction, p. 19 (Gaiser, p. 11).

9. K. F. Hermann "Über Platos schriftstellerische Motive," *Ges. Abh. u. Beiträge z. class. Literatur u. Altertumskunde* (Göttingen, 1849) esp. pp. 287f. (reproduced by Gaiser, pp. 39f.). Consult also the recent contribution of W. Luther "Die Schwäche des geschriebenen Logos," *Gymnasium* 68 (1961) esp. pp. 536ff. See also in addition the detailed critical analysis of Schleiermacher and of Hermann in F. Ueberweg, *Untersuchungen über die Echtheit und Zeitfolge platonischer Schriften*, (Vienna, 1861), pp. 56-70 (with indications of a characteristic error of translation committed by Schleiermacher, pp. 18f.). The relationship between the oral and the written in Plato, to use the terminology of Aristotle, would be that of homonymy.

10. The characterization of Schleiermacher's interpretation of the *Phaedrus* given by H. von Stein is, without wanting to be, ironic and illuminating: "certainly none of his predecessors was able to draw as much as he from this text" (*Sieben Bücher*, III, p. 354, note 1).

11. In a significant way the criticism of writing contained in the *Phaedrus* (276 E; see also Appendix, 1.1) also includes, by implication, the masterpiece of Plato, the *Republic* (consult *Republic* 376D, 501E, and on this, Luther, loc. cit.).

12. Hermann, "Über Platos," p. 288 (Gaiser, p. 40).

13. Consult the differences of times (1:30!) in the passage of the *Phaedrus* 276 B (see Appendix, 1.1).

14. Schleiermacher assumes, instead, "that Plato's object was also to bring the still ignorant reader to a state of knowledge" Introduction. p. 19 (Gaiser, p. 12, Dobson, p. 17). [The references to William Dobson are to the Arno Press edition of *Schleiermacher's Introductions to the Dialogues of Plato* (New York: Arno Press, 1973) for the convenience of the reader.]

15. Volume I 1, p. 75.

16. Volume I 1, p. 231 (p. 232^2).

17. The critical judgment of K. Jaspers concerning the literary dialogue converges with the general criticism of the written work of Plato (*Philosophie*. Vol. II, Berlin-Heidelberg-New York, 1973^4, p. 115: "Therefore the Platonic dialogues are not expressions of the communication of possible existential experiences, but only of the dialectical structure of rational knowledge"). Concerning this, see also E. Hättich, "Denken als Gespräch. Der philosophische Dialog und die Grundlagen der Dialektik." Dissertation (Innsbruck, 1961), p. 259.

18. For the argumentation which follows consult especially *APA* pp. 393-96, *Retract.*, pp. 148-54, *GF*, pp. 124-28 (with a detailed treatment).

19. So, for example, Vlastos, *Gnomon* 35 (1963), p. 653 (now also in G. Vlastos, *Platonic Studies* [Princeton, 1973], p. 395). Naturally, this could also not be a specific prerogative of the philosopher (consult G. J. De Vries, *A Commentary on the Phaedrus of Plato*, [Amsterdam, 1969], p. 262, who attributes this capacity to all authors).

20. *Phaedrus* 278B4ff.: εἰδώς, ἔχων, δυνατός: D8: ἔχοντα, consult the *logos* ἐν αὐτῷ in 278A4. Such a logos can be "discovered" (εὑρεθείς, in correspondence with the objective expression τιμιώτερα and others like it), for which an explanation that refers simply to the *spontaneity and the interior vitality of the author* is excluded as insufficient. This is imposed likewise by the fact that all authors that possess interior spontaneity and vitality would be *eo ipso* (by that fact) philosophers in the Platonic sense. So, as soon as the specifically Platonic theory of the Ideas enters into play—and this, note, is necessarily required by the total context of the *Phaedrus*—the "coming to the assistance" is referred to a different and higher level of being. Applied to Plato himself, who wrote concerning the theory of Ideas, this involves analogous conclusions, they refer to something that "is of still more value" beyond the theory of Ideas. The concepts of δίκαια, καλά and ἀγαθά mentioned in the context, which must constitute the object of oral teaching (276C, 277D10f., 278A, in each case with the significant final position in which ἀγαθά is placed), must therefore be subjected, in that situation, to a further explanation, as already the Republic, to which the end of

the Phaedrus clearly refers (especially 276E), hints in a sufficiently clear fashion (506A: the guardians of the ideal State must know δικιά τε καὶ καλὰ ὅπῃ ποτὲ ἀγαθά ἐστιν with the following reference to the Idea of the Good, whose essence—τί ποτ̓ ἐστὶ τἀγαθόν—however, in 506D E [Appendix, 2.4] expressly remains hidden "by now," while, on the contrary, it is revealed by the oral doctrine περὶ τοῦ ἀγαθοῦ and with it the relation—not simply subordinating—between justice and beauty, on the one hand, and the Good, on the other, becomes explicated and explained; concerning this see later). A hint of the duality of values (and hence, implicitly, to the opposed principle!) is found in *Phaedrus* 277E1. (See all the passages of *Phaedrus* mentioned in Appendix, 1.1).

21. T. A. Szlezák, "Dialogform und Esoterik. Zur Deutung des platonischen Dialogs 'Phaidros,'" *Museum Helveticum* 35 (1978):18-32, esp. pp. 22ff. Idem, "Sokrates' Spott über Geheimhaltung. Zum Bild des φιλόσοφος in Platons 'Euthydemos'," *Antike und Abendland* 26 (1980) 75-89. Also by the same author see "Plotin und die geheimen Lehren des Ammonios," in *Esoterik und Exoterik der Philosophie*, ed. Holzhey-Zimmerli (Basel-Stuttgart, 1977), pp. 52-69, esp. p. 67.

22. G. J. De Vries in his criticism of Szlezák did not take into account at all this ("Helping the Writings," *Museum Helveticum* 36 [1979]:61). The original way to "come to the assistance of one's writings" is in an actual conversation. It can be imitated also in a literary medium, that is, in the form of a dialogue or debate, in which the *topos* is taken up (just as it is in parallel passages). Lastly, as in the *Phaedrus* 278 (see Appendix, 1.1), the rendering of assistance can come into play also in the relationship between oral and written discourse. The meaning of the *topos* referred to the *content* is the same in all three cases. (Consult the reply of Szlezák to De Vries, in *Museum Helveticum* 36 [1979]:164). When, then, De Vries, in a new article ("Once more Helping the Writings," *Museum Helveticum* 37 [1980]:60) maintains, moreover, that coming to the assistance on the part of the philosophical author has no place in dialectical discourse, he clearly goes contrary to the text (ἔλεγχος) and to the context of the *Phaedrus* (consult the question and answer in reference to writings in 275D, λέγων αὐτός in 278C6 as in 278A2, the philosopher as essentially a dialectician in 276Eff., with the rejection of all speeches ἄνευ ἀνακρίσεως καὶ διδαχῆς [277E9] in 278B2, taken up anew with οὐκοῦν in B7). The fact escapes De Vries, too, that, if it were as he says, then the expression ἐφ᾽ οἷς ἐσπούδακεν of 278C8 (consult A5) could no longer be explained by him (sc., not even by formal dialectic). See also all the passages in the Appendix, 1.1.

23. Aristotle, *De caelo* A 10.279b32ff. (Speusippus, frag. 54 a-b Lang; frags. 94-95 Isnardi Parente, and Xenocrates, frag. 54 Heinze). The argument shows, by a mathematical example, the regressive move to a higher level: cosmogony is made to fit as a particular case in the universal "generation" of atemporal realities in the system of Platonic-Academic derivation (consult the parallels in Xenocrates, frags. 33 and 68 Heinze and Sextus Empiricus, *Adv. math.* 10.255, LCL 3:335 (*Test. Plat.* 32 Gaiser, reproduced in Appendix, 3.12 as well as on p. 426 Findlay). The objection that here Plato is not speaking but only his followers is removed by what is said in *Phaedrus* 276E7f., 278A6-9; see also Appendix, 1.1 (consult ἑαυτοῖς, Arist. loc. cit.).

24. *Phaedrus* 234E3f., 235B4f., 269Ef. Consult Szlezák on these passages in *Museum Helveticum* 35 (1978):27-30 with the pertinent interpretations. The attempt

of De Vries, *Museum Helveticum* 36 (1979):62 to refer the first two documents to the characterization of the person of Phaedrus and consequently to eliminate the importance with respect to what is said in *Phaedrus* 278 (see Appendix, 1.1), errs because of the objectively ironic function of the expressions in relation to the words of Socrates that follow, which are in point of fact "more ample." The nexus is still more clear *in the prophecy after the fact* of Socrates speaking of Isocrates, contained in the *Phaedrus* 279A, which immediately follows the antagonism between the rhetoricians and the philosophers (*Phaedrus* 278; consult Appendix, 1.1) and which this writer of discourses endows with "a philosophical impulse to something greater," and in this—even if said in an ironic manner—has a clearly *content-oriented significance*. Consult in addition, *Phaedrus* 274A.

25. Let us note the expressions παιδιά-σπουδή, εἴδωλον-μίμησις-ἀλήθεια (*Republic* 599D, 600E, 602C, 603A, 608A, and *Phaedrus* 278C5!) with the same example (Homer). For the relations between the *Republic* and the *Phaedrus*, see P. Friedländer, *Platon*, I (Berlin, 1964^3), pp. 125ff.; W. Luther, *Die Schwäche* cited in note 9, pp. 538f.

26. For more details, consult what we said in *GF*, pp. 125ff.

27. Consult especially *Phaedrus* 278C (see also Appendix, 1.1), with the *Seventh Letter* 344C (also Appendix, 1.2) with the references to the written laws of the legislator. The fact that the *Seventh Letter* 344Df. (see Appendix, 1.2) affirms the uselessness of help for the memory through writing ὑπομνήματα with respect to the theory of the principles, corresponds to the overcoming of the hypomnematic level, which the *Phaedrus* 278 (see Appendix, 1.1) addresses.

28. For more details, see what we said in *Retr.*, pp. 152ff., with an even better treatment in *GF*, p. 127 (the polemic response of G. Vlastos, *Platonic Studies*, pp. 399-403, is rendered otiose because of what we explained here).

29. W. G. Tennemann, *Geschichte der Philosophie*, Vol. II (Leipzig, 1799), pp. 204ff.

30. Consult Introduction to the *Phaedrus*, Vol. I 1, p. 75; Dobson, pp. 291ff.

31. Consult Vol. II 2, p. 520^2 (note to page 315). In the first edition Schleiermacher even wanted to change the text.

32. Vol. III 1, p. 39.

33. Vol. II 2, pp. 357ff. (pp. 369ff. of the second edition) and Vol. II 3, pp. 5ff. (pp. 8f. of the second edition).

34. In this section Tennemann is not cited by name, but he is cited several times in the context of the Introduction (for example pp. 1 and 27 [Gaiser, pp. 1 and 16f.] where Schleiermacher says that Tennemann represents the contrary to the position he has taken; clearly also at pp. 16f. [Gaiser, pp. 9f.]).

35. Introduction, pp. 11-15. In other places Schleiermacher hypothesized the possibility that the students of the Academy were instructed by fuller expositions than the material contained in the dialogues; see Introduction, p. 21 (Gaiser, p. 13); notes to the *Gorgias*, Vol. II 1, p. 485 (p. 493^2); Introduction to the *Philebus*, Vol. II 3, pp. 130f. (p. 131^2). Consult Chapter 2, note 6.

36. Introduction, p. 15 (Gaiser, p. 9). And in agreement with what is said earlier: "they would be at a loss to discover anything in the whole region of philosophy upon which some opinion, either directly and distinctly, or at least as far as a notice

of the principles goes, is not to be met with in these writings" (Introduction, pp. 13f.; Gaiser, p. 8; Dobson, p. 11).

37. Equally vague is the argument that "the works collectively are hardly intelligible, and consequently must allow that Plato might as easily have committed to them what was most difficult and mysterious in his wisdom, as what was otherwise" (Introduction, p. 13; Gaiser, p. 8; Dobson, p. 11).

38. Introduction, p. 11 (Gaiser, p. 6), keep in mind the conjunction expressly used by Schleiermacher, "consequently."

39. In a significant fashion Schleiermacher tries to combine the expressions "esoteric" and "exoteric," understood in a new way, with the nature more or less qualified of the *reader* (Introduction, p. 21; Gaiser, p. 13; Dobson, p. 2). Instructive, in addition, is that the analytical procedure applied by Tennemann to the philosophical content is characterized as "amorphous" (Introduction, p. 15; Gaiser, p. 9; Dobson, p. 2).

Chapter 2

1. W. Dilthey, *Leben Schleiermachers*, ed. M. Redeker, esp. Vol. I 2 (Berlin, 1970³), pp. 37-52; H. G. Gadamer, "Schleiermacher als Platoniker," in *Kleine Schriften*, Vol. III (Tübingen, 1972), pp. 141-49, also translated into French with the title: "Schleiermacher Platonicien," in *Archives de Philosophie* (1969):28-39.

2. See also in this regard the rich presentation of material by E. N. Tigerstedt, *The Decline and Fall of the Neoplatonic Interpretation of Plato. An Outline and Some Observations. (Comm. Hum. Litt.* 52 [Helsinki 1974], with further bibliography). By the same author see also *Interpreting Plato* (Stockholm, 1977). Consult my review of the two books of Tigerstedt in *Ph. R.* 14-22.

3. F. D. E. Schleiermacher, "Hermeneutik, nach den Handschriften neu ausgegeben und eingeleitet von H. Kimmerle," *Abh. Heidelberger Akademie d. Wiss., phil.-hist. Klasse* [1959/2]:32, 80, 155f.; F. Schleiermacher, *Hermeneutik und Kritik*, ed. F. Lücke [Berlin, 1838] (*Sämmtliche Werke*, Vol. I 7), pp. 20ff. (published also in the pocketbook edition, ed. M. Frank [Frankfurt, 1977], pp. 85ff.). Consult also on this J. Wach, *Das Verstehen. Grundzüge einer Geschichte der hermeneutischen Theorie im 19. Jahrhundert*, Vol. I (Tübingen, 1926), pp. 109, 120; P. Szondi, *Einführung in die literarische Hermeneutik* (Frankfurt, 1975), pp. 153f., 178ff., 190.

4. Introduction, p. 6; Gaiser, p. 3; Dobson, p. 2.

5. Schleiermacher distanced himself from the Neoplatonists, once again, in the Introduction, p. 13; Gaiser, p. 8; Dobson, p. 2.

6. "Reden über die Religion," *Vierte Rede*, pp. 99f. *Philos. Bibliothek* 255, (Hamburg: Meiner, 1970), which is reprinted from the first edition of 1799; *Hermeneutik und Kritik*, pocketbook edition, cited, pp. 233f.; see also pp. 103, 132, 158f. and earlier Chapter 1, note 35.

7. Consult J. Wach, *Das Verstehen*, cited Vol. I, pp. 90, 101.

8. Introduction, pp. 6, 17. See also the Introductions to the *Phaedrus*, Vol. I 1, p. 65; to the *Lysis*, Vol. I 1, pp. 174, 177; and to the *Protagoras*, Vol I 1, pp. 222, 230f.; to the *Charmides*, Vol. I 2, p. 8 (6²); to the *Parmenides*, Vol. I 2, p. 98 (96f.²); to the *Apology*, Vol. I 2, pp. 184-88; to the *Gorgias*, Vol. II 1; pp. 7 (11²), 14-17 (13-15²), 19 (17f.²), notes to p. 471²; to the *Theaetetus*, Vol. II 1, p. 177; to the *Symposium*, II 2, p. 361, and so on.

9. Letter to Reimer in the Spring of 1803, in *Aus Schleiermachers Leben in Briefen,* ed. L. Jonas and W. Dilthey, Vol. III (Berlin, 1861, reprinted 1974) p. 336 (where it reads: "I love him infinitely").

10. This is said at the end of the essay on Lessing of 1797 (the second edition is from 1800), in *Kritische Friedrich-Schlegel-Ausgabe,* Vol. II, ed. H. Eichner (Paderborn, 1967), pp. 415f.

11. F. Schleiermacher, *Über die Religion. Reden an die Gebildeten unter ihren Verächtern,* Philos. Bibliothek 255 (Hamburg, 1970) (reprinted from the first edition of 1799), pp. 92-6.

12. F. Schleiermacher, *Ästhetik,* ed. R. Odebrecht (Berlin-Leipzig, 1931), p. 115; consult also pp. 17, 29, 118, as well as the "Abhandlungen zur Ästhetik" of 1831/32 in *Sämmtliche Werke,* Vol. III 3, Reden und Abhandlungen, ed. L. Jonas (Berlin, 1835), pp. 186, 220.

13. F. Schleiermacher, *Geschichte der Philosophie, aus dem handschriftlichen Nachlass,* ed. H. Ritter, (Berlin, 1839) = *Sämmtliche Werke,* III 4, 1, pp. 97-111, esp. pp. 98 and 110.

14. Introduction, p. 40.

15. Introduction, p. 40.

16. "Brouillon zur Ethik (1805/6)," pp. 98f. Braun (see note 60); *Hermeneutik und Kritik,* pocketbook edition, cited p. 168; *Hermeneutik,* ed. Kimmerle, pp. 41, 43, 78f.

17. W. Dilthey, *Leben Schleiermachers,* Vol. II 2 (= *Ges. Schriften,* XIV 2), ed. M. Redeker (Berlin, 1966), pp. 683, 685f., 781ff. In the text of the Introduction the terms *intention* (*Absicht*) and *composition* (*Komposition*) correspond to this. This analysis of the aesthetic of production is a complement to the aesthetic consideration of the "type of effect produced by writing" (Introduction, p. 40).

18. Consult *Ästhetik,* ed. R. Odebrecht, pp. 31ff., and in addition *Hermeneutik und Kritik,* pocketbook edition, cited pp. 181ff., 217ff. (in the aesthetic of Schleiermacher the form of the dialogical presentation of philosophical themes is expressly assigned to the "meditation" stage, ibid., p. 220).

19. Concerning the three fundamental elements of the art that result (excitation [*Erregung*], sentiment [*Gefühl*], enthusiasm [*Begeisterung*]—model [*Urbildung*]—development [*Ausbildung*]) and their mutual relation with each other, consult *Ästhetik,* ed. R. Odebrecht, pp. 36ff., 150; *System der Sittenlehre,* ed. A. Schweizer (*Sämmtliche Werke,* III 5), pp. 251-55; *Abhandlungen zur Ästhetik* of 1831/2 (*Sämmtliche Werke,* III 3, ed. L. Jonas), pp. 182, 194ff.

20. Consult note 12.

21. *Dialektik,* ed. L. Jonas, *Sämmtliche Werke,* III 4, 2, pp. 444.

22. *Friedrich Schlegel's Philosophische Vorlesungen aus den Jahren 1804 bis 1806, aus dem Nachlass,* ed. C. J. H. Windischmann, Erster Band (Bonn, 1836), pp. 361-86 (Philosophie des Plato). Now in *Kritische Friedrich-Schlegel-Ausgabe,* Vol. XII: Philosophische Vorlesungen. Erster Teil, ed. J. J. Anstett (Paderborn, 1964), pp. 207-26. Consult the briefer "Charakteristik des Plato," in "Geschichte der europäischen Literatur (Pariser Vorlesungen von 1803/04"), in the *Kritische Friedrich-Schlegel-Ausgabe,* Vol. XI, ed. E. Behler (Paderborn, 1958), pp. 118-25.

23. The possibility of formulating the highest principle in Plato in a didactic fashion is, however, also denied by Schleiermacher (see the *Lecture of 1812* [cited in note 13], p. 98, where he says: "Therefore it is not possible to understand Plato, except that we take into account the essence of myth, which means that the myth substitutes for the doctrinal expression of absolute unity as a positive thing and hence also for the expression of the relations of the unity with the totality, because this doctrinal expression in words is impossible except that universal perfection is achieved." (Consult Introduction to the *Plato*, p. 7; Gaiser, p. 3; concerning the role of not-knowing in Plato). Schleiermacher also recognized in Plato different degrees of irony (Introduction, p. 23; Gaiser, p. 14; and the Introduction to the *Protagoras*, pp. 226f.), but Schleiermacher gives less weight to this than Schlegel.

24. Concerning this issue see J. Körner, *F. Schlegel, Neue philosophische Schriften* (Frankfurt, 1935), pp. 1-114; E. Behler, "Einleitung zu F. Schlegel, Studien zur Philosophie und Theologie," in *Kritische Friedrich-Schlegel-Ausgabe* Vol. VIII (Paderborn, 1975), pp. xxi-clii. For the influence on Schlegel's picture of Plato,see E. Behler, in *Kritische Friedrich-Schlegel-Ausgabe*,Vol. IX (aderborn,1958) pp. 307f.

25. W. Dilthey, *Leben Schleiermachers*, Vol. I 2, pp. 37-42. See, further, H. von Stein, *Sieben Bücher* (consult Chapter 1, note 5), Vol. III, pp. 359f. (for the position of the art); H. Süskind, *Der Einfluss Schellings auf die Entwicklung von Schleiermachers System* (Tübingen, 1909), pp. 96ff., 138ff., 222ff., 244ff., 274f. (detailed, but in part outmoded).

26. *Kritische Friedrich-Schlegel-Ausgabe*, Vol. III, p. 334 (par. 8); reprinted also in W. Dilthey, *Leben Schleiermachers*, Vol. I 2³ (Dilthey, *Ges. Schriften*, XIII 2) pp. 62f. Consult further the relation of Schleiermacher in the "Letter to Boeckh of June 18, 1808," in *Briefwechsel Friedrich Schleiermachers mit August Boeckh und Immanuel Bekker* (Mitteilungen aus dem Litaturarchive in Berlin), N.F. 11, ed. H. Meisner (Berlin, 1916), p. 26 (in Dilthey, ibid., p. 70).

27. Reprinted in ibid., p. 63.

28. *Aus Schleiermachers Leben in Briefen*, ed. L. Jonas and W. Dilthey, Vol. III, p. 362.

29. In Dilthey, *Leben Schleiermachers*, Vol. I 2³, p. 64.

30. "Letter to Boeckh" (consult note 26), p. 31. *Platons Werke*, Vol. I 1 (Berlin, 1817²), note p. 382, and Vol. III 1 (Berlin, 1828) note p. 571.

31. *Geschichte der Philosophie* (consult note 13), p. 98. Compare, for example, the construction of the Hegelian philosophical system into logic, "philosophy of reality" (*Realphilosophie*) and encyclopedia.

32. *Hermeneutik und Kritik*, pocketbook edition, pp. 182-84. Consult in this regard W. Dilthey, *Leben Schleiermachers*, Vol. II 2, pp. 660ff. ("Fichte and the Origin of the Thought Capable of Reforming Hermeneutics").

33. Introduction, pp. 49f., Gaiser, pp. 35f.

34. Introduction, pp. 21f., 46, 49; Gaiser, pp. 13f., 29, 31.

35. Introduction, p. 49; Gaiser, p. 31; Introduction to the *Gorgias*, Vol. II 1, pp. 6ff. (4ff.²).

36. Edition of the Wissenschaftliche Buchgesellschaft of Darmstadt, Vol III: *Schriften von 1801-1804*, esp. p. 514 (with the deduction of the concept) and pp. 520, 540f., 546.In Hegel the expression *Realphilosophie* is not to be found before 1805.Concerning the division of philosophy into physics and ethics in Schelling, consult Vol. II, p. 648 (of 1801).

37. Reproduced in *Aus Schleiermachers Leben in Briefen*, ed. L. Jonas and W. Dilthey, Vol. IV, pp. 579-93.

38. Vol. I 2, p. 92 (91^2).

39. Vol. I 2, p. 95 (93^2).

40. Vol. I 2, p. 96f. (95^2).

41. Vol. II 1, p. 178. Consult in this regard the degrees of manifestation of the self in the *System of the Transcendental Idealism of 1800* of Schelling (in the edition of the Wissenschaftliche Buchgesellschaft of Darmstadt, Vol. II, *Schriften von 1799-1801*, pp. 331ff., 450ff.).

42. Consult note 13.

43. Schleiermacher combines together here the two "constructive" expositions of the *Republic* and the *Timaeus*. So already also in the Introduction to the *Sophist*, Vol. II 2 (1807), p. 130 (136^2), where we read: "the necessary being one and being the one in the other of being and knowledge. In the sphere of philosophy there is nothing greater," with the relative compenetration of the opposites, of which he speaks at p. 131 ($137f.^2$); analogous statements can be read in the Introduction to the *Republic*, Vol. III 1 (1828), p. 40 (where he speaks of the "identity of being and consciousness").

44. *Geschichte der Philosophie* (cited in note 13), p. 105.

45. *Sämmtliche Werke*, Vol. III 2, esp. pp. 67f., 113.

46. *Sämmtliche Werke*, Vol. III 2, p. 145.

47. *System des transzendentalen Idealismus*, pp. 386f.

48. Consult Introduction to the translation of the *Sophist*, Vol. II 2 (1807), p. 131 ($137f.^2$), where we read: "so that for the highest being itself there can be no opposite," "how, hence, in effect the essence of each true philosophy is here expressed, does not need any further exposition."

49. W. Dilthey, *Leben Schleiermachers*. ed. M. Redeker, Vol. I 1, (1970^3), pp. 313ff., 332ff., 344ff., 365ff., 371ff. (on this consult the Introduction of Redeker, p. xxiii); Vol. I 2 (1970^3), pp. 39ff. 132f., Vol. II 1, (1966), p. 16ff., 28.ff., 47, 152ff., 451ff.

50. Consult note 70.

51. W. Dilthey, "Denkmale der inneren Entwicklung Schleiermachers," in *Leben Schleiermachers*, Vol. I (1870) pp. 98f., 103, 117, 129, 131 (where a judgment can be found on Schelling's *Ueber die Weltseele* of 1798), pp. 134, 138; the works of Schelling are defined as "of great importance," especially in regard to the *System des transzendentalen Idealismus*, ("Letter of October 20, 1800," in *Aus Schleiermachers Leben in Briefen*, III, p. 237); the *Darstellung meines Systems der Philosophie* of Schelling of 1801 is judged to be "very ingenious and very well done," and he adds: "I expect a great deal from it" (in *Schleiermacher als Mensch*, ed. H. Meisner, Vol. 1, [Gotha, 1922], p. 222); for reading the *Bruno* of Schelling see the letter of June 15, 1802, in *Schleiermacher*

als Mensch, Vol. 1, p. 247; see also in this regard the end of the review of Schelling, about which we gave information in note 37, just as Schlegel's letter of reply of September 15, 1802, in *Aus Schleiermacher Leben in Briefen*, Vol. III, p. 322. In the letter of December 15, 1804 (in *Schleiermacher als Mensch*, Vol. 2, p. 29) we read that Schleiermacher "prefers Steffens even to Schelling."

52. W. Dilthey, *Leben Schleiermachers*, Vol. I 1, p. 373. Consult *Reden über die Religion* (Philos. Bibliothek, p. 255), pp. 3f., where he speaks of the constitution of the world as beginning from opposites, with the hierarchical progression through the stages from the inanimate to the animate; pp. 95f., where he speaks of the philosophy of nature and transcendental philosophy in the reciprocal action of the one on the other. (The second edition of the *Reden* of 1806 is still much closer to Schelling).

.53. In *Schleiermacher als Mensch*, Vol. 1, p. 331 (in the letter of December 14, 1803, where we read, on the contrary, that Schelling "is of an incomparable richer nature").

54. Consult the judgment of Schlegel in the *Athenäums-Fragments* (1798-1800) on "the proper vocation of Schelling" to refer philosophy to its fundamental powers, that is, to poetry and practical action (in *Kritische Friedrich-Schlegel-Ausgabe*, Vol. II, ed. H. Eichner (Paderborn, 1967), p. 216, n. 304.

55. Concerning this see W. Dilthey, *Leben Schleiermachers*, Vol. II 1 (Berlin, 1966), p. 451. The permanent philosophical criticism of Schleiermacher is connected to the preëminence given to the religious factor, on which see H. Süskind, *Der Einfluss Schellings* (consult note 25), pp. 274f., 285ff. The letter of Schleiermacher to Count Dohna of 1804 certainly referred to both of these factors (so we read: "Schelling, with whom, notwithstanding an apparent great agreement, I am so much in opposition "), in *Schleiermacher als Mensch*, Vol. 1, p. 334. Consult also the same, p. 338 (where we read: "Schelling is repugnant to me because of his character").

56. Nevertheless *The Doctrine of the Faith*, with the fundamental religious fact that consists in the sentiment of an unconditioned dependency present in man, offers certain parallels with specific themes of the late philosophy of Schelling.

57. Consult note 51.

58. *Caroline, Briefe aus der Frühromantik* (correspondence of Caroline Schelling), ed. G. Waitz, Vol. II (1871), pp. 37, 41, 109, 177, 207. Consult on this also H. von Stein, *Sieben Bücher* (consult, Chapter 1, note 5), Vol. III, p. 377, and, for the utilization by Schelling of Schleiermacher's *Plato*, the same, pp. 393f.

59. *Schelling-Ausgabe* of the Wissenschaftliche Buchgesellschaft of Darmstadt, Vol. III: *Schriften von 1801-1804*, pp. 475, 501.

60. F. Schleiermacher, *Sämmtliche Werke*. Vol. III 5: *Entwurf eines Systems der Sittenlehre aus Schleiermachers handschriftlichem Nachlass*, ed. A. Schweizer (Berlin, 1835); F. D. E. Schleiermacher, *Werke*, Zweiter Band, *Entwürfe zu einem System der Sittenlehre*, new ed. O. Braun (Philos. Bibliothek, Vol. 137), Meiner (Leipzig, 1913).

61. Paragraphs 126, 132-137, 153-154 in *Sämmtliche Werke*. Vol. III 4, 2: *Dialektik* (of 1814), ed. L. Jonas (Berlin, 1839), pp. 69ff.; consult also pp. 317ff., 396ff., 521ff. Consult F. Schleiermacher, *Dialektik* (of 1822), ed. R. Odebrecht (Leipzig, 1942) reprinted (Darmstadt, 1976), pp. 299ff.

62. An exposition of the foundations of the ontology of Schleiermacher is offered by H. Jørgensen, "Die Ethik Schleiermachers," in *Forschungen zur Geschichte*

und Lehre des Protestantismus, ed. E. Wolf, Zehnte Reihe, Vol. XIV (München, 1959), esp. pp. 11-20 (with the related illustrations in the sphere of the various sciences, with the exception of aesthetics and hermeneutics). Concerning the epistemological aspects consult F. Weber, *Schleiermachers Wissenschaftsbegriff. Eine Studie auf Grund seiner frühesten Abhandlungen* (Gütersloh, 1973), esp. pp. 49-98.

63. See the summary paragraphs 254-57, pp. 244-56 of the edition of A. Schweizer. The elementary categories of expression, the representation and the symbol are based on the doctrine of absolute identity, paragraphs 25-30; the concept of the symbol is applied to (finite) reason and nature, being contained in each other and being one, that reproduces the absolute identity, paragraphs 126-33 ("every form of union of reason and nature is a symbol"). Concerning the concept of symbol in Schleiermacher consult M. Redeker, in W. Dilthey, *Leben Schleiermachers*, Vol. II 1, pp. xlviii-l: "Among the presuppositions of this system belongs hence the metaphysics of the unification of reason and nature, ideal and real." This distinguishes Schleiermacher from the treatment of the terms symbol, expression, representation found in A. W. Schlegel, *Vorlesungen über schöne Literatur und Kunst* held at Berlin, in 1801/2, esp. Vol. I (Heilbronn, 1884), pp. 85-93. Schelling, moreover, used the notion of "symbol" beginning from 1797, the concepts of "expression" and "representation" beginning from 1802. The system of science of Schleiermacher, ethics, understood as a philosophy of the spirit and reason (anthropology), also includes aesthetics and hermeneutics.

64. Consult especially pp. 45-49, 181-92, in the edition of O. Braun (see on p. 45 the symbolization of the ideal in the real as a result of the artistic presentation, and at p. 50 the identity of the ideal and the real world in intuition and representation).

65. *Brouillon*, pp. 181, 186; *Tugendlehre*, p. 48 of the edition of O. Braun; *Sittenlehre*, par. 255, pp. 247ff. of the edition of A. Schweizer; F. Schleiermacher, *Ästhetik*, ed. Odebrecht, pp. 65, 119, 13 ("A cosmic aspect of art which stands in relation to the creative nature this is the highest point of our research").

66. For example, *Brouillon*, pp. 99, 122, 125, 127, 129, 131.

67. Ibid., p. 187. Concerning the unconscious in knowledge and creativity, consult ibid., pp. 215f.; consult also p. 171.

68. *Ästhetik*, pp. 9, 23f., 13 Odebrecht.

69. For the division of the "sciences of reality" into ethics and the philosophy of nature, in regard to what concerns the concepts of reason and nature, consult pp. 79f., 86, 132, 191, 234. For the concept of identity between the real and the ideal consult pp. 87, 96, 104, 121, 132, 150f., 170, 175, 177, 192, 199, 202, 206, 213, 216 note, 232. For the relatively opposed consult pp. 48, 88ff., 96, 109, 126, 195, 208f., 214ff., 218 and passim, for the doctrine of the "powers," consult pp. 93, 105, 151, 160, 178ff., 218ff. and throughout in the *Tugendlehre*. For the unity of the theoretical and the practical, consult pp. 50, 59, 152, 216, 230.

70. F. E. D. Schleiermacher, *Grundlinien einer Kritik der bisherigen Sittenlehre*, new edition by O. Braun (Leipzig 1911), p. 37; consult pp. 34ff.

71. Schleiermacher, in this work, nevertheless has deliberately avoided taking into consideration the position of Schelling to which he is quite close (in the Letter

of June 10, 1803 he had also expressly pointed that "in this work there is no hint of a Schellingianism," in *Schleiermacher als Mensch*, Vol. 1, p. 304).

72. Introduction, p. 16, Gaiser, pp. 9f. Similarly the example of the chrysalis, Vol. II 3, p. 13 (12^2).

73. See Schleiermacher, *Ästhetik*, ed. Odebrecht, pp. 94, 110f., for the "organic" perfection of the work of art (the whole and the parts representing one another reciprocally).

74. Ibid., p. 77 (consult p. 79). See what was said earlier, pp. 17.

75. Schleiermacher explains, against the reproaches of plagiarism lodged by Schlegel in a letter, addressed to one of his students, the philologist August Boeckh, of 1808 (consult, note 26), that at the beginning of 1801 he had already dispatched to Schlegel his translation of the *Phaedrus* "together with an Introduction, which in substance contained the same things as the present one." Whether Schleiermacher by this title "Introduction" alludes to his Introduction to the entire *Plato* and not to the individual Introduction concerned with the *Phaedrus* is not certain; nevertheless other statements of Schleiermacher attest that even up to the end of 1803 he worked on the general Introduction (Letter to the editor Reimer of November 11, 1803, in *Schleiermacher als Mensch*, Vol. 1, pp. 319f.: "Now working on the Introduction to the *Plato* and proposing to myself to be as diligent as possible. I foresee, however, the necessity of still rewriting the Introduction a few times"). Besides it should be pointed out that in the letter to Boeckh, Schleiermacher is concerned exclusively with the philological problems about the authenticity and arrangement of the Platonic writings and not with questions regarding the artistic form. Schleiermacher, however, already in *Vertraute Briefe über F. Schlegels Lucinde* of 1800, maintained some of the starting points belonging to the philosophy of identity (in Schleiermacher, *Kleine Schriften und Predigten*, Vol. I, ed. H. Gerdes (Berlin, 1970), p. 134, with the central thesis of the identity of body and spirit). For the *Reden über Religion* of 1799, see note 52. Schelling had developed the starting points of the philosophy of identity beginning from 1795, and he had presented them in their fundamental outline in the *Ideen zu einer Philosophie der Natur* of 1797. Schleiermacher began from the onset of the 1790s with a professed Spinozism, which, however, through the thought of Fichte, was bending inevitably toward a philosophy of identity. Schelling, actually, had written his metaphysics of art in the *System of Transcendental Idealism* of 1800, but he had already espoused it several times in his lectures at Jena (Schelling, *Ausgewählte Werke*, Wissenschaftliche Buchgesellschaft [Darmstadt, 1967], Vol. II: Schriften von 1799-1801, p. 334). Perhaps he alludes to the lectures of the winter semester of 1798-1799 and the summer semester of 1799; consult H. J. Sandkühler, *F. W. J. Schelling* (Metzler:Stuttgart, 1970), p. 68. Schleiermacher was, in this period, also in personal contact with Schelling (Letter of August 29, 1800 in *Schleiermacher als Mensch*, Vol. 1, p. 187, where we read: "give my regards to Schelling also").

76. F. Schlegel, *Philosophische Vorlesungen 1804-1806*, ed. Windischmann, Vol. I (Bonn, 1836), pp. 373-84. In the *Kritische Friedrich-Schlegel-Ausgabe*, Vol. XII, ed. J. J. Anstett (Paderborn, 1964), pp. 216-25.

77. This escapes H. G. Gadamer in his attempt to base the unity of the reception of Plato on the part of Schleiermacher on dialectics (*Schleiermacher als Platoniker* [cited note 1], pp. 141-49). But, actually, it is not the dialectical method, but the philosophy

of identity of Schleiermacher, that explains both the monism and the reevaluation of the artistic form (not only of the dialogue!) in Schleiermacher's picture of Plato. The relation now apparent becomes clear simply by taking into consideration the writings on ethics and aesthetics, which were not taken into account by Gadamer. (It is probable that the general critical edition of the work of Schleiermacher, which is at its beginning, would bring further clarifications on the questions treated in this part of the book. I hope to use it, for this purpose, in the future).

78. The work of art, even in Plato, really possesses an ontological status, but a relatively low and derivative one without having any specific representative function for philosophy, as, instead, the metaphysics of art establishes for the philosophy of identity. The work of art, in fact, with respect to other beings is not privileged, but, on the contrary, hierarchically subordinated. The Platonic concept of "mimesis," in other words, proceeds in an exactly opposite direction to that proposed by modern symbolization.

Chapter 3

1. A. Boeckh, "Kritik der Uebersetzung des Platon von Schleiermacher," *Heidelbergische Jahrbücher d. Literatur für Philologie* etc. I 1 (1808), now in A. Boeckh's *Gesammelte Kleine Schriften, Siebenter Band: Kritiken* (Leipzig 1872), pp. 1-38, esp., pp. 5-9.

2. Boeckh continues: "The characteristic that distinguishes the esoteric is based, hence, not on the objects, not even solely on the exterior form of the lecture, but on the greater or lesser degree of explication of scientific exposition." The examples in context show that Boeckh tried an intermediate way between Schleiermacher and the old conception of a radical difference of essence between the exoteric and the esoteric, on the basis that each is opposed to the other without any connection between them or relationship. The same holds, on the other hand, for the two apparently contradictory statements that are found in the *Lectures on the History of Philosophy* of Hegel, Vol. II (*Sämtliche Werke*, Vol. 18, ed. Glockner, 1941²). On p. 179, on the one hand, we read that in Aristotle 'the philosophy of Plato [is found] in a more accessible form," while, on the other hand, on p. 180, we read that "even if one talks with somebody in a somewhat superficial fashion, the idea is always contained there hence in philosophy there is never the purely exoteric." Boeckh and Hegel disassociate themselves from a conception that considers the esoteric and exoteric as *completely* different and incommensurable and that consequently philosophically devalued the exoteric, just as Schleiermacher diassociated himself already (he says of the esoteric that "it was not completely different from the writings," Introduction, p. 15; Gaiser, p. 9). But Boeckh and Hegel are distinguished from the traditional conception in a more precise fashion than Schleiermacher. (Tennemann also, censured by Hegel, at least at the end of his exposition, admitted the affinity of the two traditions: *Geschichte der Philosophie*, Vol. II [Leipzig, 1799], pp. 221f.). The unhistorical attempt to find the "esoteric" in the deep "speculative" sense, contained in the text of the dialogues happens but once in Hegel (consult Vol. 18, p. 238; with p. 184).

3. Bonn 1823 (Ph.D. Dissertation).

4. Ibid., pp. 68f.

5. Ibid., p. 2: *"qui autem contendunt integram Platonis doctrinam in eius dialogis contentam esse, aut non meminerunt plura Aristotelem ex magistri doctrina tetigisse, quorum ne vestigia quidem in dialogis Platonicis reperiuntur, aut Stagiritae parum fidei tribuerunt."* (Those who maintain that the whole Platonic doctrine is contained in his dialogues, either do not remember that Aristotle reports many doctrines from his teacher that do not even reveal an [identifiable] trace in the Platonic dialogues, or have too little faith in the Stagirite"). And on p. 68: *"adhuc ignorata aut certe neglecta erant."* (Hitherto ignored or certainly neglected").

6. Brandis has not then, subsequently, developed the comparison, but, in his *Handbuch der Geschichte der griechisch-römischen Philosophie*, Vol. II 1 (Berlin, 1844), pp. 180f., 306-27, has defended, once again, the indirect tradition against Zeller. But Brandis here accepted the late dating proposed by Zeller and Hermann.

7. Leipzig, 1826.

8. Ibid., p. 2: *"tamquam commenta posteriorum aspernantes."* ("contemning it as fictions of later people").

9. Ibid., pp. 94ff.

10. Ibid., p. 6: *"sicut prioribus dialogis quasi praeparat posteriores posterioribus evolvit priores, ita et in scholis continuasse sc. Platonem dialogos, quae reliquerit, absolvisse, atque omnibus ad summa principia perductis, intima quasi semina aperuisse"* ("just as the prior dialogues somewhat prepared for the later ones, and the later ones evolved from the prior, thus Plato continued in his school lectures the dialogue, and completed what remained, all leading to the highest principles, in some way revealing the most profound seeds"). Trendelenburg, hence, like Schleiermacher, admits a general plan, which, however, also includes the activity of the oral teaching in the Academy. Consult p. 94.

11. *De Platonis et Aristotelis in constituendis summis philosophiae principiis differentia* (Leipzig, 1828); idem, *Aristoteles Physik. Übersetzt und mit Anmerkungen begleitet* (Leipzig, 1829), esp. pp. 271ff., 393ff., 431ff., 471ff.; idem, *Aristoteles von der Seele und von der Welt, Übersetzt und mit Anmerkungen begleitet* (Leipzig, 1829), pp. 123ff. The review in *Jahrbücher für wissenschaftliche Kritik* 72 (1832), pp. 568ff., is also very important.

12. Heidelberg, 1839.

13. Ibid., pp. 552ff.

14. Ibid., pp. 554, 711ff.

15. Ibid., pp. 553f., 710 note 744.

16. "Über Platos schriftstellerische Motive," in *Gesammelte Abhandlungen und Beiträge zur class. Lit. und Altertumskunde* (Göttingen, 1849), pp. 281-305; now reprinted in Gaiser, pp. 33-57.

17. *Die Geschichte der alten Philosophie in den letztverflossenen 50 Jahren* (1843) in E. Zeller, *Kleine Schriften*, I (Berlin, 1910), pp. 1ff., esp. pp. 29-38, 41 on the *Plato* of Schleiermacher. Idem, *Schleiermacher in der ersten Hälfte seines Lebens* (1871, apropos the volume of Dilthey, *Leben Schleiermachers*), in *Kleine Schriften*. III (Berlin, 1911), pp. 385-401. Idem, *Friedrich Schleiermacher* (1859, for the twenty-fifth anniversary of his

death), in E. Zeller, *Vorträge und Abhandlungen geschichtlichen Inhalts* (Leipzig, 1865), pp. 178-201.

18. *Platonische Studien* (Tübingen, 1839; reprinted Amsterdam, 1969), III, pp. 197-300. The citation is on p. 300 and similarly on p. 293; Schleiermacher is cited on p. 205. The adversaries are Brandis, Trendelenburg, and Weisse.

19. In this way also the aperçu of Schlegel (consult p. 18ff.) that Plato's students misunderstood him is concretized.

20. Concerning what Aristotle says in *Physics* IV 2, p. 269, Zeller has prepared the way for his successors in the reduction of the differences of the two traditions to terminological differences.

21. Consult pp. 166f. Also succeeding interpreters of Plato take up again in an acritical mode, the depreciation of number, expressed by Hegel, in comparison with dialectic and bring it to bear against a picture of a "Pythagoreanizing" Plato.

22. *Sämmtliche Werke*, III 3, ed. L. Jonas (Berlin, 1835), pp. 306-33, esp. pp. 315, 328f.

23. II (1846^1), pp. 210ff., 237ff., 316f.

24. See also Zeller's declaring the *Laws* spurious in 1839, which he later retracted.

25. Consult II 1 (1963^6), pp. 726, 750-760, 946ff., 998.

26. II (1846^1). p. 217; II 1 (1859^2). p. 618; II 1 (1963^6), p. 951.

27. That Zeller was not of an artistic nature is attested to by H. Diels in his obituary for the Berlin Academy (also printed in E. Zeller, *Kleine Schriften*, III, p. 478).

28. II 1 (1963^6), pp. 497ff., 510, 569ff. (where he speaks of the "ingenious work of Schleiermacher"); consult II (1846^1), pp. 139ff. and *Kleine Schriften*, I, p. 30.

29. II 1 (1963^6), pp. 484ff., 572ff.; on the *Seventh Letter* see, II 1 (1963^6), pp. 485f., note 1.

30. II 1 (1963^6), pp. 497ff., 518ff., esp. p. 522.

31. II 1 (1963^6), pp. 584f., 587. Zeller adds only the propaedeutic as fourth part, and with this expressly detached himself from Schleiermacher (*Kleine Schriften*, I, p. 37).

32. II 1^6, pp. 581f. (with reference to Hegel).

33. E. Zeller, *Kleine Schriften*, I, p. 38; III, p. 399.

34. II 1 (1859^2), pp. 323f., note 4; consult further II 1 (1963^6), pp. 484f., note 3.

35. Depending on information of W. Christ, who was part of the doctoral examining committee for Shorey ("Platonische Studien," *Abh. d. Bayr. Ak. d. Wiss.* 17 [1886]: 454), Shorey went to Munich with a recommendation of an old American student of Christ, Dr. Sterrett. Now J. R. S. Sterrett (1851-1914), who taught at various American universities beginning in 1886, had studied classical philology for many years in Germany before 1880, at Leipzig, and Munich (where he had pursued the doctorate), as well as at Berlin. It is obvious that he must have met Zeller in person.

36. P. Shorey, *What Plato Said* (Chicago, 1933), p. 566; idem, *Platonism Ancient and Modern* (Berkeley, 1938), passim.

37. K. Prantl, *Uebersicht der griechisch-römischen Philosophie* (Stuttgart, 1854), pp. 66-106 (the Chapter entitled "Plato"), repeats even down to the details the Introduction of Schleiermacher to the *Plato* and the picture of Plato traced there (three classes of writings, three degrees of explanation in the work—also the chronology corresponds fully with that of Schleiermacher—threefold subdivision of philosophy, system in the writings, unity of philosophy and poetry, rejection of a secret doctrine). For the interpretation of Christ, see the presentation of Plato in his *Geschichte der griechischen Literatur* (München, 1889), pp. 328-54. Yet, Prantl found in Shorey's treatment of Aristotle's reports concerning the ideal numbers "a hypercritical attitude" (*Acts of Promotion* O I—65p of the *Archives of the University of Munich* of May 15, 1884).

38. "De Platonis idearum doctrina atque mentis humanae notionibus commentatio," Dissertation (Munich, 1884), p. 20.

39. Ibid., p. 59: "*nonnisi per mythos et simulacra opiniones suas adumbrare quasi ludens per mythos et fabulas.*—Eius libri lectorem sicuti viva praeceptoris vox mentem cogitando intendere cogunt. Quapropter λαβόντες ψυχὴν προσήκουσαν φυτεύουσιν καὶ σπείρουσι μετ' ἐπιστήμης λόγους (Plato, Phaedrus 276E) Plato poeta et dialecticus idem philosophorum philosophus manebit, perfectissimum atque nunquam assequendum exemplar eis qui cogitant propositum." ("he presents his opinions only through myths and images almost playfully through myths and fables.—His books just as a living teacher force the reader to concentrate his thinking. On which account 'they select a soul of the right type, and in it they plant and sow words founded on knowledge' Plato poet and at the same time dialectician remains the philosopher of all philosophers, giving a most perfect and never to be achieved exemplar to them who *think*.") It is to be noted that Shorey, here, as Schleiermacher, ignores the criticism of writing by Plato and tries to transfer the superiority of oral conversation to the artistic form of the literary dialogue.

40. Shorey maintains here a unitary picture of Plato as does Schleiermacher (hinted at already in the Dissertation, on p. 21). But, in this point, there manifestly exists a casual coincidence (on this see what Shorey himself says in *What Plato Said*, p. 66).

41. *The Unity of Plato's Thought* (Chicago, 1903; reprinted 1968), pp. 6, 43, note 298, and so on.

42. "De Platonis idearum doctrina," pp. 31-9; consult *The Unity of Plato's Thought*, pp. 82-5. See in addition the review by Shorey of J. Stenzel, *Zahl und Gestalt bei Platon und Aristoteles* (1924) concerned with the unwritten doctrine, in *Classical Philology* 19 (1924): 381ff. In the great succeeding work, *What Plato Said* (1933), he does not even consider it critically (not without consistency, since it belongs, according to Shorey, to that which Plato "did *not* ever say").

43. Also the monographs of Brandis and Trendelenburg of 1823 and of 1826 are noted by Shorey.

44. *The Unity of Plato's Thought*, p. 34, note 222.

45. "De Platonis idearum doctrina," p. 37, with reference to Zeller, II 2, p. 221^2

46. Ibid., pp. 44f., note 4.

47. One exception is constituted by Plato, *Parmenides* 136D, which, however, is limited ("De Platonis idearum doctrina," pp. 44f., note 4).

48. "De Platonis idearum doctrina," pp. 32ff.: "*delira illa opinio, futilissima illa hariolatio, nugae.*" Idem., *The Unity of Plato's Thought*, p. 82: ("intolerable logomachy, nonsense"); ibid., p. 84: ("pitiful scholasticism.") Again in *Classical Philology* (cited in note 42), p. 382: "corrupt, doubtful and (!) metaphysical texts abstract German metaphysics."

49. Also J. Cook Wilson, with his article "On the Platonist Doctrine of the ἀσύμβλητοι ἀριθμοί," *The Classical Review* 18 (1904): 247-60, who like Shorey was a precursor of Cherniss, in 1873/4 had studied at Göttingen, in Germany, under the direction of R. H. Lotze, who was later a colleague of Zeller at Berlin. (Consult the obituary of H. W. B. Joseph in *Proceedings of the British Academy*, London,7 [1915-16], esp. p. 557). Wilson discussed the issue, several times, referring to the Zeller of the *Greek Philosophy*, although there is probably a historical connection with the thesis of Shorey in regard to the Ideal Numbers, repeated in the book of 1903, with which he is in agreement.

50. R. M. Jones, "The Platonism of Plutarch," diss. (Chicago, 1916), Preface. G. M. Calhoun, "Athenian Clubs in Politics and Litigation," diss. (Chicago-New Orleans, 1913), prefatory note. H. F. Cherniss, *The Platonism of Gregory of Nyssa*, University of California Publications in Classical Philology II 1 (1930), p. 65, bibliographical note. In this regard see P. Shorey in *Classical Philology* 25 (1930): 298. The two major works of Cherniss (*Aristotle's Criticism of Presocratic Philosophy* and *Aristotle's Criticism of Plato and the Academy*) are dedicated to R. M. Jones, the second also to Calhoun. Consult E. M. Manasse, "Bücher über Platon" II: "Werke in englischer Sprache," *Philosophische Rundschau*, Beiheft 2 (1961): 86: "Cherniss is not a direct pupil of Shorey, but his work clearly reveals, how strong the influence of Shorey in America has endured."

51. Consult the preceding note.

52. Shorey, "De Platonis idearum doctrina," pp. 11-20; Cherniss, *The Philosophical Economy of the Theory of Ideas* (1936), reproduced in *Studies in Plato's Metaphysics*, ed. R. E. Allen (London-New York, 1965), pp. 1-12.

53. Shorey, Ibid., p. 54; Cherniss, *Aristotle's Criticism of Plato and the Academy* (Baltimore, 1944; New York, 1962³), pp. 46f., 575ff.; idem, *The Riddle of the Early Academy* (Berkeley-Los Angeles, 1945, 1962²), pp. 53ff.

54. Even some individual explanations, as the noted attribution to Xenocrates of the doctrines contained in the report of Aristotle, *De anima* A 2.404b16ff. *Test. Plat.* 25A Gaiser, are found in embryo already in Shorey ("De Platonis idearum doctrina," pp. 35f., note 4).

55. C. J. De Vogel, *Problems Concerning Later Platonism* (1949) reprinted in De Vogel, *Philosophia, Vol. I: Studies in Greek Philosophy* (Assen, 1970) with the title "Problems Concerning Plato's Later Doctrine," p. 291. A. Mansion in *Mededelingen van de kon. Vlaamse Academie voor wetenschappen, letteren en schone kunsten van Belgie, klasse der letteren* (Brüssel, Jaargang 16, 1954) Nr. 3, p. 17. H. Krämer, *APA*, p. 445. V. E. Alfieri, *Atomos Idea* (Florence, 1953), p. 30 (Galatina, 1979²), p. 39. E. Berti, *Rivista critica di storia della filosofia* 20 (1965): 233.

56. See the emphatic conclusion of the second lecture of Cherniss in *The Riddle*, p. 59: after the destructive criticism there remains "the Plato of the dialogues still extant in their entirety."

57. Consult pp. 3ff.

58. L. Robin, *La théorie platonicienne des idées et des nombres d'après Aristote* (Paris, 1908; reprinted Hildesheim, 1963), Introduction, pp. 4f.

59. At first in *Revue philosophique de la France et de l'étranger* 43 (1918): 177-220, 370-415; also printed separately (Paris 1919); reprinted in L. Robin, *La pensée hellénique des origines à Épicure*, ed. P. M. Schuhl (Paris, 1942, 1967²), pp. 231-336.

60. For an evaluation of Robin and his French predecessors, consult the work of E. M. Manasse, "Bücher über Platon, III: Werke in französischer Sprache," *Philosophische Rundschau*, Beiheft 7 (1976): 191-205; consult also pp. 159ff.

61. In his book *Studien zur Entwicklung der platonischen Dialektik von Sokrates zu Aristoteles* (Breslau, 1917; Darmstadt, 1961³).

62. *Platons Selbstbiographie* (Berlin-Leipzig, 1928), pp. 41-46.

63. "Plato's System of Philosophy," at first in *Proceedings of the Seventh International Congress of Philosophy*, ed. G. Ryle (London, 1931), pp. 426-31, reprinted in H. Gomperz, *Philosophical Studies* (Boston, 1953), pp. 119-24.

64. *Annali della R. Scuola Normale Superiore di Pisa*, Vol. I 30, 3 (Pisa, 1930). By the same author see also: "Nuovi studi intorno alla dottrina platonica delle idee numeri," *Annali della R. Scuola Normale Superiore di Pisa*, 2, no. 6 (1937): 111-27.

65. The work was published at Regensburg in 1949, but it was already finished in manuscript form in 1942, and only because of the war it was not published immediately.

66. J. Burnet, *Greek Philosophy. Part I: Thales to Plato* (London 1914), 1955⁹, Chapter 16 "The Philosophy of Numbers," pp. 312-24; consult pp. 214f.

67. C. J. De Vogel, "Problems Concerning Later Platonism," *Mnemosyne* 4, no. 2 (1949), pp. 197-216 and 299-318; reprinted in C. J. De Vogel, *Philosophia*, pp. 256-92. Sir David Ross, *Plato's Theory of Ideas* (Oxford, 1951), the Chapter, "Plato's 'Unwritten Doctrines'."

68. Consult *APA* IV 1 "Die Frage nach der historischen Realität einer esoterischen Philosophie Platons," esp. pp. 412-47 (written without the knowledge of the contribution of De Vogel, and, hence, independent of it, but yet confirming its results). Consult on the individual questions also K. Gaiser, *Quellen*, pp. 31-84, H. Krämer, *PHP*, p. 300, note 246; *Eidos*, p. 145, note 104; in addition, J. N. Findlay, *Plato. The Written and Unwritten Doctrines* (London, 1974), Appendix, 2., "Critical Note on the views of Harold F. Cherniss," pp. 455-73 is of fundamental value. A direct response on the part of Cherniss or any of his followers has not been forthcoming.

69. Consult pp. 5ff.

70. For what follows, consult our many works, which offer solid support for what we have presented synoptically in the text: *APA*, pp. 22ff., 400-04, 457-68; *Retr.*, pp. 143-48; *GF*, pp. 115-24; *AAW*, pp. 221-23; *Ph. R.*, pp. 4f. (against Isnardi Parente), 7f., 16-20 (against Tigerstedt); *Epekeina*, pp. 22ff. (against von Fritz).

71. This expression ἄκρα καὶ πρῶτα does not allude to all the objects "*in se*" (that is, to the "fifth" of the *excursus* [consult the *Seventh Letter*, 342A7ff., Appendix, 1.2], the Ideas as such), since (*a*) these are different from their linguistic expression (λόγοι and ὀνόματα are different), and hence as such they remain essentially unspoken and unwritten, while Plato admits the freedom to write or not to write about that to which he alludes (*b*) the ἄκρα and the πρῶτα are included in the "very briefest" formulas of all (πάντων ἐν βραχυτάτοις κεῖται), the reason why writings recalling them to memory (ὑπομνήματα) would be superfluous (but consequently possible): 344D9-E2 (consult Appendix, 1.2). By this very special characteristic, a reference to a (linguistically formulated) general theory of Ideas is also excluded, so much more since Plato himself has written many times concerning this theme. Further information about this issue can be found in my *AAW*, pp. 221f.

72. Concerning what the *Statesman* 285Ef. says on finality of the dialectical exercises (precisely the comprehension of the μέγιστα and τιμιώτατα, which insofar as they are ἀσώματα are without an adequate εἴδωλον and sufficient αἰσθηταὶ ὁμοιότητες and need, therefore, a particular training). The relation with the *Excursus* of the *Seventh Letter* has been observed several times.

73. For example, *Protagoras*, 357B (Appendix, 2.1); *Charmides*, 169A-D; *Meno*, 76Ef. (Appendix, 2.2); *Phaedo*, 108D, 114C; *Republic*, 506Df., 509C (consult 435D, 611Bf.); *Parmenides*, 136D (Appendix, 2.6), *Sophist*, 254C (Appendix, 2.7); *Statesman*, 262C, 263B, 284D (Appendix, 2.8); *Timaeus*, 28C, 48C (Appendix, 2.9), 53D (Appendix, 2.10), 68Bff. On this see *APA* pp. 389-92; K. Gaiser, *Menon*, pp. 346ff.; idem, "Platons Farbenlehre" in *Synusia f. W. Schadewaldt* (Pfullingen, 1965): 173-222. A detailed interpretation of many of these passages has been done by T. A. Szlezák.

74. Consult pp. 7ff.

75. Consult pp. 220, note 11, and p. 9.

76. *Laws* VII 810B5-7; see already *Lysis* 204D4f. ποιήματα-συγγράμματα).

77. The expression σμικρὰ ἔνδειξις of 341B is explained and clarified by the words δείξων, δεινκύς of 340B7f., C7, 341A6; see 345B1f. (consult Appendix, 1.2).

78. That the comparative πάμπολυ κυριώτεροι (!) makes reference only to a relative competence of the followers, is contrary to the context of the passage. Since Plato to judge the philosophical quality of his fundamental doctrines appeals to his followers as authorities, he would have paralyzed the argument, if he had wished at the same time to limit their competence. To which is added the experience that Plato expresses in the context; that is, that there are processes of communication that achieve good and that are obtained by the actual reaching of the noetic evidence (even in the case of Dionysius, Plato maintains this as possible, that he might have achieved an "adequate knowledge": 345B1, 7ff., Appendix, 1.2).

79. With the gnomic Aorist, that is, on the basis of *repeated* experiences.

80. The School of Tübingen recently no longer places the ἀκρόασις of Plato about which Aristoxenus speaks (*Harmonika*, 44 Marquard, 39 Da Rios, *Test. Plat. 7*, Appendix, 3.1]) *On the Good* on the same level as the activity of teaching within the Academy presupposed in the *Seventh Letter* of Plato, but together with the greater number of scholars, it refers rather to a historical event that took place only once. On the contrary, the School of Tübingen takes the position with regard to the informa-

tion of Simplicius about the tradition of the school concerning the unwritten doctrine (*Test. Plat.* 8 and 23B Gaiser, Appendix, 3.2 and 3) as referring to the regular teaching activity of Plato within the Academy. (On this point, see the arguments advanced in *Ph.R.*, p. 16; consult K. Gaiser in *Phronesis* 25 [1980]:26). However, the dating of the public lecture of which Aristoxenus speaks is not settled within the School of Tübingen. Gaiser places the event about which Aristoxenus speaks after the *Seventh Letter* ("Plato's Enigmatic Lecture On the Good," *Phronesis* 25 [1980]: 5-37; consult also "La teoria dei principi in Platone," *Elenchos* 1 [1980]: esp. 69ff.). Krämer instead sees in that event an experience from Plato's youth, which was echoed in the *Republic* 506Df., Appendix, 2.4), just as in the whole theory of teaching and learning of the *Seventh Letter* (cf. *Ph. R.*, pp. 16-18, note 33). In this connection there is also a different evaluation of the concept of the "esoteric." While in the 1960s and 1970s the School of Tübingen has increasingly preferred the expression "within the Academy" (*innerakademisch*), Gaiser has returned now to a pregnant use of the term *esoteric*. The discussion continues. On the basis of the following reasons (along with those expressed in *Ph.R.*), I would opt for a not late dating as more probable: (*a*) Plato, in the case of a late dating, would have repudiated the foundations of the *Seventh Letter*, without any reasons being handed down for this step;(*b*) the way in which Aristoxenus and Aristotle present the anecdote, indicates a failure of Plato as a teacher, and not an intentionally provoked event (as *after* the *Seventh Letter* would have to be assumed);(*c*) it is not probable that Plato a priori, that is, without a corresponding experience, must have considered his own fundamental doctrines as ridiculous and worthy of contempt by the uninitiated (as done in the *Republic* VI and in the *Seventh Letter*);(*d*) a failure of the famous head of the Academy, which was Plato's position at 350 BCE, would have left some traces even outside the Academy, but not a failure of Plato as a beginner; that is, at the time of the foundation of the Academy or even before it.(*e*) The expression εἰς φῶς προαγαγεῖν of 341D7f. (see Appendix, 1.2) is referred, in the linguistic use that was made by Plato at the time of the *Seventh Letter*, unequivocally to literary publication: just as for example at *Laws* IV 722E. The passage does not exclude, hence, a preceding *oral* exposition to the uninitiated.

81. Also the expression τὰ μέγιστα of 341B1 (see Appendix, 1.2) in connection with μαθήματα of C6 (see Appendix, 1.2) corresponds to the μέγιστον μάθημα of the *Republic* (505A), that is, to the Idea of the Good. In the "whole" of the Platonic philosophy (340Bf.; see Appendix, 1.2) there must be included, moreover, the theory of principles, which was in any case professed at the period of the *Seventh Letter*. Also Aristotle in the *Protrepticus* (frag. B35 Düring, *Test. Plat.* 34 Gaiser, Appendix, 3.26) used the expression ἄκρα καὶ πρῶτα, properly in reference to the ultimate elements (that is, the principles) of the unwritten doctrine (the reference has been recognized for some time). For further hints, see *GF*, pp. 117-20. In favor of the connection existing between the *Seventh Letter* and the unwritten doctrine of Plato (*On the Good*) can be found, among others, E. Howald, *Die Briefe Platons* (Zürich, 1923), p. 45; H. Gomperz, *Platons Selbstbiographie*, pp. 44f.; F. Novotný, *Platonis Epistulae commentariis illustratae* (Brno, 1930), pp. 215-17; G. R. Morrow, *Studies in the Platonic Epistles, with a translation and notes,* Illinois Studies in Language and Literature, XVIII (Urbana, Ill., 1935, 1962²), pp. 66f.; R. S. Bluck, *Plato's Seventh and Eighth Letters, edited with Introduction and Notes* (Cambridge, 1947), pp. 120, 122, 135; H. G. Gadamer, *Sitzungsberichte Heidelberg*, 1964/2, pp. 6, 30ff.; R. Muth, "Zur Bedeutung von Mündlichkeit und

Schriftlichkeit der Wortkunst," *Wiener Studien* 79 (1966): 249ff.; H. Gundert, "Zum philosophischen Exkurs im 7. Brief," in *Idee und Zahl. Studien zur platonischen Philosophie* (Abh. Heidelb. Ak. d. Wiss., Philos.-hist. Klasse), Jahrg. 1968, 2. Abh., pp. 85ff.; hinted at also in G. Pasquali, *Le Lettere di Platone* (Florence 1938, 1967²), pp. 83, 93, 105.

82. Consult for example *Metaphysics* A 6 (*Test. Plat.* 22A Gaiser, Appendix, 3.9). The only passage in which Aristotle admits an evolution of the doctrines of Plato professed within the Academy (*Metaphysics* M 4.1078b9) does not concern the theory of principles, but only the theory of Idea-numbers. But even this development remains limited and chronologically undetermined, since it only affirms that Plato "at the beginning" did not conceive the Idea as structured in a mathematical manner. (A late dating even of the Idea-numbers certainly cannot be drawn from this, because the negation of "at the beginning" is not at all "at the end," but includes the entire tract of time that is not "at the beginning"). For a more detailed analysis of the problem related to this passage see *GF*, pp. 110f., note 20; consult *APA*, p. 35.

83. Consult note 68. See also, J. N. Findlay, *Plato and Platonism. An Introduction* (New York, 1978).

Chapter 4

1. Consult, for example, A. Boeckh, *Enzyklopädie und Methodenlehre der philologischen Wissenschaften*, ed. E. Bratuscheck (Leipzig, 1886; reprinted Darmstadt, 1966), Erster Hauptteil, p. 240: "*Quivis praesumitur genuinus liber, donec demonstretur contrarium.*" ("Each book is presumed to be genuine, until the contrary can be demonstrated").

2. C. Krehbiel, "Grundgedanken und Materialien zu einer Theorie des onus probandi der Diskussion," Dissertation (Tübingen, 1968).

3. Some examples, E. Zeller, 1839 (consult pp. 32ff.), p. 299: Aristotle "could have produced this change in the doctrines of Plato handed down by him"; H. Cherniss, *The Riddle*, p. 48, "since he [Aristotle] did not appreciate the significance of Plato's ideal numbers, much of what he says concerning them may not be evidence of Plato's opinions"; consult also p. 43. M. Isnardi Parente, *Studi sull'Accademia platonica antica* (Florence, 1979), pp. 96, 101, 103, 111, 114, 146, 192 note 204. The same author writes in *Phronesis* 26 (1981): 144: "*Serait-il hasardé de supposer que la doctrine des idées-nombres trouve son point de départ dans une lecture 'académicienne' ou 'xénocratéenne' du Timée?*". ("Would it be daring to suppose that the doctrine of idea-numbers found its beginning in an 'Academic' or 'Xenocratean' lecture of *Timaeus*?") The arbitrariness of the inference is shown, then, in the fact that the proposals of the individual authors clearly differ among themselves: whereas Zeller explained the highest principle of unity of which the reports speak by the change of a predicate of the Good ("The Good is one") into a definition ("The Good is the One"), Shorey thinks, instead, that Aristotle drew it from the *Parmenides* of Plato, while Cherniss thinks, for his part, that he drew it from the *Sophist* (by analogical reasoning that states that just as all the Ideas participate in Being, so they also participate in the One, and with this reasoning Aristotle would have misunderstood the equality and parity of the highest genera by giving a privileged position to the One).

4. But here also it is uncertain whether Xenocrates—as Cherniss admits—interpreted Plato on the basis of Speusippus, or whether, instead, he recognized the deviations of Speusippus and hence expressly corrected Plato.

5. M. Isnardi Parente tried to repair this disagreement by maintaining that Plato could be "interpreted" through his followers, but that at the same time the followers could not be interpreted through other intermediaries (*Phronesis* 26 [1981]: 144, note 4). However, to prescind from the fact that, as has been shown earlier, the hypothesis of "interpretation" is not sufficient to explain the indirect tradition, the statements in question about the relations between Speusippus and Xenocrates are in no way correct (not even about the relations between Xenocrates and his followers and the other Academics). Actually Xenocrates could have "interpreted" his predecessor Speusippus, and hence have influenced Aristotle exactly as in the case of Plato. The same observation holds, naturally, about the thesis of the "deformation"—motivated both for polemical or theoretical reasons—on the part of Aristotle himself. So, the fact that, notwithstanding, the reports of Aristotle are accepted concerning the doctrines of Speusippus, but not those of the same Aristotle concerning the doctrines of Plato, and that, hence, the critics conduct themselves differently in the two cases, depends exclusively on the dogmatic and acritical postulation of Schleiermacherianism, on the basis of which the writings of Plato constitute the single valid evidence for the interpretation of the thought of Plato.

6. So also Cherniss himself, *The Riddle*, p. 29. Cherniss, indeed, also tried to present as a mere hypothesis the interpretation of his adversaries that Plato had taught doctrines in the Academy that he had not written; but this is based on a clear contempt for the self-testimonies of Plato and on an unsustainable reduction and isolation (which goes back to Zeller) of the passage in which the ἄγραφα δόγματα are mentioned by Aristotle, *Physics* 209b13ff., 35ff. (*Test. Plat.* 54A; = Appendix, 3.4; see the criticism that aroused the criticism of Cherniss in this regard in *APA*, pp. 416-19) and then, on the lack of attention for the unmistakable traces of the activity of the oral teaching of Plato in the reports of Aristotle (for example, on the indivisible lines in *Metaphysics* 990a20ff. *Test. Plat.* 26A), concerning which what Ross says in *Plato's Theory of Ideas*, pp. 145-47 is fundamental.

7. The fact that, for example, the clear report deriving from a monograph on Plato by Hermodorus, a follower of Plato himself, concerning the material principle and the doctrine of the categories of Plato (*Test. Plat.* 31 Appendix, 3.13), becomes unduly transformed into a "philosophy of Hermodorus," about which the ancient traditions knew nothing, is to be understood simply as a grotesque consequence of Schleiermacherianism (see, finally, again, M. Isnardi Parente in *Phronesis* 26 [1981]: 139ff.). On the basis of these premises, also the reports of Aristotle and Theophrastus concerning the Presocratics would become, as a logical consequence, worthwhile for their own philosophies, or (all things being equal) it would be necessary to speak about a philosophy of Diogenes Laertius or Sextus Empiricus. (Concerning the report of Hermodorus, see, now, the detailed exposition, that we gave to it in the new edition of *Ueberweg* [consult further, note 14], Chapter 7).

8. On the basis of such foundations, a corrupt passage in the *Oedipus Rex* of Sophocles could prove that this tragedy is not Sophoclean, and that furthermore a Greek literature does not exist, and so on.

9. Consult the clarifications of J. A. Brentlinger "The Divided Line and Plato's Theory of Intermediates," *Phronesis* 8 (1963):146-66 and of Findlay, *Plato*, pp. 188, 190 (both with reference to the ontological difference between shadows and images with respect to the things themselves in the *Republic* 516A, 532B, see also 534A, probably referring to astronomy and to musicology, on the one hand, and to arithmetic and to geometry on the other). Consult on this also J. Annas, *Archiv f. Geschichte d. Philosophie* 57 (1975):146-66.The research of Robin, De Vogel, Ross, Wilpert, Gaiser and Annas converge in the interpretation according to which the "identification" of the Ideas and Numbers in the Aristotelian reports should not be understood in a strictly logical sense, and vice versa, the "reduction" of the Ideas to Numbers in Theophrastus, *Metaphysics* 6b13ff. (consult Appendix, 3.8), presupposes a numerical structuring of the Ideas, so that in this way the supposed contradiction between the two informants is resolved in the *structure of the relations* λόγοι) within the sphere of the universals in virtue of its participation in the ideal numbers. Concerning the relations existing between the indivisible lines, the points-unities and the divisible to infinity great-and-small that underlies them (for example *Test. Plat.* 23B Appendix, 3.11) what we have said in *PHP*, p. 300, note 246 is fundamental. Consult further the instructive reflections of K. Gaiser, "Widerspruch oder Aspektverschiedenheit?" in *PUL*, added to the second edition, pp. 579-81. On the tendency of Cherniss to isolate particular aspects and on the construction of abstract antitheses, see what we said in *APA*, p. 446 (with documents among which we point out for example the change of the quantity of the judgments that Cherniss produces with respect to the reports of Aristotle, *Physics* IV 2 [Appendix, 3.4]: Cherniss, in this case, falsifies a deductive judgment [the *chora* {space} of the *Timaeus* is the great-and small] transforming it into a judgment of identity [the *chora* and the great-and-small are mutually identical, that is, the great-and-small is only *chora* and nothing else], and by beginning from this he deduces "contradictions" with regard to other kinds of the great-and-small contained in other relations; in this regard see the critical remarks that we made in *APA*, pp. 416f.). Consult also what we said in *Ph.R.*, pp. 18-21.

10. This has not been understood in addition to H. Cherniss, *The Riddle*, pp. 18f. and M. Isnardi Parente, *Studi sull'Accademia platonica antica*, pp. 92ff., 104f., unfortunately also by E. M. Manasse, *Bücher über Platon. III: Werke in französischer Sprache*, pp. 198, 201 and frequently. More detailed observations in regard to this question are to be found in my review of the book of M. Isnardi Parente, in *Archiv für Geschichte der Philosophie* 64 (1982): 76-82. The latest attempt by M. Isnardi Parente to find at all cost a contradiction between the doctrine of the Ideas and the doctrine of the principles, or at least to maintain that the doctrine of the Ideas becomes superfluous as a result of the doctrine of the principles (consult, *Phronesis* 26 [1981]: 141), is denied by the tradition of the history of philosophy, which begins from Neoplatonism and continues through the Fathers until it reaches the new Idealism (consider the relation between the transcendental apperception or the Absolute and the categories), but it is contradicted even by the writings of Plato (consult *Republic* 509B). The affirmation of Isnardi Parente, found on page 150, note 23, that the Idea of the Good of the *Republic* could not be brought into relationship with the theory of the principles, ignores the fact that the principles, insofar as they are intelligible universals ("unity in itself" etc.), have obviously, themselves an ideal character. (Likewise unconvincing is the attempt to clarify the restrictions of the theory of Ideas about

which Aristotle speaks in the *De ideis*, which is shifted from the dialogues, by the theory of the principles and in such a way to classify the latter as post-Platonic, which goes against the explicit testimonies of the tradition. In fact, it is difficult to see how the further reduction to the principles, for example, with respect to *artifacts*, should lead necessarily to the elimination of the ideal models. M. Isnardi Parente, moreover, does not take into account the fact that an important restriction of the theory of Ideas effectively connects with the theory of the principles [in its aspect of reduction to elements] and is still expressly attested in this respect for Plato himself [οἱ κομίσαντες Dirlmeier translates exactly: "the founders"] by Aristotle, *E.N.* I 4.1096a17ff. Appendix, 3.22; consult also III 23; for the reference of this text to Plato consult also H. Flashar, "Die Kritik der platonischen Ideenlehre in der Ethik des Aristoteles," in *Synusia für W. Schadewaldt* (Pfullingen, 1965), pp. 228, 240f.; see also *Eidos*, p. 144f. with note 104).

11. *Sophist* 254C (Appendix, 2.7); see 255E1 and on this, what we said in *Ph. R.*, pp. 30-33.

12. In this respect see the fundamental clarifications of J. N. Findlay, *Plato*, Appendix, 2.: "Critical note on the views of Harold F. Cherniss," pp. 455ff., esp. pp. 471-73. See also *APA*, p. 446.

13. R. Mondolfo, *Problemi e metodi di ricerca nella storia della filosofia* (Florence, 1952), pp. 114-17, see also pp. 111ff.

14. The fullest exposition that has been done on the doctrines of the Ancient Academy is now found in H. Krämer, *Ueberwegs Grundriss der Geschichte der Philosophie*. New edition, *Die Philosophie der Antike*, Vol. 3: *Ältere Akademie -Aristoteles -Peripatos*, ed. H. Flashar (Basel: Schwabe, 1983), pp. 1-174.

15. An analogous situation is encountered vis-à-vis Democritus, given that the foundations of the atomistic doctrine are accessible to us only through the doxographical tradition, that is, by an indirect tradition.

16. Consult on this H. Krämer, "Grundsätzliches zur Kooperation zwischen historischen und systematischen Wissenschaften," *Zeitschrift f. philos. Forschung* 32 (1978): esp. 323, 333ff. It is obvious, that the greatest degree of certitude possible in the interpretation of an author can be achieved only by taking into account all the testimonies which are available.

17. Consult pp. 9 and 41 and also p. 236, note, 73.

18. And if the *justification* adopted for reasons of discretion in the *excursus* (342A-344D = Appendix, 1.2), finally, is pointed out as a "myth," in this case it is necessary to note,(a) that the decisive affirmations on the fact of the discretion are found before and after the *excursus*,(b) that the *excursus* is problematic not in its content of truth (λόγος ἀληθής, 342A3f.), but only because of the incompleteness of the succinct exposition and the difficulty of the issue (consult G. Pasquali, *Le Lettere di Platone*, p. 102). Plato had evidently furnished the justification in more detailed manner in the ambit of his oral teaching activities, as can be seen from 342A5: πολλάκις ὑπ' ἐμοῦ καὶ πρόσθεν ῥηθείς (for the relation with the oral teaching see J. A. Post, E. Howald, H. G. Gadamer, J. Kerschensteiner, in their commentaries on the *Seventh Letter*). The critical statements of the *Seventh Letter* about writing hence, on a further level—that is, within the ambit of "orality"—can be grounded in a still more precise manner and clarified (but cannot be surpassed).

19. The term συγγράφειν means literally "to write," "to put down into writing"; the term σύγγραμμα hence means the "written," "written note or work," "writing."

20. *Laws* VII 810B5-7.

21. Just as, for example, Galen 16.532 (Liddell-Scott-Jones, *A Greek-English Lexicon*, s. v. ὑπόμνημα, nr. 5c) with an exact explanation, which is fundamental for the explanation of the same passage under the word σύγγραμμα, which is very brief, and, therefore, can perhaps lead to error). On the problem T. A. Szlezák, *Museum Helveticum*, 35 (1978): esp. 25f., has written in a final and probably conclusive fashion.

22. In αὐτοῦ τέχνην, *Seventh Letter* 341B4 (see Appendix, 1.2), Plato undoubtedly accentuated the first word. (In this respect it is probable that in the term *techne* is hidden a reference to Dionysius or the source of Plato, see what we said in *GF*, p. 122, note 54). In addition in the text there are no opportunities to hold that the other writers, of whom Plato speaks in 341B5ff. (see Appendix, 1.2), or future writers, about which he makes a judgment in C1 (see Appendix, 1.2), have written treatises or will write treatises. The attempt of M. Isnardi Parente to connect σύγγραμμα especially to the writings of the legislator ("La VII Epistola e Platone esoterico," *Rivista critica di storia della filosofia* [1969]: esp. 418, reprinted in Isnardi Parente, *Filosofia e politica nelle Lettere di Platone* {Naples, 1970}, esp. p. 151) does not succeed, because Plato cited the written work of the legislator, in the *Seventh Letter* 344C, just as in the *Phaedrus* 278C, only by way of illustration, but for the rest he expressly condemns also all the other types of συγγράμματα (ibid.).

23. L. Sichirollo in M. Untersteiner, *Problemi di filologia filosofica* ed. L. Sichirollo and M. Venturi Ferriolo (Milan, 1980), p. 32, seems not to recognize accurately either the *Seventh Letter* or the discussion about it. In any case, his argument corresponds approximately to one in which the existence of Australia would prove the fact that a fifth continent does not exist. This, together with the onesided and misleading report of the revision, is much more deplorable because it occurs in a book on method and the editor, with that, repudiates the position that the author M. Untersteiner (who is worthy of the highest respect and could no longer personally take part in publishing the book because of his lack of sight) had taken expressly in the text. The theses of E. A. Havelock of the passage from an oral culture to a written culture applied to the Greeks (*Preface to Plato* [Cambridge, Mass., 1963), which Sichirollo thought he could bring into evidence against the School of Tübingen, had been discussed by scholars such as R. Harder, F. G. Kenyon, W. C. Greene, and W. Luther a long time before, and as such had also been accepted by the School of Tübingen (consult for example what is said in *Ak²*, p. 207, note 14, while these authors are not found either in Havelock, or in Sichirollo). The same holds also for the results of W. Jaeger relative to the prehistory of the writings of the philosophical schools (Ak², p. 208). On the documentation of K. Gaiser which shows the existence of a tradition of protreptic writings see pp. 72f.

24. Consult Republic 435D, 509C7-10 (before the simile of the divided line; Appendix, 2.5), 530D, 532D, 533A, 534A, 611Bf.

25. The *Timaeus* is notoriously connected to the *Republic*. The words with which Plato introduces the central part of the dialogue and in which he says that he does not wish to speak about the principles (48C carried on in 53D = Appendix, 2.9 and

10) corresponds almost verbatim to that of the *Republic* VI 506D-E (= Appendix, 2.4); see *GF*, pp. 130f. That which is concealed in the central part of the *Timaeus*, refers, however, clearly to the dimensional system (53D = Appendix, 2.10) and to the indeterminate principle of the great-and-small of the unwritten doctrines (compare the expression τὰ λεγόμενα ἄγραφα δόγματα of Aristotle, *Physics* 209b15 [see Appendix, 3.4] with τὰ δόγματα and δοκοῦντα of the *Republic* 506B9, E2, 509C3, [see Appendix, 2.4 and 5] and the *Timaeus* 48C6 [see Appendix, 2.9]. Quite similar is the correspondence between the τί ἐστι that is concealed in the *Republic* 506D8f. [see Appendix, 2.4] and the "essence" [οὐσία] of the Good in the form of the One, in the Aristotelian report in *Metaphysics* N 4.1091b14f.).

26. See *APA*, p. 454, where it is pointed out that the importance of the unwritten doctrines does not diminish the philosophical status of the dialogues; consult pp. 67, 69f.

27. For more detail see pp. 106f. (with the demonstration that the *Parmenides* even to those for whom the thematic is known can recall to mind only some aspects of the unwritten doctrines, while it is silent in agreement with what is said in the self-testimonies of Plato for other aspects, and, hence, the whole as such).

28. H. Meissner, *Der tiefere Logos Platons* (Heidelberg, 1978). Consult on this book the pertinent review by T. A. Szlezák in *Gnomon* 52 (1980): 301-4.

29. *Seventh Letter* 344D9ff. (see Appendix, 1.2).

30. There is no doubt that modern philosophical criticism must judge theoretically Plato's teaching method as well as his philosophy and the relations existing between them as well. In fact, since such criticism, at times, reflects the situation of the epoch, contemporary history also cannot help but be conditioned by it.

31. The position of the problem concerning the thematic of the principles in this perspective appears, once again, somewhat like a kind of literary *topos* among other *topoi*, with which one can dispense eventually.

32. The limits of "fair play" and of scientific permissiveness are completely at odds in these cases in which unpleasant publications (for example *Retr.* and *GF*) or particular arguments are intentionally ignored by adversaries, as has frequently occurred.

33. All this escapes authors like von Fritz, whose aversion to the unwritten doctrines is motivated by expressly "political" reasons, in the background of which there stands an unresolved conflict between historicism and humanism: ancient history—in this case Plato—must be taken seriously and at the same time must be in agreement with the proper ideals, and precisely with the republican ideals of the eighteenth century; it is, in comparison with the political philosophy of Plato, an evident ahistorical anachronism. (For the criticism of von Fritz' taking of positions in relation to the unwritten doctrines, see our detailed review in *Epekeina*, pp. 22ff.).

34. Instructive also in this respect is B. Barber, "Resistance by Scientists to Scientific Discovery" in *Sociology of Science* , ed. B. Barber and W. Hirsch (New York, 1962), pp. 596-602.

Chapter 5

1. *"Si quelcun reduisoit Platon en système, il rendroit un grand service au genre humain"* ("If anyone were to reduce Plato to a system, he would render a great service

to humankind"), G. W. Leibniz, "Letter to Rémond," in *Die philosophischen Schriften von G. W. Leibniz*, ed. C. J. Gerhardt, Vol. III (Berlin, 1887; reprinted in 1978), p. 637.

2. The fundamental anthropological concept of Schleiermacher that to know and to act (produce) both represent a symbolizing relation of subject-object that is based on the absolute unity of subject-object in God (for example, in *Brouillon zur Ethik* of 1805/06, p. 187, Braun) refers, in what concerns the artistic form of the Platonic writings, both to the aspect of the aesthetic of production (artistic production!) and to the aspect of the aesthetic of reception (to understand is to know!).

3. A. Solignac and P. Aubenque, "Une nouvelle dimension du Platonisme. La doctrine 'non-écrite' de Platon," *Archives de Philosophie* 28 (1965): 251-65.

4. Remember the subdivisions (*diaereses*), a precise echo of which is found in the *Divisiones Aristoteleae*, ed. H. Mutschmann (Leipzig, 1906), or the diaeretic exercises, which had a place in the Academy under the direction of Plato, about which comedy informs us (for example *Athen.* II 59D-E = *Test. Plat.* 6).

5. H. Gundert, in several of his works and especially in *Der platonische Dialog* (Heidelberg, 1968), esp. pp. 15ff. goes back to this reflection—not without the danger of over-estimating it. The concept of the "serious play" of the dialogues, which is found in other authors, is oriented in the same direction.

6. J. Stenzel, "Literarische Form und philosophischer Gehalt des platonischen Dialoges," 1916, in *Studien zur Entwicklung der platonischen Dialektik*, pp. 123ff. also in *Kleine Schriften* (Darmstadt, 1956) pp. 32ff.; P. Friedländer, *Platon* (Berlin, I/II 1964³) [American version of first volume trans. Hans Meyerhoff, 1969², and second volume in 1964 of the German edition of 1957²]. III 1960² [American version of third volume trans. Hans Meyerhoff, of the 1960² German edition, all in the Bollingen Series of Princeton University Press]; R. Schaerer, *La question platonicienne* (Neuchâtel, 1938, 1969²); V. Goldschmidt, *Les dialogues de Platon. Structure et méthode dialectique* (Paris, 1947, 1963²); H. Gundert, *Der platonische Dialog*, also his *Dialog und Dialektik. Zur Struktur des platonischen Dialogs* (in the collection *Studien zur antiken Philosophie*, ed. Flashar-Gundert-Kullmann, 1 (Amsterdam, 1971) (first in *Studium Generale* 21 [1968]: 295ff., 387ff.); H. L. Sinaiko, *Love, Knowledge, and Discourse in Plato* (Chicago-London, 1965); Stanley Rosen, *Plato's* Symposium (New Haven and London, 1968); R. Burger, *Plato's* Phaedrus. *A Defense of a Philosophic Art of Writing* (University of Alabama Press, 1980), by the same author, *The Phaedo. A Platonic Labyrinth* (New Haven and London: Yale University Press, 1984). See also, among others, P. Merlan, "Form and Content in Plato's Philosophy,"*"Journal of the History of Ideas* 8 (1947): 406ff., reprinted in P. Merlan, *Kleine philosophische Schriften* (Amsterdam, 1976), pp. 26ff.

7. *Seventh Letter* 344D9 (see Appendix, 1.2).

8. K. Gaiser, *Protreptik und Paränese bei Platon. Untersuchungen zur Form des platonischen Dialogs* (Stuttgart, 1959).

9. Consult the preceding note.

10. The *Laws* are considered especially as a manual for the instruction of youths and a model for the choice of further reading (811Cff.; on this see H. Görgemanns, "Beiträge zur Interpretation von Platons Nomoi," *Zetemata* 25 [Munich, 1960]).

11. This is connected with the fact that the literary dialogue is not directed, like an actual dialogue, only to the partners present, but by a special refraction, it is also directed to somebody outside itself, to its reader as if he were the third participant.

12. R. Wiehl, "Dialog und philosophische Reflexion," *Neue Hefte für Philosophie*, ed. Bubner-Cramer-Wiehl, Heft 2/3: *Dialog als Methode* (Göttingen, 1972), pp. 41-94, esp. pp. 81ff.

13. Consult *Symposium* 209A-E.

14. The same holds for the probable epideictic function of which see under 4.

15. E. Schmalzriedt, *Platon. Der Schriftsteller und die Wahrheit* (Munich, 1969).

16. The further task of Platonic research oriented to the study of the artistic form of the dialogue could consist in the specification and determination of the various hypomnematic, protreptic, propaedeutic, didactic, endeictic, or epideictic parts and aspects and their synergistic action in the individual dialogues. As a result the function of the writings would probably be revealed often as being polyvalent. Also the relation between the written work and the unwritten doctrine could still be interpreted in a more precise manner on the basis of the central parts of the great dialogues and it could be brought to fruition for a concrete comprehension of the morphology of the Platonic dialogues and in addition of the literary technique of Plato (starting points in this sense can be found in *APA*, pp. 481-86). To the question aroused by Schmalzriedt, that is, how the philosophical aspect can express itself in the literary dialogues, in this way a response is possible the results of which would be certified and guaranteed by the unwritten doctrine.

Chapter 6

1. Concerning what follows, see especially what is said in *APA*, pp. 249-318; *Ak*[2], pp. 209-20; *PD*, passim; *GF*, pp. 139-46; *Epekeina*, pp. 1-15; *VPA*, pp. 348-50; *Ph.R.*, pp. 32-34; Gaiser, *PUL*, pp. 41-172.

2. *Test. Plat.* 22A = Appendix, 3.9.

3. This does not exclude that the principles themselves are universals and that, hence, they have an ideal character.

4. *Test. Plat.* 50 (on the Platonic character of the report see W. Burkert, *Weisheit und Wissenschaft* [Nürnberg, 1962], pp. 19, 56f.; Gaiser, *PUL*, p. 531; *Epekeina*, pp. 4f.); see Aristotle, *Met.* N 2.1089a2ff.

5. Fundamental concerning this point O. Töplitz, "Das Verhältnis von Mathematik und Ideenlehre bei Plato," *Quellen und Studien zur Geschichte der Mathematik, Astronomie und Physik* B I 1 (1931): 3ff., reprinted in *Zur Geschichte der griechischen Mathematik*, ed. O. Becker, Wege der Forschung, 33 (Darmstadt, 1965), pp. 45ff. ; J. Stenzel, "Zur Theorie des Logos bei Aristoteles," *Quellen und Studien*, pp. 34ff., reprinted in J. Stenzel, *Kleine Schriften zur griechischen Philosophie*, pp. 188ff.

6. The original Platonic terms seem to be the following: περατοῦν, ὁρίζειν and ἰσάζειν. See *Test. Plat.* 22B (Appendix, 3.10), 23B (Appendix, 3.11), 28b fin., 32, par. 277 (Appendix, 3.12); see Aristotle, *Met.* 989b18, 1081a25, 1083b23f.; Xenocrates frag. 68 Heinze and Speusippus quoted in Iamblichus, *De communi mathematica scientia* c. IV p. 16, 17f. Festa (frag. 88 Isnardi Parente).

7. Concerning this, see now W. Schwabe, "'Mischung' und 'Element' im Griechischen bis Platon," *Archiv für Begriffsgeschichte*, Supplementheft 3 (1980).

8. *Test. Plat.* 50 (*melius ente* probably expresses the Greek phrase κρεῖττον τοῦ ὄντος, see *Republic* 509B; on the theme see Speusippus, frag. 34e Lang (frag. 57 Isnardi Parente, Aristotle, *Met.* 1092a14f.), and quoted in Iamblichus, *De communi mathematica scientia*, c. IV, pp. 15, 7ff. Festa (frag. 72 Isnardi Parente); on this see what we said in *Epekeina*, pp. 4-6 and *Archiv für Geschichte der Philosophie*, 64 (1982): 79. For the characteristic of the material principle (of the great-and-small) of being below being see *Test. Plat.* 31 (Appendix, 3.13, to the end), on the basis of the book on Plato of the follower of Plato named Hermodorus. (For the interpretation see H. Krämer, "Die Ältere Akademie" in *Ueberwegs Grundriss*, Vol. III, par. 7, 130).

9. Consult what we said in *Epekeina*, pp. 6-15.

10. The quantification of the relations is simply a consequence of the mathematical aspect of the Greek concept of *logos* that is structurally connected to dialectic as the fundamental method of philosophy (on this see H. G. Gadamer, "Platons ungeschriebene Dialektik," in *Idee und Zahl*, Abh. Heidelb. Akad. d. Wiss., 1968/2, pp. 14ff., reprinted in H. G. Gadamer, *Kleine Schriften* [Tübingen, 1972], III, pp. 33ff.).

11. *Test. Plat.* 30 = Appendix, 3.8 (= Theophr. *Met.* 6b13f.). All the Ideas, in virtue of their relations, are determined in a numerical way ("Idea-numbers"), but only some Ideas are the Ideas of numbers (Ideal Numbers).

12. *Test. Plat.* 22A (Appendix, 3.9), 22B (Appendix, 3.10), 23B (= Appendix, 3.11), 32 (= Appendix, 3.12), 59, 60. Concerning the process of generation of the Ideal Numbers, in modern studies numerous theories have been developed, of which, nevertheless, none has hitherto received general acceptance. It is possible that Plato himself has not presented any definitive solution, but that he left this question, which from the philosophical point of view is subsidiary, programmatically in suspension. For an orientation on this issue, we refer to the discussions that can be found in P. Wilpert, *Zwei aristotelische Frühschriften*, pp. 157ff., 202ff. and in K. Gaiser, *PUL*, pp. 115ff., 363ff. Concerning the little that has been related on the generation of the remaining Ideas see *Test. Plat.* 30 = Appendix, 3.8 (consult *Republic* 509B and what is said pp. 100ff.).

13. This is to be drawn from the "division of the yard" of which *Test. Plat.* 23 B (Appendix, 3.11) speaks and from the theory of the indivisible lines that *Test. Plat.* 26A, 36 (Xenocrates, frag. 42 Lang) addresses. At any rate, it seems that Plato did not use a sufficiently clear distinction, in this case, between the different levels of the material principle (consult *Test. Plat.* 28b, esp. 1090b32ff.).

14. Plato preferred, in the area of geometry, the expression *indivisible line* (*Test. Plat.* 26A), because the mathematical point was defined as a limit without extension; in the sphere of "physics," instead, he preferred the traditional term of *monad-point* (for example, *Test. Plat.* 22B, 23B; Xenocrates as the first has spoken also here of indivisible lines). Consult on this theme *PHP*, p. 300, note 246.

15. *Test. Plat.* 25A (Aristotle, *De an.* 404b18ff.). Just as mathematical numbers are based on ideal numbers, so also geometrical figures and stereometricals are grounded on ideal figures. Both of these themes have been carefully examined by Robin (consult p. 39) and K. Gaiser, *PUL*, first part. Gaiser, moreover, beginning from

the intermediate position of the soul, advanced the proposal that the entire hierarchical arrangement of realities could be conceived as organized according to the model of a series of dimensions.

16. *Test. Plat.* 22B (Appendix, 3.10), 31 (Appendix, 3.13), 32 (Appendix, 3.12), 43 (Appendix, 3.27), 44a (Appendix, 3.29). (The hypothesis of a "dependence" from the *Sophist* 255C12f., is already excluded simply by the fact that Plato himself in other passages, as in *Statesman* 284D1f. [Appendix, 2.8], alludes to the respective reduction to the principles, but avoids speaking of it).

17. *Test. Plat.* 39A-42B (Appendix, 3.14-21); see 35b, 45, 61 (κίνησις-στάσις); see Aristotle, *Met.* B 1.995b20-24; Γ 2.1005a12-18 and moreover *Test. Plat.* 32, par. 261 (consult Appendix, 3.12). Consult C. Rossitto, "La possibilità di un'indagine scientifica sugli oggetti della dialettica nella *Metafisica* di Aristotele," *Atti dell'Instituto Veneto di Scienze, Lettere ed Arti, a. 1977/78*, T. 136 (1978): 363ff., esp. pp. 366f., 377. There is an allusion to the reduction to the principles in the simile of the divided line of the *Republic* in the notion of entities that "depend" on the principle (τὰ ἐκείνης sc., τῆς ἀρχῆς ἐχόμενα 511B8; consult the things "derived" [ἑπόμενα] from the ἀρχαί in the report of Aristotle, *Met.* 1084a32ff. *Test. Plat.* 61, on which see what we said in *PD*, pp. 409ff.).

18. The expression is justified in the *Republic* 516A6ff. (μετὰ τοῦτο-ὕστερον δέ-ἐκ δὲ τούτων; consult 532A).

19. For the principles of Plato understood as the most universal genera (τὰ μάλιστα καθόλου, τὰ πρῶτα ἀνωτάτω γένη) see Aristotle, *Met.* B 3.998b17-21 with b9-11; Δ 3.1014b6ff.; K 1.1059b27ff.; M 8.1084b14, 25, 31; consult A 2.982a21-26; Γ 2.1004b34-1005a2 (Appendix, 3.16); Sextus Empiricus, *Adv. math.* X 274f. (Appendix, 3.12).

20. Consult for example Aristotle, *Met.* M 8.1084b18-32; in addition 998b9, 1059b21ff.; *Test. Plat.* 22B (Appendix, 3.10), 32 (consult Appendix, 3.12).

21. *Test. Plat.* 10, 30, 32 and 22B (Appendix, 3.6, 8, 10, and 12) as well as Aristotle, *Eth. Eud.* I 8.1218a24ff. (Appendix, 3.25) along with a16ff. (Appendix, 3.25). Testimony number 10 (Appendix, 3.6) contains a fragment of a methodological reflection referring to the procedure (with the distinction of two kinds of argument—λόγοι—Dalways in accord with the corresponding position and the related procedure). Other documents integrate one another in a complementary fashion; for example, *Test. Plat.* 7 = Appendix, 3.1 (*anodos*) and 22A = Appendix, 3.9 (*kathodos*).

22. Also the distinction by Kant of the concepts of the a priori and the a posteriori can be referred in the ultimate analysis beyond Aristotle back to Plato himself.

23. *Test. Plat.* 7 = Appendix, 3.1; consult also 22A = Appendix, 3.9 (Aristotle, *Met.* A 6.987b27-29 and 1086a11f.) on the mathematical entities that are "in the middle" between Idea-numbers and individual entities.

24. *Test. Plat.* 25A; consult Plato *Timaeus* 34B, 36E and what Gaiser says in *PUL*, pp. 44ff.

25. For example, *Test. Plat.* 22B, 23B, 33a, 34 (Appendix, 3.10, 11, 7, 26); consult Aristotle, *Met.* B 1.995b22; Γ 2.1005a16.

26. For example, *Test. Plat.* 22B, 23B, 32 (par. 269), 33a, 34 (Appendix, 3.10, 11, 12, 7, 26).

27. On this consult earlier p. 91. The role of mathematics and its axiomatic system is connected to this—it is constituted through interaction with Platonic philosophy, as a model-sphere and "a sphere of verification" for ontological dialectic. (For this see Gaiser, *PUL*, pp. 305ff. and what we say in *GF*, p. 140, note 118. The function of mathematics as a "sphere of verification" is enclosed within the order of knowledge.)

28. On this see P. Merlan, "Zwei Bemerkungen zum aristotelischen Plato," *Rheinisches Museum für Philologie* 111 (1968): 1-15, reprinted in *Kleine philos. Schriften* (Hildesheim-New York, 1976), pp. 259-73. A fuller treatment can be found in H. Happ, *Hyle. Studien zum aristotelischen Materiebegriff* (Berlin-New York, 1971), pp. 147-76; consult 262ff.

29. *Test. Plat.* 38; on this see A. D. Steele, "Über die Rolle von Zirkel und Lineal in der griechischen Mathematik," *Quellen und Studien zur Geschichte der Mathematik, Astronomie und Physik* B III (1936): esp. 328ff. The system of the concentric spheres of Eudoxian astronomy that Plato is said to have inspired (*Test. Plat.*, 16), with its reduction of the irregularities of the planetary motions to regular circular movements, is precisely influenced by the Platonic philosophy of the elements.

30. The special principles emerge in a particularly accentuated way in Speusippus, and unlike in Plato, they have the tendency toward becoming autonomous.

31. Aristotle, *Met.* Δ 6.1016b18ff.

32. *Test. Plat.* 35a.

33. Consult ibid., 15-18, 21.

34. Consult ibid., 6.

35. In this regard, the fact that increasing concreteness can involve a susceptibility to ever greater criticism must be taken into account.

36. It is not obvious from the systematic viewpoint that Plato must place the Good on the level of the principles and not subordinate it to the One as *one kind of unity*, like the Idea of being and the other Meta-Ideas, as, for example, was actually done by his successor Speusippus. In this the Socratic problematic of the virtue (*arete*) of the soul can clearly be seen as the start of the Platonic theory of being and the principles and it keeps at length united at its foundation the outlines of the Platonic problematic.

37. *Test. Plat.* 7 (Appendix, 3.1) is, for example, clear.

38. Ibid., 51 = Appendix, 3.24 (where the identity of ἕν and of ἀγαθόν in the sense that the first constitutes the essence is explained), similarly *Test. Plat.* 22A (Aristotle, *Met.* A 6 fin. [Appendix, 3.9]), 61 (*Met.* 1084a35). On the identity see, in addition, Aristotle, *Eth. Eud.* I 8.1218a20f., 25 (Appendix, 3.25); Met. Λ 10.1075a34ff.; consult Theophrastus, *Met.* 11a27ff.; Aristotle, *De philosophia*, frag. 6 Walzer and Ross frags. 3 and 11 Untersteiner.

39. Aristotle, *Eth. Eud.* I 8.1218a15ff. = Appendix, 3.25. On the Platonic character of the relation, see J. Brunschwig, "EE I8.1218a15-32 et le περὶ τἀγαθοῦ," *Unter-*

suchungen zur Eudemischen Ethik, Akten des 5. Symposium Aristotelicum (Berlin, 1971), pp. 197-222. Consult E. Berti, ibid., p. 168, note 33.

40. *Test. Plat.* 34 = Appendix, 3.26 (Aristotle, *Protr.* frag. 5 Walzer and Ross, B33 Düring): τἀγαθά ἐστι ὡρισμένα καὶ τεταγμένα (καὶ) γνωριμώτερα.

41. *Test. Plat.* 32, par. 268 = Appendix, 3.12 (in the framework of the categorial reduction), further developed and specified until the achieving of the doctrine of the *mesotes* and virtue in *Test. Plat.* 44a/b = Appendix, 3.29-31 (*Div. Arist.*, Cod. Marc. Nr. 68 Mutschmann and Diogenes Laertius 3.104-5, LCL 1.367, 369; consult Cod. Marc. 23). For the status of the tradition E. Hambruch, *Logische Regeln der platonischen Schule in der aristotelischen Topik* (Berlin, 1904), pp. 11ff., remains fundamental. For more details see what we said in *APA*, pp. 287-98. The fact that the *Div. Arist.*, (Appendix, 3.29), different from *Test. Plat.* 32, par. 268 (Appendix, 3., 12), with respect to determinate opposites (for example, between good and evil) admit the existence of a mean (for example, that which is neither good nor evil), and that further they admit the existence of opposites between the things that are neither good nor evil, hardly constitutes a contradiction, but only a precision. In fact, also in *Test. Plat.* 32 (Appendix, 3.12) the principle of the excluded middle between the opposites holds undoubtedly uniquely within the *specified* realms of the real; for example, the necessity that a thing be either healthy *or* ill, alive *or* dead, holds only in the sphere of organic entities, but not likewise for inorganic entities (consult *Div. Arist.*otle, cited: ὅπερ τῆς ζωῆς δεκτικόν ἐστιν!). The fact that the *Div. Arist.*otle, place in relief the existence of spheres of reality of different and unspecified types, by making an issue for a thorough discussion exactly the existence of *things that are neither good nor evil*, is quite in agreement with Platonic thought, since Plato, following the Socratic tradition, in the dialogues frequently places next to the ἀγαθόν and the κακόν likewise that which is οὔτε ἀγαθὸν οὔτε κακόν (for example, *Lysis* 216f.; *Gorgias* 467E; *Symposium* 202Af.; *Republic* 584Dff., 609B; on this theme see Hambruch, *Logische Regeln*, p. 12 and note 5). The fact, then, that these things which are *indifferent* can be equally structured according to the schema of the opposites, corresponds to what was said in the *Republic* 479B, 523Dff., and in the *Philebus* 12Ef. (where the same examples are found again which were used in the *Div. Arist.*). The reduction to the doctrine of the principles takes place, therefore, in this case, very probably, through the numerical structuring of the corresponding ideal models. Vice versa the "mean" between the correlatives of the *more* and *less* is not really correlative (see the following note), but belongs in an unequivocal way to the *same* sphere of reality to which these belong, which pass from more to less through the mean and the equal and vice versa.

42. *Test. Plat.* 31 = Appendix, 3.13 (on the basis of the book on Plato of Plato's follower, Hermodorus). The distinction of limited and unlimited is referred here to relative being (πρὸς ἕτερα) in general, hence to the opposites just as to the correlatives. (The limited considered from the logical viewpoint is not a correlative, but an opposite explicitly). The fact that the "mean" (μέσον), as ἱκανόν, σύμφωνον between the correlatives, which has a positive value, in *Test. Plat.* 32, par. 268 (consult Appendix, 3.12), does not lead back as the positive opposites, through equality, to Unity, with much probability based on the evident presupposition that, in this case, it can be treated only as a positive opposite. This mean, also here, from the logical viewpoint is *not* a correlative, but in comparison with correlatives is like a (positive)

opposite. The positivization that consists in the equalization of the correlatives of *more* and *less*, which in the examples are very close to those of the *Philebus* of Plato, can, moreover, be derived not from the dyad, but only from unity. And it *must be* thus, because according to the *Test. Plat.* 32, par. 276 (consult Appendix, 3.12), "everything" must be explained by both principles (just as it is said in *Test. Plat.* 23B [Appendix, 3.11] for the "limitation"). And, in effect, Plato hints to such a reduction in the *Statesman* 284D1f. (Appendix, 2.12).For the rest, the pseudo-Pythagorean texts parallel to *Test. Plat.* 32 par. 268 Appendix, 3.12 (for example, *De oppos.*, *Pseudo-Kallicratides*, *Pseudo-Metopus*, in Mullach and in Thesleff), as the doctrine of the categories and the principles in context proves, go back to the same tradition (consult what we said in *UGM*, p. 25, note 14; see also T. Szlezák, *Pseudo-Archytas über die Kategorien* [Berlin, 1972], pp. 129-33), while the terminology that can be connected with the categorial division in general found in Sextus Empiricus himself through the New Academy goes back to the Ancient Academy, and, in the final analysis, to Plato (on this see what we said *PHP*, pp. 75ff., with the treatment of the modifications).

43. Aristotle, *Eth. Eud.* I 8.1218a22 (Appendix, 3.25). (Concerning the character of limitation of the καλόν, consult *Met.* 1078a36ff. with the reference to the περὶ τοῦ ἀγαθοῦ of Aristotle in a marginal note of the *Codex Parisinus*). Note that the monads, which are specified as good in reference to the unity (which is the Good), in the relation contained in the *Eudemian Ethics*, in other contexts are presented as "limited" by unity, see *Test. Plat.* 23B, at the end (Appendix, 3.11).

44. See K. Bärthlein, *Die Transzendentalienlehre in der alten Ontologie* Vol. I (Berlin, 1972), pp. 80-102, 379 on the Platonic-Academic, and non-Aristotelian, origin of the doctrine of the transcendentals.

45. *Republic* 534B-C; *Seventh Letter* 342Aff. (Appendix, 1.2).

46. *Test. Plat.* 35b fin. (consult 47A); Aristotle, *Statesman* frag. 79 Rose (πάντων γὰρ ἀκριβέστατον μέτρον τἀγαθόν ἐστιν, completing Plato, *Statesman* 284D2 = Appendix, 2.8); consult Aristotle, *Met.* 1052b15ff., 1053b4ff., 1054a26ff. (*Test. Plat.* 41A = Appendix, 3.18), 1087b33, 1088a4; Plato, *Protagoras* 357B (Appendix, 2.1), *Republic* 504C (with B and E), *Laws* 716C (consult *Sophist*, 228Cf., *Philebus* 64Df., 66A), *Test. Plat.* 36 (Xenocrates, frag. 42 Heinze). For what follows, see *PD*, passim, and especially pp. 432ff.

47. *Theaetetus* 201Eff., 205Cff.; consult also Aristotle, *Met.* 1014b3-11.The admission of a supreme genus of "measure," to which the principle must also be subordinated, would lead to an infinite regress in the sense of "the third man argument" (on this see below pp. 139ff.). All the relations of particular measures are understood only by going back to the relation of the "principal" measure. And this must be explained in terms of itself.

48. More precisely, as "the most exact measure," "absolute measure of all multiplicity in general."

49. For example, by Menaechmus, frag. V Schmidt.

50. Aristotle, *Anal. post.* I 3; consult *Anal. post.* I 8 and in addition, *Topics*, VI 4.

51. *Meno* 76A7: the figure (σχῆμα) is "the limit (πέρας) of the body in three dimensions."

52. This lack of differentiation of ethics and ontology that is specifically Platonic is not always expressed in an adequate manner in the reports of Aristotle and the Peripatetics, since they stand chiefly on the ground of first philosophy and physics. In them, because of the logic of the division of philosophy into different disciplines, a separation is to be found in what in Plato was still conceived in a strictly unitary fashion. But the task for the historian who is to reconstruct and integrate what has been divided takes place in some smaller measure, too, in what is found throughout the written works of Plato by the mediation of those dialogues like the *Parmenides* and the *Sophist*, on the one hand, and the *Symposium* and the *Phaedrus*, on the other.

53. *Seventh Letter* 341C (see Appendix, 1.2).

54. For example, *Laches* 194Eff.; *Protagoras* 360D; Hippias Minor 397Bff.; *Phaedo* 97D; *Phaedrus* 261Cff.; *Laws* 816Df.; *Seventh Letter* 344B1f. (see Appendix, 1.2); consult Aristotle, *Topics* A 14.105b5f., Met. Γ 2.1004a9ff., etc.

55. The dialectical method comprehends globally, hence, the plurality of methods, that is to say, the method of *elementarizing* and that of *generalizing*. It follows that it cannot simply be identified with the *method of generalizing*.

56. *Div. Arist.*, nr. 65 Cod. Marc.; Aristotle, *Met.* 1005a16ff. combined with 995b21ff.

57. The *Test. Plat.* 11 is very instructive in this regard for the unwritten doctrine; consult also *Phaedrus* 278D (Appendix, 1.1); *Seventh Letter* 344A8f., B7f. (see Appendix, 1.2). (Consult in regard to this what we said in *APA*, p. 464, and, for further clarifications, what we said in *Ak.*, pp. 225-27, 230).

58. Consult pp. 83, 85.

Chapter 7

1. Consult pp. 5ff. and 42ff.

2. On the problematic character of the concept of evolution, the contribution of K. Oehler is fundamental, "Der Entwicklungsgedanke als heuristisches Prinzip der Philosophiehistorie," *Zeitschrift für philos. Forschung*, 17/4 (1963): 604ff.

3. The decisive contacts and resolutions fall in this period for Plato (the contacts with Socrates, Euclides of Megara, Archytas, and a little later, the founding of the Academy).

4. For further explanations consult what we said in *APA*, pp. 29-35, 532f.; *Retr.*, pp. 163-66; *Ak.* pp. 221-23; *AAW*, p. 224.

5. Consult *Theaetetus* 183E.

6. *Protagoras* 357B (Appendix, 2.1); on this passage see *APA*, pp. 490-493; *Meno* 76Ef. (Appendix, 2.2), on this passage see Gaiser, *Menon*, pp. 347ff.; consult pp. 339ff., 379ff., 388ff., 393.

7. For example, the Idea of the Good in the *Republic* (505A) is indicated as something that "is often heard," and the Ideas in the *Phaedo* (76D, 100B) as something that "has been spoken about many times"; and if Aristophanes already toward the end of the 390s in the *Ecclesiazusae* (vv. 590ff.) alludes to the community of families, which, according to Aristotle (*Politics* B 7.1266a34ff.; 12.1274b9ff.), Plato was the first

to profess, then there one needs to take account of the fact that some central concepts of the *Republic* go back to twenty years earlier.

8. Also in this case, the relation of contrariety is falsified in a relation of contradictoriness, that is, in that relation which is based on the principle of the excluded middle. Consult pp. 58f.

9. In this regard see W. Jaeger, *Aristoteles, Grundlegung einer Geschichte seiner Entwicklung* (Berlin, 1955²), p. 13. There is no lack of examples which would lead in the direction of this convergence: μέτρον and μετρητική of the *Protagoras* (357B = Appendix, 2.1) are brought to light for the first time in the *Republic*, the diaeretic articulation of the ideal cosmos hinted at in the *Republic* 511Bf., is passed over in silence until the *Sophist* and the *Statesman* and the mathematical structure of the soul (the μακροτέρα ὁδός of the *Republic* 435Cf.; see 504Af., 611Bff.) is manifested for the first time in the *Timaeus*. For further references, consult H. Erbse, "Über Platons Methode in den sogenannten Jugenddialogen," *Hermes* 96 (1968): esp. 35ff.; H. G. Ingenkamp, "Laches, Nikias und Platonische Lehre," *Rheinisches Museum* 110 (1967): 234-47, and the basic observations of W. Schulz, "Das Problem der Aporie in den Tugenddialogen Platons," in *Die Gegenwart der Griechen im neueren Denken, Festschrift für Hans Georg Gadamer zum 60. Geburtstag* (Tübingen, 1960), pp. 267ff., as well as that which we have done in *APA*, pp. 532f.; *GF*, p. 129, note 77. That Plato retracted these limits in his later works, in a conscious manner, seems to be confirmed also in the *Laws*, where he clearly returns again to posit such limits farther on.

10. Consult pp. 237-38, note 81.

11. Consult *APA* pp. 35f., 329-41.

12. In this respect consult G. Reale, *Per una nuova interpretazione di Platone. Rilettura della metafisica dei grandi dialoghi alla luce delle "Dottrine non scritte"* (Milan: Vita e Pensiero, 1989⁶) [American version trans. J. R. Catan, forthcoming].

13. For what follows see what we said in *APA*, pp. 135-45, 473-80, 533ff.; *Ak.* p. 214f., 221; *PD*, passim; *GF*, pp. 128-34; *Epekeina*, passim; *Ph.R.* pp. 30-32 and the contribution of K. Gaiser, cited in note 23.

14. Consult p. 220, note 11 and p. 9.

15. *Republic* 435D, 506D-E, 509C5ff. (Appendix, 2.4/ 5), 530D, 532D, 533A, 534A, 611B-C; with this see *Timaeus* 48C, 53D (Appendix, 2.9, 10).

16. In a different case, the simile of the sun would be a limping one for this central point, that is, it would be without any specific *tertium comparationis* (known third thing for comparison).

17. The attempt of E. De Strycker ("L'idée du bien dans la '*République*' de Platon," *L'antiquité classique* 39 [1970]: 450-67, esp. 455, note 23), to base on the Aristotelian report in *Eud. Eth.* I 8.1218a15ff. (Appendix, 3.25), the explanation in a teleological mode of the *Republic* 509B, makes use of the unwritten doctrines, and must consequently also admit the "generation" of the Ideas (the Ideal Numbers) in the background of the *Republic*. Moreover, the teleological metaphor of the report (the "tending" of numbers toward the One-Good) cannot supersede the generation and the derivation of the Ideas from the principles, for the simple fact that it, in the context of the report, belongs to the order of knowledge, and *presupposes* hence as *already present* the existence of numbers, which is deducible only according to the

order of the degrees of being. The affirmation of the *Republic* 509B, on the other side, is much more radical, and as such is connected in an unequivocal manner together with the reports that speak of generation according to the ordering of being.

18. That the definition of the Good is not absolutely "inexpressible" but that Plato makes Socrates intentionally silent on this point, results from the following facts and allusions contained in the text. (1) The "opinion" (δοκοῦν) of Socrates must not be expressed in words, as has been explicitly explained, not for reasons of principle, but only "now" and "in the actual circumstances," affirmations that would be incomprehensible, if the definition of the Good could not be formulated in an absolute sense. (2) Socrates, with the affirmation that the Good is beyond being, even offers a partial revelation of his thought, which he had from the beginning said he did not wish to reveal. (3) Formulas that express the intention of wanting to conceal certain things are found in the beginning of the simile of the divided line (509C = Appendix, 2.5) just as in a series of other passages of the *Republic* (consult note 14; with the parallel texts also in the *Timaeus*, which belongs to the same trilogy), which cannot be explained on the assumption of the "ineffability" of the Good, since they refer to different themes. (4) The reasons for which he does not wish to speak about the essence of the Good in the *Republic* 506D-E (Appendix, 2.4 is explained and founded down to the very details by the theory and the experience contained in the *excursus* of the *Seventh Letter* (uselessness of the direct communication of the Good—διελθεῖν, *Republic* 506D5, 509C6 [see Appendix, 2.4, 5] is placed in relation to the *Seventh Letter* 341A8, 345A7, ἐξηγεῖσθαι 345D4 [see Appendix, 1.2]—for those who are not prepared, both in oral discourse and in writing, by reason of the fact that the means of communication are not understood, and consequently, are "ridiculed" [see *Republic* 506D8 = Appendix, 2.4, and the corresponding passage of the *Seventh Letter* 343C8 = Appendix, 1.2], as for example, the name and definition). "Name" (ὄνομα) and "definition" (λόγος) of the Good are, then, clearly presupposed in the *Republic* (see 534B-C!) as well as in the *Seventh Letter*. (5) The theme of ridiculousness, which is encountered in *Republic* 506D8 (see Appendix, 2.4), returns in 517A-D in reference to the philosopher *who is in possession of knowledge*, but who, once he returns to the cave, remains incomprehensible to those who are not in possession of knowledge and is killed like Socrates. (6) The dialectical method would have to be rejected as invalid, if already on such a preliminary level as exposed in the *Republic* that still precedes an effective completion of the dialectic ascent, it must be acknowledged as insufficient and has to abdicate in favor of a language constituted by similes. (7) The theme of "ineffability," the "difficulty in speaking about it" is not at all a Platonic theme, but rather a Neoplatonic, and, especially, a modern one.

19. For example, *Republic* 422E, 423A, 445C, 462Aff., 551D, 557Cf. The fact that Plato hints at the unity and stability of the State and its ontological foundations (on the mixed constitution see, pp. 112f.), is far from modern political pluralism, but answers to the well-known instability of the relations in the ancient polis, against which other theorists of the State, among the ancients, also tried to respond.

20. *Republic* 443E1, 554D, 561E; see *Phaedrus* 230A, and *Epinomis* 992B6f.

21. *Republic* 370Af., 374Aff., 392Cff., 406C, 407A, 415Aff., 421C, 423D, 445C.

22. *Test. Plat.* 34 (Appendix, 3.26) and Aristotle, *Eud. Eth.* 1 8.1218a2ff. (Appendix, 3.23); consult pp. 86f.

23. Clearly, for example, this emerges from Aristotle, *Eud. Eth.*, loc. cit.

24. Concerning this issue, K. Gaiser, "Die Rede der Musen über den Grund von Ordnung und Unordnung: Platon, Politeia VIII 545D-547A," in *Studia Platonica. Festschrift für H. Gundert* (Amsterdam, 1974), pp. 49-85, esp. pp. 80ff. is fundamental.

25. Consult on this in addition to what is said in *APA*, pp. 135ff., 324ff., 536ff., 554f., also H. Gomperz, *Platons philosophisches System* (consult Chapter 3, note 62), pp. 123f. Consult also J. M. Crombie, *An Examination of Plato's Doctrines* (London, 1962-63), II, pp. 450f.; J. N. Findlay, *Plato*, pp. 184f., 190.

26. *Test. Plat.* 25A = Aristotle, *De anima* A 2.404b22 (νοῦν μὲν τὸ ἕν). A little different is the "unity of consciousness" in the soul in the *Theaetetus* 184D3.

27. Consult the connection of the συμμετρία of the (rational) soul with its capacity to achieve the truth (ἀλήθεια) in *Sophist* 228.

28. For example, the hints about the μακροτέρα ὁδός in 435D, newly taken in 611Aff., in the proof for the immortality of the soul (οἷον δ᾽ ἐστὶν τῇ ἀληθείᾳ, see *Phaedrus* 246A).

29. The opposite conjecture of K. von Fritz, that the Good is also a principle of knowledge, because without the preference given on the part of the knower to the good or to the better it is not possible for any knowledge to result (*Phronesis* 11 [1966]: 150), is not justified by the text of the *Republic* for two reasons: (*a*) the virtue (*arete*) of the soul spoken about there is already given in its *capacity* and *power* of knowing, and, hence, *precedes* the respective objects of knowledge, just as the acts of choosing among these; (*b*) the act of preference or choice among the "chaos of impressions" (K. von Fritz, *Studium Generale* 14 [1961]: 616) is inadequate for the intuition of the intelligibles and, rather than to this, it corresponds to sensualism and to the doctrine of the criterion, which is characteristic of the doctrine of knowledge of Hellenistic philosophy. The numerical arrangement of the rational soul, on the basis of the fundamental principle of "like with like," is in correspondence with the ordering of being and with its structure. Insofar as the soul distinguishes, that is, enumerates and counts, it is, consequently, itself numerically determined (so J. Stenzel and H. G. Gadamer explain it).

30. *Republic* 505Bff., 506B2ff., with the following continuation in the simile of the sun in 508Ef.

31. For example, *Republic* 476A, 478B10ff., 479A, 507B; *Parmenides* 131B5, C9f., 132A1ff., B 2, 5, C4, 133B1, 135B3ff., C9f.; *Phaedo* 78D5, 80B2; see also *Symposium* 211E4; *Cratylus* 439C, 440B; *Philebus* 14Dff.; *Euthyphro* 5D3f., 6D11.

32. The Platonic term to express this concept was, perhaps (as for the correlatives), συνυπάρχειν, to which corresponds in the negative a συναναιρεῖσθαι.

33. *Test. Plat.* 50; consult the parallel Aristotle, *Met.* N 2.1089a2ff., and for the details, see the interpretation we give in *Epekeina*, pp. 6-17.

34. The text of the *Republic* 509C1 (consult Appendix, II 5) contains even an intimation of unity, when Socrates' partner, on hearing that the Idea of the Good is beyond being, responds with an exclamation of wonder ῝Apollon (aÂ-pollaÈ: not-many, the Pythagoreans understood the monad in an allegorical sense as Apollo = aÂpoÈfasiw tv n pollv n). For those who were familiar with the teaching the allusion to the doctrine was unmistakable. The status of the unity that is beyond

being means, in the concrete, *that it is nothing limited like every being, but that it itself is limiting and limit* ("measure": meÈtron). One ought not to conclude from this that it itself is nonexistent, just as one ought not to conclude from its function of being a ground of truth that it is entirely beyond truth and of itself unknowable. The text of the Republic, especially the myth of the cave, belies this point for point (consult 505A: meÈgion maÈuhma! 511B, 516B, 517C, 518C, 532B, 533A: ayÂtoÈ toÈ aÂlhueÈw, 534B, 540A). The properties of "limitation" belong to unity, as that which constitutes the limit itself, per eminentiam (surpassingly).

35. On the incompleteness of the exposition of the simile of the divided line, see the express suggestion in the *Republic* 509C = Appendix, 2.5 (συχνά γε ἀπολέιπω!). This incompleteness can be confirmed, for example, by the fact that the intermediate ontological status of the mathematical entities, of which the reports tell us (for example, Aristotle, *Met.* A 6 [*Test. Plat.* 22A = Appendix, 3.9], in the *Republic* can be drawn only from a brief hint contained in the myth of the cave (516A; see 534A: shadows and images); see now the clarifications of J. A. Brentlinger, *Phronesis* 8 (1963): 146-66; J. N. Findlay, *Plato*, pp. 188 and 190; see, moreover, J. Annas, *Archiv für Geschichte der Philosophie* 57 (1975): 146-66.

36. Consult the report of Aristotle, *Met.* M 1084a32ff. with the distinction of the principles and their derivatives: τὰ ἑπόμενα, which are illustrated by the Meta-Ideas movement and rest.

37. See on this Ž. Marcović, "La théorie de Platon sur l'Un et la Dyade indéfinie et ses traces dans la mathématique Grecque," *Revue d'histoire des sciences*, VIII, 4 (1955): 289ff. (A German version can also be found in *Zur Geschichte der griechischen Mathematik*, ed. O. Becker, pp. 308ff.) The "figures" mentioned in the simile of the divided line (σχήματα, referring preferentially to the series of polygons) make reference not so much to a generalizing reduction but to an elementarizing reduction, and the same must primarily be admitted for the κοινωνία, the συγγένεια and the οἰκειότης of the mathematical disciplines, of which the *Republic* 531D and 537C speaks (for the special elements and the special principles that are here at the basis and for their relationship with unity as fundamental measure, consult pp. 84ff.). Among the "related" concepts about which C5 speaks (καὶ ἄλλα τούτων ἀδελφά), the mathematical concept of "similarity" as intermediate between equality and inequality could have a role.

38. The interpretation of K. von Fritz, *Phronesis* 11 (1966): 150, which tries to directly connect mathematics with the Good by the concept of "choice," "preference," "refinement," and similar ones does not do justice to the text of Plato (in fact it does not consider the methods of mathematics, but the deduction and definition of some of its fundamental *concepts*).

39. Consult in B3f. the definition of the dialectician as ὁ τὸν λόγον ἑκάστου λαμβάνων τῆς οὐσίας. That there should be such a *logos* also for the Good is in agreement with the theory of teaching and learning of the *Seventh Letter* (342Aff., esp. 342D4, 344A8 [see Appendix, 1.2] for the ἀγαθόν).

40. For the interpretation of the passage, see the further clarifications that we made in *PD*, pp. 425f., note 78. For the definition of the Good in the indirect tradition, see pp. 87ff.

41. Consult p. 237-38, note 81.

42. In any case, the basic ontological conception, that is, the limitation of multiplicity by unity, in this passage is suggested also for the sphere of the intelligibles, independently from the degree of thematization of the principle opposed to unity. The fact, then, that the (universal) principle opposed to the unity in the *Republic* on the basis of this passage can be only inferred, does not at all constitute an argument against the grounding of this work on the unwritten doctrines. In fact, (*a*) in the concept of the "unwritten doctrines" is implied by definition that not all is expressly stated or even only hinted at in the written works. Moreover (*b*) the numerous hints about the "unsaid" and the hermeneutic potential of the indirect tradition that is otherwise unattainable and rightly so for the central books of the *Republic*, secure in substance, that the masterpiece of Plato—in agreement with the programmatic affirmations of the *Phaedrus* and the *Seventh Letter*—presupposes the unwritten doctrines.

43. *Gorgias* 504A3f., B2, 506D5ff., and in addition *Symposium* 186A-188E, 209A7f. (In the discussion by Eryximachus good love and bad love, as principle of order and principle of disorder represent unity and multiplicity.)

44. *Symposium* 207D5, 6, 7, E3f., 208A2, 6f., 8f.

45. The discussion of Aristophanes prefigures in mythical form the original whole, the unity and unitary essence of man, which in the speech of Diotima is also the object and end of Eros: 191D2, 192E 1, 2, 3, 8, 193A1; see 192D6, E10.

46. In particular, the fifth hypothesis is a parody of the second, making affirmations concerning a nonexistent unity appear possible by the dialectical method, and this from the viewpoint of multiplicity (unlike the first hypothesis, on the basis of which no multiplicity is opposed to unity); the sixth hypothesis corrects this, by making us see that from not-being follows the impossibility of any relation (and therefore agreeing in the results, but again not in its basic reason, with the first hypothesis). The seventh hypothesis caricatures the third, feigning the admission of the existence of a nonexistent unity (probably a criticism of atomism), a fiction that in the eighth hypothesis is discovered and resolved (the relation of these two hypotheses is analogous to the relation between the sixth and the fifth and as a result is in agreement with the fourth, but with a more radical reasoning: the impossibility of any relation is maintained not on the basis of the isolation, but on the nonexistence of unity; and in this it is the corresponding opposite of the first hypothesis: as the existence of only unity is inconceivable, so also the existence of only multiplicity is inconceivable).

47. In particular, the Meta-Ideas play a central role (but without being reduced to the principles), and it seems that there is an allusion to the doctrine of the *minima* (164E3ff.).

48. The theory of the *hypomnemata* of the *Phaedrus* is limited by the affirmations of the *Phaedrus* 278C-D = Appendix, 1.1 (and similarly in the *Seventh Letter* 344D9ff. = Appendix, 1.2). Also the *Parmenides* takes account of this restriction.

49. The fact that "difference" or "otherness" of the *Sophist* already presupposes participation in unity seems to be the result of the central theoretical third hypothesis of the *Parmenides* (158D).

50. The same thing holds, in a corresponding manner, for the principle opposed to unity.

51. This holds also for the copulative use or for the identifying use of the *is*, which always indicates relations, that is, wholes and unities or in other words unity in multiplicity. The *logos* as affirmation (*logos* also means relation!) can for this reason be presented also as a genus of being (*Sophist* 260A), because the word being (ὄν) expresses also relations of being.

52. L. Robin, *Études sur la signification et la place de la physique dans la philosophie de Platon*, pp. 177ff., 370ff., reprinted in *La pensée hellénique*, pp. 231ff. J. Stenzel, *Zahl und Gestalt*, pp. 71ff., 123f. Gaiser, *PUL*, pp. 41ff., 145ff. C. F. von Weizsäcker, *Die Einheit der Natur* (Munich, 1971), pp. 474ff.; also *Der Garten des Menschlichen. Beiträge zur geschichtlichen Anthropologie* (Munich-Vienna, 1977), pp. 171ff., 326ff., 335ff. Consult *GF*, p. 130, note 85.

53. Aristotle, *Physics* 209b15ff., 33ff. (*Test. Plat.* 54A = Appendix, 3.4). Consult also Theophr. *Met.* 6a28f. (*Test. Plat.* 30 = Appendix, 3.8). The words that introduce the central part of the *Timaeus* and say that it will not speak of determinate things (48C = Appendix, 2.9), may refer also to the integration of space into the theory of the principles.

54. The second kind, which is the more important of the fundamental triangles, contains in the relations of angles (1:2:3) and relations of squares (1:3:4, and consequently the relations of the sides 1:2:√3) the four fundamental numbers of the Tetraktys, in the relations of the sections of the diagonals of the figures of two and three dimensions, moreover, it contains the musical intervals of the fifth (3:2) and the fourth (4:3). The first type of fundamental triangle produces by the progressive squaring of the hypotenuse (that is, of the diagonal of the square) the powers of two, whereas the second type of triangle, by the progressive doubling of the line which divides in half the side (understood as *cathetus*) produces the powers of three. Consult for the details Gaiser, *PUL*, pp. 112, 156.

55. *Test. Plat.* 25A = Aristotle, *De an.* 404b16ff.

56. Concerning the structure of the principles in the ordering and the deduction of the fundamental colors in *Timaeus* 67C-68D, see K. Gaiser "Platons Farbenlehre," in *Synusia für W. Schadewaldt*, esp. pp. 180ff. (with considerations on a further completion in the Academy of Plato).

57. *Test. Plat.* 7 = Appendix, 3.1 together with 16 (with the request of Plato to the mathematicians to relate the movements of the planets by harmonic analysis, that is, elementarizing, to circular movements and in this way to simplify them).

58. Consult *Timaeus* 50Cf., for the difference from the theory of the principles of a dialectical-universal character, consult *VPA*, pp. 331ff.

59. Concerning this, see the full presentation which we have given in *APA*, Chapters II and III. The terminology of the *special doctrine* of the categories may be seen also in *Philebus* 51C6f., D7f.

60. The most important documents are: *Laws* III 691-702, IV 712-715, VI 756-757 and the *Eighth Letter* 354f.

61. Concerning the concept of order as found in the late dialogues (except the *Timaeus*), see for example, *Phaedrus* 230A, 238A, 264C, 268D, 269C; *Philebus* 26B, 64B;

Statesman 273Bff., 308C. The "determinate mean" with respect to the structure of the order of being has the same relation that the part has to the whole or the element to the compound and has therefore characteristics that are closer to those of a principle (to speak more specifically, it is ontologically "prior," and if "eliminated" the order will also be "eliminated" as a whole but not vice versa). For a more detailed analysis in this regard, see *APA*, pp. 321ff., 333ff.

62. Consult *Philebus* 64ff. with the related analysis of the "determinate" human good on the basis of the quantitative-limiting, qualitative-aretological, epistemological (64B, E, 65A, B) and ontological aspects (64B3).

63. With typical words, Plato says that he does not wish to speak of a determinate thing 76E-77A = Appendix, 2.2 (note the word play with ἕν-πολλά in relation to the mysteries!). Let us refer, once again, to the penetrating interpretation of the dialogue made by K. Gaiser, *Menon* (with the supplement of 1968 reprinted in the volume of essays ed. Wippern).

64. The same must be said also for the numerical relations within the sphere of the universals that proceed in the same direction and for their ultimate foundation in the principles as ultimate elements of the order of numbers.

65. *Republic* 511Bff., 516Aff., 532Aff., 540Af.; *Parmenides* 136B-E; *Sophist* 254Bf.; *Statesman* 285D-286B.

66. *Sophist* 217Aff., 254B, consult 253E; *Statesman* 257Af.; on the function of these references, see what we said in *APA*, pp. 247ff., 316f., 484, and already F. M. Cornford, *Plato's Theory of Knowledge* (London, 1935), p. 169.

67. The alternative formulated by A. Graeser, namely that in the unwritten doctrine in relation to the dialogues is "either a system of a wholly different type, or only a dimension of a more elevated order" (*Zeitschrift für philos. Forschung* [1980]: 676), is consequently to resolve in favor of the second member of the distinction.

68. One must, however, always take into account the possibility that the indirect tradition is also limited by a choice made among oral doctrines professed by Plato in his teaching. (On the relations between the *Republic* and the *Ecclesiazusae* of Aristophanes, see what we said on p. 257, note 7.)

69. Also this shows the insensitivity of the attempt to eliminate the political doctrine of Plato and in a particular way his project of the ideal State, by considering them in a utopian or even ironic fashion. (That Plato maintained as possible a realization of the ideal State, at least a realization that would approximate it, although only under conditions that would be particularly favorable and that he maintained his project as necessary and obligatory even independently of historical and geographical conditions, is demonstrated in the passage of the *Republic* 499Cf.). The limits to the claim to rule by philosophy and philosophers arise, in part, from the differences between divine and human wisdom and, in part, from the dual structure of the doctrine of the principles.

70. We must pay attention to this in a special way if, from the "open" and "experimental" character of the writings and the lack of stable terminology, some try to draw consequences concerning the whole of Platonic philosophy.

Chapter 8

1. Concerning what follows, see what we said in *APA*, Chapter, V, ("Platon und Parmenides").

2. That the term *arche*, as a philosophical term, was used for the first time in Plato, was demonstrated by A. Lumpe, "Der Terminus 'Prinzip' (ἀρχή) von den Vorsokratikern bis auf Aristoteles," *Archiv für Begriffsgeschichte* 1 (1955): 108ff.

3. K. Albert, *Griechische Religion und platonische Philosophie* (Hamburg, 1980), esp. pp. 39-49 ("Hen"); consult pp. 27, 71, 106f., 117ff., 122. Albert (see, for example, p. 38) refers Plato on individual points directly to the religious-theological tradition (without the mediation of the Presocratics). See also K. Albert, *Die ontologische Erfahrung* (Ratingen, 1974), pp. 46ff. (on the experience of the One and Being in Plato).

4. Consult pp. 79f., 100f.

5. *Test. Plat.* 45; consult 46A. Anaximenes, *DK* 13A5; 6, par. 3; 8; Parmenides, *DK* 28B8, vv. 22ff., 44ff., Zeno, *DK* 29B1-3; Melissus, *DK* 30B7, par. 8. Anaxagoras, *DK* 59B3.

6. *Test. Plat.* 22A = Appendix, 3.9 Aristotle, *Met.* A 6.987b25ff.

7. For what concerns the philosophical foundation of the theory of the proportions of Eudoxus, see, pp. 78f. and 141f. For more details about the different prefigurations of the great-and-small, see what we said in *APA*, pp. 258ff., 512, note 49, 536, note 86.

8. The dualism of the two "worlds" (τόποι), that of the intelligible and that of the sensible, from the beginning does not coincide with that of the two principles, but intersects with it. The dualism of the two "worlds" can rather be deduced from the dualism of the principles by the admission of different relations of mixture and with degrees of one with respect to the other. Consult what we said on p. 81f., and for more details, see what we said on pp. 144ff.

9. Plato tried to integrate in the generalizing Socratic method of definition that elementarizing aspect belonging to the Presocratic tradition, represented especially in the Pythagoreans but in the Atomists as well, including Anaxagoras and Empedocles, to reach the most universal starting points.

10. What H. Boeder, "Zu Platons eigener Sache," *Philosophisches Jahrbuch*, 76 (1968): 37ff., wrote in this respect is instructive.

11. It is, therefore, wholly erroneous to put into opposition the image of Plato drawn from the indirect tradition and the Socraticism of Plato from the dialogues. This is a mistake, not only, because of (*a*) the reasons hinted at earlier, but moreover because (*b*) the very sphere of "orality" that the unwritten refers to is the consequence of the Socratic method, and, further, because (*c*) the primacy of the Socratic inheritance is shown in an unmistakable fashion in the main theme of the unwritten doctrine (*On the Good*). On the other side, it is, vice versa, to take into account that the written work of Plato contradicts in some way the nonliterary way of life of Socrates (remember the end of the *Phaedrus*) and that in the course of the thematic development of the writings themselves the symbolic figure of Socrates recedes in an increasing fashion, while other protagonists emerge into the foreground of the

dialogue (Parmenides, the Eleatic Stranger, the Pythagoreans Timaeus and Hermocrates, the Athenian host of the *Laws*, and so on).

12. *Laws* 716C; see the debate about the *summum bonum* (the highest good) in the *Republic* 505Bff., 506B2ff., 508E3ff., 509A6ff. (with the allusion to the character of the "measure" that is proper to the Good itself in 504Cff.).

13. The antecedent of the doctrine of the One-Good of the Socratic school of Megara, referred to by H. Gomperz and independently from him also by me, after the clarifications of K. von Fritz and K. Döring no longer has a strong proof, since now the influence of the Eleatic school on the Megaric is put in doubt ("one," in the Megaric school, probably is only predicated of the Good).

14. The *Republic* itself, as is known, presupposes already in some readers previous knowledge of the Good (504E7f., 505A3).

15. J. Stenzel, *Studien zur Entwicklung der platonischen Dialektik*, pp. 3ff.

16. For example, *Gorgias* 503E.

17. The superessentiality of unity itself, derived from the radical transformation of the Eleatic disjunction, presupposes already the previous clarification of these problems.

18. Plato hence follows the maxim that the ultimate principle can be only that which is *akin* in essence to that which is the principled and not that which is *equal* in essence and that hence between the principle and that which is subject to the principle there is necessarily a difference in their *status*. Moreover, the systematic consequence also emerges here, by which, in Plato, this approach carries philosophy also to a precise claim to political power.

19. For what follows, see what we said in *APA*, Chapter VI ("Platon und Aristoteles"); *UGM*, Chapter II ("Struktur und geschichtliche Stellung der aristotelischen Nus-Metaphysik"); *GSAM*, passim; *Denkbewegung*; *VPA*; *Eidos* and in addition: "Grundfragen der aristotelischen Theologie," I/II, *Theologie und Philosophie* 44 (1969): 363-82, 481-505; "Grundbegriffe akademischer Dialektik in den biologischen Schriften von Aristoteles und Theophrast," *Rheinisches Museum* 111 (1968): 293-333; a review of E. Berti, *Dalla dialettica alla filosofia prima* (Padua, 1977), in *Archiv für Geschichte der Philosophie* 62 (1980): 199-204; K. Gaiser, *PUL*, pp. 308-31; H. Happ, *Hyle. Studien zum aristotelischen Materiebegriff*, Chapters 2 and 4, par. 6.

20. On this point, P. Merlan, *From Platonism to Neoplatonism*, Chapter VII, has opened a new path.

21. And not, instead, the relation of πρòς ἕν (*analogia attributionis*) [analogy of attribution], as the preceding interpretation incorrectly maintained.

22. P. Merlan, "Zwei Bemerkungen zum Aristotelischen Plato," *Rheinisches Museum* 111 (1968): 1ff. (*Kleine philos. Schriften*, pp. 259ff.); H. Happ, *Hyle*, pp. 262ff.

23. The apparently inadequate explanation of the ontological nexus is clarified by beginning from the characteristic of the series in which the members *per definitionem* (by definition) are referred to the first and, in addition, from the fact that the arrangement of the levels of being in the form of a series, for contemporary philosophers was evident of itself.

24. Speusippus, frag. 32 Lang, = frags. 45-47 Isnardi Parente, frag. 68 Tarán. See what follows in the text.

25. Aristotle, *Met.* Λ 1 still allows a glimpse of the first stage, since the categories are organized not as πρὸς ἕν, but as ἐφεξῆς, that is, as a regular series. In this regard, moreover, observe that the number ten of the categories in the early Aristotle is inspired by the model of the series of Ideal Numbers of the Academy; i.e., the number ten.

26. On the Platonic-Academic origin of the Aristotelian doctrine of the principles, especially of the triadic schema of the *eidos-hyle-steresis*, see M. Gentile, *La dottrina platonica delle idee numeri e Aristotele*, pp. 106ff., 117ff.; E. Berti, *La filosofia del primo Aristotele*, pp. 315f., 554ff.; idem, *Aristotele: Dalla dialettica alla filosofia prima*, Chapters V-VII. Further explanations are found in H. Krämer, *VPA*, pp. 331ff.; in particular on the concept of *hyle*, see H. Happ, *Hyle*, Chapters 2, 4, and 8.

27. The analogical relationship which remains, especially in Aristotle, *Met.* Λ 4-5, refers to the model of the particular principles of Speusippus. The cosmological aspects of the doctrine of the principles are connected to the Academic interpretation of the *Timaeus*, to which also belongs the conception of the divine mind of the Demiurge, which is transformed by Aristotle in the conception of the Unmoved Mover.

28. Consult pp. 80f.

29. Again the nonreducibility of the categories to subordinate genera or to principles that corresponds to the general weakening of *generalizing* thought is connected to this. On the connection between the Aristotelian doctrine of the categories and the Platonic division of being, see P. Merlan, *Philologus* 89 (1934) 35ff., now in *Kleine philos. Schriften*, pp. 57ff.; M. Isnardi Parente, in *Rivista di filologia* 96 (1968): 131ff.; H. Krämer, *VPA*, pp. 340ff.; E. Berti, *Aristotele: Dalla dialettica alla filosofia prima*, pp. 186ff.

30. For example, in the relation of "power" among numbers or dimensions, but also in the Speusippian conception of the relation of the various levels of being. The most important point of difference is the primacy of the actual over the potential in Aristotle. Consult Gaiser, *PUL*, pp. 430f.; K. Bärthlein, "Über das Verhältnis des Aristoteles zur Dynamislehre der griechischen Mathematiker," *Rheinisches Museum* 108 (1965): 35ff.; M. Isnardi Parente, in *Rivista di filologia* 96 (1968): 141ff.; H. Krämer, *VPA*, pp. 342f.

31. See what we said in *APA*, Chapter III. This was acknowledged by W. Jaeger in 1961 in personal correspondance with the author, and, in addition, by I. Düring, *Aristoteles* (Heidelberg, 1966), pp. 457, 460, 465 and by the same author in *Realencyclopädie der class. Altertumswissenschaft*, Suppl. XI, 1968, s. v. Aristoteles, coll. 283f.; F. Dirlmeier, *Aristoteles, Werke in deutscher Übersetzung*, ed. E. Grumach, Vol. 7: *Eudemische Ethik* (Berlin-Darmstadt, 1979³), pp. 142f., 504; G. Bien, *Die Grundlegung der politischen Philosophie bei Aristoteles* (Munich, 1973), pp. 114f.; consult in addition the conjecture that was already advanced by O. Gigon, Introduction to *Aristoteles, Die Nikomachische Ethik* (Zürich, 1951), p. 49; consult also J. Lohmann, "Vom ursprünglichen Sinn der aristotelischen Syllogistik," *Lexis* 2, no. 2 (1952): 205ff. On the contrary, the attempt to devalue the influence of the Platonic indirect tradition on the structure of value or of the *mesotes* in Aristotle on the part of W. Fiedler, *Analogiemodelle bei Aristoteles* (Amsterdam, 1978), pp. 222ff. is mistaken and off the mark. Fiedler ignores the categorial origin of the doctrine of the "mean" from the

NOTES

theory of the opposites of Plato and the Academy, which belongs to the systematic of the principles (see especially what we said in *APA*, pp. 348f., where we clarify the influences of the Platonic doctrines of the opposites in the *Topics*, and in the *Eudemian Ethics* unlike those in the *Nicomachean Ethics*; see, in addition, Speusippus, frag. 60a-b Lang = frags. 108-109 Isnardi Parente), just as the unequivocal parallels of the biological writings (see, in this regard, what follows earlier in the text). The same holds for the status of the tradition in the passages regarding the argument which are found in the *Div. Arist.* (esp. Cod. Marc. 68 = Appendix, 3.29), clarified by Hambruch, *Logische Regeln der Platonischen Schule*, pp. 11ff., and the arguments adduced in *APA*, pp. 352ff., 225ff., 367f. (the *topos* of the "limited" in the Ethics [on this also, see *Test. Plat.* 31 = Appendix, 3.13], inaccuracy in the practical sphere in Plato, and similar ones). Moreover, the necessary distinction between a general conception of the mean proper to value and a particular doctrine of the ethical *mesotes* is not found in Fiedler. On the problem of the reduction of the mean proper to values referred to in *Test. Plat.* 32, par. 268 (consult Appendix, 3.12), to unity itself, which only if seen in the general context of the Platonic systematic can be judged (Fiedler interprets differently and consequently is wrong, pp. 223f., note 4), see p. 249-50, note 42 (see also p. 249, note 41). The weakness of Fiedler is shown, among others, in the contradictory insistence on the prejudice according to which Aristotle had in general followed "the things themselves" in the phenomenological sense, on the one hand, and, on the other, in the affirmation according to which he would be the inheritor of the whole Greek tradition, without proceeding to the necessary distinctions between the prephilosophical and the philosophical tradition.

32. Consult *Rheinisches Museum* 111 (1968): 293ff. ("Grundbegriffe akademischer Dialektik in den biologischen Schriften von Aristoteles und Theophrast"), with further arguments. For the relationship in question, in addition to *Physics* A, *Metaphysics* I 3, and I 7 are important.

33. Just as, for example, the linking together of the Aristotelian apodeictic (*An. Post.* I) to the methods of demonstration in mathematics is related to the methodology and the systematic of the circle of the Platonic Academy (F. Solmsen and others).

34. The attempt that still is met, inspired by the influence that Aristotle has had historically, to make Aristotle himself appear as an original genius without a history by isolating him from the Academy and Plato, reduces his belonging to the circle of the Academy to a purely empty fact, and from the philosophical viewpoint is based on not recognizing the fact that the doctrine of the *eidos*, the sphere of transcendence, and the method of the distinction of different meanings (fundamental for the analysis of being) would not have been possible except that there had been Platonic dialectic.

35. Fundamental, in this regard, is the destructive criticism of the theory of both the principles and numbers found in *Met.* M, N (and A 9) and which eliminates the autonomous existence of mathematical entities. Corresponding to it in *Physics* Z is the refutation of the doctrine of the *minima* in favor of the doctrine of the continuum, as well as the elimination of the ontology of geometrical dimensions from the cosmological doctrine of the elements and the bodies in the *De caelo* (Γ). A dequantified notion of the "series" is found then in the succession of the levels of being (οὐσίαι), as well as in the succession of the powers of the soul in the *De anima*

(B 3), or in the succession of the unmoved Movers in the *Metaphysics* Λ 8, but also in any type of analogy (including the analogy of the relation of πρὸς ἕν) and, finally, in the principle of degrees (more or less) of biology.

36. K. Bärthlein, *Die Transzendentalienlehre* excludes, correctly, for this reason, Aristotle contrary, to the Academy of Plato, from the circle of upholders of the doctrine of the transcendentals.

37. The practical philosophy of Aristotle, therefore, was engaged in an emphatic fashion with the notion of the "human good" (the treatment of the same theme in the *Philebus* of Plato is of a different, less radical type). On the concept, connected to this of the "exclusion" of all that which is not a human good, see the pertinent explanations by G. Bien, in *Die Grundlegung der politischen Philosophie bei Aristoteles*.

38. This is drawn by the programmatic inspection of W. Schwabe, " 'Mischung' und 'Element' im Griechischen bis Platon," *Archiv für Begriffsgeschichte*, Supplementheft 3 (1980):12, 253.

39. For more details, see what we said in *PHP*, Chapters I, III, and IV. A further synthesis is given in *Die Platonisch-akademische Prinzipienlehre in der hellenistischen Philosophie* (forthcoming).

40. On the development and modification of the unwritten doctrine of Plato in the Ancient Academy, see now the exposition of H. Krämer in the already cited new edition of Ueberweg, Vol. 3, 1983.

41. On both of these arguments, see T. Szlezák, *Platon und Aristoteles in der Nuslehre Plotins* (Basel-Stuttgart, 1979), esp. pp. 110ff. (exemplary from the methodological viewpoint, in what concerns the results to which he comes concerning the reelaboration, from the side of Plotinus, of basic classical texts, but not definitive in regard to the reception of the "Neopythagorean"-Hellenistic tradition, for example, the monistic transformation of the theory of principles).

42. On this point, see what we said in the final Chapter of *UGM*, passim.

Chapter 9

1. The concept of Quine of ontological relativity (conditioned by language), which is found prefigured in a general manner in Hamann, Humboldt, Whorf, Sapir, Weisgerber, and others, has a legitimate place here. In particular, the linguistic conditioning of the ontological foundation in Plato and Aristotle has been investigated by Trendelenburg, von Fritz, Benveniste, C. H. Kahn, E. Tugendhat, and still others.

2. The fact that nonapophantic types of discourse, as in other ontologies of this type were scarcely considered depends on this. The Eleatic-Platonic ontology of names is explained by J. Hintikka by the adaptation of propositions to the objects of sensorial perception: "Knowledge and its Objects in Plato," in *Patterns in Plato's Thought*, ed. J. M. E. Moravcsik (Boston, 1973), pp. 1ff.; further developments are to be found in A. Graeser, "On Language, Thought, and Reality in Ancient Greek Thought," *Dialectica* 31 (1977): 359ff., esp. 384ff.

3. Consult pp. 80f. That the dependent forms of being are also employed in Aristotle as being, even if this does not receive its justification from the structure of

language ('the house is blue', not 'the blue is'; consult E. Tugendhat, *Vorlesungen zur Einführung in die sprachanalytische Philosophie* [Frankfurt, 1976], pp. 44ff., English translation, *Traditional and Analytical Philosophy*, [Cambridge, 1982]), is explained by the fact that Aristotle passed through the ontology of the predicates of Platonism (this is also, hence, encountered in the categorial division of Plato).

4. A comparison between generative propositional grammar and the Platonic generative processes, consequently, is hardly useful. The character of being a predicate of "unity in itself" is noted expressly in the Aristotelian report in *Met.* 1084b31, 1085b8 (τὸ κατηγορούμενον ἕν). L. Hickman, *Modern Theories of Higher Level Predicates. Second Intentions in the Neuzeit* (Munich, 1980) is fundamentally concerned with scholasticism and the modern age, but nevertheless refers repeatedly to Aristotle, although not explicitly to the position of Plato, who from the theoretical viewpoint is more important.

5. The conjecture of J. Lohmann (*Musike und Logos* [Stuttgart, 1970], pp. 5f., 9, 95) that the Greek and Platonic term, which means "element" (στοιχεῖον), is connected to the verb στείχω ('to proceed' and by association with the fundamental dynamic meaning of a "passage," a "stage") in a chronological succession, cannot certainly be verified; consult on the contrary, W. Schwabe, "'Mischung' und 'Element' im Griechischen bis Platon." *Archiv für Begriffsgeschichte*, Supplementheft 3 (1980): 90f., who maintains firmly as meaning the static "member of a series," which perhaps is derived from the example of the sun-dial (pp. 97f.: "a point on the curve of the sun-dial shadow").

6. For the Academic schema of the relation existing between definition (the signified) and name (expression), see Speusippus, frag. 32 Lang = frags. 45-47 Isnardi Parente = 68 Tarán; Aristotle, *Cat.* 1.

7. With this it would be illicit to conceive that dialectic analyzes some meanings, understood as entities immanent to the language, independently from an object that transcends language. The *logos* (definition), which is distinct from the linguistic sign (name) as critically clarified meaning reproduces rather an ontological nexus, to which dialectic refers in a primary way (see on this the *Sophist*). In the doctrine of Ideas the meanings of modern semantic theory are distinct from the word but "are connected with the referential object" (A. Graeser, *Platons Ideenlehre* [Bern, 1975], p. 40), even if Plato, in the "capacity of designating" (δύναμις) proper to a name, recognizes also a sphere of signification of words (on this, see K. Gaiser, *Name und Sache in Platons 'Kratylos'* [Heidelberg, 1974], pp. 41f., 90), in which the *logos* understood as definition again returns.

8. So it is inescapable that of a series of synonymous terms only one is maintained and the remainder are eliminated. The fact that Plato, in the dialogues, frequently seems to avoid a terminological fixation of the language is strictly connected with the predominant character of the order of knowledge in the ambit of the written works (consult p. 113).

9. Aristotle, *Met.* N 1 (esp. 1087b17ff.) draws our attention to the preoccupation of the Platonic-Academic dialecticians with choosing for a characterization of the principles, in the sphere of the linguistic material at their disposal, a terminology that would guarantee a maximum result in universalizing.

10. In this last are conceptually united singularity and simplicity, while the meaning of unicity in the sense of totality (consult H. Rickert, *Das Eine, die Einheit und die Eins* [Tübingen, 1924²], esp. pp. 72ff.), in Plato, is subordinated.

11. Consult p. 116. The problems that arise from the Platonic conception, which concern chiefly the relation of "intension" and "extension" or—especially with respect to the structural mutiplicity of meanings involved in the definition of the principles—of sense and signification (reference), brings us to further reflections, but the tradition does not abound in elements to guide our judgment. Plato cannot, surely, be placed within a theory of extensionality of modern coinage by which the notion of intensions would be eliminated.

12. Porphyry developed the interpretation of the unity as "Being" (εἶναι) in his commentary on the *Parmenides* of Plato, and hence refers, in this, directly to Plato himself and not just generically to Platonism.

13. On this last point K. Gaiser, *Name und Sache*, pp. 121ff., and D. Markis, "Platon und das Problem der Sprachphilosophie," *Zeitschrift für philos. Forschung* 2 (1978): 286ff., agree.

14. This holds for the material principle, but not for the series of numbers derived from it (in spite of its prototypical limitation to the decade that is done in many passages: *Test. Plat.* 24, 25A, 61; but consult Aristotle, *Met.* 1073a19f.).

15. On this Aristotle, *Met.* 991b13-21, 1092b13-25 is clear.

16. The operations of calculation or theorizing about calculation are not to be linked with this.

17. V. Hösle, "Platons Grundlegung der Euklidizität der Geometrie," *Philologus* 126 (1982): 184-97.

18. Consult pp. 121f.

19. On this point R. A. Eberle, *Nominalistic Systems* (Dordrecht, 1970), pp. 24ff. is instructive.

20. If the principles are presented each as a class constituted by only one member, then that can also be said by the terms of *extension* and *intension*.

21. *Theaetetus* 201D-202C, 205Cff.; consult Aristotle, *Met.* 1014b3ff.

22. *Republic* 534B-C; *Seventh Letter* 342A-344B.

23. Actually the difference is very small if the fact is taken into account that Aristotle, for example, for the "axiom of axioms" that is, for the *principium contradictionis* (principle of contradiction), admits an elenchic-dialectical "demonstration" in a kind of apagogic sense (*Metaphysics* Γ 4). The circular proof beginning from that which is derived from the principles, which is achieved primarily in the order of knowledge, constitutes equally a nonrigorous proof of this type and, hence, has an affinity to the Aristotelian procedure. Conforming to that, in the Anal. post. I 3 (see the preceding text) Aristotle rejects only the notion that circular reasoning possesses the attributes of a canonical and rigorous proof (72b25ff.).

24. Frag. 5 Schmidt (Proclus, In Eucl. Elem. comm. 72,23ff. Friedlein), consult frag. 7; on this, see J. Barnes, "Aristotle, Menaechmus, and Circular Proof," *Classical Quarterly* 70, ns. 26 (1976): 278-92.

25. H. Hasse-H. Scholz, *Die Grundlagenkrise der griechischen Mathematik* (Char-lottenburg, 1928), pp. 17, 24f.; H. Stachowiak, *Rationalismus im Ursprung. Die Genesis des axiomatischen Denkens* (Vienna-New York, 1971), pp. 117f.

26. Consult pp. 87f. On the whole thematic treated comprehensively, see *PD*, passim, esp. pp. 432ff.

27. Plato, *Meno* 76A "a figure is the limit of a body in three dimensions": σχῆμα πέρας στερεοῦ; see the critical analysis which is made by Aristotle in the *Topics* 141b19ff. (διὰ τῶν ὑστέρων τὰ πρότερα δηλοῦσιν with the same example), 142a17ff.

28. Plato believed that with this he also had solved the hermeneutic problems associated with intersubjective communication, although the admission of the exist-ence of different degrees of evidence reduced anew this criteriological base (*Seventh Letter*, excursus; the essential calling in question of the unanimity of such evidence is not found, however in Plato; only the skepticism of the Hellenistic Age has reflected on this point, although putting aside, as complementary, the hermeneutic problems of communication).

29. Moreover, the *logos* in the signification of "relation" of being already includes, in any case, a numerical component (consult H. G. Gadamer, "Platons ungeschriebene Dialektik," in *Idee und Zahl*. [Abh. Heidelb. Akad. d. Wissenschaf-ten], 1968/2, pp. 13ff.). But the series of numbers is constituted only from the principles and therefore cannot be applied to the principles themselves.

30. *Republic* 436D; *Sophist* 230B, 249B, 259D.

31. The *Parmenides* presupposes the principle of the excluded middle (prin-cipium exclusi tertii). Consult Aristotle *Met.*, 1011b24f.

32. See the formulation in *Stoicorum veterum fragmenta* II 65.

33. Consult the formulation in *Test. Plat.* 32, par. 275 Appendix, 3.12 (τὸ γὰρ ἕν πρώτως αὐτὸ ἑαυτῷ ἴσον).

34. Consult in this regard Theophrastus, *Met.* 4b12f., 9a21f. (8a19f.; on the Platonic-Academic background of these passages, see H. Krämer, "Zum Standort der Metaphysik Theophrasts," in *Zetesis for E. De Strijcker* [Antwerpen-Utrecht, 1973], pp. 211f.).

35. Opposition, difference, and identity presuppose multiplicity in the sense of the principle opposed to unity. Unity and duality considered together do not constitute, however, a derived multiplicity, and, in this sense consequently, in their reciprocal relation they cannot be considered *either* as different *or* as opposed *or* as identical. But insofar as there is a connection and, at the same time, a difference between them, these exist by virtue of unity and duality themselves, i.e., by way of self-application.

36. Consult the documentation in *Studies in Plato's Metaphysics*, ed. R. E. Allen, (New York-London, 1965), or in G. Vlastos, *Platonic Studies*, pp. 335-65; and in addition A. Graeser, *Platons Ideenlehre*, pp. 33ff. For the relation existing between self-predication and the argument of infinite regress seen from the theoretical viewpoint, consult in addition J. Passmore, "The Infinite Regress," in *Philosophical Reasoning* (London, 1970²), pp. 19-37.

37. Aristotle, *Met.* 990b17ff., 1079a14ff., 1087b23ff.; Alexander of Aphrodisias, *In Met.* 81.7f. Hayduck, in the new critical edition of D. Harlfinger, p. 24f. (in W. Leszl,

Il 'De Ideis' di Aristotele e la teoria platonica delle idee [Florence, 1975] = *De ideis*, frag. 3 = Ross frag. 187 Rose).

38. Aristotle, *Nic. Eth.* 1096a17ff. Appendix, 3.22 (on this, see H. Flashar, "Die Kritik der platonischen Ideenlehre in der Ethik des Aristoteles," *Synusia für W. Schadewaldt*, 1965, pp. 228, 240f., note 25); consult the parallel in *Eth. Eud.* 1218a1ff. Appendix, 3.23.

39. Placing on the same level the Ideas and singular things or principles and the things that are derived from the principles with an infinite regress involved, to use modern terminology, is a category-error or contrary to the "theory of types."

40. The expression is not used here in a technical sense; that is to say, it is not used in the sense of a *modus ponens* (affirming the antecedent).

41. Therefore, a general concept of number (a number-genus) does not exist, for example, for the number series.

42. In this regard, see the pertinent clarifications of M. Frede, "Prädikation und Existenzaussage, Platons Gebrauch von 'ist' und 'ist nicht' im *Sophistes*," *Hypomnemata* 18 (1967), according to whom Plato does not have a theory of different meanings of *is* and *is not*, but only uses them in different ways; consult also U. Hölscher, "Der Sinn von Sein in der Älteren griechischen Philosophie," *Sitzungsberichte d. Heidelb. Akad. d. Wissenschaften* 1976/3, pp. 32ff.

43. Aristotle, *Anal. post.* A 2; 10.

44. Speusippus, frags. 46-47 Lang = frags. 36-37 Isnardi Parente (with the related comment at pp. 250ff.) = frags. 72 and 74 Tarán (with comment at pp. 422ff.).

45. A. Szabó, "Was heisst der mathematische Terminus ἀξίωμα?," *Maia*, n.s. 12 (1960): 89ff.; idem., "Axiom," in *Historisches Wörterbuch der Philosophie*, ed. J. Ritter, Vol. 1 (Basel-Stuttgart, 1971), coll. 737-741.

46. K. von Fritz, "Die APXAI in der griechischen Mathematik," *Archiv für Begriffsgeschichte* 1 (1955): 13-103, reprinted in K. von Fritz, *Grundprobleme der Geschichte der antiken Wissenschaft* (Berlin-New York, 1971), pp. 335-429.

47. K. von Fritz, ibid., pp. 420, 423, 427.

48. K. von Fritz, "Platon, Theaetet und die antike Mathematik," *Philologus* 87 (1932), reprinted with an addition (Darmstadt, 1969), pp. 98ff.; H. Stachowiak, *Rationalismus im Ursprung*, pp. 62, 87, 93, 101ff.

49. Consult pp. 101ff. The "hypotheses" of which the *Republic* VI-VII speaks are understood primarily as enunciations of existence, to which however are connected in the downward path (511Bf.) definitions and proofs (consult the "secure foundation" of 533D1). A systematic construction of mathematics was certainly pursued in the Academy (consult *Republic* 531D, 537C, where κοινωνία, συγγένεια, and οἰκειότης of the mathematical disciplines are spoken about), but without achieving their complete axiomatization and deduction.

50. Consult pp. 78ff.

51. Aristotle, *Met.* Γ 1005b33f.; on the position of these propositions in the ambit of first philosophy, see *Met.* B 2.996b26ff., Γ 3-8, K 5-6.

52. Consult W. Schwabe, "'Mischung und 'Element'," pp. 173ff., 219ff., 253 (among the other with reference to *Phaedo* 101E, *Laws* 626D, 790C, to the hypothetical procedure of the dialogues and to the indirect tradition).

53. For *Phaedo* 101E consult also A. Lumpe, *Der Terminus 'Prinzip'*, p. 108.

54. *Test. Plat.* 54A = Appendix, 3.4 = Aristotle, *Phys.* 209b14f. (τὰ λεγόμενα ἄγραφα δόγματα).

55. Plato, *Sophist* 263Dff.; Ps. Plat. *Def.* 414C.

56. *Seventh Letter* 344E2 (consult Appendix, 1.2). In another passage (341B4, [consult Appendix, 1.2], perhaps as a citation?) Plato even applies the expression τέχνη ("a system of rules or propositions," "complex of doctrines").

57. On the question of a philosophical axiomatic in our time, consult E. Rogge, *Axiomatik alles möglichen Philosophierens* (Meisenheim, 1950); F. Austeda, *Axiomatische Philosophie. Ein Beitrag zur Selbstkritik der Philosophie* (Berlin, 1962).

58. E = *essence* (οὐσία) resp. existence, U = *unitas*, Û = *non-unitas*, ∈ = copula, means here in particular a relation of participation in the opposites in different respects.

59. P. Duponchel, *Hypothèses pour l'interprétation de l'axiomatique thomiste* (Paris, 1953), pp. 132ff., 153ff.; L. Oeing-Hanhoff, "Axiom," *Historisches Wörterbuch der Philosophie*, ed. J. Ritter, Vol. 1, col. 743.

60. E = *essence* (οὐσία), B = *bonitas (arete)*, V = *veritas*; u = *unum* (Monad, Henad), understood in the sense of the *definitum* (that which is defined) (ὡρισμένον, πεπερασμένον) and *commensuratum* (that which is measured) (μεμετρημένον, μέτριον).

61. u = *unum* in the sense explained in the preceding note, û = *non-unum*, > = greater than, < less = than.

62. The axioms of equality have, both in Euclid (Book I) and Aristotle (for example, *Met.* K 4, *Top.* H 1, *Anal. post.* I 10), a fundamental importance.

63. R = *relation* between the members of a hierarchical succession (*a, b*, etc.).

64. On the medieval axiom *omne ens est aut simplex aut compositum* (all that which is is either simple or composite), consult L. Oeing-Hanhoff, "Axiom," (consult note 59).

65. R = *relation* between the members of a hierarchical series; *a'* = *universal* that which is beyond the members of a hierarchical series (as for example, the 'third man' beyond individual men and the Idea of man).

66. On the question of an axiomatization of the syllogistic, see G. Patzig, *Die Syllogistik des Aristoteles* (Göttingen, 1968³), pp. 136ff., 197.

67. H. Stachowiak, *Rationalismus im Ursprung* (consult note 25), esp. pp. 132-35.

68. For more details in this regard consult pp. 84ff. and 88.

Chapter 10

1. P. Natorp, *Platons Ideenlehre* (Darmstadt, 1961³, Leipzig, 1903¹), pp. 188-216.

2. Ibid., pp. 433-56. The unity itself, in fact, is here recognized as a fundamental determination of thought (for example, p. 449), but, then, it is smoothened with respect to the numerous other determinations of thought (for example, p. 245).

3. According to Natorp, Aristotle always misunderstood Plato—both his writings and his oral teachings—in an objective-dogmatic sense (ibid., Chapter 11).

4. The "Metakritischer Anhang" (Metacritical Appendix) added to the second edition of 1920 shows Natorp on the way to Neoplatonic mysticism; but also this correction of the picture of Plato is inadequate for a comparison with a historically grounded transcendental philosophy.

5. Aristotle, *Met.* 1016b19ff. (in the Platonic-Academic context of the Chapter on ἕν; on the Platonic character of what is said here, consult J. Stenzel, *Zahl und Gestalt*, pp. 158f.).

6. *Test. Plat.* 34 = Appendix, 3.26 = Aristotle, *Protrep.* B33 Düring. Consult also the reflection in *Philebus* 64Ef., (ἀλήθεια is placed in relation to μετριότης and συμμετρία).

7. Ibid., (B36 Düring). For the interpretation, see E. De Strycker, in *Aristotle and Plato in the Mid-Fourth Century. Acts of the First Symposium Aristotelicum*, ed. I. Düring and G. E. L. Owen (Göteborg, 1960), esp. pp. 98ff.

8. P. Natorp, *Philosophische Systematik* (Hamburg, 1958), pp. 313, 370ff.; H. Wagner, *Philosophie und Reflexion* (Munich-Basel, 1980³), pp. 32ff., 100, 121ff., 206ff.; H. Holz, *System der Transzendentalphilosophie im Grundriss* I (Freiburg-Munich, 1977), pp. 28f., 46f., 99ff., 341, 345, 348ff.

9. On the function of criticism of language exercised by the principles, see pp.133 and 135.

10. *Theaetetus* 184D (μία τις ἰδέα); *Republic* 508Ef. (ἐπιστήμη and γνῶσις are said to be "good-formed", that is, akin to the Good); *Sophist* 228C; *Test. Plat.* 25A = Aristotle, *De anima* 404b22 (correlation of νοῦς and monad).

11. The same thing holds for certain points that emphasize the contribution of thought and its spontaneity that are found in the Aristotelian theory of abstraction and of the actualizing function of thought (on this consult H. Happ, *Hyle*, pp. 51-55), and that, actually, have transcendental character, but are far from the radical revolution based on the concept of subject achieved by modern criticism. (Accentuated more than necessary, instead, is the character of receptivity of the theory of consciousness of the ancient world in K. Oehler, *Die Lehre vom noetischen und dianoetischen Denken bei Platon und Aristoteles* [Munich, 1962; Hamburg, 1985²].

12. Kant, *Kritik der reinen Vernunft* B131.

13. For the distinction of the two aspects, see D. Henrich, "Identität und Objektivität. Eine Untersuchung über Kants transzendentale Deduktion," *Sitzungsberichte Heidelb. Akad. d. Wissenschaften*, 1976/1, pp. 55ff.

14. The transformation into the subjective attitude can be observed in another way in the forms of unity of reflective judgment in the third Critique of Kant, which revive certain teleological aspects of the structure of reality proper to Plato. The interpretation of the beautiful as a symbol and as a preparatory stage of the good and, on the other hand, the affinity of moral law and of the *principium contradictionis* (principle of contradiction) converge in the sense of a unity of reason, which is an analogous thematic with the polyvalence of the Platonic theory of the principles.

15. Consult pp. 117f.

16. *Republic* 533C8f. (ἵνα βεβαιώσηται must be referred either to the hypotheses or to dialectic itself, and not to the ἀρχή, which, on the contrary, produces the security of the foundation).

17. In this, in either case, the starting points for a coherence theory of truth are present; consult *Kritik der reinen Vernunft* A104-106; H. Wagner, *Philosophie und Reflexion*, pp. 72f., 217f., 255f. and pp. 165ff.

18. Consult note 17.

19. H. Wagner, *Philosophie und Reflexion*, p. 335; D. Henrich, *Identität und Objektivität*, p. 111; H. Holz, *System der Transzendentalphilosophie*, I p. 365, and frequently; M. Hossenfelder, *Kants Konstitutionstheorie und die transzendentale Deduktion* (Berlin-New York, 1978), esp. pp. 117ff., 157. Similarly, also the analytic transcendental philosophy in Strawson, Bennett, and others.

20. Consult p. 257, note 51.

21. *Kritik der reinen Vernunft* A125-130.

22. The apparent chronological succession goes back instead to a hierarchical succession of being; that is, to the ontological dependence (πρότερον-ὕστερον φύσει).

23. For example, in the *Prolegomena*, or in the *Grundlegung zur Metaphysik der Sitten*.

24. W. Röd, "Die Idee der transzendentalphilosophischen Grundlegung in der Metaphysik des 17. und 18. Jahrhunderts," *Philosophisches Jahrbuch* 79 (1972): 56ff.

25. J. P. Strawson, *Individuals* [London, 1959] (differently in *The Bounds of Sense* [London, 1966]). Here also the theory of subjectivity passes into a second line behind to the transcendental conditions of the identification (which, historically considered, can be placed in relation to the Platonic category of unity).

26. Consult pp. 82f.

27. Ancient Idealism as well as the new is characterized by the *deduction* of the complex of the categories *from a unitary principle* and in this is different from the tradition of Aristotelianism, which places the categories on a par with each other, without going back to a common foundation. Both types of categorial constitution have always had supporters, and they still have to this day.

28. M. Heidegger, *Schellings Abhandlung über das Wesen der menschlichen Freiheit* (1809) ed. H. Feick (Tübingen, 1971), pp. 27-74 (p. 33: "He who speaks then of a system of Plato or a system of Aristotle, falsifies history and is barred from the way that leads to the inward movement of this philosophizing and the comprehension of its claim to truth").

29. Ibid., p. 39. Heidegger not only did not take into account Hellenistic philosophy and Neoplatonism, but in what concerns Plato himself he based himself exclusively on the picture of Plato painted by Schleiermacher resting on the dialogues, without taking into consideration the indirect tradition. On the contrary T. W. Adorno, in the metaphysics of number of the indirect tradition, correctly recognized the tendency to achieve the "completion" and the "continuity" of the system and the "availability" of the world for man ("Zur Metakritik der Erkenntnistheorie," *Gesammelte Schriften* 5 [Frankfurt, 1970], pp. 17-19).

30. The distinction of Kant between dogmatic and systematic (*Kritik der reinen Vernunft* B 673, 765f.) corresponds perfectly also to the philosophy of Plato; for the difference between the degrees of validity and the degrees of coherence in Plato consult pp. 91f.

31. Consult pp. 82f., 84; also pp. 87ff.

32. That Plato took into account the fundamental differences between regression and progression can be drawn from *Test. Plat.* 10 = Appendix, 3.6 (consult p. 247, note 21).

33. For example, *Monadology*, par. 32, consult par. 37f.; *Theodicy*, par. 44; *Principles of Nature and of Grace*, par. 7 (referring to being and to being-in-a-determined-way: existence and essence).

34. *Kritik der reinen Vernunft* B145/46: "Of the peculiarity of our intellect to achieve the unity of apperception a priori only by the categories and only by this given type and this given number of themselves, one cannot furnish a further grounding, as well as we cannot furnish it for the fact that we have these functions for judgments and no others, or for the fact that space and time are the unique forms of our possible intuition."

35. Consult on this M. Hossenfelder, *Kants Konstitutionstheorie*, pp. 132ff.

36. D. Henrich, *Identität und Objektivität*, pp. 94ff.; consult also P. Rohs, "Transzendentale Apperzeption und ursprüngliche Zeitlichkeit," *Zeitschrift f. philos. Forschung* 31 (1977): 191ff.; by the same author, *Die Vernunft der Erfahrung* (Königstein/Taunus, 1979); also *Die Zeit des Handelns* (Königstein/Taunus, 1980), pp. 37ff.; R. Aschenberg, "Über transzendentale Argumente. Orientierung in einer Diskussion zu Kant und Strawson," *Philosophisches Jahrbuch* 85 (1978): esp. 357, criticizes Henrich.

37. Consult R. Aschenberg, *Sprachanalyse und Transzendentalphilosophie* (Stuttgart, 1982), pp. 392ff.; see also p. 138.

38. Consult pp. 83, 144f.; see pp. 135f.

39. H. Holz, *System der Transzendentalphilosophie* I, p. 218, speaks of a "relation of mutual conditioning" (in diverse respects) between foundation and that which is founded. H. Wagner, *Philosophie und Reflexion*, p. 127 distinguishes, consequently, between foundation and condition.

40. Plotinus, *Enneads* VI 8 (for the interpretation, see what we said in *UGM*, pp. 398ff.); further on one will speak of *aseity* (being of itself) and of *causa sui* (the self-caused).

41. On this, see especially R. Bubner, "Zur Struktur eines transzendentalen Arguments," *Kant-Studien* 65 = *Sonderheft Akten des 4. Internationalen Kant-Kongresses* (Mainz, 1974), Teil I, pp. 15-27.

42. Consult pp. 139-40f.

43. The characterization of pure unity as the Good itself corresponds to the axiological perspective. That Plato, with a certain incoherence, has placed the concept of being under the concept of unity, and accentuated the difference in a marked fashion, is a fact that must be explained chiefly on the basis of historical influences; consult pp. 79, 100f.; see p. 248, note 36.

44. Moreover, each of the two principles can be known and received only in relation to that which is principled and, hence, always, at the same time, in relation also to the transcendental condition of the corresponding opposite principle. (This is one of the implicit results of the dialogue *Parmenides*.)

45. Aristotle, *Met.* Γ 3ff. To this is linked, for example, R. Aschenberg, *Sprachana-lyse und Transzendentalphilosophie*, pp. 383ff.;, see, besides, H. Holz, *System der Transzendentalphilosophie*, I, p. 263.

46. Aristotle, *Anal. post.* I 3. On this see pp. 88, 137f.

Chapter 11

1. On this, see now especially W. Beierwaltes, *Platonismus und Idealismus* (Frankfurt, 1972), pp. 144ff., 154ff. (Plotinus and Proclus compared to Hegel); also *Identität und Differenz* (Frankfurt, 1980) (from Plato up to Hegel and Adorno).

2. Let us remember the works of Dodds, Armstrong, Merlan, De Vogel, Theiler, Krämer (*UGM*) and Szlezák, mentioned on p. 126.

3. J. N. Findlay, *Plato*; see also my review of this book in *Philosophische Rundschau* 27 (1980): 25-29. Consult also J. N. Findlay, *Ascent to the Absolute. Metaphysical Papers and Lectures* (London-New York, 1970), pp. 248ff. Little profit was involved in the inclusion of the indirect tradition in W. Künne, "Dialektik und Ideenlehre in Platos 'Parmenides'. Untersuchungen zu Hegels Plato-Deutung." Dissertation (Heidelberg, 1975) (further developed in W. Künne, "Hegel als Leser Platos. Ein Beitrag zur Interpretation des Platonischen 'Parmenides'," *Hegel-Studien* 14 [1979]: 109ff.).

4. G. W. F. Hegel, *Gesammelte Werke* (Kritische Hegel-Ausgabe), Band 7, 1971: *Jenaer Systementwürfe II*, ed. R.-P. Horstmann and J. P. Trede. See also G. W. F. Hegel, *Jenenser Logik, Metaphysik und Naturphilosophie*, ed. G. Lasson (Philos. Bibliothek, 58), reprinted 1967. For the relation with Plato, see K. Rosenkranz, "Hegel's ursprüngliches System 1798-1806," *Literarhistorisches Taschenbuch*, ed. R. E. Prutz, 2. Jahrgang (1844): 155-242, esp. pp. 167ff.; R. Wiehl, "Platos Ontologie in Hegels Logik des Seins," *Hegel-Studien* 3 (1965): 157-80. The meaning of the concept of logic as first philosophy, in Hegel, is linked, probably, to the tripartition of philosophy into logic, physics, and ethics in the Academy of Plato (Xenocrates, frag. 1 Heinze).

5. G. W. F. Hegel, *Vorlesungen über die Geschichte der Philosophie*, Vol. 2 = *Sämtliche Werke, Jubiläumsausgabe*, ed. H. Glockner, Vol. 18, pp. 240ff.; *Phänomenologie des Geistes*, ed. Hoffmeister (Meiner-Verlag), p. 57; *Wissenschaft der Logik*, ed. G. Lasson (Meiner-Verlag), I, p. 87. The speculative interpretation of the *Parmenides* already started in the article concerned with skepticism of 1802 (G. W. F. Hegel, *Suhrkamp-Werkausgabe*, Vol. 2: *Jenaer Schriften 1801-1807*, esp. pp. 228f. in what concerns the *Parmenides*). On Hegel's discussion of Plato, see in addition: D. Markis, "Epekeina Ousias. Platon und die Platoninterpretation Hegels," Dissertation (Frankfurt, 1967); G. Duso, *Hegel interprete di Platone* (Padua, 1969), pp. 17ff., 61ff.; J. Delhomme, "Hegel et Platon," in *Hegel et la pensée grecque*, published under the editorship of J. d'Hondt (Paris, 1974), pp. 85ff.; J.-L. Vieillard-Baron, *Platon et l'Idéalisme allemand (1770-1830)* (Paris, 1979), pp. 129ff., 225ff., 373ff.; K. Düsing, "Ontologie und Dialektik bei Plato und Hegel," *Hegel-Studien* 15 (1980): 95-150. In what concerns in particular Plato in

the *History of Philosophy* of Hegel, see M. Isnardi Parente, "Noterelle marginali alle hegeliane lezioni sulla storia della filosofia. La dottrina platonica delle Idee," *La cultura* 9 (1971): 145ff.

6. *Vorlesungen über die Geschichte der Philosophie*, Vol. 1 = *Jubiläumsausgabe*, Vol. 17, pp. 260-72, 276f.; *Wissenschaft der Logik*. I, pp. 208-10 Lasson (referring to *Test. Plat.* 22A and 32 = Appendix, 3.9 and 12); on this, see also the dissertation of Künne, pp. 81f. Consult the corresponding reception by Schelling (following Brandis) in F. W. J. Schelling, *Philosophie der Mythologie* (Darmstadt, 1976), Vol. I 324, 392, 396, 423f., 433f., 448, Vol. II 59. Idem., *Philosophie der Offenbarung* (Darmstadt, 1974), Vol. I 61 note.

7. *Vorlesungen über die Geschichte der Philosophie*, Vol. 1 = *Jubiläumsausgabe*, Vol. 18, pp. 179f., 185, 230, 249; consult also what we said on p. 230-31, note 2. Some have occasionally called attention to the fact a twofold tradition exits, with regard to Hegel, as with Plato. But, the weight of the two traditions in a certain sense is reversed, since the works that have been written by Hegel himself (the *Phenomenology of the Spirit* and the *Logic*, unlike the manuscripts concerned with various individual branches of philosophy that go back to his pupils), contain the foundations of his philosophy.

8. On the whole problem, see H. G. Gadamer, *Hegel und die antike Dialektik* (1961), now in Gadamer, *Hegels Dialektik* (Tübingen, 1971), pp. 7ff.; D. Markis, *Epekeina Ousias*, pp. 55ff., 154ff.; G. Duso, in *Il Pensiero* 2 (1967): 206ff.; concerning the last reference, see what K. Düsing, *Ontologie und Dialektik*, pp. 120ff., 138ff., 148f., has said. The speculative Hegelian interpreation of Plato is found again in some Neo-Hegelians of the twentieth century like J. Wahl or B. Liebrucks; in a critical reelaboration can it be found also in H. G. Gadamer, R. Wiehl, and in G. Duso.

9. For example, *Wissenschaft der Logik*. I, p. 87, 163f., consult also p. 92. On this, see G. Maluschke, "Kritik und absolute Methode in Hegels Dialektik," *Hegel-Studien* Beiheft 13 (1974): 52ff. In the vision of the problem of the application of dialectic, R. Bubner, "Dialog und Dialektik oder Plato und Hegel," in *Zur Sache der Dialektik* (Stuttgart, 1980), pp. 124ff., defends the Platonic dialogue against the Hegelian concept of method, certainly without—in this following Schleiermacher—going back from the literary dialogue to the process of the true dialogue.

10. *Logik*, I, pp. 46f.

11. Chiefly the conception of the educative process sketched in the *Republic* and the description of the degrees of knowledge of the imperfect consciousness found in the *Theaetetus*, which can be interpreted as a prelude to the *Phenomenology* of Hegel are added to the unwritten doctrines. Also for the theoretical relation between system and history there are some parallels. The philosophy of history, which K. Gaiser has drawn from the *Statesman* and from Book Eight of the *Republic* for Plato (*Platon und die Geschichte* [Stuttgart, 1961]; idem., *PUL* [second part "Geschichte und Ontologie"]; again, *Die Rede der Musen* [p. 254, note 24]) allows us to see that the foundation of the process of history was based on the theory of principles, insofar as such a process is maintained in motion by a cyclical polarization due to the structure of the principles (to the growing prevalence of the principle opposed to unity corresponds a growing reflection on the sphere of the principles itself). Plato, like Hegel, sees himself as an exponent of a chronologically concluding period, with the difference that for Hegel the general movement is linear, while, in Plato, it proceeds

only cyclically, and, moreover, with the further difference that, in Plato, the historical evolution is not speculatively and dialectically structured.

12. *Jubiläumsausgabe*, Vol. 18, pp. 243, 245 (on the *Parmenides*); Vol. 17, pp. 260, 269f. (on *Test. Plat.* 32 = Appendix, 3.12). Consult *Logik*, II, pp. 488f. That the "first philosophies are the most impoverished and abstract," "keeping only to the generals," Hegel underlined, on principle, in the introduction to the *History of Philosophy* (*Jubiläumsausgabe*, Vol. 17, pp. 69ff.).

13. On the theme of the "reversed world" or the "inverted world" (*verkehrte Welt*) in Hegel, see the summary pages of H. G. Gadamer, *Hegels Dialektik*, pp. 31ff.

14. The system of the follower of Plato, Speusippus, which has been occasionally compared to that of Hegel (for example, by R. Berthelot, *Évolutionisme et Platonisme* [Paris 1908], pp. 271ff.), since, in Speusippus, the "perfection" takes place only with the realization of the universal process in the levels of reality deduced from the principles (frag. 34 Lang; frags 53-58 and frag. 72 Isnardi Parente = frags. 42-44 Tarán), belongs actually to Plato, because even in Speusippus the result of the process is not a foundation and principle, and the principles, notwithstanding their abstraction, support the highest level of being and the rank of that which is in itself primary.

15. J. N. Findlay, in his volume on Plato, frequently cited, tries to bring historical Platonism close to Hegelianism, by taking into pure unity not only the sensible contingents but also the Ideas and the principle opposed to unity, considering them as abstractions. This reconstruction of Plato, nevertheless, overleaps the Aristotelianizing of Hegel, whose absolute Idea has no parallel in Plato (while it has some in the immanent form and in the composite and, moreover, in the thinking of thinking of the unmoved Mover of Aristotle). The actualistic Idealism of Croce and Gentile, which are linked to Hegel, have taken up the reproach of abstraction, lodged by Hegel against metaphysics, and tried to direct it against Hegel himself. See, for example, G. Gentile, *L'atto del pensare come atto puro* (Florence, 1937²); also, *La riforma della dialettica hegeliana* (Florence, 1954³). (*Opere complete*, Vol. 27), pp. 227ff.; B. Croce, *Logica come scienza del concetto puro* (Bari, 1909).

16. Consult K. Düsing, "Das Problem der Subjektivität in Hegels Logik," *Hegel-Studien* Beiheft 15 (1976): 336ff.

17. On this, see especially K. Hartmann, "On Taking the Transcendental Turn," *Review of Metaphysics* 20 (1966/67): 223ff.; also "'The 'Analogies' and after," in *Proc. of the Third Intern. Kant Congress, Rochester 1970*, pp. 47ff.; idem., "Die ontologische Option," in *Die ontologische Option*, ed. K. Hartmann (Berlin, 1976), pp. 1ff. In addition, H. Holz, *System der Transzendentalphilosophie im Grundriss*, II, pp. 72ff.; R. Aschenberg, *Sprachanalyse und Transzendentalphilosophie*, pp. 403ff.

18. The structuring of the pure concept and of the absolute Idea in the *Logik* follows the progressive degrees of relation beginning with the logic of being through the logic of essence to the logic of the concept; in the categorial development the concept achieves the highest degree of relation with itself.

19. *Logik.* I, p. 59.

20. Ibid., I, p. 57f.

21. Consult p. 135.

22. For example, in the article on natural law of 1803 (*Suhrkamp-Werkausgabe*, Vol. 2, pp. 456f.), *Jenenser Logik*. Meiner-Ausgabe (Philos. Biblioth., 58), pp. 1ff., 33f., 132ff.; on this, see R. Wiehl, *Platos Ontologie*, pp. 172ff. See *Phänomenologie*, ed. Hoffmeister, p. 126, and still *Logik*. II, p. 495 (the unity of the one and the many).

23. *Logik*. I, p. 59;, see the definition of the ground as unity of identity and diversity in the *Enzyklopädie*, par. 121.

24. *Logik*, I, p. 209 (on the basis of the pseudonymous Life of Pythagoras in Photius, *Bibl. cod. 249*, with *Test. Plat.* 22A in context); *Vorlesungen über die Geschichte der Philosophie*. 1, *Jubiläumsausgabe*, Vol. 17, p. 271 (referring to *Test. Plat.* 32 = Appendix, 3.12, with the judgment that is read on p. 261: "Unity is identity, universality duality is difference, the particular. These determinations still hold today in philosophy"; and further, on pp. 269f., it is affirmed that "in their relations the absolute essence, the richness and the organization of the natural world as well as the spiritual is covered and what is God in the speculative sense, that is, the thing most high is expressed in these ordinary words, the most profound thing in these well-known words the most rich thing in the poverty of these abstractions").

25. Findlay, in his *Plato*, has curtailed the basic dual structure of Plato to bring Plato closer to Hegel; but note that Hegel himself is based on a structural analogy to Plato (identity and nonidentity). Against such attempts at a neutralization, in the monistic sense of Plato's dualistic principles, with pertinent arguments, see F. Kümmel, *Platon und Hegel zur ontologischen Begründung des Zirkels in der Erkenntnis* (Tübingen, 1968), pp. 121ff. (The admission of a super-unity is disproved by the fact that later monism, on the contrary, had to deduce the duality from unity.)

26. Only between the two aspects of the opposite principle, the great and the small, does Plato acknowledge a sort of "dialectical" passage (in the Hegelian sense), in fact an unforeseen leap, which, however, lacks a speculative synthesis and which hence remains confined within the limits of thesis-antithesis (and therefore within the limits of "exterior reflection"). See Plato's *Eighth Letter* 354D/E; consult *Republic* 562Bff., 563Ef.; Aristotle, *Eth. Eud.* 1234a34ff.; on this, see my *APA*, p. 188.

27. For the distinction of the terms concerning the three degrees of the *Logik*, see *Enzyklopädie*, par. 240.

28. *Logik*, II, p. 27 (Lasson). Both Hegel and Plato conceive of identity primarily as self-identity (see *Sophist* 254D, 256B1; Hegel, *Logik*, II, pp. 26ff.).

29. Consult pp. 81f. 84, 87ff.

30. See also, for example, H. Holz, *System der Transzendentalphilosophie*, I, pp. 307ff., 315f., 322ff. The same holds for the relation of multiplicity and difference in a corresponding fashion.

31. H. Rickert, *Das Eine, die Einheit und die Eins*; W. Flach, *Negation und Andersheit* (Munich, 1959). Consult B. Croce, *Logica* (Bari, 1909). The position of Hegel is defended and accepted by R. Kroner and K. Hartmann.

32. On the meaning of the modern notion of "to determine" as "to isolate" from infinity E. Braun, "Die transzendentale Selbstreflexion des Wissens. Gegenstand und Methode der Wissenschaftslehre J. G. Fichtes," Dissertation (Tübingen, 1972), pp. 275ff., is illuminating.

33. For example, *Logik* II, pp. 58f. (contradiction is "that which is more profound and more essential").

34. Following this contemporary tendency, H. G. Gadamer tries to give to the opposite principle of the indefinite dyad, within the ambit of the Platonic doctrine of the principles, a privileged position ("Platons ungeschriebene Dialektik," in *Idee und Zahl* (Abh. Heidelb. Akad., 1968/2), esp. pp. 28ff., reprinted also in *Kleine Schriften*, III, pp. 47ff.; idem., *Die Idee des Guten zwischen Plato und Aristoteles.* (Sitzungsberichte Heidelb. Akad., 1978/3), p. 57; [*The Idea of the Good in Platonic and Aristotelian Philosophy*, trans. P. Christopher Smith [New Haven: Yale University Press, 1986]). An instructive comparison of Adorno with the tradition is found in W. Beierwaltes, *Identität und Differenz* (Frankfurt, 1980), pp. 269-314 ("Adornos Nicht-Identisches"). On the irruption of the difference (which is "life") in the structures of identity, oriented on a mathematical model, of classical philosophical construction in the sphere of post-Kantian philosophy, see the summary exposition of B. Taureck, *Das Schicksal der philosophischen Konstruktion* (Vienna-Munich, 1975), esp. pp. 264ff.

35. The de-Platonization of philosophy in the course of the modern age could be indeed described as a triumph of duality (that is, of the Platonic principle opposed to unity).

36. Consult pp. 106ff.

37. *Vorlesungen über die Geschichte der Philosophie. Jubiläumsausgabe* Vol. 18, p. 230; consult p. 179 (in the amplified version of the text published by [Leiden:Bolland, 1908]).

38. Consult pp. 144f.

39. The good, in Hegel, belongs to the logic of the concept. A deduction of the good corresponding to the Hegelian development of the concept is found, unlike in Plato, in outline in Speusippus, pupil and successor to Plato, who, however, has formulated and expressed some Platonic theoretical starting points only in a more marked manner. (See note 14).

40. *Test. Plat.* 10 = Appendix, 3.6 (consult p. 247, note 21).

41. Consult pp. 83, 84f., what we said about the iletic and categorial *plus* of the individual levels of being. On the hierarchical succession of the forms of movement what Gaiser, *PUL*, pp. 173ff., says is instructive.

42. On this *Logik* I, pp. 109, 397f.; II, pp. 4ff., 240ff., 260ff., 484ff. is fundamental.

43. From the unrelated (from that which has a relation only with itself) to the related and, within the whole of this, from the opposites to the correlatives. (A kind of relation to itself belongs to "being" in the Hegelian *Logik*, this also has been demonstrated by R. E. Schulz-Seitz, "'Sein' in Hegels Logik: 'Einfache Beziehung auf sich'," in *Wirklichkeit und Reflexion, Walter Schulz zum 60. Geburtstag* (Pfullingen, 1973), pp. 365ff. This corresponds, in Plato, to the self-relation of the unrelated and linked to this, to the concept of being, while unity itself remains absolutely unrelated in both authors; Hegel, *Logik* I, pp. 159, 210). Moreover, Hegel has interpreted the Platonic sequence on the basis of the *Test. Plat.* 32 = Appendix, 3.12 (Sextus Empiricus, *Adv. math.* X 263ff. *LCL* 3.339) and has judged it favorably. (In the *Vorlesungen über die Geschichte der Philosophie. 1. Jubiläumsausgabe*, Vol. 17, p. 265, it reads in fact: "This shows already a developed reflection"; consult also p. 268; p. 267 reads:

"universal logical determinations, which now and always are of the greatest importance." A detailed comparison with the *Logik* of Hegel would be very desirable). In another sense, the absolute Idea of Hegel could be compared with the soul in Plato, which, analogously, represents the most complex level of the intelligible world.

44. A sequence of degrees of common consciousness can be found in the different attempts at the definition of knowledge of the *Theaetetus*.

45. On the correspondence between *Logic, Phenomenology,* and the *Encyclopedia* (with the *Realphilosophie*), see now especially B. Puntel, "Darstellung, Methode und Struktur. Untersuchungen zur Einheit der systematischen Philosophie G.W.F. Hegels," *Hegel-Studien*, Beiheft 10 (1973). On the function of the *Phenomenology* in the complex of the system, see H. F. Fulda, *Das Problem einer Einleitung in Hegels Wissenschaft der Logik* (Frankfurt, 1965).

46. Consult p. 152.

47. *Phänomenologie*, Vorrede, p. 21 (ed. Hoffmeister); *Enzyclopädie*, par. 14 and par. 445 to the end.

48. Consult pp. 79 and p. 246, note 10, and 135. Refer, in addition, to the works of O. Töplitz and J. Stenzel that, in this regard, have opened a new approach.

49. Consult also *Enzyclopädie*, par. 259 (with detailed criticism). Aristotle is here a precursor of Hegel, with his criticism of the metaphysics of numbers belonging to Platonism. Consult in addition, for example, *Logik* I, pp. 207ff.; II, pp. 258f., 262; *Phänomenologie*, pp. 36ff., 212, 538f.

50. Consult note 4. This distinguishes both of the coherence theories of truth from formal or scientific types as, for example, the holism of Quine; see the exposition of N. Rescher, *The Coherence Theory of Truth* (Oxford, 1973), from the analytic viewpoint.

51. Consult pp. 150ff.

52. An allusion is made in the *Republic* 534B/C to this; on which, see *PD*, pp. 440f.

53. *Logik* I, pp. 114ff.; consult *Enzyclopädie*, par. 256; on this, see, for greater detail, the dissertation of Künne (cited in note 3), pp. 117ff. (Some modern critical philosophers of the theory of the dimensional series of Plato are accustomed to neglect intentionally the fact that Hegel has accepted this theory). If Hegel on the basis of the finitization of the modern infinitesimal and integral calculus attributes to mathematics a true infinite (that is, a qualitative infinite) and opposes to it the false infinite of metaphysics, then it must be said that the principle of multiplication and gradation of Plato belongs without doubt to this last form of the infinite. All mathematical entities already presuppose, in Plato, the constitutive action of unity itself and, therefore, are not, as in Hegel, infinite, but finite.

54. Hegel used these two concepts in different contexts with different meanings. He is not interested in a *synopsis* of a Platonic type.

55. *Logik* I, pp. 199ff.; II, pp. 35ff. Vice versa the particular doctrine of the categories appears in the logic of being (I, pp. 106ff.: being in itself and being for another).

56. For example, *Logik* I, pp. 341f., 384. The relation between quantity and quality emerges especially in the section at pp. 379ff. ("Knotenlinie von

Massverhältnissen") and at pp. 384ff. ("Das Masslose"). On the reference of Hegel to the Platonic concepts of measure and limit, see G. R. G. Mure, *A Study of Hegel's Logic* (Oxford, 1959), pp. 75f.; A. Doz, in *Hegel, La théorie de la mesure,* trans. and commentary A. Doz (Paris, 1970), pp. 113f.; see, in addition, the *Vorlesungen über die Geschichte der Philosophie. 2, Jubiläumsausgabe,* Vol. 18, pp. 239f.

57. *Logik* I, pp. 336ff.; *Enzyklopädie,* paragraphs 107-11.

58. From another point of view, note that 'measure' already is included by 'existence' (*Dasein*): "All that which exists has a measure" (*Logik* I, p. 343).

59. See the work of A. Doz, cited in note 56, pp. 15ff.

60. *Logik* I, p. 387 (together with the concept of order). For the numerical determination of measure and order in Plato, see *Philebus* 25Af., 25D; Aristotle, *Eth. Eud.* 1218a18ff. and p. 99.

Chapter 12

1. For example, in C. Ritter, *Platon,* Vol. II (Munich, 1923), pp. 287ff., where a comparison can be found between the theory of Ideas with modern theories, and, especially on pp. 312ff. with Husserl (but still without taking into consideration the *Ideen zu einer reinen Phänomenologie und phänomenologischen Philosophie* of 1913); P. Natorp, "Husserls 'Ideen zu einer reinen Phänomenologie,'" in *Logos* 7 (1917-18): 224ff. reprinted in *Husserl* ed. H. Noack (Wege der Forschung, 40) [Darmstadt, 1973], pp. 36ff., esp. pp. 43ff. To the Platonic Ideas Husserl himself made reference, for example, in *Erfahrung und Urteil,* ed. Meiner 1976[5], p. 411, although in a manner "free of all metaphysical interpretations."

2. For the Neo-Kantian criticism, see F. Kreis, *Phänomenologie und Kritizismus* (Tübingen, 1930); R. Zocher, *Husserls Phänomenologie und Schuppes Logik, Ein Beitrag zur Kritik des intuitionistischen Ontologismus in der Immanenzidee* (Munich, 1932); H. Wagner, "Kritische Betrachtungen zu Husserls Nachlass," *Philosophische Rundschau* 1 (1954): 1ff., 93ff. For the neo-Hegelian criticism, see K. Hartmann, "The 'Analogies' and After," *Proceedings Third Intern. Kant Congress. Rochester 1970,* esp. pp. 59f.; also by Hartmann, "Sartres Phänomenbegriff," (*Phänomenologische Forschungen,* Vol. 9, 1980), pp. 163ff. For the defense of the phenomenological position, see E. Fink, "Die phänomenologische Philosophie Edmund Husserls in der gegenwärtigen Kritik," *Kant-Studien* 38 (1933): 319-83 (authorized by Husserl himself).

3. Plato, *Parmenides* 132Bf.

4. Plato, *Seventh Letter* 342A-D = Appendix, 1.2 (ἐν ψυχαῖς ἐνόν). The context offers, then, further points of comparison with the concept of noetic evidence.

5. Plato, *Seventh Letter* 344D4f. = Appendix, 1.2 (τὰ περὶ φύσεως ἄκρα καὶ πρῶτα).

6. *Philosophie der Arithmetik,* p. 91.

7. Ibid., p. 175.

8. Ibid., pp. 130f. The affinity with the "implicit definition" in Hilbert is clear.

9. Ibid., p. 102; consult p. 91.

10. H. Rickert, *Das Eine, die Einheit und die Eins,* esp. pp. 72ff.

11. See, for example, *Logische Untersuchungen*, I, pp. 242ff.; II, 1, pp. 225, 252; II 2, pp. 139ff.; *Ideen*, III, pp. 97f.; "Formale und transzendentale Logik" (*Husserliana*, XVII, 1974), pp. 91ff.; *Erfahrung und Urteil*, (see note 1), p. 408.

12. *Logische Untersuchungen*, II 1, pp. 275ff.; "Ding und Raum. Vorlesungen von 1907" (*Husserliana*, XVI), pp. 33ff., 186ff.

13. That, for Husserl, it is not a question of a supersensible intuition, but of a concrete comprehension (*Erfüllung*), is demonstrated by E. Tugendhat in his analysis of the categorial intuition (*Der Wahrheitsbegriff bei Husserl und Heidegger* [Berlin, 1970^2], pp. 126ff.).

14. For example, in *Logische Untersuchungen*, II 2, pp. 139, 150f., 184.

15. *Ideen*, I (*Husserliana*, III, 1950), pp. 372ff.

16. *Ideen*, I, p. 371; *Erfahrung und Urteil*, p. 418; *Ding und Raum*, p. 265.

17. *Erfahrung und Urteil*, pp. 419, 432ff., 458ff.

18. In this regard the clarifications of W. Beierwaltes, *Identität und Differenz* (Frankfurt, 1980), pp. 138-41 are of fundamental importance.

19. Consult p. 135. For further detail, see P. Hadot, *Porphyre et Victorinus*, Vol. II (Paris, 1970), pp. 104ff.

20. M. Heidegger, *Was ist Metaphysik?* (Frankfurt, 1965^9); *Brief über den Humanismus* (Frankfurt, 1954^2), pp. 112ff.; on this, see E. Tugendhat, "Das Sein und das Nichts," in *Durchblicke, für M. Heidegger zum 80. Geburtstag* (Frankfurt, 1969), pp. 152ff. The inseparability of being and nothing has been taken from Heidegger by Sartre, but with a different emphasis.

21. W. Schulz, "Über den philosophiegeschichtlichen Ort Martin Heideggers," *Philosophische Rundschau* 1 (1953-4): 65ff., 211ff., reprinted in *Heidegger*, ed. O. Pöggeler (Köln-Berlin, 1970^2), pp. 95ff., esp. pp. 106f., 117ff.

22. Consult esp. M. Heidegger, *Der Satz vom Grund* (Frankfurt, 1978^5), esp. pp. 181ff., 204ff.; emphasized in a little different manner in (*Identität und Differenz* (1957), or in *Unterwegs zur Sprache* (Frankfurt, 1975^5), pp. 258ff. ("*Ereignis*" [event], is like "*Offenheit*" [opening] and "*Lichtung*" [clearing, or perhaps better effulgence], only a different word to indicate *Being* [*Sein*] itself, which is in strict relation with its dynamic and temporal sense). A summary exposition and further developments are found in W. Röd's, "Grund," in *Handbuch philosophischer Grundbegriffe*, Vol. 3, Studienausgabe (Munich, 1973): 654ff.

23. *Test. Plat.* 25A offers a detailed coordination (with a gradation of the cognitive powers).

24. On the limitations that, by reason of the circumstances we mentioned follow in regard to the criticism of Plato by Heidegger, see what we said in *APA*, pp. 478, 555, 570, note 45. On the second point, see W. Beierwaltes, *Identität und Differenz*, pp. 5, 134ff.

Chapter 13

1. On the ontological interpretation, based on the theory of the principles, of the *Symposium*, see what is said on pp. 104. (For example, Eros as the tendency toward self-actualization, in Plato, is undoubtedly to be interpreted in an ontological sense.)

2. Consult *Phaedrus* 275Ef., 278C. On these passages T. A. Szlezák is fundamental: "Dialogform und Esoterik. Zur Deutung des platonischen Dialogs 'Phaidros'," *Museum Helveticum* 35 (1978): esp. 21ff.; consult also pp. 8f.

3. On the *onus probandi* (burden of proof) that belongs to those who assume skeptical attitudes toward the indirect tradition, see what we said on pp. 50ff.; on the principle on the basis of which the intrinsic importance of the tradition (concerning the theory of the principles) supplies and counterbalances the inferior quality of the indirect tradition with respect to that which is direct, consult pp. 55f.

4. For example, H. Kuhn, "Platon und die Grenze philosophischer Mitteilung," in *Idee und Zahl*, 167, note 25; F. F. Repellini, "Gli Agrapha Dogmata di Platone: La loro recente recostruzione e i suoi presupposti storico-filosofici," *Acme* 26/1 (1973): 51ff., esp. pp. 81ff. (among others erroneously connecting the doctrine professed by Plato within the Academy, which is not at all irrational, with the irrationalism of Heidegger); consult also L. Sichirollo, in M. Untersteiner, *Problemi di filologia filosofica*, p. 32, who follows Repellini.

5. Consult *APA*, p. 570 (where a comparison with Heidegger may be found); *Akad.*, p. 218; and *UGM*, p. 210 (where a comparison with N. Hartmann to explain certain aspects of the unwritten doctrines can be found).

6. On the other hand, note that the sense of direction of the hierarchy of levels, in ancient Platonism and in Neoplatonism, goes from high to low, while in Hartmann, as well as in Boutroux, on the contrary, it goes from low to high. The reproach made to the interpretation of the School of Tübingen to follow Hartmann implies an allusion, at least within the sphere of the German language, to the fact that the philosophy of Hartmann was quickly antiquated and obsoletized after his death in 1950. The suspicion arises that the attempt to relate the picture of Plato reconstructed by the School of Tübingen to Hartmann—and not to Heidegger—is nothing other than one of the strategic moves of Scheiermacherianism, which tends to devalue the indirect tradition. The criticism by us in the final Chapter of APA against Aristotle beginning with the viewpoint of Plato, was intended also as a criticism of N. Hartmann from the viewpoint of Heidegger (which, evidently, does not exclude a defense of Plato against Heidegger). From this it should be clear how little already even then (1959), Hartmann did play a role as an interpretative model.

7. Beyond everything, modern philosophical criticism does not have any competence with regard to the existence and authenticity of the tradition itself. Therefore on the simple basis of a judgment of value, it cannot reject totally that Plato would have professed determinate philosophical doctrines.

8. See the warning in *GF*, pp. 149f., unfortunately it remains, evidently, without much influence.

9. For example, W. Wieland, in the introduction to *Antike*, in the collection *Geschichte der Philosophie in Text und Darstellung* (Stuttgart: Reclam Verlag, 1978), p. 27 (where he writes explicitly: "slightly relevant from the point of view of philosophy(!)"); consult idem, "Platon und der Nutzen der Idee. Zur Funktion der Idee des Guten," *Allgemeine Zeitschrift für Philosophie* 1 (1976) esp. pp. 31-3; see, in addition, what is written by G. Patzig, *Vernünftiges Denken*. Gedächtnisschrift für W. Kamlah, ed. J. Mittelstrass and M. Riedel (Berlin-New York, 1978), p. 450 note 5;

consult also J. Mittelstrass, "Platon," in *Klassiker der Philosophie. I*, ed. O. Höffe (Munich: Beck, 1981), p. 60. Patzig and Wieland know the unwritten doctrine of Plato perhaps only by having heard it spoken about and, precisely, as participants in a conference held at Heidelberg in 1967, papers from which have been published in *Idee und Zahl*. From that, in any case, Patzig is "very far" (loc. cit.), as he shows in his continuing to speak of the "lectures held in Plato's old age." He is far away from an at least superficial grasp of a knowledge of the self-testimonies of Plato and from the testimonies of other authors, who do not offer at all minimum information for such a dating. The same thing holds for the contemporary discussion regarding the philosophical content of the indirect tradition, which Patzig so far, evidently, has neglected to consult; on this, see pp. 185. The attempt of Wieland to reduce the problem of the indirect tradition of Plato to "philology" (loc. cit.), fails, moreover, by taking into account the numerous comments of a philosophical character on the indirect tradition, both in antiquity and in the modern period; on this, see pp. 185 and p. 282, note 14.

10. K. von Fritz, in his aversion fueled chiefly by political reasons, also appeals to the "philosophical sterility of the schematisms" of the indirect tradition (*Schriften zur griechischen Logik*, Vol. II: *Logik, Ontologie und Mathematik* [Stuttgart-Bad Cannstatt, 1978], p. 65, note 8), using a citation from Gadamer in a way that is evidently erroneous and deceptive and making it over into its exact contrary (see the original tenor of the words of Gadamer in *Sitzungsberichte Heidelberger Akademie der Wissenschaften, 1964/2*, p. 31). Von Fritz, evidently, does not grasp that by rejecting as sterile the development and fulfillment of the synoptic-generalizing dialectic that is presented in the indirect tradition, likewise he rejects as sterile Platonic dialectic in general, also in the way in which it is presented in the dialogues since Plato expressly states that "the synoptic is the dialectician and the nonsynoptic is not" (*Republic* 537C7). Von Fritz, as well, avoids consideration about the way he ought to judge the "schematisms" also found in Aristotelian, Stoic, Neoplatonic, Kantian, Hegelian, or analytic philosophies, if they were subjected to likewise superficial criteria of judgment. (On the positive judgment of Hegel about the Platonic concepts, consult pp. 157, p. 275, note 24, p. 276-77, note 43.)

11. *Allgemeine Zeitschrift für Philosophie* 1 (1976): 19-33, and esp. pp. 31ff.; in the volume cited earlier of the Reclam edition (note 9), pp. 182ff.

12. This rule of restrictive interpretation ("A sensible thinker can have thought only as we think") can be checked in Wieland also elsewhere (it is a kind of "uncontrolled mixture of areas of interest").

13. The opinion that Plato would separate dialectic (the theory of Ideas) from mathematics in the *Republic*, but not, instead, in the unwritten doctrines, is not correct. As the most recent discussion on this issue has demonstrated, the intermediate position of the mathematical objects between the Ideas and sensible things in the *Republic* is at least ambiguous, while in the Aristotelian reports they are expressly specified as "intermediate" (μεταξύ!). Only a passage of the simile of the cave (*Republic* 516A) hints at an agreement with the "intermediate" position of which Aristotle speaks. (Consult the already cited article of Brentlinger, in *Phronesis* 1962).

14. In what concerns Hegel consult, pp. 156f., 160f., 166f. A. N. Whitehead, "Mathematics and the Good," in *The Philosophy of Alfred North Whitehead* ed., P. A.

Schilpp (Lasalle, Ill., 1951²), pp. 666-81; T. W. Adorno, "Zur Metakritik der Erkenntnistheorie" (1934-37), *Gesammelte Schriften*, Vol. 5 (Frankfurt, 1970¹), pp. 17-19; K. R. Popper, *Conjectures and Refutations* (London, 1969³), pp. 91f., note 55; C. F. von Weizsäcker, *Die Einheit der Natur* (Munich, 1971), pp. 474-91; idem., *Der Garten des Menschlichen. Beiträge zur geschichtlichen Anthropologie* (Munich-Vienna, 1977), pp. 171ff., 326ff., 335ff.; Findlay, *Plato*, the final Chapter; idem., *Plato and Platonism. An Introduction* (New York, 1978). For what concerns the philosophical discussion, see also J. Annas, *Aristotle's Metaphysics, Books M and N, Translated with Introduction and Notes* (Oxford, 1976), esp. pp. 2 and 42ff. For the interpretation or the position taken by philosophers such as Tennemann, Brandis, Trendelenburg, Weisse, Stenzel, H. Gomperz, Wilpert, Gadamer and French historians of philosophy before and after Robin, consult pp. 29ff., 38ff.

15. For what concerns the marxist discussion, consult T. V. Vasiljeva in *Voprosy Filosofii* 11 (1977): 152-60 (consult Appendix, IV, nr. 154).

16. In this there would already be an acknowledgement on principle, which evidently shall be avoided at the start.

17. See, in this regard, the pertinent remarks of A. Graeser, *Platons Ideenlehre* (Bern, 1975), p. 133, note 32. On the contrary, one prefers to keep (as, for example, by G. Patzig) to the popularizing expositions of the theory of Ideas, for example, that of Book Five of the *Republic*, from which can evidently be drawn whatever one desires.

18. "The indirect tradition is philosophically weak, because it does not properly derive from Plato—and since it is philosophically thin, for this reason it cannot properly be Platonic." And so vice versa: "The philosophy of the dialogues is significant, because it is unequivocally Platonic—and since it is significant, it represents the authentic position and genuine philosophy of Plato." Conforming to this type of reasoning, the aporias encountered in the written works are considered expressions of a profound meaning, while, on the contrary, in the indirect tradition they are considered as expressions of claptrap. The contradictions, in the written works, are considered as expressions of a vigorous stirring of thought, instead, in the unwritten tradition, they are considered as indices of philosophical impotency, or falsifications and untrustworthiness of the tradition, and so on. In this way of reasoning the evidence and the simplicity of that which is familiar becomes wrongly a criterion of measure against that which is unfamiliar and hence still to be studied and assimilated.

19. F. Schlegel, *Philosophische Vorlesungen 1800-1807, Kritische Friedrich-Schlegel-Ausgabe*, Vol. XII, ed. J. J. Anstett (Paderborn, 1964), *Philosophie des Plato*, esp. p. 211: "His loss [sc., of the book on the unwritten doctrines of Plato] does not at all seem to have that importance which is ascribed to it" it "would furnish little new things and little of interest about his philosophy."

20. In the case of Democritus this would have the consequence of necessarily negating that he would have had an atomic theory, since this doctrine has been transmitted to us solely by the doxographers; and we must then make the theory of the atoms begin only with Epicurus.

21. W. Wieland, Introduction to the volume *Antike*, (see note 9), p. 27 (the indirect tradition "does not even achieve proximity to the level of reflection that instead suffuses the dialogues"); J. Mittelstrass, *Platon*, (see note 9), p. 60 ("from the

philosophical viewpoint, that is, measured with Plato's own criteria of dialogical and methodical philosophizing, these systematizations [of the indirect tradition] must be placed far behind the doctrines of the dialogues"). Wieland acknowledges curiously in his book, *Die aristotelische Physik* (Göttingen, 1970²), p. 289, note 10, in the Platonic theory of the indivisible lines that belongs to the unwritten doctrines, "a mathematical abstraction greatly developed" with respect to the Aristotelian theory of the continuum. Moreover, the position taken by K. H. Ilting in *Phronesis* 13 (1968): 29 is very instructive. He defends the dialogues, affirming that they are "on the same plane of philosophical reflection" as the unwritten doctrines. The tendency, which in Mittelstrass is still present (consult in this regard, *GF*, p. 140, note 118), even if not in a consistent way, corresponding to a tendency that arises from Schleiermacherianism, which tends to make the responsibility of the systematic character of the unwritten tradition go back to the circle of the pupils of Plato, is destined to fail, because it is not in a condition to bear the *onus probandi* (burden of proof) demanded in this case and in particular because it is refuted by the doctrinal distinctions regularly established by Aristotle between Plato and the other Academics (see the fundamental remarks made in this regard on pp. 51f.). That Aristotle would have substantially discussed the doctrines encountered in the dialogues and not those unwritten and orally taught by Plato within the Academy (as would be for Mittelstrass, *Platon*, p. 39) is incorrect (consult, for example, the opposed judgment of W. Jaeger, *Studien zur Entstehungsgeschichte der Metaphysik des Aristoteles* [Berlin, 1912], pp. 140f.; see also Aristotle, *Physics* A and *Metaphysics* A, M, N).

22. This procedure, applied once more to the in many respects analogous position of Democritus, would lead to the conclusion that the atomic theory—unlike the moral doctrines that are partially preserved in their original formulation—must be considered negatively from a philosophical point of view, because it has lost its original form of presentation. The disastrous consequences that would follow for every kind of doxography are clearly evident.

23. The inverting of the importance of what results from the affirmations of Plato is characteristic, in fact the theory of the principles strictly linked to the method proper to Plato, that is, to the oral method, is subordinated to the derived and secondary method of the literary dialogues and of their content.

24. The literary dialogue, according to Plato, does not even possess a role in communication! (See what is said on pp. 6ff., and p. 73 with respect to the *Phaedrus*.)

25. A significant example is to be found in the attempt by H. Kuhn to defend the picture of Plato influenced by the philosophy of life and existentialism of his generation against the claims of the indirect tradition that go well beyond, by a criticism of the indirect tradition, not sufficiently sophisticated and hence misleading, taken from Cherniss ("Platon und die Grenze philosophischer Mitteilung," in *Idee und Zahl*, pp. 151ff.). W. Wieland in the meantime has written a book on Plato (*Platon und die Formen des Wissens* [Göttingen:Vandenhoeck-Ruprecht, 1982], in which he continues to follow the tendencies explained earlier and preserves in all points the objections already raised. Since our work was already in press when the Weiland's book was published, we reserved answering his arguments to another place: See Appendix, 4, Nr. 184 ("Kritische Bemerkungen zu den jüngsten

Äusserungen von W. Weiland und G. Patzig über Platons Ungeschriebene Lehre,"
Rivista di Filosofia neo-scolastica 74/4 [1982]:579-92).

In her posthumous work, *Rethinking Plato and Platonism* (Leiden: Brill, 1986;
1988[2]), the late Professor C. J. De Vogel committed to her views about the unwritten
doctrines, which had been formed by the location of Platonic scholarship during the
twenties and thirties of this century, has published a feeble defense of them. To be
sure, De Vogel was always, with Robin and against Cherniss, an advocate of the
authenticity of the indirect Platonic tradition but, at the same time, remained a
follower of the wide-spread evolutionism concerning Plato's thought, inherited from
nineteenth century scholarship, beginning from her doctoral dissertation, "Een
keerpunt in Plato's denken" (1936), and, consequently, a follower of a late dating of
the unwritten doctrines. Now, her last work, unfortunately, lacks a critical account
of more sophisticated criteria for the evolutionistic hypthesis that formerly were
applied to Plato that are required by the recently changed situation of Platonic
scholarship. Instead, the author continues suggesting some highly hypothetical
assumptions about the philosophical—and not only literary—evolution of Plato's
thought, which are not very convincing, but are, at least, interchangeable with
others. Especially, she has not taken into account the fact that we cannot simply draw
conclusions from the written work to the unwritten doctrines, which would presuppose that the latter, nevertheless, in a certain sense are represented by the dialogues
and, therefore, not really unwritten. Second, one misses coherent interpretations of
the self-testimonies of Plato as well as of the allusions of the written work to the
unwritten (except solely *Protagoras* 356/7) or, at least, detailed comments on the newer
discussions thereof. When the author occasionally maintains that in the self-testimonies Plato meant only the ineffability of his ultimate doctrines (18, 66), this results
from a simplistic reading of the texts, which testify, on the contrary, that Plato really
taught these doctrines with success (*Eighth Letter*) or claimed to be able to do so
(*Phaedrus* 278C/D). The same holds for the conjecture, suggested as an alternative
and proposed in the following rhetorical question: "Would not the insufficiency of
the hypothesis (!) have been the reason why Plato never wrote it down?" (35),
because Plato expressly stresses the high value of his doctrines (e.g., *Seventh Letter*
345B) and gives quite different reasons for not writing them down. Further, there
are manifest prejudices in favor of the written work, leading to an asymmetry in the
mutual relation of explication and clarification between the two branches of Platonic
tradition. So De Vogel, repeatedly, underlines the hermeneutic role of the dialogues
for the unwritten doctrines (e.g., pp. 32ff., and p. 115), but nowhere provides any
discussion, let alone an instance, of the probabilities of success by the utilization of
the indirect tradition for a better understanding of the written works of Plato. Plato,
thus, remains a *Plato dimidiatus* [*a halved Plato*]. This depends, at least in part, on an
insufficient appreciation of the dialectical character of the "schemata" and "fossilized
summaries" delivered by the indirect tradition, which, in reality, offer an insight into
the completion and fulfillment of the dialectical movement of the dialogues. To this
is joined the futile attempt at "rectifying" the bipolarity of the two principles
contained in the reports, by opposing it to the dialogues, on the one side, and by
stressing reports with a tendency to monism in Hermodorus (Appendix, 3.13) and
Sextus Empiricus (Appendix, 3.12), on the other. But there are clear traces of a
fundamental dualism also in the dialogues (*Seventh Letter* 344A8f., *Parmenides*,

Philebus, for *Republic* VI consult now G. Reale, *Platone* (Milan, 1987⁵), pp. 321ff.), whereas Hermodorus undoubtedly presupposes the original dualism and he reserves only the term 'principle' for the active part, which is, however, probably the cosmological demiurgic principle in comparison with the cosmological material substrate; it is, then, not a question of the ultimate ontological principles at all. But even this conceded, Hermodorus' ambiguous report is counterbalanced and neutralized by Speusippus' report (*Test. Plat.* 50 Gaiser), where, on the contrary, not the One, but the indeterminate Duality is the principle. The only testimony (in Sextus), where the latter is really derived from the One, is as is generally recognized-dependent on a Neo-Pythagorean and ultimately a Stoic tradition that cannot be traced back, therefore, to a "true" monistic Plato, and this even less so, because otherwise Aristotle and Theophrastus together with the followers of Plato in the Ancient Academy would all have misunderstood the "true" Plato, before he would have been taken up in the right way by those neo-Pythagoreans. Actually it is obvious that here normative premises on the side of Professor De Vogel have misled the unprejudiced inventory of the historical facts. For the rest, the original bipolarity, that is, the fundamental structural dualism of both principles, does not imply, of course, that they are equal and of the same rank (see Chapter 6, p. 77). Further, De Vogel's reports on Platonic scholarship within the last decades are not always reliable. For example, the Tübingen School is neither dependent on H.G. Gadamer nor on H. Gomperz (see pp. 29, 38, 47, 185, n. 14), the theses enumerated (p.116) are not supported by Tübingen scholars or, at least, are misunderstood, as are nearly all the putative differences between K. Gaiser and me, and the main thesis of my book *Der Ursprung der Geistmetaphysik* (1967²) is *not* that the Aristotelian God thinks the world, but quite the contrary. The title of my paper *Retraktationen* (1964, see Appendix, 4, Nr. 78), of course, is not to be understood in the modern but in the more general sense of ancient Latin. Finally, it is to be regretted, that De Vogel did not take into consideration the research after about 1975, prescinding from a few exceptions; and, hence, she does not present the actual state of affairs in recent scholarship. At any rate, then, it would be quite erroneous and even fatal to consider De Vogel's book as a sufficient substitute for the original study of the schools of thought and the individual authors discussed therein.

Select Bibliography on the Problematic of the Unwritten Doctrines of Plato (In Chronological Order)

Brucker, J. *Historia critica philosophiae a mundi incunabulis ad nostram usque aetatem deducta.* I, Leipzig, 1742, pp. 659-63.

Tiedemann, D. *Geist der spekulativen Philosophie.* II, Marburg, 1791, pp. 192-98.

Tennemann, W. G. *System der platonischen Philosophie.* I, Leipzig, 1798, pp. 128-41; II, 1794, pp. 295-98.

Buhle, J. G. *Lehrbuch der Geschichte der Philosophie und einer kritischen Literatur derselben.* II, Göttingen, 1797, pp. 45-50.

Tennemann, W. G. *Geschichte der Philosophie.* II, Leipzig, 1799, pp. 205-22.

Schlegel, F. *Geschichte der europäischen Literatur, Pariser Vorlesungen 1803/4, Kritische Friedrich-Schlegel-Ausgabe.* Vol. XI, 1958, pp. 118-25.

Schlegel, F. *Die Entwicklung der Philosophie in zwölf Büchern. Kölner Vorlesungen 1804/5, Kritische Friedrich-Schlegel-Ausgabe.* Vol. XII, 1964, pp. 207-26. *Platons Werke von F. Schleiermacher.* I-III, Berlin, 1804 ff.[1], 1817 ff.[2], 1855[3].

Boeckh, A. *Kritik der Uebersetzung des Platon von Schleiermacher.* Heidelbergische Jahrbücher der Literatur für Philologie usw, I 1 (1808), now in A. Boeckh, *Gesammelte Kleine Schriften.* Siebenter Band: *Kritiken,* Leipzig, 1872, pp. 1-38.

Brandis, C. A. *Diatribe academica de perditis Aristotelis libris de ideis et de bono sive philosophia,* Bonn, 1823.

Trendelenburg, A. *Platonis de ideis et numeris doctrina ex Aristotele illustrata.* Leipzig, 1826.

Weisse, C. H. *De Platonis et Aristotelis in constituendis summis philosophiae principiis differentia.* Leipzig, 1828.

——*Aristoteles Physik. Übersetzt und mit Anmerkungen begleitet.* Leipzig, 1829, pp. 271-76, 393-405, 431-50, 471-74.

——*Aristoteles von der Seele und von der Welt. Übersetzt und mit Anmerkungen begleitet.* Leipzig, 1829, pp. 123-43.

Zeller, E. *Platonische Studien.* Tübingen, 1839 (reprinted Amsterdam, 1969), III. *Die Darstellung der Platonischen Philosophie bei Aristoteles.* pp. 197-300.

Hermann, K. F. *Über Plato's schriftstellerische Motive.* in *Gesammelte Abhandlungen und Beiträge zur classischen Literatur und Altertumskunde.* Göttingen, 1849, pp. 281-305, reprinted in Gaiser, K. ed. *Das Platonbild. Zehn Beiträge zum Platonverständnis.* Hildesheim, 1969, pp. 33-57.

Brandis, C. A. *Handbuch der Geschichte der griechisch-römischen Philosophie.* Vol. II 1, Berlin, 1844, pp. 180 f. 306-27.

Zeller, E. *Die Philosophie der Griechen*. Vol. II, Tübingen, 1846[1], pp. 210 ff.

Shorey, P. *De Platonis idearum doctrina atque mentis humanae notionibus commentatio.* Dissertation München, 1884, reprinted in Shorey, P. *Selected Papers*. ed. with an introduction by L. Tarán, New York, 1979.

———*The Unity of Plato's Thought*. Chicago, 1903 (reprinted 1968).

Wilson, J. Cook, "On the Platonist Doctrine of the ἀσύμβλητοι ἀριθμοί," *The Classical Review* 18 (1904):247-60.

Robin, L. *La théorie Platonicienne des idées et des nombres d'après Aristote.* Paris, 1908 (reprinted Hildesheim, 1963).

Jaeger, W. W. *Studien zur Entstehungsgeschichte der Metaphysik des Aristoteles.* Berlin, 1912, pp. 131-48: *Die Publikation der Lehrschriften.*

Robin L. "Études sur la signification et la place de la physique dans la philosophie de Platon," *Revue philosophique de la France et l'Étranger* (1918, 1967[2]):177-220, 370-415; separate edition Paris, 1919; reprinted in L. Robin, *La pensée hellénique des origines à Épicure.* Paris: Schuhl, 1942 (1967[2]), pp. 231-336. Translated into German in part in J. Wippern, ed., *Das Problem der ungeschriebenen Lehre Platons* (Wege der Forschung, 186) Darmstadt 1972, pp. 261-98.

Natorp, P. *Platos Ideenlehre. Eine Einführung in den Idealismus.* 1922[2], reprinted 1961, pp. 433-56.

Frank, E. *Plato und die sogenannten Pythagoreer.* Halle, 1923, Darmstadt, 1962[2].

Stenzel, J. *Zahl und Gestalt bei Platon und Aristoteles.* Leipzig-Berlin, 1924, 1933[2], Darmstadt 1959[3].

Taylor, A. E. *Plato. The Man and His Work.* London, 1926, 1956[7], Chapter 19: "Plato in the Academy Forms and Numbers," pp. 503-16.

———"Forms and Numbers. A Study in Platonic Metaphysics," I, *Mind* 35 (1926):419-40; II, *Mind* 36 (1927):12-33; reprinted in *Philosophical Studies.* London, 1934, pp. 91-150.

Shorey, P. "Forms and Numbers Again," *Classical Philology* 22 (1927):213-18.

Thompson, D'Arcy W. "Excess and Defect: Or the little More and the little Less," *Mind* 38 (1929):43-4.

Töplitz, O. "Das Verhältnis von Mathematik und Ideenlehre bei Plato," *Quellen und Studien zur Geschichte der Mathematik, Astronomie und Physik.* Abt. B, Vol. I (1929/31):3-33; reprinted in O. Becker, ed., *Zur Geschichte der griechischen Mathematik* (Wege der Forschung 33) Darmstadt, 1965, pp. 45-75.

Stenzel, J. "Zur Theorie des Logos bei Aristoteles," *Quellen und Studien zur Geschichte der Mathematik, Astronomie und Physik.* Abt. B, Vol. I (1929/31):34-66; reprinted in J. Stenzel, *Kleine Schriften zur griechischen Philosophie* Darmstadt, 1956, 1966[3], pp. 188-219.

Becker, O. "Die diairetische Erzeugung der platonischen Idealzahlen," *Quellen und Studien zur Geschichte der Mathematik, Astronomie und Physik.* Abt. B, Vol. I (1929/31):464-501.

Stenzel, J. *Metaphysik des Altertums, Handbuch der Philosophie.* I D, München-Berlin, 1929/31, pp. 128-51.

Gentile, M. "La dottrina platonica delle idee numeri e Aristotele," *Annali della R. Scuola Normale Superiore di Pisa* I 30/3, Pisa (1930):3-216.

Gomperz, H. "Platons philosophisches System," in *Proceedings of the Seventh International Congress of Philosophy*, ed. G. Ryle, London (1931):426-31; reprinted in

J. Wippern, ed. *Das Problem der ungeschriebenen Lehre Platons* (Wege der Forschung, 186) Darmstadt, 1972, pp. 159-65. English version: "Plato's System of Philosophy," in H. Gomperz, *Philosophical Studies*. ed. D. S. Robinson and P. Merlan, Boston, 1953, pp. 119-24.

Cornford, F. M. "Mathematics and Dialectic in the *Republic* VI-VIII," *Mind* 41 (1932):37-52, 173-90; reprinted in R. E. Allen, *Studies in Plato's Metaphysics*. London-New York, 1965, pp. 61-95.

Merlan, P. "Beiträge zur Geschichte des antiken Platonismus," *Philologus* 89 (1934):35-53, 197-214; reprinted in P. Merlan, *Kleine philosophische Schriften*. Hildesheim-New York, 1976, pp. 51-87.

Klein, J. "Die griechische Logistik und die Entstehung der Algebra," *Quellen und Studien zur Geschichte der Mathematik, Astronomie und Physik*. Abt. B, Vol. III (1936):18-105, 122-235. English version, *Greek Mathematical Thought and the Origin of Algebra*, trans. E. Brann, Cambridge, Mass., 1968.

Whitehead, A. N. *Mathematics and the Good* (1936) in P. A. Schilpp ed., *The Philosophy of Alfred North Whitehead*. New York, 1951², pp. 666-81.

Gentile, M. "Nuovi studi intorno alla dottrina platonica delle idee numeri," *Annali della R. Scuola Normale Superiore di Pisa* II 6 (1937):111-27.

Wilpert, P. "Neue Fragmente aus Περὶ τἀγαθοῦ," *Hermes* 76 (1941):225-50; reprinted J. Wippern ed., *Das Problem der ungeschriebenen Lehre Platons* (Wege der Forschung, 186) Darmstadt, 1972, pp. 166-200.

Wielen, W. van der, *Die ideegetallen van Plato*. Amsterdam, 1941.

Brommer, P. "De numeris idealibus," *Mnemosyne* III 11 (1943):263-95.

Cherniss, H. *Aristotle's Criticism of Plato and the Academy*. I, Baltimore, 1944, 1946², New York, 1962³.

———*The Riddle of the Early Academy*. Berkeley-Los Angeles, 1945, 1962². German version trans. J. Derbolav, Heidelberg, 1966; Italian version trans. L. Ferrero, Firenze, 1974.

Junge, G. "Platos Ideen-Zahlen," *Classica et Mediaevalia* 10 (1948):18-38.

Vogel, C. J. de, "La dernière phase du Platonisme et l'interprétation de M. Robin," in *Studia Varia Carolo Guilielmo Vollgraff a discipulis oblata*. Amsterdam, 1948, pp. 165-178; reprinted with the title: "La dernière phase du Platonisme et l'interprétation de Léon Robin," in C. J. de Vogel, *Philosophia. I. Studies in Greek Philosophy*. Assen, 1970, 243-55. German version in J. Wippern ed., *Das Problem der ungeschriebenen Lehre Platons* (Wege der Forschung, 186) Darmstadt, 1972, pp. 201-16.

Wilpert, P. *Zwei aristotelische Frühschriften über die Ideenlehre*. Regensburg, 1949.

———"Platons Altersvorlesung über das Gute," *Philosophisches Jahrbuch* 59 (1949):1-13.

Vogel, C. J. de, "Problems Concerning Later Platonism," *Mnemosyne* IV 2 (1949):197-216, 299-318; reprinted in J. Wippern ed., *Das Problem der ungeschriebenen Lehre Platons* (Wege der Forschung, 186) Darmstadt, 1972, pp. 41-87. Modified version with the title, "Problems Concerning Plato's Later Doctrine," in C. J. de Vogel, *Philosophia. I*. Assen, 1970, pp. 256-92.

Bröcker, W. "Plato über das Gute," *Lexis* II 1 (1949):47-66; reprinted in J. Wippern ed., *Das Problem der ungeschriebenen Lehre Platons* (Wege der Forschung, 186) Darmstadt, 1972, pp. 217-39.

Vogel, C. J. de, *Greek Philosophy. A Collection of Texts. Vol. I: Thales to Plato.* Leiden, 1950, 1963[3].

Ross, W. D. *Plato's Theory of Ideas.* Oxford, 1951, 1953[2].

Wilpert, P. "Eine Elementenlehre im platonischen Philebos," in *Studies Presented to David Moore Robinson on His Seventieth Birthday.* II, St. Louis, 1953, pp. 573-82; reprinted in J. Wippern ed., *Das Problem der ungeschriebenen Lehre Platons* (Wege der Forschung, 186) Darmstadt, 1972, pp. 316-28.

Martin, G. "Platons Lehre von der Zahl und ihre Darstellung durch Aristoteles," *Zeitschrift für philosophische Forschung* 7 (1953):191-203.

Vogel, C. J. de, "On the Neoplatonic Character of Platonism and the Platonic Character of Neoplatonism," *Mind* 62 (1953):43-64; reprinted in C. J. de Vogel, *Philosophia.* I. Assen, 1970, pp. 353-77.

Merlan, P. *From Platonism to Neoplatonism.* The Hague, 1953, revised 1960[2], 1968[3].

Vogel, C. J. de, "A la recherche des étapes précises entre Platon et le Néoplatonisme," *Mnemosyne* IV 7 (1954):111-22.

Marcovič, Ž. "La théorie de Platon sur l'Un et la Dyade indéfinie et ses traces dans la mathématique grecque," *Revue d'Histoire des Sciences et de leurs applications* VIII, 1955. German version in O. Becker ed., *Zur Geschichte der griechischen Mathematik* (Wege der Forschung 33) Darmstadt, 1965, pp. 308-18.

Saffrey, H. D. Περὶ φιλοσοφίας *d'Aristote de la théorie platonicienne des idées et des nombres.* (Philosophia antiqua, VII) Leiden, 1955, 1971[2].

Becker, O. "Zwei Untersuchungen zur antiken Logik," *Klassisch-philologische Studien* 17, Wiesbaden (1957):1-22: "Zum Problem der platonischen Idealzahlen (eine Retraktation)."

Lasserre, F. "Nombre et connaissance dans la préhistoire du platonisme," *Museum Helveticum* 15 (1958):11-26.

Vogel, C. J. de, "La théorie de l'ἄπειρον chez Platon et dans la tradition platonicienne," *Revue philosophique de la France et de l'Étranger* 84 (1959):21-39; reprinted in C. J. de Vogel, *Philosophia.* I, Assen, 1970, pp. 378-95.

Kucharski, P. "Les principes des Pythagoriciens et la dyade de Platon," *Archives de Philosophie* 22 (1959):175-91, 385-431.

Krämer, H. J. *Areté bei Platon und Aristoteles. Zum Wesen und zur Geschichte der platonischen Ontologie* (Abhandlungen d. Heidelberger Akademie der Wissenschaften, philosophisch-historische Klasse, Jahrgang 1959, Nr. 6), Heidelberg, 1959; Amsterdam, 1967[2].

Strycker, E. de, "On the First Section of Fragment 5a of the *Protrepticus*. The Logical Structure and the Platonic Character of the Doctrine," in *Aristotle and Plato in the mid-fourth Century* (Papers of the *Symposium Aristotelicum* held at Oxford in August 1957), ed. I. Düring, and G. E. L. Owen, Göteborg, 1960, pp. 76-104.

Gaiser, K. *Platon und die Geschichte.* Stuttgart, 1961.

Gauss, H. *Philosophischer Handkommentar zu den Dialogen Platos.* III 2, Bern, 1961, pp. 146-54: "Platos Altersvorlesung über das Gute."

Berti, E. *La filosofia del primo Aristotele.* Padua, 1962.

Burkert, W. *Weisheit und Wissenschaft. Studien zu Pythagoras, Philolaos und Platon,* Nürnberg, 1962, Chapter 1; American version in, *Lore and Science,* trans. E. L. Minar, Cambridge, Mass., 1971.

Brentlinger, J. A. "The Divided Line and Plato's 'Theory of Intermediates'," *Phronesis* 8 (1963):146-66.

Gaiser, K. *Platons Ungeschriebene Lehre. Studien zur systematischen und geschichtlichen Begründung der Wissenschaften in der Platonischen Schule. Mit einem Anhang: Testimonia Platonica. Quellentexte zur Schule und mündlichen Lehre Platons.* Stuttgart, 1963, 1968².

Lesky, A. *Geschichte der griechischen Literatur.* Bern, 1963², pp. 585ff.

Liebich, W. in Nestle-Liebich, *Geschichte der griechischen Literatur.* Vol. II, Berlin, 1963³ (Sammlung Göschen Vol. 557), pp. 11-25.

Krämer, H. J. "Die platonische Akademie und das Problem einer systematischen Interpretation der Philosophie Platons," *Kant-Studien* 55 (1964):69-101, reprinted in K. Gaiser *Das Platonbild. Zehn Beiträge zum Platonverständnis.* Hildesheim, 1969, pp. 198-230.

———"Retraktationen zum Problem des esoterischen Platon," *Museum Helveticum* 21 (1964):137-67.

Gadamer, H. G. *Dialektik und Sophistik im siebenten platonischen Brief* (Sitzungsberichte der Heidelberger Akademie der Wissenschaften, philosophisch-historische Klasse 1964/2), Heidelberg, 1964; reprinted in H. G. Gadamer *Platos dialektische Ethik und andere Studien zur platonischen Philosophie.* Hamburg, 1968, pp. 221-247. American version in *Dialogue and Dialectic: Eight Hermeneutical Studies on Plato,* trans. P. Christopher Smith, New Haven-London: Yale University Press, 1980, pp. 93-123.

Hager, F. P. "Zur philosophischen Problematik der sogenannten ungeschriebenen Lehre Platons," *Studia Philosophica* 24 (1964):90-117.

Theiler, W. "Einheit und unbegrenzte Zweiheit von Plato bis Plotin," in *Isonomia. Studien zur Gleichheitsvorstellung im griechischen Denken* ed. J. Mau and E. G. Schmidt, Berlin, 1964, 1967², pp. 89-109; reprinted in W. Theiler *Untersuchungen zur antiken Literatur.* Berlin, 1970, pp. 460-83.

Gaiser, K. "Platons *Menon* und die Akademie," *Archiv für Geschichte der Philosophie* 46 (1964):241-92; reprinted in J. Wippern ed., *Das Problem der ungeschriebenen Lehre Platons* (Wege der Forschung, 186) Darmstadt, 1972, pp. 329-93.

Vries, G. J. de, "Marginalia bij een esoterische Plato," *Tijdschrift voor Philosophie* 26 (1964):704-19.

Krämer, H. J. *Der Ursprung der Geistmetaphysik. Untersuchungen zur Geschichte des Platonismus zwischen Platon und Plotin.* Amsterdam, 1964, 1967².

Berti, E. "Una nuova ricostruzione delle dottrine non scritte di Platone," *Giornali di metafisica* 19 (1964):546-57. German version in J. Wippern ed., *Das Problem der ungeschriebenen Lehre Platons* (Wege der Forschung, 186) Darmstadt, 1972, pp. 240-58.

Oehler, K. "Der entmythologisierte Platon. Zur Lage der Platonforschung," *Zeitschrift für philosophische Forschung* 19 (1965):393-420; reprinted in K. Oehler *Antike Philosophie und byzantinisches Mittelalter. Aufsätze zur Geschichte des griechischen Denkens,* München, 1969, pp. 66-94, and also in J. Wippern ed., *Das Problem der ungeschriebenen Lehre Platons* (Wege der Forschung, 186) Darmstadt, 1972, pp. 95-129.

Untersteiner, M. "Studi Platonici. Il *'Carmide '*," *Acme* 18 (1965):19-67; reprinted in M. Untersteiner *Da Omero ad Aristotele. Scritti minori.* Series 2, Brescia, 1976, pp. 347-416.

Berti, E. Review in *Rivista critica di storia della filosofia* 20 (1965):231-35. German version with the title: "Über das Verhältnis von literarischem Werk und ungeschriebener Lehre bei Platon in der Sicht der neueren Forschung," in J. Wippern ed., *Das Problem der ungeschriebenen Lehre Platons* (Wege der Forschung, 186) Darmstadt, 1972, pp. 88-94.

Gaiser, K. "Platons Farbenlehre," in *Synusia. Festgabe für Wolfgang Schadewaldt zum 15. März 1965.* Pfullingen, 1965, pp. 173-222.

Baumgartner, H. M. "Von der Möglichkeit, das Agathon als Prinzip zu denken. Versuch einer transzendentalen Interpretation zu *Politeia* 509b," *Parusia. Studien zur Philosophie Platons und zur Problemgeschichte des Platonismus. Festgabe für J. Hirschberger.* Frankfurt, 1965, pp. 89-101.

Solignac, A. and Aubenque, P. "Une nouvelle dimension du Platonisme. La doctrine <non écrite> de Platon," *Archives de philosophie* 28 (1965):251-65.

Muth, R. "Zur Bedeutung von Mündlichkeit und Schriftlichkeit der Wortkunst," *Wiener Studien* 79 (1966):246-60.

Fritz, K. von, "Die philosophische Stelle im siebten platonischen Brief und die Frage der 'esoterischen' Philosophie Platons," *Phronesis* 11 (1966):117-53; reprinted in K. von Fritz *Schriften zur griechischen Logik,* Vol. 1 (Problemata, 70), Stuttgart, 1978, pp. 175-214.

Krämer, H. J. "Über den Zusammenhang von Prinzipienlehre und Dialektik bei Platon. Zur Definition des Dialektikers *Politeia* 534 B-C," *Philologus* 110 (1966):35-70; reprinted in J. Wippern ed., *Das Problem der ungeschriebenen Lehre Platons* (Wege der Forschung, 186) Darmstadt, 1972, pp. 394-448.

Krämer, H. J. "Aristoxenos über Platons Περὶ τἀγαθοῦ," *Hermes* 94 (1966):111f.

Düring, I. *Aristoteles. Darstellung und Interpretation seines Denkens.* Heidelberg 1966. Italian version by P. Donini, Milan, 1976.

Dönt, E. *Platons Spätphilosophie und die Akademie. Untersuchungen zu den platonischen Briefen, zu Platons "Ungeschriebener Lehre" und zur Epinomis des Philipp von Opus.* (Sitzungsberichte der Österreichischen Akademie der Wissenschaften, 251/3), Vienna, 1967 (see also in this regard the review of H. J. Krämer in *Anzeiger für die Altertumswissenschaft* 21 [1968], pp. 221-25.)

Krämer, H. J. "Zur geschichtlichen Stellung der aristotelischen Metaphysik," *Kant-Studien* 58 (1967):313-54.

——"Das Problem der Philosophenherrschaft bei Platon," *Philosophisches Jahrbuch* 74 (1967):254-70.

Fritz, K. von, "Zur Frage der esoterischen Philosophie Platons," *Archiv für Geschichte der Philosophie* 49 (1967):255-68; reprinted in K. von Fritz *Schriften zur griechischen Logik,* Vol. 1 (Problemata, 70) Stuttgart, 1978, pp. 215-24.

Merlan, P. "Τὸ ἀπορῆσαι ἀρχαϊκῶς (Arist. *Met.* N 2, 1089a1)," *Philologus* 111 (1967):119-21; reprinted in P. Merlan *Kleine philosophische Schriften.* Hildesheim-New York, 1976, pp. 235-37.

Isnardi Parente, M. "Studi e discussioni recenti sul Platone esoterico, l'Accademia antica e il Neoplatonismo," *De Homine* 22/23 (1967):217-40; reprinted with the title: "Platone esoterico nella literatura critica recente," in M. Isnardi Parente *Filosofia e politica nelle lettere di Platone*. Naples, 1970, pp. 113-46.

Dempe, H. "Platon und die moderne Philosophie," *Gymnasium* 74 (1967):510-28, esp. pp. 524 ff.

Gadamer, H. G. "Platons ungeschriebene Dialektik," in *Idee und Zahl. Studien zur platonischen Philosophie* von H. G. Gadamer, K. Gaiser, H. Gundert, H. J. Krämer, H. Kuhn, ed. H. G. Gadamer and W. Schadewaldt, (Abhandlungen der Heidelberger Akademie der Wissenschaften, philosophisch-historische Klasse, 1968/2), Heidelberg, 1968, pp. 9-30; reprinted in H. G. Gadamer *Kleine Schriften*, III. Tübingen, 1972, pp. 27-49. [American version in *Dialogue and Dialectic: Eight Hermeneutical Studies on Plato*, trans. P. Christopher Smith, New Haven-London: Yale University Press, 1980, pp. 124-55]

Gaiser, K. "Quellenkritische Probleme der indirekten Platonüberlieferung," in *Idee und Zahl*, pp. 31-84.

Gundert, H. "Zum philosophischen Exkurs im 7. Brief," in *Idee und Zahl*, pp. 85-105.

Krämer, H. J. "Die grundsätzlichen Fragen der indirekten Platonüberlieferung," in *Idee und Zahl*, pp. 106-50.

Kuhn, H. "Platon und die Grenze philosophischer Mitteilung," in *Idee und Zahl*, pp. 106-50.

Boeder, H. "Zu Platons eigener Sache," *Philosophisches Jahrbuch* 76 (1968):37-66.

Merlan, P. "War Platons Vorlesung 'Das Gute' einmalig?," *Hermes* 96 (1968):705-09; reprinted P. Merlan *Kleine philosophische Schriften*, Hildesheim-New York, 1976, pp. 88-92.

————"Zwei Bemerkungen zum aristotelischen Plato," *Rheinisches Museum*111 (1968):705-9; reprinted P. Merlan *Kleine philosophische Schriften*. Hildesheim-New York, 1976, pp. 259-73.

Pépin, J. "Redécouverte de Platon," *Preuves* n. 206 (1968):76-84.

Krämer, H. J. "Grundbegriffe akademischer Dialektik in den biologischen Schriften von Aristoteles und Theophrast," *Rheinisches Museum* 111 (1968):293-333.

Schwarz, F. F. "Platon-Esoterik und Akademie. Zum derzeitigen Stand der Forschung," *Die Allgemeinbildende Höhere Schule* 17 (Vienna, 1968):149-53.

Ilting, K. H. "Platons 'Ungeschriebene Lehren': der Vortrag 'über das Gute'," *Phronesis* 13 (1968):1-31.

Vries, C. J. de, "Aristoxenos über Περὶ τἀγαθοῦ," *Hermes* 96 (1968):124-26.

Routila, L. "Agrapha Dogmata." *Ajatus* 31 (1969):63-92.

Krämer, H. J. "ΕΠΕΚΕΙΝΑ ΤΗΣ ΟΤΣΙΑΣ. Zu Platon, *Politeia* 509 B," *Archiv für Geschichte der Philosophie* 51 (1969):1-30.

Merlan, P. "Bemerkungen zum neuen Platobild," *Archiv für Geschichte der Philosophie* 51 (1969):111-26; reprinted in P. Merlan *Kleine philosophische Schriften*. Hildesheim-New York, 1976, pp. 93-108.

Isnardi Parente, M. "La VII epistola e Platone esoterico," *Rivista critica di storia della filosofia* 24 (1969):416-31; reprinted in M. Isnardi Parente *Filosofia e politica nelle lettere di Platone*, Naples, 1970, pp. 147-67.

Gaiser, K. ed. *Das Platonbild. Zehn Beiträge zum Platonverständnis* (contains articles of F. Schleiermacher, K. F. Hermann, P. Natorp, J. Stenzel, W. Jaeger, F. Solmsen, N. Hartmann, H. Gundert, H. J. Krämer, H. Kuhn), Hildesheim, 1969.

Schmalzriedt, E. *Platon. Der Schriftsteller und die Wahrheit*. München, 1969.

Strycker, É. de, "L'idée du Bien dans la *République* de Platon," *L'antiquité classique* 39 (1970):450-67.

Lohmann, J. *Musiké und Logos. Aufsätze zur griechischen Philosophie und Musiktheorie.* Stuttgart, 1970, pp. 95ff.

Happ, H. *Hyle. Studien zum aristotelischen Materie-Begriff.* Berlin-New York, 1971.

Weizsäcker, C. F. von, *Die Einheit der Natur.* München, 1971, pp. 474-91.

Scolnicov, S. "On the Epistemological Significance of Plato's Theory of Ideal Numbers," *Museum Helveticum* 28 (1971):72-97.

Krämer, H. J. *Platonismus und hellenistische Philosophie.* Berlin-New York, 1971.

Niewöhner, F. W. *Dialog und Dialektik in Platons "Parmenides," Untersuchungen zur sogenannten Platonischen "Esoterik"* (Monographien zur philosophischen Forschung, 78), Meisenheim/Glan, 1971.

Isnardi Parente, M. "Théophraste, Metaphysica 6 a 23 ff." *Phronesis* 16 (1971):49-64.

——"Per l'interpretazione di Aristotele. De An. 404b18 ff." in *Philomathes, Studies and Essays in the Humanities in memory of Philip Merlan,* ed. R. B. Palmer and R. Hamerton-Kelly, The Hague, 1971, pp. 146-70.

Brunschwig, J. "*EE* I 8, 1218a15-32 et le Περὶ τἀγαθοῦ," in *Untersuchungen zur Eudemischen Ethik. (Akten des 5. Symposium Aristotelicum),* ed. P. Moraux and D. Harlfinger, Berlin, 1971, pp. 197-222.

Wippern, J. ed. *Das Problem der ungeschriebenen Lehre Platons. Beiträge zum Verständnis der platonischen Prinzipienphilosophie* (Wege der Forschung, 186), Darmstadt, 1972 (with further bibliographical information up to 1971).

Watson, G. *Plato's Unwritten Teachings.* Dublin, 1973.

Gaiser, K. "Die Platon-Referate des Alkimos bei Diogenes Laertios (III 9-17)," in *Zetesis, Festgabe für É. de Strijcker.* Antwerpen-Utrecht, 1973, pp. 61-79.

Gundert, H. "'Perspektivische Täuschung' bei Plato und die Prinzipienlehre," in *Zetesis, Festgabe für É. de Strijcker.* Antwerpen-Utrecht, 1973, pp. 80-97.

Krämer, H. J. "Zum Standort der 'Metaphysik' Theophrasts," in *Zetesis, Festgabe für É. de Strijcker.* Antwerpen-Utrecht, 1973, pp. 206-14.

——"Aristoteles und die akademische Eidoslehre. Zur Geschichte des Universalienproblems im Platonismus," *Archiv für Geschichte der Philosophie* 55 (1973):119-90.

Repellini, F. F. "Gli Agrapha Dogmata di Platone: La loro recente ricostruzione e i suoi presupposti storico-filosofici," *Acme* 26 (1973):51-84.

Findlay, J. N. *Plato: The Written and Unwritten Doctrines.* London, 1974; reprinted New York: Humanities Press, 1974.

Zeller, E. and Mondolfo, R. *La filosofia dei Greci nel suo sviluppo storico. Parte II. Volume III/2: Platone e l'Accademia antica,* ed. M. Isnardi Parente, Florence, 1974.

Tigerstedt, E. N. *The Decline and Fall of the Neoplatonic Interpretation of Plato. An Outline and Some Observations.* (Commentationes Humanarum Litterarum, 52), Helsinki, 1974.

Graeser, A. "Kritische Retraktationen zur esoterischen Platon-Interpretation," *Archiv für Geschichte der Philosophie* 56 (1974):71-87.

Gaiser, K. "Die Rede der Musen über den Grund von Ordnung und Unordnung: Platon Politeia VIII 545D-547A," in *Studia Platonica, Festschrift für Hermann Gundert zu seinem 65. Geburtstag am 30.4.1974.* Amsterdam, 1974, pp. 49-85.

Annas, J. "Forms and First Principles," *Phronesis* 19 (1974):257-83.

Albert, K. *Die ontologische Erfahrung*. Ratingen, 1974, pp. 46 ff.; "Die ontologische Erfahrung bei Platon."

Annas, J. "On the Intermediates," *Archiv für Geschichte der Philosophie* 57 (1975):146-66.

Turnher, R. *Der siebte Platonbrief. Versuch einer umfassenden philosophischen Interpretation* (Monographien zur philosophischen Forschung, 125), Meisenheim-Glan, 1975.

Annas, J. *Aristotle's Metaphysics, Books M and N. Translated with Introduction and Notes*, Oxford, 1976.

Wieland, W. "Platon und der Nutzen der Idee. Zur Funktion der Idee des Guten," *Allgemeine Zeitschrift für Philosophie* 1 (1976):19-33.

Berti, E. *Aristotele: Dalla dialettica alla filosofia prima*. Padua 1977, pp. 112-42.

Tigerstedt, E. N. *Interpreting Plato* (Acta Universitatis Stockholmiensis, Stockholm Studies in History of Literature, 17), Stockholm, 1977.

Weizsäcker, C. F. von, *Der Garten des Menschlichen. Beiträge zur geschichtlichen Anthropologie*. München-Wien, 1977, pp. 171ff. 326ff. 335 ff.

Vasiljeva, T. V. "Nepisanaja filosofija Platona," *Voprosy Filosofii* 11 (1977):152-60, ["The Unwritten Philosophy of Plato," in *Problems of Philosophy*].

Szlezák, T. A. "Plotin und die geheimen Lehren des Ammonios," in *Esoterik und Exoterik der Philosophie*, ed. H. Holzhey and W. C. Zimmerli, Basel-Stuttgart, 1977, pp. 52-69.

Vasiljeva, T. V. "Nepisanaja filosofija Platona," *Obzor Akademija Nauk USSR*, Moscow (1978):91-112, ["The Unwritten Philosophy of Plato," (Review), *The USSR Academy of Sciences*, Moscow].

Guthrie, W. K. C. *A History of Greek Philosophy. V. The Later Plato and the Academy*. Cambridge, 1978, Chapter VIII, "Plato's Unwritten Metaphysics," pp. 418-22.

Szlezák, T. A. "Probleme der Platoninterpretation," *Göttingische Gelehrte Anzeigen* 230 (1978):1-38.

————"Dialogform und Esoterik. Zur Deutung des platonischen Dialogs 'Phaidros'," *Museum Helveticum* 35 (1978):18-32.

Meissner, H. *Der tiefere Logos Platons*. Heidelberg, 1978.

Findlay, J. N. *Plato and Platonism. An Introduction*. New York, 1978. German version, *Plato und der Platonismus. Eine Einführung*. Königstein-Taunus, 1981.

Gadamer, H. G. *Die Idee des Guten zwischen Plato und Aristoteles* (Sitzungsberichte der Heidelberger Akademie der Wissenschaften, philosophisch-historische Klasse), 1978/3, Heidelberg, 1978. American version, *The Idea of the Good in Platonic-Aristotelian Philosophy*, trans. P. Christopher Smith (New Haven-London: Yale University Press, 1986).

Wieland, W. ed. *Geschichte der Philosophie in Text und Darstellung. Vol. I: Antike*. Stuggart:Reclam, 1978, pp. 19ff.

Vries, G. J. de, "Helping the Writings," *Museum Helveticum* 36 (1979):60-2.

Szlezák, T. A. "What One Should Know When Reading 'Helping the Writings'. A Reply to G. J. de Vries," *Museum Helveticum* 36 (1979):164f.

Bojadžiev, C. "Problemata za Edinnoto v 'Parmenid' i 'Nepisanite učenija' na Platon," *Filosofska misŭl 5 (1979):115-20 [in Bulgarian]*, ("The Problem of the One in the 'Parmenides' and 'the Unwritten Doctrines of Plato' ").

Moukanos, D. " ὁ τρόπος τοῦ εἶναι τῶν μαθηματικῶν ἀντικειμένων κατὰ τόν Πλάτωνα καὶ τὸν Ἀριστοτέλην," *Athens*, 1979.

Beierwaltes, W. *Identität und Differenz*. Frankfurt, 1980, pp. 35-56.

Vries, G. J. de, "Once More Helping the Writings," *Museum Helveticum* 37 (1980):60ff.

Gaiser, K. "Plato's Enigmatic Lecture *On the Good*," *Phronesis* 25 (1980):5-37.

Krämer, H. J. "Neues zum Streit um Platons Prinzipientheorie," *Philosophische Rundschau* 27 (1980):1-38.

Untersteiner, M. *Problemi di filologia filosofica*, ed. L. Sichirollo and M. Venturi Ferriolo, Milan, 1980 pp. 23ff.

Gaiser, K. "La teoria dei principi in Platone." *Elenchos. Rivista di studi sul pensiero antico* 1 (1980):45-75.

Szlezák, T. A. "Sokrates' Spott über Geheimhaltung. Zum Bild des φιλόσοφος in Platons *Euthydemos*," *Antike und Abendland* 26 (1980):79-89.

Albert, K. *Griechische Religion und platonische Philosophie*. Hamburg, 1980, pp. 27 ff. 39 ff.

Schwabe, W. "'Mischung' und 'Element' im Griechischen bis Platon. Wort-und begriffsgeschichtliche Untersuchungen, insbesondere zur Bedeutungsentwicklung von ΣΤΟΙΧΕΙΟΝ," *Archiv für Begriffsgeschichte* (Supplementheft 3), Bonn, 1980.

Krämer, H. J. "Zum neuen Platon-Bild," *Deutsche Vierteljahrsschrift für Literaturwissenschaft und Geistesgeschichte* 55 (1981):1-18.

Mittelstrass, J. Chapter on "Platon" in O. Höffe, ed. *Klassiker der Philosophie. Vol. 1, Von den Vorsokratikern bis David Hume*, München, 1981, pp. 38-62.

Bojadžiev, C. "Lekcüte 'Za Blagoto' i problemata za ezoteričeskata filosofija na Platon," *Filosofska misŭl* 7 (1981):13-22 [in Bulgarian], ("The Lecture On the Good and the Problem of the Esoteric Philosophy of Plato").

Isnardi Parente, M. "Le perì ideôn d'Aristote: Platon ou Xénocrate?," *Phronesis* 26 (1981):135-52.

Hösle, V. Platons Grundlegung der Euklidizität der Geometrie, *Philologus* 126 (1982):184-97.

Wieland, W. *Platon und die Formen des Wissens*, Gottingen, 1982, pp. 38-50.

Patzig, G. *Platon*, in N. Hoerster ed. *Klassiker des philosophischen Denkens*, Band 1, Deutscher Taschenbuch Verlag (Abteilung Wissenschaft), München, 1982, pp. 9-52.

Krämer, H. J, "Kritische Bemerkungen zu den jüngsten Äusserungen von W. Wieland und G. Patzig über Platons Ungeschriebene Lehre," *Rivista di Filosofia neo-scolastica* 74/4 (1982):579-92.

Sobrevilla, D. "La doctrina no escrita de platón, según H. J. Krämer. Un informe sobre el estado de la investigación," *Logos* 30 (1982):11-47.

Aubenque, P. "La matière de l'intelligible. Sur deux allusions méconnues aux doctrines non écrites de Platon," *Revue philosophique* 2 (1982):307-20.

Yashiki, K. "Platons ungeschriebene Lehrmeinungen," *Philosophia* (Waseda University Philosophical Society) Nr. 70, (1982):215-30 (in Japanese).

Apostolopoulou, G. Review of H. Krämer, *Platone e i fondamenti della metafisica*, *Filosofia* 12 (1982):429-32.

Žunjić, S. "Nova slika Platonove metafizike," *Theoria* 26 (1983):236-41.

Berti, E. "Il Platone di Krämer e la metafisica classica," *Rivista di Filosofia neo-scolastica* 75 (1983):313-26.

Richard, M. -D. *Le traité sur le bien d'Aristote et l'enseignement oral de Platon*, Thèse pour l'obtention du doctorat de 3 ème cycle es lettres, option philosophie, Université de Paris, IV la Sorbonne, I/II, 1983.

Gaiser, K. "La biografia di Platone in Filodemo: Nuovi dati dal P Herc. 1021," *Cronache Ercolanesi* 13 (1983):53-62.

Reale, G. *Per una rilettura e nuova interpretazione di Platone, prima edizione*, Milano:CUSL, 1984.

Hösle, V. "Zu Platons Philosophie der Zahlen und deren mathematischer und philosophischer Bedeutung," *Theologie und Philosophie* 59/3 (1984):321-55.

———"Hegels 'Naturphilosophie' und Platons 'Timaios' - ein Strukturvergleich," *Philosophia naturalis* 21/1 (1984):64-100.

———*Wahrheit und Geschichte. Studien zur Struktur der Philosophiegeschichte unter paradigmatischer Analyse der Entwicklung von Parmenides bis Platon*, Stuttgart-Bad Cannstatt, 1984, pp. 447-623.

Gaiser, K. *Platone come scrittore filosofico. Saggi sull'ermeneutica dei dialoghi platonici*, con una premessa di M. Gigante, Napoli, 1984.

Szlezák, T. A. "Aufbau und Handlung der platonischen 'Politeia'," *Antike und Abendland* 30 (1984):38-46.

Bojadžiev, C. "Plato's Unwritten Doctrine," Sofia 1984 (in Bulgarian)

Aristotele ed altri: Divisioni. Introduzione, traduzione e commento di Cristina Rossitto, Padova, 1984, pp. 20-23, 341 ff.

Isnardi Parente, M. "Il Platone *non scritto* e le autotestimonianze. Alcune note a proposito di un libro recente," *Elenchos* V (1984):201-9.

Wesoly, M. "Swiadectwa niespisanej nauki Platona (I): Traktat Arystotelesa 'O Dobru'," *Meander* 4 (1984):169-83.

———"Swiadectwa niespisanej nauki Platona (II): Pryncypia a typy ontologiczne," *Meander* 6 (1984):281-92.

Ferber, R. *Platos Idee des Guten*, Sankt Augustin, 1984, pp. 17, 157 ff.

Isnardi Parente, M. Review of H. Krämer, *Platone e i fondamenti della metafisica*, *Gnomon* 57 (1985):120-27.

Lisi, F. L. *Einheit und Vielheit des platonischen Nomosbegriffs. Eine Untersuchung zur Beziehung von Philosophie und Politik bei Platon*, Beiträge zur Klassischen Philologie Heft 167, Königstein-Taunus. 1985.

Szlezák, T. A. *Platon und die Schriftlichkeit der Philosophie. Interpretationen zu den frühen und mittleren Dialogen*, Berlin-New York, 1985.

Erler, M. "Platons Schriftkritik im historischen Kontext," *Altsprachlicher Unterricht* 28/4 (1985):27-41.

Schmitz, H. *Die Ideenlehre des Aristoteles*, Bonn, 1985, Vol. II: *Platon und Aristoteles*.

Reale, G. *Per una nuova interpretazione di Platone. Rilettura della meta fisica dei grandi dialoghi alla luce delle "Dottrine non scritte", seconda edizione* (per intero rifatta e molto ampliata) Milano Edizioni cusl Marzo 1986, terza edizione (con l'aggiunta di nuovi indici) Giugno 1986, quarta edizione (riveduta e con l'ulteriore aggiunta di nuovi indici) Ottobre 1986, quinta edizione Ottobre 1987, sesta edizione Novembre 1989. [An American edition is forthcoming, *A*

New Interpretation of Plato. A Re-reading of the Metaphysics of the Great Dialogues in the Light of the "Unwritten Doctrines" trans. J. R. Catan.

Böhme, G. "Symmetrie: Ein Anfang mit Platon," in *Symmetrie. Katalog der Ausstellung Mathildenhöhe*, Darmstadt, 1986, pp. 9-16.

Soleim, V. "A Greek dream—to render women superflous," *Social Science Information* 25 (1986):67-82, especially pp. 73f.

Eder, W. "Die ungeschriebene Lehre Platons: Zur Datierung des platonischen Vortrags 'Über das Gute'," in *Studien zur Alten Geschichte*, Siegfried Lauffer zum 70. Geburtstag am 4. August 1981 dargebracht, Roma, 1986, Vol. I pp. 209-35.

Gaiser, K. "Platons Zusammenschau der mathematischen Wissenschaften," *Antike und Abendland* 32 (1986):89-124.

Richard, M. D. *L'enseignement oral de Platon, Une nouvelle interprétation du Platonisme*, Préface de Pierre Hadot, Paris, 1986.

Krämer, H. J. Review of M. Isnardi Parente, Studi sull'Accademia Platonica antica (Firenze, 1979), *Archiv für Geschichte der Philosophie* 64 (1982):76-82.

——"Mutamento di Paradigma nelle ricerche su Platone. Riflessioni intorno al nuovo libro su Platone di Giovanni Reale," *Rivista di Filosofia neo-scolastica* 78/3 (1986):341-52.

——*La nuova immagine di Platone*, Napoli, 1986.

De Vogel, C. J. *Rethinking Plato and Platonism*, Leiden, 1986, pp. 3-92, 119-27.

Richard, M. D. "La méthode exégètique de Schleiermacher dans son application au Platonisme," in M. Tardieu, ed. *Les règles de l'interprétation*, Paris, 1987, pp. 209-25.

Krämer, H. J. Review of R. Ferber, *Platos Idee des Guten* (Sankt Augustin, 1984), *Philosophisches Jahrbuch der Görres-Gesellschaft* 94 (1987):196-201.

Erler, M. *Der Sinn der Aporien in den Dialogen Platons*, Berlin-New York, 1987.

Montserrat i Torrents dels Prats, J. *Las transformaciones del Platonismo*, Bellaterra, 1987, pp. 17-36.

Reale, G. *Storia della filosofia antica*, Vol. II, Platone e Aristotele, Milano 1987₅, pp. 102-155, 272 ff. 344 ff.

Berti, E. "Principali tendenze negli studi recenti di filosofia antica," *Filosofia oggi*, anno x, n. 4 (1987):535, 538, 541.

Beierwaltes, W. "Term 'Hen' " in *Reallexikon für Antike und Christentum*, Lieferung 107 (1987):449-50.

Yashiki, K. "The Report of Aristoxenus on Plato's Lecture on the Good," *Methodos*, 19 (1987):40-6 (in Japanese).

Migliori, M. "Il recupero della trascendenza platonica e il nuovo paradigma,"*Rivista di Filosofia neoscolastica*, 79/3 (1987):351-81.

Szlezák, Th. A. "Platons 'undemokratische' Gespräche," *Perspektiven der Philosophie*, 13 (1987):347-68.

Bubner, R. "Theorie und Praxis bei Platon, *Gymnasium*, Beiheft 9 (1987):63-76.

Gaiser, K. "Platonische Dialektik-damals und heute," *Gymnasium*, Beiheft 9 (1987):77-107.

Wesoly, M. "Swiadectwa niespisanej nauki Platona (III): Argumenty przeciwko pismu," *Meander*, 42/3 (1988):79-93.

Gaiser, K. (ed.), *Supplementum Platonicum. Die Texte der indirekten Platonüberlieferung*, Band 1: Konrad Gaiser, "Philodems Academica, Die Berichte über Platon und die Alte Akademie in zwei herkulanensischen Papyri" Stuttgart-Bad Cannstatt, 1988.

———*La metafisica della storia in Platone, Introduzione e traduzione di Giovanni Reale*, Milano, 1988.

———"Platons esoterische Lehre," in P. Koslowski, ed., *Gnosis und Mystik in der Geschichte der Philosophie*, Zürich-Münster, 1988, pp. 13-40.

Szlezák, T. A., *Platone e la scrittura della filosofia*, Introduzione e traduzione di Giovanni Reale, Milano, 1988, 1989².

Krämer, H. J. "Fichte, Schlegel und der Infinitismus in der Platondeutung," *Deutsche Vierteljahrsschrift für Literaturwissenschaft und Geistesgeschichte*, 62 (1988):583-621.

———Review of T. A. Szlezák, "Platon und die Schriftlichkeit der Philosophie," in *Perspektiven der Philosophie*, 14 (1988):417-39.

Heitsch, E. "Platon über die rechte Art zu reden und zu schreiben," *Mainzer Akademie der Wissenschaften und der Literatur, Abhandlungen der geistes-und sozialwissenschaftlichen Klasse, Jahrgang 1987 Nr. 4*, Wiesbaden-Stuttgart, 1987.

Szlezák, T. A. Review of E. Heitsch, "Platon über die rechte Art zu reden und zu schreiben," (1987), *Gnomon* 60 (1988):390-8.

Movia, G., "La Diairesi nel *Sofista*," *Rivista di Filosofia neo-scolastica* 80 (1988):331-78; 501-48.

Wesoly, M., "Swiadectwa Niespisanej Nauki Platona (IV): Odsylacze w Dialogach do dialektyki pryncypiow," *Meander*, 43/8 (1988):287-306.

Bares Partal, J. d. D., *Matematicas y Ontologia en Platon: El Testimonio Aristotelico*, Universidad de Valencia, 1988, 465pp.

Szlezák, T. A., "Gespräche unter Ungleichen. Zur Struktur und Zielsetzung der platonischen Dialoge," *Antike und Abendland*, Vol. 34 (1988):99-116.

Krämer, H. J. "Neue Literatur zum neuen Platonbild," *Allgemeine Zeitschrift für Philosophie*, 14/1 (1989):59-81.

———*Dialettica e definizione del Bene in Platone. Interpretazione e commentario storico-filosofico di 'Repubblica' VI, 534B3—D2*. Traduzione di Enrico Peroli, Introduzione di Giovanni Reale, Milano, 1989.

Kranz, M. *Das Wissen des Philosophen. Platons Trilogie 'Theaitet,' 'Sophistes,' und 'Politikos.'* Dissertation, Tübingen, 1986, published 1989.

Albert, K. *Über Platons Begriff der Philosophie*, Sankt Augustin, 1989.

Gaiser, K. "Das Gold der Weisheit. Zum Gebet des Philosophen am Schluss des 'Phaidros'," *Rheinisches Museum* 132 (1989):105-40.

Szlezák, T. A. "Die Lückenhaftigkeit der akademischen Prinzipientheorien nach Aristoteles' Darstellung in Metaphysik M und N," in A. Gaiser, ed. *Mathematics and Metaphysics in Aristotle, Akten des X. Symposium Aristotelicum 1984* (Bern/Stuttgart, 1987):45-67.

Burnyeat, M. F. "Platonism and Mathematics. A Prelude to Discussion," loc.cit. pp. 213-40.

Isnardi Parente, M. "ΤΑ ΜΕΤΑ ΤΑΣ ΙΔΕΑΣ: Figures idéale ou premières figures?," ibidem, pp. 261-80.

Thesleff, H. "Platonic Chronology," *Phronesis* 34/1 (1989):1-26.

Königshausen, J. H. "Grundsätzliches der platonischen σκεψις von guter Rede und guter Schrift im Phaidros," in *Perspektiven der Philosophie*, Band 14 (1988):109-27.

Isnardi Parente, M. *L'eredità di Platone nell'Accademia antica*, (Naples/Milan, 1989).

———"La akroasis di Platone," *Museum Helveticum*, 46 (1989):146-62.

Heitsch, E. "τιμιώτερα," *Hermes* 117 (1989):278-87.

Ferber, R. "Warum hat Plato die 'ungeschriebene Lehre' nicht geschrieben?," in *Atti del II Symposium Platonicum, Università degli Studi di Perugia, 1-6 September 1989*, pp. 1-26.

Krämer, H. "Zur aktuellen Diskussion um den Philosophiebegriff Platons," *Perspektiven der Philosophie*, Band 16 (1990):1-20.

INDICES

Names Of The Ancient Authors Cited

Names of Modern Authors Cited

Sartre, J. P. 278, n. 2, 279, n. 20.
Schaerer, R. 38, 39, 71, 74, 244, n. 6.
Schelling, C. 277, n. 58.
Schelling, F. W. J. 20, 21, 23-27, 161,
225, n. 25, 226-27, nn. 36, 41, 51-56,
227, n., 59, 228, n. 63, 229, nn. 71,
75, 270, n. 28, 273, n. 6.
Schilpp, P. A. 282, n. 14.
Schlegel, A. W. 228, n. 63.
Schlegel, F. W. J. 4, 5, 17-20, 23, 26,
27, 31, 34, 37, 49, 57, 63, 186, 224-
25, nn. 10, 22, 23-26, 227, nn. 51,
54, 228, n. 63, 229, n. 75, 230, n. 76,
232, n. 19, 283, 19.
Schleiermacher, F. E. D. 3-7, 9-13, 15-
27, 29-35, 37, 38, 41, 42, 47, 49, 54,
56-60, 63-67, 73-75, 127, 175, 186,
187, 188, 219, nn. 1, 6, 7, 9, 220, nn.
10, 14, 222, nn. 31, 34, 45, 223, nn.
38, 39, 3, 5, 224, nn. 11-13, 18, 225,
nn. 23, 26, 226, n. 43, 227, nn. 51,
55, 58, 60, 61, 228, nn. 62, 63, 65,
70, 229, nn. 71, 73, 75, 230, 77, 2,
231, n. 10, 232, nn. 17, 18, 28, 31,
233, nn. 37, 39, 40, 244, n. 2, 271, n.
29, 273, n. 9.
Schmalzriedt, E. 38, 73, 245, nn. 15,
16.
Schmidt, M. C. P. 251, n. 49, 266, n.
24.
Scholz, H. 266, n. 25.
Schuhl, P. M. 39, 235, n. 59.
Schulz, W. 252, n. 9, 279, n. 21
Schulz-Seitz, R. E. 277, n. 43.
Schwabe, W. 142, 241, n. 14, 246, n. 7,
263, n. 38, 264, n. 5, 268, 52.
Schweizer, A. 25, 224, n. 19, 227, n.
60, 228, nn. 63, 65.
Scott, R. 242, n. 21.
Shorey, P. 34-38, 232-33, n. 35, 233,
nn. 36, 37, 39, 40, 42, 43, 234, nn.
49, 50, 52-54, 283, n. 3.
Sichirollo, L. 242, n. 23.
Sinaiko, H. L. 38, 244, n. 6.
Sneed, J. P. 49.
Socher, J. 29.
Solignac, A. 244, n. 3.

Solmsen, F. 262, n. 33.
Spinoza, B. 23, 25, 26, 161, 162.
Stachowiak, H. 266, n. 25, 267, n. 48,
268, n. 67.
Steele, A. D. 248, n. 29.
Steffens, H. 23, 227, n. 51.
Stegmüller, W. 49.
Stein, H. von 219, n. 5, 220, n. 10, 225,
n. 25, 227, n. 58.
Stenzel, J. 34, 38-40, 71, 110, 119, 184,
233, n. 41, 244, n. 6, 246, n. 5, 254,
n. 29, 257, n. 52, 260, n. 15, 269, 5,
277, n. 48, 282, n. 14.
Sterrett, J. R. S. 232, n. 35.
Strauss,, D. F. 32.
Strawson, J. P. 270, nn. 19, 25.
Süskind, H. 225, n. 25, 227, n. 55.
Szabó, A. 267, n. 45.
Szlezák, T. A. 8, 126, 221, nn. 21, 22,
24, 236, n. 73, 242, n. 21, 243, n. 28,
250, n. 42, 263, n. 41, 272, n. 2, 280,
n. 2.
Szondi,, P. 223, n. 3.

Taureck, B. 276, n. 34.
Tennemann, W. G. 9, 11, 222, nn. 29,
34, 223, n. 39, 230, n. 2, 282, n. 14.
Theiler, W. 272, n. 2.
Thesleff, H. 250, n. 42.
Tigerstedt, E. N. 223, n. 2, 236, n. 69.
Töplitz, O. 245, n. 5, 277, n. 48.
Trede, J. P. 272, n. 4
Trendelenburg, F. A. 30, 31, 231, n.
10, 232, n. 18, 233, n. 43, 263, n. 1,
282, n. 14.
Tugendhat, E. 263, n. 1, 264, n. 3, 279,
n. 13, 20.

Ueberweg, F. 219, n. 9, 239, n. 7, 263,
n. 40.
Untersteiner, M. 242, n. 23, 249, n. 38,
280, n. 4.

Vasiljeva, T.V. 282, n. 15.
Venturi, Ferriolo M. 242, n. 23.
Vieillard-Baron, J.-L. 273, n. 5.
Vlastos, G. 139, 220, n. 19, 222, n. 28,
267, n. 36.

Index of the Agreements between the Collection of the Testimonia Platonica of Gaiser and Krämer

Gaiser 7 = Krämer 1

Gaiser 8 = Krämer 2

Gaiser 10 = Krämer 6

Gaiser 22A = Krämer 9

Gaiser 22B = Krämer 10

Gaiser 23B = Krämer 3 and 11

Gaiser 30 = Krämer 8

Gaiser 31 = Krämer 13

Gaiser 32 = Krämer 12

Gaiser 33a = Krämer 7

Gaiser 34 = Krämer 26

Gaiser 39A = Krämer 14

Gaiser 39B = Krämer 15

Gaiser 40A = Krämer 16

Gaiser 40B = Krämer 17

Gaiser 41A = Krämer 18

Gaiser 41B = Krämer 19

Gaiser 42A = Krämer 20

Gaiser 42B = Krämer 21

Gaiser 43 = Krämer 27 and 28

Gaiser 44a = Krämer 29

Gaiser 44b = Krämer 30 and 31

Gaiser 51 = Krämer 24

Gaiser 54A = Krämer 4

Lacking in the Collection of Gaiser:

Krämer, Appendix 1.1—2

Krämer, Appendix 2.1—11

Krämer, Appendix 3.5, 22, 23, 25